Beyond Adversary Democracy

BEYOND
ADVERSARY
DEMOCRACY

Jane J. Mansbridge

Basic Books, Inc., Publishers

NEW YORK

Library of Congress Cataloging in Publication Data

Mansbridge, Jane J
    Beyond adversary democracy.

    Bibliography: p. 378
    Includes index.
    1.   Democracy.   2.   Local government—Vermont—Case
studies.   3.   Crisis intervention (Psychiatry)—United
States—Case studies.   I.   Title.
JC423.M353   323'.042   79-3129
ISBN: 0-465-00657-4

Contents

I V
Conclusion

Preface

THIS BOOK deals with two great themes in American political thought: democracy and equality. When I started work on it in 1969, I intended to do two or three case studies of how the small egalitarian New Left groups that were then spreading across the country made their decisions. The book has changed in several ways over the ensuing ten years. I early added a study of a Vermont town governed by a traditional town meeting, then gradually reduced the other groups I was interested in to one, a "participatory" workplace. But I also changed the book's purpose dramatically. My case studies convinced me that both popular and academic thinking about democracy contained a number of fundamental contradictions. I therefore spent several years sorting out traditional conceptions of what democracy is and what it ought to be, and developed a new way of thinking about democracy that indicates when different conceptions of it are appropriate. The book's ultimate aim is now to demonstrate the theoretical and practical value of this new approach to a very old subject.

Both my discussion of democratic ideals and my case studies of democracy in action use unfamiliar concepts that are likely to confuse some readers. Since many people find a new concept easier to understand if they know how and why it developed, this preface describes the evolution of my thinking. The remainder of the book sets forth my argument in a more systematic way, beginning with an analysis of democratic ideals, then moving to case studies of the town meeting and the participatory workplace, then returning to the question of how democratic institutions ought to function if they want to live up to their members' ideals.

In the late 1960s, every major American city and every rural area to which young people had migrated could claim a host of free schools, food co-ops, law communes, women's centers, hot lines, and health clinics organized along "participatory" lines. I had been a member of several such groups; in all of them, internal struggles over equality and elitism had left the groups in disarray.

Most members of these organizations attributed inequality and the pain it caused to the warped personalities of particular individuals and, ultimately, to the destructive effect of a capitalist society on the individual personality.¹ These explanations had some force. But I also believed—and still believe—that certain kinds of inequality would appear in any society, no matter what its ideology or social system, and that egalitarian organizations would have to find ways to deal with this fact. It seemed to me that in any nonhierarchical organization that encompassed more than fifteen or so members those who were most central to the organization's communication network, who expressed themselves best at meetings, and who had been members of the organization longest would inevitably exert more power over collective decisions than others did.

Since I was fundamentally sympathetic to the egalitarian impulses that shaped these organizations, I wanted to find techniques, like occasional referenda or decentralizing to small groups, that would help them implement their ideals. Second, I also wanted to help them shift the blame for those inequalities that proved ineradicable from individuals to structures, thereby reducing personal acrimony among participants. I therefore set out to do a series of case studies that would serve as models for such collectives. I deliberately looked for deviant cases—collectives that were larger than a ten- to fifteen-member primary group but that still did not have an obvious elite. I expected these collectives' successes to suggest solutions to problems that most collectives had failed to solve. At the same time, I felt I could better test my thesis—that certain kinds of inequality were difficult or impossible to abolish—by looking at the most successful collectives than by looking at failures.

The late 1960s were also the heyday of the "community control" movement, when radicals dreamed of decentralizing political power to participatory governments at the neighborhood level. In a New England town meeting, I could study a local government that already dealt with issues like schools, roads, traffic, fire and police protection, garbage, and zoning in an egalitarian, participatory fashion. The town meeting had been an inspirational symbol of American democracy since before the Revolution. Yet surprisingly, no one had ever analyzed its operations in detail.² Because I wanted a town where, at least initially, "the people" seemed to govern, I passed up the Massachusetts and Connecticut town meetings I attended, which were run by an obvious professional and business elite, and settled on a Vermont town with 350 adult residents. I call this town "Selby."

My next goal was to find a radical workplace that had successfully confronted the challenge of inequality. I believed that a workplace would provide the most promising conditions for egalitarian decision making: a fairly stable membership with both access to information and a sizable stake in the outcome of decisions. While most of the participatory workplaces I investigated were dominated by a readily identifiable elite with greater experience, access to money, or other hard-to-redistribute resources,[3] in 1973 I discovered a "crisis center" whose forty-one paid employees had deposed its founding elite and ran their organization on an extremely egalitarian basis. I used this group, which I call "Helpline," for my second case study.

These two cases differed in many crucial respects. The town had nearly nine times as many adult "citizens" as the workplace and had been in existence nearly forty times longer. But the workplace touched its members' daily lives far more deeply, for the decisions at work set the members' salaries, determined what work they would do, and selected future members of the group. The workplace was also committed to a version of democracy far more egalitarian than the town's. While both workplace and town made all major decisions in face-to-face meetings of the entire membership, the workplace made its decisions by nominal consensus, whereas the town had a formal majority rule. Finally, membership in the workplace was more nearly voluntary since most of its members were young and found changing jobs relatively easy.[4] I settled on two such drastically different organizations on the grounds that their differences provided a stronger test of the inevitability of certain kinds of political inequality than would two similar organizations.[5]

My initial approach to both of these democracies reflected the political preoccupations of the time. In 1970, internal political discussion in the participatory democracies of the New Left focused on issues of equality. But the town meeting and the collective I was studying shared two other features besides a nominal commitment to equality. They made decisions in face-to-face assembly and, at least in part, by consensus. Although a commitment to either equality or liberty could mandate both consensus and face-to-face assembly,[6] the ultimate concern of the participatory democracies I know best seemed to me to be "fraternity"—or, as they preferred to call it, "solidarity," "community," or "sisterhood."

Rereading Aristotle's *Nicomachean Ethics* two years into my study, I was arrested by the Greek maxim, "Friendship is equality." The maxim captured perfectly the link between equality and solidarity that I had seen in these collectives. The equality of friendship is not an impersonal, quantitative, universalistic ideal. It involves a quality of human relations, not an equal quantity of power, money, or other resources. The equality of friendship is an equality of mutual respect, binding one person to another.

According to Aristotle, the Greeks also saw friendship as the necessary basis of the state. Equality, consensus, face-to-face contact, and, I would add later, common interest were distinguishing features of that friendship. Since many radical collectives in the 1960s and 1970s had started as groups of friends, it seemed to me that they had simply codified, when it became necessary, the mode of operations they were already pursuing. As friends, they had treated one another as equals, had met face to face, and had made decisions by consensus. When the group became more formal, took on a name, or admitted newcomers, the members continued to try to treat one another as friends and to turn their earlier informal ways of coming to decisions into rules.

This line of thinking led eventually to the major conclusion of this book: the model of democracy unconsciously adopted by the participatory democrats of the late 1960s and early 1970s, which I call "unitary" democracy, was in essence and in form directly opposed to the model of democracy that I, like most Americans, had grown up with, a model I call "adversary" democracy. Unitary democracies are like friendships. They assume a high degree of common interest. They are distinguished by consensus, face-to-face assembly, and an emphasis on a rough equality of respect among the members. Adversary democracies, on the other hand, are compatible with large-scale polities in which the members do not know or care for one another. They assume conflicting interests. They are distinguished by majority rule, the secret ballot, and an emphasis on the equal protection of the members' interests rather than on equal respect.

As Aristotle helped me to understand modern participatory democracies, so they helped me to understand—and I think clarify—a theoretical dilemma that goes back to the ancient Greeks. Ever since Plato set down his criticisms of democracy in *The Republic*, theorists have disputed the degree to which the democratic ideal requires that citizens share power equally. The members of my participatory workplace were deeply committed to equality; the members of my town meeting were also relatively egalitarian. Yet most members of both groups accepted disparities in power under certain circumstances. In my first study, the town meeting, I often attributed the citizens' acceptance of inequality to self-deception. When Selby's less powerful citizens told me that they did not mind others running the town because the people who ran the town were "just like I am" or because "we're all friends here," I dismissed their reactions as a form of "false consciousness." But when I studied the crisis center a few years later, its less powerful members said much the same thing. This time, to my surprise, I believed them. When they said they trusted those who exerted more power than they, I felt their trust justified. The difference between Selby and Helpline, I realized, was that I believed the citizens of Selby had conflicting interests, while the members of Helpline had predominantly common interests. Because I believed that the members of Helpline had common interests, I assumed that the less powerful members could in most instances count on the more powerful to protect their interests. At least for this purpose, equal power was unnecessary.

Once I began to think in terms of common and conflicting interest, I realized that Selby's citizens probably had more common interests than I had previously recognized. On the spectrum from predominantly unitary to predominantly adversary polities, Selby lay to the adversary side of Helpline, but it was nonetheless far more unitary than the national government or even the typical local government.

It took me almost five years to figure out that democratic organizations took different forms when their members had common rather than conflicting interests. My failure to recognize the centrality of interests earlier had at least two sources, both of which may also affect readers' willingness to accept my argument. First, democratic theory has had remarkably little to say about the spectrum from common to conflicting interests. This may be because the term "interest" has so many different implications that no single definition can cover all conventional usages, and theorists are understandably reluctant to emphasize a concept they cannot define rigorously. Second, when modern political scientists have taken account of interests, they have almost always assumed that individual interests were in conflict. They have made this assumption partly because they were preoccupied with the nation-state, where conflict is highly visible and often unavoidable, rather than with smaller groups. My conclusion that members of certain kinds of democracies had predominantly common interests thus required a sharp break with the way I had been trained to think about democracy. It will require most Western readers to make an equally sharp break with their prior assumptions.

Two final caveats may help orient the reader. First, while much of this book is devoted to criticizing what I call adversary democracy and to explaining what I call unitary democracy, I am not "for" unitary democracy or "against" adversary democracy. I believe that every polity contains both common and conflicting interests and that every polity therefore needs both unitary and adversary institutions to make democratic decisions. Unitary democracies that ignore or suppress conflicting interests can do as much damage both to themselves and to their members as can adversary democracies that ignore or fail to develop their members' common interests.

Second, while I began this book as an investigation of "participatory" democracies, my argument has very little in common with the "participatory" critique of democratic "elitism" that emerged during the 1960s. What I call adversary democracy is not synonymous with democratic elitism since the ideals of adversary democracy are fully consistent with, and may well require, the active participation of all citizens to ensure that their interests are protected equally. Nor is what I call unitary democracy simply a matter of widespread participation. On the contrary, when interests coincide participation is sometimes unnecessary and irrelevant.

Because my attempt to distinguish these two forms of democracy requires a frame of reference employed at the moment neither by the right nor by the left, and neither by political scientists nor by practitioners of participatory democracy, the vocabulary and the analytic concepts are to some extent new and the analysis is far from complete. Most of the material presented here will therefore be a detailed description of the way people act, feel, and think in two quite different small democracies near the unitary end of the spectrum.

Political theorists have not ordinarily paid much attention to the way ordinary people think about normative issues. My experience writing this book has convinced me that this is a mistake. The men and women I interviewed were often confused, but many of them made heroic efforts to live up to their ideals, reformulating them as they discovered their limitations through painful experience. By looking at what happens to an ideal under stress, theorists can obtain what I think of as an "exploded diagram" of its inner meanings and potentialities. In the case of political equality, for example, the ideal turns out to be both subtler and somewhat more practical than theorists have traditionally assumed. This experience convinced me that field studies of what happens to various ideals when people try to live by them could prove useful in clarifying a wide range of normative questions. One aim of this book is to persuade other theorists that my "empirical" approach to doing theory is not just a symptom of personal idiosyncrasy but a widely applicable method.

I have many debts as I finish this book. The first, and strongest, is to the people of Selby and Helpline, who shared their understanding with me. The second is to the extraordinary number of friends and colleagues who have read what I had written and have given me both support and criticism. Those who have, at some point in the past ten years, read earlier drafts of the manuscript include Peter Bachrach, Frank Bryan, John Case, Richard Flacks, Susan Horn-Moo, Ira Katznelson, Helen Lambert, Nathan Leites, Seymour Martin Lipset, Georgia Mansbridge, Ronald Mansbridge, Kenneth Miller, Harvey Molotch, Benjamin Page, Carole Pateman, David Riesman, Evelyn Riesman, Thomas Scheff, Kay Schlozman,

Preface

Steven Soldz, Margaret Svenchenko, Sidney Verba, Aristide Zolberg, and several members of Helpline. I would particularly like to thank Thomas Schrock and Brian Barry. I did not always take their advice, but their criticism and encouragement helped me greatly in the theoretical sections of this book. To Christopher Jencks, who read most of the manuscript more than once, discussed the issues with me, suggested phrasing when my mind flagged, typed, and took care of our son, I have an enormous debt.

I am also grateful to the National Science Foundation, whose post-doctoral grant enabled me to begin the research that led to this book; to the Institute for Policy Studies, whose support financed my first year of interviewing; to the University of California at Santa Barbara, whose warm welcome, colleagues, typing funds, and a quarter's leave sustained me at a crucial moment; and, finally, to the University of Chicago, whose Social Science Research Division provided funds for the computer analysis, whose leaves of absence gave me time to write, and whose tradition of intellectual inquiry and colleagueship forced me to rethink and to rewrite more often than I care to recall.

This book has been typed more than once. Among the typists to whom, over the years, I have been particularly grateful are Marjorie Peach, Irene Goodsell, and Oneita Wilde. For computer help, I relied on the goodwill and skills of Marianne Winslett. For crucial support in the final, harried months of getting the manuscript together, I thank Nancy Walker and her friends.

The following publishers have kindly granted permission to reprint the parts of chapters 6, 17, and 21 that originally appeared, respectively, in their journals:

"Conflict in a New England Town Meeting," *The Massachusetts Review* 17, no. 4 (winter 1976). Copyright © 1976 by The Massachusetts Review, Inc. Reprinted with permission.

"Acceptable Inequalities," *British Journal of Political Science* 7 (1977). Reprinted by permission of Cambridge University Press.

"The Limits of Friendship," *Participation in Politics: NOMOS XVI,* ed. Pennock and Chapman. Reprinted by permission of the publishers, Lieber-Atherton, Inc. Copyright © 1975; all rights reserved.

I

The Argument

Chapter 1

Introduction

THE WEST believes that it invented democracy, and that institutions like Parliament, representation, and universal adult suffrage are synonymous with democracy itself. Every American schoolchild knows that when you set up a democracy you elect representatives—in school, the student council; later, senators, representatives, councilmen, assemblymen, and aldermen. When you do not agree, you take a vote, and the majority rules. This combination of electoral representation, majority rule, and one-citizen/one-vote *is* democracy. Because this conception of democracy assumes that citizens' interests are in constant conflict, I have called it "adversary" democracy.

Every step in this adversary process violates another, older understanding of democracy. In that older understanding, people who disagree do not vote; they reason together until they agree on the best answer. Nor do they elect representatives to reason for them. They come together with their friends to find agreement. This democracy is consensual, based on common interest and equal respect. It is the democracy of face-to-face relations. Because it assumes that citizens have a single common interest, I have called it "unitary" democracy.

These two conceptions of democracy persist, side by side, in every modern democracy. The adversary ideal and the procedures derived from it have dominated Western democratic thinking since the seventeenth century. But unitary ideals and procedures continue to influence the way legislative committees, elected representatives, major institutions like the Supreme Court, and local democracies actually act. In crises of legitimacy, citizens often revert to the unitary ideal, as young people did in the small participatory democracies that flourished in America in the 1960s and early 1970s.

These two conceptions of democracy are not only different, but contra-

3

dictory. Yet those who talk and write about our democratic ideals never distinguish them. They assume either that adversary democracy is the only legitimate form of democracy or that unitary democracy is the ideal form and adversary democracy a compromise between the unitary ideal and the exigencies of practical politics. The main argument of this book is that both the unitary and the adversary forms of democracy embody worthy democratic ideals, although each is appropriate in a different context.

If decisions are legitimate only when they are "democratic," it is important to recognize that democracy can come in these two different forms. When interests conflict, a democratic polity needs adversary institutions. When interests do not conflict, unitary institutions are more appropriate. The most important single question confronting any democratic group is therefore whether its members have predominantly common or conflicting interests on matters about which the group must make decisions.

In developing this general argument, based in part on case studies of a New England town meeting and a small democratic workplace, I will reach several conclusions regarding both unitary and adversary democracies. I will first try to persuade cynical readers that, despite the drawbacks of the participatory democracies of the late 1960s and early 1970s, these relatively unitary institutions filled human needs that adversary institutions cannot fill. Second, I will try to show that the failures of unitary democracies often derive from their refusal either to recognize when interests conflict or to deal with those conflicts by adversary procedures. Third, turning to adversary democracies, I will argue that their legitimating logic requires that citizens' conflicting interests all be protected equally. Substantively, this ideal demands a greater equality in economic and social resources than is now found in any nation-state. Fourth, I will argue that the adversary ideal can often be better met by what the Europeans call consociational democracy than by majority rule.

Table 1 summarizes the major differences between adversary and unitary democracy. In an adversary democracy, where citizens' interests conflict, those citizens find it hard to agree on any principle for resolving differences other than counting each individual's interests equally, weighing them up, and choosing the policy that accumulates the most weight (majority rule). The ideal of equality in an adversary democracy is quantitative, part of the weighing process, and mandates that in a decision each individual's interests have equal weight. When interests conflict, a secret ballot minimizes the cost to individuals of pursuing their interests.

In a unitary democracy, the similar interests of the citizenry allow

TABLE 1

Models for the Democratic Polity:
Unitary versus Adversary Democracy

	Unitary Democracy	Adversary Democracy
Assumption:	Common interests	Conflicting interests
Central egalitarian ideal:	Equal respect	Equal protection of interests
Decision rule:	Consensus	Majority rule
Level of intimacy:	Face-to-face contact	Secret ballot

them to make their decisions by consensus. Because they need not worry about weighing each individual's interests equally in the decision, the kind of equality that concerns them is qualitative—the feeling of equal respect that prevails among friends. The unitary process of making decisions consists not in the weighing of votes but in the give and take of discussion in a face-to-face setting. All three distinguishing features of a unitary democracy—equal respect, consensus, and face-to-face meetings of the whole—encourage members to identify with one another and with the group as a whole. This process of identification in turn helps develop common interests.

Readers may well feel skeptical about the unitary ideal. Clearly, no two individuals can have completely common interests. The claim that people have common interests can, moreover, be a way of misleading the less powerful into collaborating with the more powerful in schemes that mainly benefit the latter. Since what I call the adversary revolution in political thought, which began in the seventeenth century, Westerners have increasingly accepted conflicting interests as an inalterable fact. This development in political thinking paved the way for creating democratic institutions on a national scale. But the increasing legitimation of conflicting interests should not blind us to the fact that most human relationships are still built on common interests.

An analysis of interests is central to understanding the contradictions of both democratic theory and democratic institutions. Recognizing the centrality of interests allows us, for example, to reject the frequent claim that democracy implies or requires that all citizens have equal power.[1] When citizens have the same interests, as they do in unitary democracies, they do not need equal power to protect their interests against one another since each will promote the interests of the others. Instead, they need equal respect, or equal status. When citizens have conflicting interests, as they do in adversary democracies, they again do not need

5

equal power with everyone in the polity. They need to have their interests protected equally, which they can sometimes do better through giving power to a representative than by trying to retain power themselves. The issue of the distribution of power is important in both unitary and adversary democracies, but equal power is always a means, and not the only means, of achieving some other end.

Recognizing the centrality of interests also helps us to understand some of the apparent contradictions in our national institutions and to judge these institutions more realistically. The Supreme Court, for example, appears at first glance to be the very antithesis of democracy. It allows "nine old men" to exercise enormous discretionary power over the lives of their fellow citizens, leaving them virtually unaccountable to anyone. Yet those who believe in democracy are only occasionally hostile to the Court as an institution. The reason for this is partly political: the Court has recently favored egalitarian causes like racial equality with greater consistency than has any other institution of government. But the fundamental rationale for the Supreme Court is that, while its members have far more power than ordinary citizens, their interests coincide with the interests of the citizenry as a whole. To the extent that members of the Court have different interests from the rest of the citizenry, their powers are incompatible with democratic ideals. Thus, the Court's decisions, while often controversial in the short run, are supposed to promote our common interests in the long run. To the extent that the Court succeeds in doing this, and in gaining popular recognition for its success in this role, it enhances its own legitimacy.

Finally, recognizing the centrality of interests helps us make sense of our ambivalent attitude toward representation, and more particularly toward Congress. Unlike the Supreme Court, Congress is explicitly designed to deal with situations where interests conflict, often irreconcilably. In situations of this kind, we cannot judge Congress according to whether or not it promotes the common interest, since no common interest exists. Instead, we must ask how it resolves conflicting interests. The logic of adversary democracy is that every citizen's interests are as legitimate as every other's, that "each shall count for one, and none for more than one." The goal of Congress or of any other democratic legislature must therefore be to protect everyone's interests equally. This is often impossible in making a single decision, on which some must win and others lose. But the goal of equal protection can be approximated in the long run through explicit or implicit bargains that ensure a group whose interests are sacrificed at one point that it will be compensated later on. In moments of conflict the legitimacy of a democratic legislative body ultimately depends on its ability to produce proportional outcomes of this kind, even though popular thinking condemns as logrolling the bargains that make these proportional outcomes possible.

Today, as national governments become increasingly involved in managing all aspects of society, and as citizens become aware of the degree to which decisions made in a nation's capital can benefit or harm them, there is a constant threat that the government will lose its legitimacy. If citizens believe that government is legitimate only as long as it is "democratic," it then becomes critically important to clarify precisely what we mean when we demand that decisions be made in democratic fashion. My argument is that we actually mean two different things when we speak of "democracy" and that we will not be able to deal effectively with crises of legitimacy until we recognize that neither conception is appropriate under all circumstances. The task confronting us is therefore to knit together these two fundamentally different kinds of democracies into a single institutional network that can allow us both to advance our common interests and to resolve our conflicting ones.

Chapter 2

Unitary versus Adversary Democracy

THIS CHAPTER describes the unitary conception of democracy, without which one cannot understand the behavior of the two small democracies that I examine in later chapters. It argues that the unitary ideal extends traditional conceptions of friendship to the political realm, and that unitary democracy is the oldest and longest lived form of human organization. With the rise of mercantilism and the spread of market relations in the seventeenth century, the unitary conception of democracy began increasingly to be supplanted by an adversary conception. Since this adversary revolution political theorists have more and more tended to see adversary democracy as the only possible kind of democracy and to dismiss unitary ideals as a by-product of nostalgia or popular ignorance. Yet because the unitary ideal remains a fundamental part of human experience, citizens and a minority of theorists in almost every era have tried to revive it. The chapter concludes by tracing the evolution of unitary thinking since the adversary revolution and the persistent reappearance of unitary forms.

The Basis in Friendship of Unitary Democracy

The strength of unitary democracy derives partly from its simplicity: it makes formal and extends to the level of a polity the social relations of friendship. The Greeks were aware of this connection. With the phrase,

"Friendship [*philia*] appears to hold city-states together,"[1] Aristotle illuminates the bond between citizens in a unitary polity. Friendship has a meaning close to love. It is a relation with other human beings that almost everyone has enjoyed, and it is a good in every culture. Drawing from the experience of friendship, a democrat could easily believe that relations between citizens ought to be like relations between friends. Friends are equals. They choose to spend time together. They share common values. They expand in each other's company. So, too, in a democracy based on friendship, participants are equal in status; the costs of participation, of which some make so much, do not feel heavy. Citizens "fly to the assemblies" as if to meet their friends. They value the time they spend on their common affairs. They share a common good, and are able, as a consequence, to make their decisions unanimously. The characteristics of unitary democracy—equal respect, face-to-face contact, common interest, and consensus—are from this perspective nothing but the natural conditions that prevail among friends.

Any polity based on friendship must be a democracy, for it is based on a fundamental equality among its members. Friends are always equals. In all cultures, friendship demands a rough equality of respect. Friends need not be equal in every quality that they value; indeed, in order for the union to be anything but narcissistic, each must bring to it qualities that the other does not have. Friends must be complementary, rather than the same. But for a friendship to be viable, the total respect that friends hold for each other must be roughly equal. Friendships do not form between individuals who recognize between them a distinct inferiority or superiority. Because friendship is, next to the family, the closest relation between human beings, it becomes a "natural" or "organic" basis for democracy, just as the family is the natural metaphor for legitimating a monarchy.

Unitary democracy is not only egalitarian, in this sense of equality of respect; it is also consensual. Adversary democrats, who tend to equate consensus with suppression, should think first of their own friendships. Friends make their decisions by consensus, reaching a decision by drawing together subtle preferences, intensities, and information. Among friends, everyone's pleasure is reduced if any one of the group cannot join them or goes along reluctantly. For each individual, the pleasure of the collective experience outweighs his or her individual preferences. Equally important, the friends make each other's pleasure their own. Because the group's unity has a value for each individual greater than the value of most differences in individual preferences, a group of friends will rarely, if ever, settle its decisions with a vote. Voting symbolizes,

9

reinforces, and institutionalizes division. Voting produces a result that excludes the minority, whose interests the others have partly made their own, while a decision by consensus includes everyone, reinforcing the unity of the group.

Consensus can only work among friends because by and large they have common interests. Their private interests tend to coincide, they sometimes subordinate their private interests to the friendship they have formed together, and they often take up each other's interests as their own. For, as Aristotle observed, "Those who wish well to their friends for their sake are most truly friends."[2]

The face-to-face interaction of friends helps to create and to maintain their common interests. Friends enjoy the drama of each other's existence and value the time they spend together rather than resenting it. They come to respect and to know one another by piecing together, over time, informal cues derived from their intimate contact. Without such contact, friendship usually withers. Thus, for a polity built on friendship face-to-face assemblies are a benefit as well as a cost. These four central features of friendship—equal status or respect, consensus, common interest, and face-to-face contact—recur in unitary democracies throughout history.

The Original Unitary Democracy

Unitary democracy almost certainly has a longer history than any other form of government. For more than 99 percent of our existence, we human beings lived in hunter-gatherer bands, which in all probability practiced unitary democracy.

We know relatively little about the hunter-gatherers of earlier times. What we do know derives from archaeological finds, from accounts of European travelers and explorers who recorded some characteristics of hunter-gatherer groups when they first encountered them, and from systematic studies of anthropologists on the handful of hunter-gatherer tribes that have survived into the twentieth century. But these three sources of evidence agree on one point: the remarkable degree of economic equality among hunter-gatherers. More recent evidence suggests a comparable degree of political equality. At least in the past few centuries, hunter-gatherers have habitually made their decisions as equals, by consensus, and in face-to-face meetings. It seems fairly safe to infer that hunter-gatherers always operated as unitary democracies.[3]

The economic equality in hunter-gatherer bands supports this political equality. These bands, both now and probably back to their earliest origins, divide up any major catch after a hunt. Sharing eliminates the need for storage and permits greater mobility. As for gathering, two to four hours of collecting fruits and nuts usually provides amply for a family. In hard times, the custom of sharing a catch allows the whole band, excepting the very oldest and the very youngest members, to survive. When food becomes extremely scarce, the bands leave their oldest members behind and move on, and mothers smother their new-borns. Those who stay with the band share the food. The hunter-gatherers have a similar pattern of equality in possessions. The constant mobility of a band makes possessions more a burden than an asset, and each adult can make housing, bedding, clothing, and even cooking and carrying utensils quickly from naturally available materials. A family therefore carries with it little more than a few ornaments, spare flints, skin blankets, and a bag.[4]

At least in modern bands, equality in political status parallels this equality in food and possessions. Each adult male comes to the band's decision-making council as an equal. Some bands have no head at all; others select an older man to act as a peacemaker and arbitrator in the council, not to hold a higher rank or exercise any formal power. This fundamental equality in status does not necessarily imply equal influence on decisions. The opinions of an individual who combines skill in hunting and in warfare with the personal qualities of generosity, kindness, self-control, experience, and good judgment may well carry more weight than those of other men. But the influence of such a man does not derive from a position of formal authority, entails no obligation on the part of other members of the band, and is not accompanied by any marks or perquisites of higher status.[5]

This kind of equality in political status is not new. The first Europeans in Tierra de Fuego, the Great Lakes region, and the Canadian plains reported, in the words of one, that the Indians they met would not "endure in the least those who seem desirous of assuming superiority over others."[6] Even war parties chose only a temporary leader. No member of the war party was obliged to accept the leader's direction, and after the action, the war leader would sometimes participate in a formal ceremony divesting him of whatever unequal standing he had acquired.[7]

There are two principal exceptions to this general pattern of equality among hunter-gatherers. First, women never attended councils or enjoyed political equality. Second, since age bespeaks experience in these societies, older males were apt to speak with more weight. But relations among families and among men of the same age were essentially equal. Even among men of different ages there was a kind of equality, for the young were not without experience and would inevitably acquire more.

This portrait of equality among the hunter-gatherers runs counter to the usual impression that primitive social organizations are hierarchical, and that equality is a modern preoccupation. Most people's picture of primitive social organization is not based on the hunter-gatherers, however, but on settled societies that engage in some form of agriculture. These societies, which have usually had some form of hierarchy, are in the long view of human history a relatively recent phenomenon.

European and American intruders also confused the picture when they forced hunter-gatherers to adopt some form of hierarchy. As recently as 1965, the federal government insisted that the Potawatami Indians in Topeka, Kansas, elect a formal leader before they could receive poverty funds. None of the Indians wanted to elect a leader, and none wanted to be one. According to the assistant director of the local Office of Economic Opportunity, "Some of them even commented, 'You'll never get an Indian to be a leader!' "[8] The adult males of the tribe insisted on equality of status.

The hunter-gatherers also make their decisions face to face, sometimes shoulder to shoulder, wrist to wrist, and arm to waist. Some hunter-gatherers are "extremely dependent emotionally on the sense of belonging and companionship,"[9] a sense reinforced by their frequent touching. While their intimacy does not eliminate conflict between individuals and families, a hunter-gatherer band often works as if the interests of the members of a band are similar. Questions of when to move to a different camp or in what direction to hunt have one more or less correct answer, and discussions are expected to discover the course of action best for all. In such societies, even personal conflicts can be settled in a way that is "best." Hunter-gatherer bands reach consensus because their interests generally coincide, because the members of the band are emotionally and economically interdependent, and because a relatively static culture prescribes a common interpretation of events.

In short, decision making in a hunter-gatherer council is egalitarian, face to face, and consensual. It assumes that the band as a whole has a common interest. But only very small societies can make this assumption and can maintain this kind of decision making. With increasing membership, the probability of a group's achieving a common interest, and therefore genuine consensus, diminishes rapidly. The participants in a large polity may never meet, and if they do, they will usually know each other in only one role, often one that dramatizes conflicts of interest. Large-scale organization also requires a hierarchy of some sort, if only for communication. Finally, sheer numbers make impossible a face-to-face meeting of all members at once. For these and other reasons, unitary democracy has had no large-scale form.

When large-scale polities first developed, they retained the central ideal of common interest while scrapping the democratic paraphernalia of equal status, consensus, and face-to-face assembly. In chiefdoms, monarchies, and even empires, one individual often personified the whole, becoming a unifying force in the face of increasingly diverse interests. The authority structure in these unitary, but nondemocratic, polities mirrored that of hunter-gatherer families rather than that of hunter-gatherer councils. Large-scale democracies had to await the full development of a theory of adversary democracy.

Athens: The Classic Balance

The Athens of the fifth and fourth centuries B.C. owes something of its eternal fascination to the balance it achieved between adversary and unitary democracy. On the adversary side, Athenians accepted as legitimate the separate interests of citizens.[10] Aristotle argued that the city would not be a real *polis* if individual interests were identical, "all men saying 'Mine' and 'Not mine' at the same time and of the same object."[11] The Athenian assembly allowed its decisions to be made by a formal vote, with majority rule,[12] and a formal vote is the crucial mark of the legitimacy of conflict. A vote signals both the passing of a belief that decisions have a correct solution and the introduction of a procedural substitute for common interest. In ancient Athens, political clubs further institutionalized the conflict of interests by managing lawsuits and elections for their members. In votes of ostracism, for instance, these clubs acted like political machines, supplying voters with ballots of potsherd marked in advance with one man's name.[13]

Yet amidst the competing interests of individuals, the clash of rich and poor, and the organized competition of factions, Athenian citizens could still believe that the goal of their deliberations, when they met regularly face to face in the assembly, should be the common good.[14] They could even acknowledge, without deserting the ideal, that some of their number used the rhetoric of the common good to further their own interests.[15]

The ideal remained *homonoia*—unanimity, being "of one mind." Although the assembly used majority rule, it may well have made most of its decisions by consensus.[16] Aristotle, again making friendship a model for the polity, noted that "unanimity [*homonoia*], which seems akin to friendship, is the principal aim of legislators. They will not tolerate faction at any cost."[17] He evidently believed that in a polity based on friendship *homonoia* was possible, and by *homonoia*, he meant congruence of interest on "matters of consequence" in which "it is possible for both or all parties to get what they want."

> We . . . say that a city is unanimous [*homonoein*] when men have the same opinion about what is to their interest, and choose the same actions, and do what they have resolved in common.[18]

The belief that citizens could often be of one mind, having the same opinion about what is to their interest, allowed Athenian democrats to be less interested in equal power (which would help them protect their interests equally) than in maintaining the floor of equal respect that is necessary to friendship. The ancient Greeks had early recognized that equal respect, or a sense of equal worth, was the necessary basis of personal friendship. They codified this understanding in a common maxim: "Friendship is equality,"[19] and they saw equality as playing an active role in maintaining friendship, rather than being only a passive prerequisite:

> Equality, which knitteth friends to friends
> Cities to cities, allies unto allies,
> Man's law of nature is equality.[20]

Athenian democrats went further to make equal status the basis of the state.[21] In one important sense, all Athenian citizens were of equal status, for each was a Greek and, moreover, Athenian born, rather than a barbarian. Greek democratic theory, therefore, derived equality among Athenian citizens from the underlying likeness of their common birth:

> The basis of this our government is equality of birth . . . [W]e and our citizens are brethren, the children all of one another, and we do not think it right to be one another's masters or servants, but the natural equality of birth compels us to seek for legal equality, and to recognize no superiority except in the reputation of virtue and wisdom.[22]

Assuming the possibility of a common good thus made it possible for Athenian democrats to concentrate on equal status rather than on equal power. Even writers as committed to democracy as Democritus took it for granted that those who could make the greatest contribution to the common good should have the greatest power.[23]

The Adversary Revolution

By accepting some conflict as legitimate and by instituting the formal procedures of one-citizen/one-vote and majority rule, Athens became the first society to move away from unitary democracy while preserving the democratic ideal of involving all full citizens in a decision. Many other assemblies in ancient Greece, Rome, and medieval Europe also adopted the vote and a formal system of majority rule, but they probably, like the English Parliament, made most of their decisions by consensus.[24] It was not until the advent of the large-scale nation-state and the market economy that the foundations were laid for a full-fledged system of adversary democracy.

The fourteenth, fifteenth, and sixteenth centuries in Europe saw a feudal, traditional, and theoretically immutable system of "just" prices, "discovered" laws, and personal ties transformed into a national, fluid, and permanently transitory system of shifting prices, positive law, and a mobile, self-interested citizenry. Nascent capitalism required the loosening of personal ties and the legitimation of self-interest. The new market economy demanded labor and capital free to move where opportunities developed, free to contract at rates that shifted with supply and demand, and free to move on again when the market required it. Personal loyalties, local ties, and complex networks of mutual obligation obstructed this process. The machine of the market, moreover, worked on the steam of self-interest. In the incoming capitalist system, each person, pursuing a course of individual aggrandizement, was to help allocate wages, prices, and capital investment efficiently—driving wages and prices down to their lowest limits and bringing in capital or labor wherever wages or prices still hovered above the optimum dictated by supply and demand.

The new economic order required a new political ethos, for which Thomas Hobbes obligingly provided a rationale. Hobbes's seventeenth-century England was fraught with conflict. Disbanded private armies roamed the highways. Unlanded peasants became begging vagabonds on the highways or squatted in camps outside city walls, tripling the cities' populations. Local ties could no longer restrain the highwaymen, and the cities' medieval corporate laws could not oblige the newcomers outside their walls. A contemporary of Hobbes described the capitalists and drifters of this new age as loners, acting on the precept that "nature sent man into the world, without all company, but to care for one."[25] For these "masterless men," Hobbes developed a political theory based on self-interest alone. His human beings single-mindedly pursue "power after power that ceaseth only in death." But eventually, their own interests in avoiding the continuing threat to their lives in a "war of all against all" lead them to contract on equal terms with one another and to submit to a government.

It is a commonplace that Hobbes was the first theorist systematically to legitimate self-interest as the cornerstone of political life. This idea, and the atheism it was held to imply, so appalled most of his contemporaries that they made "Hobbism" grounds for expulsion from political or religious service. Nonetheless, the modern democratic institutions that developed in England at the same time that Hobbes was writing also implicitly recognized the centrality of conflict and self-interest. The traditional monarchy had managed to maintain at least the semblance of common interest even in a polity the size of seventeenth-century England. But as the monarchy lost its ability to impose its will on Parliament, Parliament became increasingly adversary in character. By 1646, Parliament had departed enough from its traditional informal practice of unanimity to begin making decisions more than half the time by majority vote.[26] A year later, the Levellers were arguing that the poor needed an equal vote in order to defend their interests.[27] Finally, in this era parties began to develop into ongoing organizations that represented a coherent group of interests with a specific ideology, and the word "party" began to lose its unsavory connotation of a faction opposed to the common good.[28]

Over the generations, the idea gradually gained acceptance that a democracy should weigh and come to terms with conflicting selfish interests rather than trying to reconcile them or to make them subordinate to a larger common good. John Locke, in the treatise that would inspire the framers of the American Constitution, borrowed more from Hobbes in this respect than he dared admit. In spite of the crucial role he sometimes gives to common interest, Locke has men unite in political society chiefly in order to protect their property against others, and he defends majority rule on the grounds that it is required by the "contrariety of interests, which unavoidably happen in all collections of men."[29]

By the next century, the framers of the American Constitution explicitly espoused a philosophy of adversary democracy built on self-interest. Although James Madison believed in the existence of a "public good" and a "true interest of [the] country," he had adopted enough of the adversary logic to conclude that no government could eliminate the "causes of faction"—self-love and self-interest combined with differing economic circumstances. The task he set the framers of the Constitution was not the abolition of self-interested behavior but the "regulation of the various and interfering interests" in a way that actually "involves the spirit of party and faction in the necessary and ordinary operations of the government."[30]

Modern political theorists have taken this line of development to its logical conclusion. In current adversary theory, there is no common good or public interest.[31] Voters pursue their individual interests by making demands on the political system in proportion to the intensity of their feelings. Politicians, also pursuing their own interests, adopt policies that buy them votes, thus ensuring accountability. In order to stay in office, politicians act like entrepreneurs and brokers, looking for formulas that satisfy as many, and alienate as few, interests as possible. From the interchange between self-interested voters and self-interested brokers emerge decisions that come as close as possible to a balanced aggregation of individual interests.[32]

At bottom, this theory of adversary democracy is remarkably similar to modern laissez-faire economics. Following a modified version of Adam Smith's *Wealth of Nations*, laissez-faire economists not only accept the "marketplace" vision of a society based on self-interest but make it an ideal. They believe either that the invisible hand of supply and demand will aggregrate millions of selfish desires into the common good, or that, because no one can know the common good, the aggregation of selfish desires is the best substitute. Like these economists, many modern political scientists also believe either that equally weighted votes, majority rule, and electoral competition can in principle aggregate millions of selfish political desires into one common good, or that, because no one can know the common good, the aggregation of selfish political desires is the best substitute.

Because both adversary democracy and laissez-faire economics are founded on self-interest, there is no room in either system for arguments that the interests of some people are better than those of others. Each individual's interests are of equal value. Politically, therefore, each individual's interests should carry equal weight. Assuming further that each individual is the best analyst of his or her interests, the adversary system settles conflicts with the formula of one-citizen/one-equally-weighted-vote. The central egalitarian ideal in an adversary democracy becomes the equal protection of interests, guaranteed by the equal distribution of power through the vote. The implication of combining the goal of equal protection of interests with the assumption that individuals always protect their own interests better than they protect other people's interests is that only a fully equal distribution of power can guarantee equal protection.

The logic of equal value, equal weight, and equal power has pushed adversary democracies both into extending the vote to more and more members of the polity and into efforts to ensure that each vote carries equal weight. This same logic inevitably produces disillusionment, however, since even an equal vote cannot guarantee equal power.

The adversary system also has another, more serious, drawback. The mechanical aggregation of conflicting selfish desires is the very core of an adversary system. But this idea verges on moral bankruptcy. It accepts, and makes no attempt to change, the foundations of selfish desire. Because interests often conflict in the modern nation-state, a fundamentally adversary system of electoral representation based on competing interests, equally weighted votes, and majority rule is probably the least dangerous method of managing these conflicting interests. Yet safety and practicality do not make this kind of democracy morally satisfying. Adversary democracies at the national level are therefore under continual pressure from their citizens to pursue unitary goals that will tie the nation together by emphasizing common interests and political friendship.

The Antiadversary Reaction

Adversary democracy is the democracy of a cynical society. It replaces common interest with self-interest, the dignity of equal status with the baser motives of self-protection, and the communal moments of a face-to-face council with the isolation of a voting machine. Such a system invites reaction.

Jean Jacques Rousseau was the first democrat to react. Repelled by what he had seen in Great Britain, he insisted that democracy be direct rather than representative. "Sovereignty," he wrote, "does not admit of representation. . . . Every law the people has not ratified in person is null and void. . . . The moment a people allows itself to be represented, it is no longer free."[33] His provision for majority rule was a reluctant acknowledgment that opinions could differ, not an endorsement of adversary democracy premised on inevitable conflicts of interest. Rousseau believed that a polity, to be worthy of the name, must be built not on conflict but on identity of interest. The common element among differing individual interests "is what forms the social tie; and . . . it is solely on the basis of this common interest that every society should be governed."[34] For

Rousseau, an adversary democracy with its base in conflicting interests was an abomination. In a central passage, he traced the three stages by which society moved from a unitary to an adversary democracy:

> As long as several men in assembly regard themselves as a single body, they have only a single will . . . there are no embroilments or conflicts of interests; the common good is everywhere clearly apparent, and only good sense is needed to perceive it. . . .
> But when the social bond begins to be relaxed and . . . particular interests begin to make themselves felt . . . opinion is no longer unanimous; the general will ceases to be the will of all; contradictory views and debates arise; and the best advice is not taken without question.
> Finally, when the State, on the eve of ruin, maintains only a vain, illusory, and formal existence, when in every heart the social bond is broken, and the meanest interest brazenly lays hold of the sacred name of "public good," the general will becomes mute; all men, guided by secret motives, no more give their views as citizens than if the State had never been; and iniquitous decrees directed solely to private interest get passed under the name of laws.[35]

If interests are identical on many matters, as Rousseau assumes they will be in a society where the social bond is strong, the polity does not require an equal distribution of power in order to protect interests equally. Accordingly, he can say that "we should understand, not that the degrees of power . . . are to be absolutely identical for everybody, but that power shall never be great enough for violence and shall always be exercised by virtue of rank and law."[36] On matters where interests are identical, equal power is irrelevant. "In a word, it is the best and most natural arrangement that the wisest should govern [read "be executives or administrators for"] the many, when it is assured that they will govern for its profit and not for their own."[37] It is a sure sign that the social bond is breaking when the wisest are no longer heeded and when "the best advice is not taken without question."

Rousseau's general will is a unitary concept, which he opposes to the "contradictory views and debates" of adversary democracy. It derives from the experience of small face-to-face democracies and makes most sense in such democracies where debate in the assembly can reveal a genuine common interest, grasped after discussion and commanding an eventual consensus. Rousseau said he saw this process at work in the Swiss face-to-face democracies; we shall see it again in the democracies reported on here.

No democratic theorist since Rousseau has opposed adversary democracy in such a thoroughgoing way. In the first quarter of the nineteenth century, however, Friedrich Hegel attacked the private self-interest on which modern "civil society" (*die burgerliche Gesellschaft*) was based. Karl Marx, adopting this part of Hegel's analysis twenty years later, traced the new ethos to capitalism, which, through the bourgeoisie, "has left remaining no other nexus between man and man than naked self-interest. . . ."[38] At the end of the century, Ferdinand Toennies argued, also along Hegelian lines, that Gesellschaft (society) represented a distinctively modern social form, which, compared to rural, feudal Gemeinschaft (community), was "a mere aggregation of its parts," where individuals are "independent of one another and devoid of mutual familiar relationships" and "everybody is by himself and isolated, and there exists a condition of tension against all others."

> In Gesellschaft every person strives for that which is to his own advantage and affirms the actions of others only insofar as and as long as they can further his interest.[39]

This critique of self-interested societies could be extended to the political institutions of adversary democracy as well. Or by equating adversary democracy with all democracy, it could lead to a rejection of democratic government itself.[40] But among the critics, only the anarchists preserved Rousseau's ideal of small-scale unitary democracy, urging a return to the politics of common interest and face-to-face assembly.[41] And in moments of crisis, citizens might resurrect the form. The Paris sections of 1792 and the Spanish communes of 1934 organized themselves as face-to-face, rather than as representative, democracies, and at least in Spain, the communes tried to make their decisions by consensus.[42]

The forms of small-scale unitary democracy reappeared in America during the late 1960s and early 1970s. These were years in which millions of people felt that existing democratic institutions had somehow failed them. As early as 1956, C. Wright Mills had said of the mass of American citizens: "They feel they live in a time of big decisions; they know they are not making any."[43] A decade later, with the escalation of the Vietnam war, this sense of estrangement had become far more intense. The percentage of all American adults believing that "people like me don't have any say in what the government does" rose from 27 percent in 1960 to 34 percent in 1966, and 40 percent in 1972.[44] Declining confidence in the traditional institutions of adversary democracy drove both academics and politicians—of the right as well as of the left—to devise schemes for community control, neighborhood government, workers' control, and decentralized socialism. Even President Richard Nixon, unwittingly picking up language the Students for a Democratic Society (SDS) had coined nine years earlier, declared in his 1971 State of the Union message: "Let us give the people a bigger voice in deciding for themselves those questions that so greatly affect their lives."[45]

But by far the most dramatic response to the growing sense of political impotence was the establishment all over Western Europe and North America of thousands of New Left collectives—ranging from free schools, health clinics, and law communes to women's centers, underground papers, and food co-ops—operating on principles completely different from those of adversary democracy. Almost without exception, these collectives assumed that their members had common rather than conflicting interests. Most adopted as well, either formally or informally, the unwritten rules of unitary democracy: face-to-face, consensual decision making and the elimination of all internal distinctions that could encourage or legitimate inequality among the members.

The rules were not universal, of course. Certain communes, organized like families rather than groups of friends, had strong leaders. Some of the larger and earlier national organizations, like SDS, allowed elected representatives to make some decisions, and some used majority rule. But almost all radical collectives insisted on equality of status. Most made their decisions face to face. Even SDS, while not always able to avoid representation, tried to decentralize most of its decisions to small, self-governing face-to-face groups. Most collectives also adopted a formal rule of consensus, insisting that any organizational action must be acceptable to all. Benjamin Zablocki, after visiting 150 communes between 1969 and 1971, reported: "If unanimity cannot be reached, the matter is tabled. I know of no commune that makes its decisions by majority vote."[46]

Perhaps the most astonishing feature of this phenomenon was its spontaneity. The New Left's affinity for the ground rules of unitary democracy was certainly not inherited from the Old Left. There were stronger precedents in anarchist history, but few in the New Left knew that history. Nor did leading New Left organizations like SDS promote these rules in a systematic way. The founding document of SDS, the Port Huron Statement, made "participatory democracy" part of the language, but it never advocated anything like the rules that actually came to govern these collectives over the following decade.[47] Although occasional pamphlets, self-help manuals, and articles in newsletters discussed the problems of face-to-face meetings, unanimous decisions, and equality among the members, the literature of this era reveals little, if any, conscious advocacy of a unitary form of organization.[48]

This history suggests that, despite its "impracticality," face-to-face, egalitarian, consensual democracy has had some staying power. Yet no one has studied such a democracy in practice. In the late 1960s and early 1970s, when "participatory democracies" of a unitary form appeared everywhere like fragile bubbles, I decided to investigate their attraction and their mechanics. It was this investigation that led me to analyze the relations among common interest, political equality, consensus, and face-to-face contact.

Chapter 3

The Inner Logic of Unitary Democracy

T O PEOPLE steeped in the adversary tradition, the very notion of unitary democracy usually appears naive and impractical. They assume that interests are always in conflict, that individuals never respect one another equally, that consensus is always a sham in which some are afraid to make their true feelings known, and that face-to-face meetings are too cumbersome to play a significant role in a modern national polity. Describing the circumstances in which these adversary assumptions do not hold true requires, first, a definition of some crucial terms.

I begin with an analysis of interests, asking when and how the members of a polity can have their interests in common. I then argue that the more the members of a polity have common interests, the less they need to protect their interests against one another and, consequently, the less they need equal power in order to protect those interests. I also argue that a high degree of common interest allows a polity to exploit the advantages of decision making by consensus rather than by majority rule and, in the smallest polities, to settle issues by face-to-face negotiation among those concerned rather than by electing representatives or relying on secret ballot referenda.

The analysis in this volume is restricted to those polities that call themselves "democracies" and to democratic theory. Polities other than democracies can also usefully be ranged along a spectrum from common to conflicting interests, but I have not extended the analysis to cover the subtleties and possible contradictions that these other forms of human association introduce. Furthermore, even nominal democracies usually restrict citizenship in important respects, and I have not analysed these restrictions. Instead, I have looked at political practice and theory only as it applied to full citizens. This means ignoring women, slaves, resident aliens, and children in ancient Greece; nonresidents and children in my Vermont town; clients and volunteer workers in my crisis center.

Interests

Pure unitary democracy would require that all participants have common interests on all matters requiring collective decision. But do individuals ever have common interests, even on the limited range of issues requiring collective decisions? And if they do, how can they tell when this is the case? Answering these questions requires a brief definition of what I mean by "interest" and "common interest."

Defining "interest" is as difficult as defining "the good." No philosopher has ever done either adequately. Indeed, interest is intimately related to the good, since one can easily argue that what is in your interest is what is good for you. Given the intractability of the problem, I will define interests as "enlightened" preferences among policy choices (that is, preferences based on full information), without insisting that this is the only defensible definition or claiming that it subsumes every legitimate use of the term.

Some will reject this definition on the grounds that interests are "objective" and can be determined independently of an individual's subjective preferences, no matter how enlightened.[1] The view that interests are objective poses no problems for my theoretical analysis. Everything I say about unitary and adversary democracies would be equally true using an objective definition of interests. Those who adopt such a definition are, however, likely to reject some of my empirical claims regarding the degree to which members of specific polities have common or conflicting interests. The degree of discrepancy between their judgments and mine will depend on the criterion they choose for defining objective interests. An ethical criterion will have one set of practical implications, a psychological criterion will have another, a Marxist criterion still another.

Others will reject my definition of interests as enlightened preferences on the grounds that one can never know what people would want if they had full information and that we must therefore rely on their actual preferences to define their interests.[2] Those who take this position will have some difficulty with my analysis of unitary democracy since the central assumption of unitary democracy is that, while its members may initially have conflicting preferences about a given issue, goodwill, mutual understanding, and rational discussion can lead to the emergence of a common enlightened preference that is good for everyone. Those who equate interests with current preferences should also be less worried than I am about situations in which unitary democracies create what I call a false consensus by manipulating their members' feelings in such a way that some members' conscious preferences do not coincide with their true interests. Nor should those who equate interests with current preferences be as worried as I am about the ways in which both unitary and adversary democracies distort preferences by restricting and manipulating the flow of information.

For purposes of this analysis, then, I will define "interests" as "enlightened preferences" among policy choices, "enlightened" meaning the preferences that people would have if their information were perfect, including the knowledge they would have in retrospect if they had had a chance to live out the consequences of each choice before actually making a decision.[3] This is not an "operational" definition, for it can never be put into practice. No one can ever have perfect information. No one can ever live out two or more choices in such a way as to experience the full effects of each and then choose between them.[4] Nevertheless, the exercise of imagining what it would be like to have experienced two or more choices suggests the kind of analysis we should conduct in trying to understand what someone's interests are. When I write of the interests of particular groups of people in my case studies, I will attempt to perform this mental experiment, taking into account not only what the individuals concerned say their preferences are, but also what their objective circumstances indicate their enlightened preferences might be.

In the discussion that follows, I intend to stretch the concept of interest, or enlightened preference, to cover a wide variety of choices, including those that involve altruistic motives, ideals, and even trivial matters of taste.[5] In regard to taste, if neither orange cake nor walnut cake is better for you, if you have full knowledge of all flavors and their consequences, if you have "lived out" the choice between orange cake and walnut cake, and if you still prefer orange cake, I will say that your enlightened preference is for orange cake. Then if the cafeteria, reduced for financial reasons to serving only one kind of cake, must make a policy choice on this matter, I will say that it is in your interest to see that it serves orange cake.[6]

In regard to altruism, I will say that, if you have made the good of another individual your own through empathy, then promoting that person's well-being is in your interest. Likewise, if you have made the good of a group your own (for example, through patriotism), I will say that promoting the group's welfare is in your interest.

Finally, I will include the fulfillment of your ideals as one of your interests. This definition of interest is broader than some of the definitions implicit in ordinary discourse. People often distinguish, for instance, between acts that promote their "interest" and acts that promote the welfare of others. They also distinguish acting on the basis of "interest" from acting on principle.[7] However, my usage is also consistent with ordinary discourse. It does not seem a distortion of meaning to speak of my having an interest in someone else's welfare or in ending famine in Biafra if I have no material stake in the outcome but have so identified myself with the achievement of these goals that they have become part of myself in the same way as my need for clean air or a higher income.[8] This usage seems especially natural in the context of adversary democracy, one of whose distinguishing features is its attempt to handle conflicts over moral as well as material interests on the basis of one-citizen/one-vote, majority rule. I will therefore use the one word, "interest," to cover all these different types of enlightened preference. "Self-regarding" or even "selfish" interest will mean a purely personal good; "other-regarding" and "public-regarding" interest will denote making the good of another individual or group one's own; and "ideal-regarding" interest will mean identifying one's own good with the realization of some principle.

Common Interests

No group of people, however small, ever has completely identical interests. Such a state would require not only that one course of action meet the enlightened preferences of every participant, but also that in every conceivable policy choice that could come before them, the enlightened preferences of every participant be the same. This condition is virtually never met.

Many groups can have a common interest on a particular policy. That is, if all the participants knew what their enlightened preferences were, they might indeed find that these preferences led them all to support one policy over another.[9] Yet the participants' interests would still not be identical. They would probably have different reasons for preferring the policy, be willing to incur different costs to gain their preference, and have different enlightened preferences about how the policy could best be implemented. These differences might well become significant as other, hardly separable issues came up for decision.

A perfect unitary democracy would, over time, require identical interests—common interests on every conceivable policy that could come before the group. Perfect unitary democracy will therefore never be found in the real world. Neither will perfect adversary democracy, which assumes conflicts of interest on all issues except the peaceful settlement of disputes. These two ideal types are simply useful end points for a spectrum on which we can array real polities. Because interests are in fact never absolutely identical, I will use the term "identical interests" only when speaking theoretically, to express the distance between an actual situation and that theoretical point. In describing real situations, I will refer to "common interests" in a particular policy or policies and to "similar interests" on a wide range of issues.

If we allow both individual and group altruism into the definition of interest, then individuals may come to have common interests for any of three reasons. First, and most obviously, their private interests and ideals can overlap either by coincidence or because they arise from similar circumstances.[10] Second, empathy can lead individuals to make one another's good their own. Individual interests do not then overlap; instead, the separate individuals fuse, in a sense, into one. Third, several individuals may adopt as their own the good not of one another but of the whole polity. This process can have two forms. The public-spirited can adopt as their own the good of others in their group, not as specific individuals, but as a collectivity. Thus they may favor a policy that promotes the group's general welfare even when it provides them with no personal benefits and may involve them in considerable cost or inconvenience.[11] A second way of making the good of the whole one's own is to adopt as one's own the goal or function of the collectivity itself. Carried to its logical conclusion, this approach could lead to decisions that were against the selfish interest of every member of the polity. Thus, if the function of an academic department were to advance knowledge, its members could in principle conclude that the best way to do this would be for them all to resign and give up their places to more competent teachers and scholars. Adopting the good of the whole is therefore in some situations clearly not quite the same thing as making the good of the other individuals in the polity one's own. Yet if two or more people make the good of the whole their own, and if they understand this good in the same way, they will have a common interest.

The degree to which there are common interests in a democracy determines many of its other features: the kind of equality it seeks, its decision rule, and the intimacy of its relations. A democracy of common interests will emphasize equality of status rather than equal protection of interests, consensus rather than majority rule, and face-to-face contact rather than the more impersonal mechanisms of referenda or electoral representation.

Equality: Equal Respect versus Equal Protection of Interests

> Friendship is seldom lasting but between equals, or when the superiority on one side is reduced by some equivalent advantage on the other.
>
> SAMUEL JOHNSON[12]

Unitary democracy requires a rough equality of respect among its members in order to preserve the bond of friendship that draws them together. Like friendships, unitary democracies are composed of equals, not because the members, out of envy or rapacity, want to tear down the prominent and share their goods, but because potential superiors and potential inferiors alike gain from stressing the ways in which they are equal. Reducing the social distance between the members ties them more tightly to one another. In a friendship, for example, the potential superior who asks to be addressed by a first name is not being altruistic; by lowering the barriers of rank, he or she hopes to foster closer communication and a less constricted relationship. The bonds thus forged make empathy easier and so facilitate the creation of a common interest.

I do not contend that all close ties between human beings require equality; families and many agricultural societies provide evidence to the contrary. Conservative social theorists like Toennies have even argued on the basis of these examples that community requires hierarchy rather than equality, because equality breaks up the only stable (hierarchical) bonds between human beings, leaving each individual equal but separate. In this argument, the mutual isolation of modern life derives in part from the modern penchant for equality.

The experience of the hunter-gatherers—or of colleagues in a tightly knit academic department—refutes the contention that bonds of community require inequalities of status. Equal status itself creates bonds, although bonds of a different kind. Children, who idolize their elders and enjoy dominating younger siblings, like best to play with others their own age; they want to be met and understood, challenged but not overwhelmed. Adults also form friendships among those with whom they feel in some way on a par, and any situation that puts people in clearly unequal roles is a threat to the friendship between them. Many individuals want the exhilaration, mutual trust, and reciprocity of working with equals. They want colleagues, not minions or bosses.

Even in modern capitalist society, this form of equality is a necessary part of personal friendship. In both of his major studies of exchange relationships, George Homans concludes that friendship requires "similarity of esteem."[13] And the same sentiment is echoed in precapitalist societies, not only in ancient Greece, but also in fourteenth-century England.[14] Indeed, the only cross-cultural anthropological study of friendship concludes that in every known society "equality—the idea of dual souls, *alter egos*—is part and parcel of friendship."[15]

This form of equality is qualitative, not quantitative. It has to do with subjective relations among human beings, with the tone, the nature, the kind of bond between them. To our modern quantitative understanding, the phrases "equal status" and "equal respect" conjure up a misleading picture of little mounds of status or respect, carefully measured and leveled so that none exceeds the others in height, width, or weight. But the equality I mean has to do with people's vivid sense of underlying identity—a sense that rebels against the idea that either person is superior or inferior to the other.[16]

Equal respect need not depend on equal ability. It can arise from moments of emotional identification. In the first flush of discovering their common history, women in the radical women's movement felt a tremendous sense of "sisterhood." To feel that all women were sisters meant that all other differences faded into insignificance beside the overwhelming understanding that they had, so to speak, grown up together— shared the same fears, troubles, ways of coping, humiliations, and joys. In the era of sisterhood, institutional reminders of the distinctions and inequalities of the larger society became intolerable. Women found too much in each other to respect.

To the extent that we feel we share experience with another, we feel alike, and hence in some sense equal. We think of this underlying experience when we say that, although human beings may be unequal in outward qualities, they are equal underneath. Our common experience allows us to view others as somehow independent of their social roles and titles, which are clearly unequal.[17] Blood brothers and sisters, unequal in skills, often feel these sentiments of identity and equality of respect. Workers, blacks, Jews, women, nationalists—all groups with a common past—can, in stressing that past, evoke feelings of identity and equality. "Fraternity" does not contradict the ideal of equality, but rests on a perception of underlying likeness.[18]

Concern with equality takes different forms in unitary and adversary democracies. While unitary democracies are primarily concerned with equal respect and equal status, the logic of adversary democracy implies a primary concern with equal protection of interests. Adversary democracy arose to resolve conflicts in situations where there was little agreement about the common good or, indeed, about the nature of the good. Without some definition of the good, there is no way of arguing that any one individual's interests have more value than any other's. Thus, there is no basis for arguing that any one individual's interests should have more weight in the political process than any other's. Whenever there is no precedent to fall back on, equality is an obvious and therefore often uncontroversial solution to the problem of distribution.[19] Equal division is a mechanical process that, in the words of Isaiah Berlin, "needs no reasons."[20] It becomes the solution of choice at moments when a society has no reasons. In politics, adversary democracy provides exactly this mechanical process: without judging between them, it weighs every citizen's interests equally.

The suffrage, distributed on the basis of one-person/one-vote, is a first step toward the equal protection of interests. But the traditional arguments for universal suffrage can always be extended to demands for equal power[21] because an equal vote will not protect one's interests unless it is backed by equal power. The logic of adversary democracy may also ultimately require the distribution of political outcomes in proportion to a group's numerical weight in the population because, at least under majority rule, equal power will not protect equally the interests of a permanent minority.

In a pure unitary democracy, where the interests of the members are identical, the adversary rationale for equal power is eliminated. Individual interests are not in conflict and therefore need not be protected equally. One group of people—the oldest members, the intellectual vanguard, the most interested, or the best administrators—can wield more power than the others and still exercise that power in the interests of all.

Arguments for unequal power, therefore, almost invariably assume that all parties have similar interests. In the doctor–patient or captain–passenger analogies frequently cited to justify unequal power, the doctor and patient are assumed to have a similar interest in curing the patient, the captain and passenger a similar interest in getting the ship safely to shore. Robert Dahl, for example, in discussing the "Criterion of Competence," makes this assumption.[22] So does John Stuart Mill in his argument for weighted votes and Edmund Burke in his argument for the unfettered representative. Because the citizens of the two small democracies studied here often believed that their interests were the same, they often felt comfortable in collective decisions where some of their number had more power than others.

On some issues, however, the interests of the members of both the town meeting and the radical workplace did conflict. So, too, do the interests of the doctor and patient or captain and passenger. When this happens, and joint decisions must still be arrived at, the rationale for unequal power collapses. In these moments, unequal power simply results in the powerful getting their way. How equally power should be divided in a democracy therefore depends partly on how similar the members' interests—private-regarding, other-regarding, and ideal-regarding—really are. By the same logic, the degree to which elected representatives in a democracy should act on mandates from their constituents or should feel free to pursue what they see as the interests of the polity as a whole also depends on the degree to which the interests—again, private-, other-, and ideal-regarding—of the citizens and the representatives are in fact similar. The greater the common interest, the less need a polity has for equal power in order to protect members' interests equally.

While no real polity is composed of members whose interests are identical, polities do vary in the degree to which their members have common and conflicting interests. When there are costs to establishing equal power, as there usually are, a democracy should force itself to pay those costs more in moments of conflicting interest than in moments of common interest.[23]

The Decision Rule: Consensus versus Majority Rule

The decision rule of consensus also baffles most people who think in adversary terms. Only a polity in which individuals have many of their interests in common can use a consensus rule on every issue without its resulting in impasse or in extreme social coercion. When individual interests are in irresolvable conflict, a consensus requirement guarantees either deadlock in favor of the status quo or social pressure on dissenters to go along.[24] These are admittedly serious drawbacks, but in practice, moments of common interest occur far more frequently than adversary theorists assume. When a decision encompasses problems with a correct solution, or when participants in a decision can sympathize with one another or make the good of the whole their own, common interests are possible. Most tribes, committees, and intimates, all groups where these conditions hold, make their decisions by reaching a consensus on each issue. Globally, consensual democracy is still at least as common as majority-rule democracy. In non-Western societies, the local village council, the corporation, and even the national legislature will consciously and frequently make their decisions by consensus. Even in Western societies, consensual decision making is far more common than we usually realize, partly because it is often disguised behind formal majoritarian procedures. The assumption of common interests and the dynamic of face-to-face contact can lead not only friends but business organizations, committees of all sorts, academic departments, and even legislatures to make most of their decisions by consensus. For most human beings, the face-to-face, consensual decision among equals is the everyday experience, and majority rule the exception.

I will use the term "consensus" to describe a form of decision making in which, after discussion, one or more members of the assembly sum up prevailing sentiment, and if no objections are voiced, this becomes agreed-on policy.[25] Although the formal logic of consensus may be technically the same as that of a "unanimity rule," the two terms conjure up quite different processes. In a consensual process, as under a strict unanimity rule, the determined opposition of one member can usually prevent collective action, and if the group acts in spite of that opposition, the dissenter will not be obligated by the group decision. But the consensual process differs in form from a strict unanimity rule in that no vote is taken, and it differs in purpose from strict unanimity rule in that people usually adopt it when they expect to agree, not when they expect to differ.

This last distinction is vital. The informal, nonquantitative, consensual process is not designed to protect individual interests. If the members of a group can acknowledge that their interests conflict, they can then agree unanimously to make a bargain, giving one part of the group the goods it desires on the condition that the other part of the group gets other goods that it desires ("side payments"). But collectivities whose members have many common interests often develop norms that make it difficult even to suggest that individual interests might conflict. Groups that are accustomed to using consensus find it hard to recognize and to legitimate conflicts of interest by allowing bargains, distributing benefits proportionately, taking turns, or making decisions by majority rule. Just like couples who feel they must act on every issue as if they were one, consensual groups often find themselves unable to shift to adversary techniques when their members' interests begin to conflict. Such groups end up either reinforcing the status quo or, in an informal and unacknowledged manner, forcing the minority to go along.

The spectrum which stretches from the unitary to the adversary polity does not end with the latter. When interests conflict on a sufficiently large number of interests and along sufficiently consistent lines, even majority rule becomes unworkable, because the losers refuse to be bound by the result. At this point, no polity is possible. Yet collective decisions are still possible on specific issues as long as all parties agree. Thus, as we shall see, the unanimity requirement appears in different forms at both extremes of the spectrum running from trust to mistrust. What I will term consensus, as distinct from a formal unanimity rule, appears only in a unitary democracy.

Level of Intimacy: Face-to-Face Contact versus the Secret Ballot

There is no logical reason why individuals who meet face to face should not see most human relations in terms of conflict, make decisions by majority vote, or stress the equal protection of interests in the resolution of those decisions. Experience teaches us, however, that in practice face-to-face contact increases the perception of likeness, encourages decision making by consensus, and perhaps even enhances equality of status. It does this in a variety of ways. On the positive side, it seems to increase the actual congruence of interests by encouraging the empathy by which individual members make one another's interests their own. It also encourages the recognition of common interest by allowing subtleties of direct communication. On the negative side, it increases the possibility of conformity through intimidation, resulting in a false or managed consensus.

Rousseau believed that the groups of peasants he saw in Switzerland "regulating affairs of the State under an oak, and always acting wisely" were "among the happiest people in the world."[26] But whatever the effects of bringing the Swiss together under an oak, bringing the members of my two small democracies together in a meeting hall did not invariably make them the happiest people in the world. When citizens have a common interest, face-to-face contact—which allows debate, empathy, listening, learning, changing opinions, and a burst of solidarity when a decision is reached—can bring real joy. But in the face of conflict, emotions turn sour.

Even in representative systems, an aversion to conflict leads citizens to avoid discussing politics; in face-to-face assemblies, similar aversions have more profound effects. Some people do not attend meetings because they know in advance that they will get upset. If they do attend, they may still need the support of a faction before they can find courage enough to enter the fray. They may hold back what they have to say until they lose control and become too angry to listen. Fear of conflict leads those with influence in a meeting to suppress important issues rather than letting them surface and cause disruption. It leads them also to avoid the appearance of conflict by pressing for unanimity. If these techniques are successful, the consensual decision that results does not reflect a common interest. For these reasons, in both the town meeting and the democratic workplace, face-to-face decision making worked better in times of common interest than it did in times of irreconcilable conflict. When a polity has to handle many questions of conflicting interest, most people prefer a secret ballot and a method of combining preferences, like referenda or electoral representation, that puts some distance between them and their opponents.

Face-to-face meetings of all citizens are in any case impossible on a nationwide level, although meetings of smaller groups can still have a significant influence on national policy. All parliamentary systems, for instance, end up with face-to-face meetings of elected representatives. Although the incentives to finding a common interest are usually partially offset by the personality, professional socialization, and structural position of the representatives, face-to-face interaction in a legislature can take on the same character as in a direct town meeting or workers' assembly. Unitary or pseudo-unitary moments in a primarily adversary system often derive from these face-to-face pressures. If decisions in industry or government were decentralized to the level of workers' councils and neighborhood assemblies, and if these assemblies met face to face, as is to some degree the case in Yugoslavia, this too would affect what is now primarily an adversary system.

Much of this volume will be devoted to a detailed analysis of unitary and adversary modes in two democracies close to the unitary end of the spectrum. These democracies are not free of conflict; indeed, these pages report mostly their moments of greatest conflict. Both democracies have learned, to some degree, to shift back and forth between unitary and adversary modes of decision making, depending on the degree to which their members' interests conflict, but neither has learned how to guarantee the equal protection of interests when conflicts erupt. In both democracies, but particularly in the town meeting, unitary procedures therefore occasionally mask actual conflicts of interest, to the detriment of citizens who are already at a disadvantage.

II

A Town Meeting Government

Chapter 4

Life in Small Town Selby

> For the first time, the ideal social
> compact was real. . . .
> —EMERSON

I WILL ARGUE that the Vermont town of Selby acts in many ways like a unitary democracy. Outwardly at least, it seems to lie closer to the unitary end of the spectrum running from common to conflicting interests than do most democracies with which the reader is familiar. This chapter briefly describes the characteristics that create common and conflicting interests in Selby. It sets the stage for a later description of the town meeting itself and the kinds of forces, both in the meeting and outside it, that make Selby's townspeople assume they have common interests.

Selby is small, and its citizens govern themselves by coming together once or more a year in a face-to-face assembly—the town meeting. These two facts lead Selby's citizens in a unitary direction. But Selby's citizens are not all alike. They have differing interests. As Americans, moreover, they have inherited a primarily adversary tradition. Selby thus throws into visible relief the struggle in any democracy between unitary and adversary forces.

The town of Selby, which carries here both a fictional name and some fictional details, lies north-northeast of Montpelier, Vermont. Without skiable mountains, the area has escaped the intensive development of Vermont's south and central areas, but the new interstate highway system, only twenty miles away, has brought summer houses—49 of the 193 houses in the town—and an increase in new residents, most of whom have emigrated from the city. Retired professionals have moved in, along with young dropouts going back to the land. Blue-collar workers from two larger towns half an hour away have bought tiny parcels of land along the highway for their mobile homes.

In spite of these changes, Selby remains in some ways a small, traditional Vermont town. Its population is a little over 500. A quarter of its people feel they know almost everyone in town. A fifth have lived in town all their lives. Most residents know their neighbors' "coupes" and pickups; they decide whether to drop in at the lunch counter of the general store by a glance at who is parked outside. As they drive past each other on the back roads, they give a small, laconic gesture of recognition, raising one finger from the hand at the top of the steering wheel. I had been interviewing in Selby only two days when an old-timer told me he had seen my car parked someplace else in town and had wondered whose it was.

Selby's back country roads are beautiful, but from the state highway to St. Johnsbury, the nearest city, the town does not betray much of its rural charm. In the 1830s, Selby's population peaked at twice what it is today. The highway, along a series of ponds and small, swift-flowing rivers, bristled with grist mills, sawmills, and fulling mills. Today, with the mills either gone or not functioning and with the population down to about 500, most of the commercial life in Selby still follows that river highway. A trailer park, thirty or so mobile homes, two small garages, a big Texaco station, and a "window service" take-out shack string along the highway on both sides of the village. Two miles outside the village, Mrs. Keppler has renovated an old sawmill, renamed it "The Country Mill," and stocked it with tourist goods. The village itself is only a half mile section of highway where the houses cluster closer together and a firehouse and neat brick post office back up against the town's old cemetery. A hundred yards down a secondary road stands a square-towered Church of Christ, a four-room school, and the decrepit Grange Hall. Among the two dozen houses that make up the village, two have signs in their windows, one proclaiming the sale of automobile and fire insurance, the other the office of the Town Clerk. This is the "retail district" of the town of Selby. There are no other churches, no newspapers, and only one store, Tyson's.

Town social life centers on Tyson's general store. In the summer, the store's green screen door bangs closed as you enter its dark coolness. There you can buy underwear, bathing caps, flannel shirts, rubber boots, strainers, sewing materials, school supplies, and basic foodstuffs. Its little lunch counter boasts a gallery of signs advising: "Don't criticize the coffee; you may be old and weak yourself someday!" "Please! Fill my mouth with worthwhile stuff, and nudge me when I've had enough," and "In God we trust; all others pay cash." The rack on the cash register offers county newspapers, beef jerky, chewing tobacco. The gas at the pump outside goes for seven cents more a gallon that it does in St. Johnsbury, a half hour drive away. This store, the gas pump, and, down the road, the renovated mill would have trouble surviving without the patronage of travelers on the state highway. But the traffic from outside is not sufficient to disrupt the local pace. At the register, someone passes a few words with the storekeeper's wife. A couple of men gather at the gas pump as one fills his pickup. At the store's lunch counter in the morning, at noon, or after work, the men stop in for coffee, hoping to see someone they know.

Away from the highway that cuts through the village stretch Selby's hills and hill farms, served by thirty-five miles of unpaved dirt roads and two blacktop roads that connect Selby to the two small towns to its north and south. On a land-use map, every acre of the land in town except for one thin strip along the state highway appears as either forest or farm. When the town was at its peak, these hills made it a thriving dairy community. In 1970, only twenty active farms survived. Three or four large, highly capitalized farms remain prosperous; the smaller ones most often continue only because their owners have not died.

The farms have been replaced by little else. Along the state highway, the garages, take-out shack, general store, and renovated mill provide the only visible commercial development. One of the town's two blacktop roads leads up into the pines toward a state forest and, on the very edge of town, a newly developed resort condominium. The second blacktop winds in the other direction, past a sales depot for farm equipment, a sign advertising pure-bred collies, and an unpainted house where a "for sale" sign on the porch sits on some sticks of broken furniture, old farm implements, and bottles. Before I started my interviews in Selby, these were the only visual cues I had as to how the people of Selby survived.

I had come to town to find out what a town meeting meant in the lives of the approximately 350 adult citizens of this small town. In the nineteenth century, Alexis de Tocqueville wrote that "Town meetings are to liberty what primary schools are to science; they bring it within the people's reach, they teach men how to use and enjoy it."[1] Lord Bryce described the town meeting as "the most perfect school of self-government in any modern country."[2] And Thomas Jefferson concluded that town meetings "have proved themselves the wisest invention ever devised by the wit of man for the perfect exercise of self-government, and for its preservation."[3] My first town meeting in Selby assured me that the issues the town had to handle that year would touch the lives of each of its citizens. Knowing this, I wanted to learn how well the citizens thought the town meeting did in settling those issues democratically.

In Selby, the adult residents of the town are the legal repository of the town's powers. Of these, I interviewed about one in five. Before my interviews, I had attended one town meeting and had collected much of the available public record data on the town. The sixty-nine people with whom I talked were a random sample of the town's residents.[4] I began our talks by asking them in a general way how they felt about town meetings, this town, and its town meeting. Although I included a number of structured questions, the interviews usually led in the directions the townspeople chose themselves. In most cases, I tape-recorded the interviews, although whenever anyone seemed uncomfortable about my request to use a recorder I took notes instead. In two interviews in which I felt even taking notes would be intrusive, I scribbled down as much as I could remember after I left. I also asked the people I interviewed to fill out a five-page questionnaire that duplicated questions asked nationwide in public opinion surveys, and fifty-four of them eventually did so.[5] The two intensive weeks in which I did the interviews left me with gratitude, respect, and something close to love for the people of Selby.[6]

Those interviews made it clear that Selby was no longer primarily a farming community. Of the sixty-nine people I interviewed, only twelve lived on operating farms; of these, only two owned farms sufficiently large and well capitalized to provide a comfortable living. Six of the others made only a sparse living from their rocky holdings, while four supplemented their farming with part-time cabinetmaking, collie breeding, and professional knitting.

The "self-employed managerial" class in my sample consisted of these four small farmer-businessmen and the owners of the Texaco station, a smaller garage, a mail-order business, a trailer park, the Country Mill, a wholesale antique business, a retail antique shop in St. Johnsbury, and a television repair service. A school superintendent, an elementary school teacher, a farm management advisor, and a poultry inspector formed what the census would call the "professional" and "salaried managerial" classes.

At least half of Selby's population might be called "working class." Four of the thirty-one men I interviewed were wage-earning craftsmen and operatives—a machinist, a welder, and two road machine operators. Two more were foremen, and two were self-employed, in carpentry and housepainting. All but the self-employed carpenter and painter worked out of town, in one of the two larger towns within driving distance or in the adjacent small towns. Five more men drove trucks—four for wages, one his own rig. One man was a repairman at the nearby state park, and another combined some state support with odd jobs like tending the cemetery.

Seven of the thirty-eight women I interviewed were secretaries or book-keepers, all but one of whom worked in St. Johnsbury, Barre, or Mont-pelier. One woman cleaned in the St. Johnsbury hospital morgue, one worked in a plastics plant in the same city, and a third held jobs as a daily cleaning lady in some of the well-to-do homes in the area.

Only three of the thirty-eight women were primarily supported by the wages of their husbands and cared for a house and family as their primary occupation. Each of these three had more than one preschool child. Ten other women, all over sixty-five years of age, were either widowed or retired. Three men had come to Selby to retire. Two women —one old and disabled, the other deserted with four children—and one old and disabled man were supported entirely by welfare.

This list of occupations reinforced my visual impression that Selby was far from self-sufficient. For many of its blue-collar and clerical workers and a few of its professionals, the town provided cheap housing, decent schooling, and beautiful surroundings, but not a place of employment. Just over half the active labor force worked out of town. Those who were not constantly on the road, like the truck drivers, drove fifteen minutes to an hour to work every day.

This lack of economic self-sufficiency has implications for Selby's politics. The town cannot be the kind of independent polis that Aristotle or Rousseau envisioned. The automobile takes Selby's citizens away each day to work; the city lures its young away for life; and the coordination of schools, roads, welfare, and the environment with those outside has gradually eroded its governmental autonomy. These changes might make a town meeting obsolete. Analogous changes in the Swiss communes, some of which also have direct, town meeting-style democracies, led one scholar to conclude that "the conditions prerequisite to a successful direct democracy have simply ceased to obtain."[7]

It is true that since the eighteenth century, and at a more accelerated pace since reapportionment of the state legislature in 1965, Vermont towns have lost to the state government many of their traditional powers over roads, schools, police, welfare, and zoning.[8] Moreover, these days citizens are likely to perceive the power not in the town's hands as more in the hands of state and federal governments than in the hands of God. Certainly in the nineteenth century, national decisions drastically affected Selby's inhabitants. During the Civil War, almost half of Selby's men between the ages of eighteen and forty-eight left home in the Union cause. Because of the national railroad grants and the Homestead Act, cheap transportation and cheap land in the West undermined Vermont farming; as a consequence, in the seventy years between 1830 and 1900, Selby's population was cut in half. But it is likely that the citizens of that era ascribed these kinds of changes more to their own decisions or to fate than they do today, when the national causes of local conditions are publicized every evening on the television news, which 81 percent of the townspeople say they watch nearly every day.

Improved communications and mobility have also reduced the importance of the town in the citizens' social lives. Selby's town meeting is no longer so important a source of entertainment as it was when farm families had no radio or television and looked forward to the March meeting as marking the end of a long, isolating winter. In the 1820s, Selby's central village was the focus of the townspeople's economic activity, boasting two stores, four taverns, a distillery, a tannery, and a variety of mills and mechanics' shops. Today, when a family leaves its television, it drives not to Selby's village center but to a drive-in movie along the state highway, a snowmobile club fifteen miles away, or a football game at the consolidated high school in the next town. For food, clothing, hardware, furniture, or other necessities, most families drive to two larger towns nearby. As individuals became more mobile, their interests became more diverse. The town Grange has closed. The "Home Dem" Club (for "home demonstration"—a rural self-help group) attracts only older women. Most of the organizations to which Selby's people now belong have a county, state, or national base.

Yet despite the erosion of the town's social and economic importance since the day its settlers held their first town meeting, a Vermont town like Selby retains local powers with important effects on the daily lives of its citizens. Within relatively nonrestrictive state guidelines, Selby's elected school directors still hire and fire the town's teachers and school bus drivers. They decide on books, curricula, physical facilities, and the frequency and routes of the school buses. The Selby town meeting votes on the school budget, and can mandate the school directors in any of the other matters. Towns still have responsibility for 65 percent of the road mileage in Vermont. They must decide how much money to spend on their roads, which roads to repair, which to pave or straighten, how often to plow in wintertime, and which roads to plow first—decisions that, in the meager economy of a Vermont town, often amount to decisions on whom to leave snowbound for three days or which dairy farmer to put out of business when a milk company's truck refuses to negotiate certain roads because of their disrepair. Towns vote on whether liquor can be sold within their boundaries or whether their residents have to drive fifteen to thirty minutes to get a drink. Towns set their own zoning regulations; make provision for their own sewage and garbage; create their own parks, cemeteries, and hospitals; institute their own local celebrations; hire their own fire and police protection; and tax themselves each year to pay for all this. They even have the power to own and operate their own water, light, heat, power, and gas facilities. In short, although they have lost a good many of their older powers, Vermont towns still have most of the powers that radical decentralists dreamed of giving city neighborhoods in the 1960s.[9]

Selby, with all its local autonomy, is not a rich town. Vermont is poor, and for years, Selby ranked among its poorer towns. While the 1970 census put Selby's per capita income at slightly more than the state average, the year before a survey labeled almost 15 percent of its year-round houses "poor" and "dilapidated," and about 20 percent of its sewage disposal systems "inadequate"—percentages above the average for the region. In the same year, Selby had a higher proportion of trailers for residences than any town in the region. Yet the town's beautiful "outback" is now acquiring value as city people with money look for rural peace and relative inaccessibility. Among the sixty-nine people with whom I talked in 1970, two families had bought large holdings within the last two years. Blue-collar workers were also moving in. While Selby appears more stable than most Vermont towns, only a fifth of those I interviewed had been born there, and half the adult population had moved to town within the last twelve years. On the basis of Selby's growing land values, the state had recently revalued local property in such a way as to declare the town richer than before and to deprive it of most of the state school support it had previously received.

These changes brought two important problems before the town's government. Losing the state school subsidy coincided with a sudden increase in the school population, as blue-collar workers helping build the interstate highway twenty miles away bought or rented small pieces of land for their mobile homes. The school budget consequently doubled in the space of three years. Since state aid fell, taxes soared. Older residents and farmers put strong pressure on the school to cut costs, and parents fought back.

The townspeople also began to think of ways to limit the increasing number of mobile homes, which usually increased the number of schoolchildren more than they increased the tax base. The newer, wealthy migrants from the city wanted zoning to protect their land. A Regional Planning Commission, created by the state and funded jointly by the state and participant towns, maneuvered for the adoption of a master regional plan. Yet instituting any zoning in a previously unzoned town like Selby would make it harder for poorer farmers to sell small pieces of their land while continuing to farm the rest. Zoning would probably also cut back on trailers, driving up the price of low-cost housing and changing the class composition of the town.

School budgets and zoning were both within the town's competence to decide and were formulated as issues to be raised, discussed, and decided at town meeting. Some potential measures were not, however, within the town's power. One farmer's wife wanted an income tax to replace the property tax, but such legislation could only be passed by the state. Other possibilities within the town's power did not fall within the town's dominant belief in individual self-sufficiency. In Selby, no one was likely to consider, let alone bring before the meeting, a proposal for cooperative manufacture, a day-care center, a remedial reading program, or even town garbage collection.

The citizens of Selby themselves constitute the only body with the power to decide every political issue in the town. When the townspeople come together each year in their own small legislature, their interests often conflict. Some conflicts never surface, but others, like the issues of schools and zoning, come to town meeting and shape the lives of the townspeople. According to the theory of adversary democracy, the town should recognize these conflicts and settle them in ways that protect each citizen's interests equally. But Selby's townspeople like to think they have a common good. They want to be friends, and can sometimes find policies that approach a common interest. Their daily contact and the atmosphere of their face-to-face town meeting reinforce their dislike of conflict and their desire to settle things unanimously. These powerful unitary pressures clash with the fact of conflict and force the Selby town meeting to combine unitary and aversary forms. Each year, gathered together in face-to-face assembly, Selby's citizens live out the tension between unitary and adversary democracy. They temper face-to-face contact with a secret ballot, consensual decision making with majority rule, and the desire for peace with tolerance for a little open strife.

The next chapter describes my first Selby town meeting—a meeting I attended before I had formulated the concepts of unitary and adversary democracy.

Chapter 5

The Town Meeting

> In a town meeting, the roots of society
> were reached. Here the rich gave counsel,
> but the poor also, and moreover, the just
> and the unjust. . . .
>
> —EMERSON

TWO WEEKS before I visited Selby for the 1970 meeting, the town report, mailed to every resident, had published the accounts of the town along with the agenda, or "warning" of the meeting. In those two weeks, the lunch counter at the general store in the village became the forum for disgruntled observations, worries about the tax rate, occasional slander, and heated discussion about the school and zoning.

On the first Tuesday in March, at 9:30 or so in the morning, one of the selectmen unlocked the doors to the little white meeting house, and the early comers, mostly old residents of the town, drifted in. They found seats in the wooden chairs lined up to face the raised dais at the front, or gathered to exchange news and speculate on the meeting's outcome. Heavy wool jackets and coats filled up some of the many empty seats; mud-laden boots, scraped at the door, still left their prints on the floor.

When I entered the meeting house, no more than fifty people had scattered themselves among the chairs, chatting with friends. Counting the chairs in the meeting hall, I realized that the little building could never seat more than half the town's potential voters. The town's electorate had in fact been too large to fit in the town meeting hall since at least 1920, when women's suffrage doubled its number. The hall needs no more space, however, since less than a third of the town's voters normally attend the meeting, a proportion that is actually slightly higher than that of most towns this size in Vermont.[1] On this particular day, ninety of Selby's 350 or so potential voters were present for at least part of the meeting.

Such a low turnout reflects one great difficulty of assembly democracy: it takes time. In small towns of comparable size, farming acreage, and population density in New York State, turnouts for town elections average 80 to 85 percent.[2] The difference is due primarily to the fact that in New York "turning out" requires little more than dropping in at the polls for a few minutes to cast one's vote. But here in Selby, many voters who attend have to give up the wages or profits of a full working day.[3]

That March in Selby, Mrs. Thresher, whom I recognized from the fruit and jellies stand outside her farm, had settled her frail frame in her usual seat[4] up at the front of the meeting hall. She was letting the young man two seats away have a piece of her mind. "I always say my mind," she told me later. "That's a thing I believe in. And I don't go telling you one thing and the other fellow something else, either." Wallace Tyson, owner of the general store, was sitting on the left sideline with Samuel Holt, Clayton Bedell, and some of the older farmers. One of the selectmen had taken his customary place on the right sideline with the men from the volunteer fire department. Along the same wall, closer to the raised platform in front, sat a row of several of the older ladies in the town, including Mrs. Tyson, Wallace's mother, who hadn't missed a meeting in ten years. Sitting on the sidelines lets you have a quick consultation with someone else on the floor, or simply leave the meeting, without much trouble. These seats also command a full view of the entire hall. People most active in town politics are likely, therefore, to choose a place on the sidelines (see Figure 1).

The meeting itself began shortly after 10:00 with the uncomplicated business of reelecting Homer Allen as the moderator to chair the meeting and Mildred Tyson as the town clerk to take the minutes. Both have held these jobs for years. The office of the moderator, an honorary one, changes hands in Selby and in other small towns only once every five or ten years. The office of town clerk is even more stable. Mildred Tyson has been Selby's town clerk for the past generation, and her father was clerk before her. In most small towns, one person remains town clerk for years because the clerk is paid little, must develop expertise in the craft, and must, for accessibility, live in the village, finding some spot in his or her house to store the documents and conduct the minor legal business of the town. This March, as usual, the vote for Homer Allen, a thin, white-haired farmer, and Mildred Tyson, whose tight white curls and

FIGURE 1
Selby's Town Meeting Hall

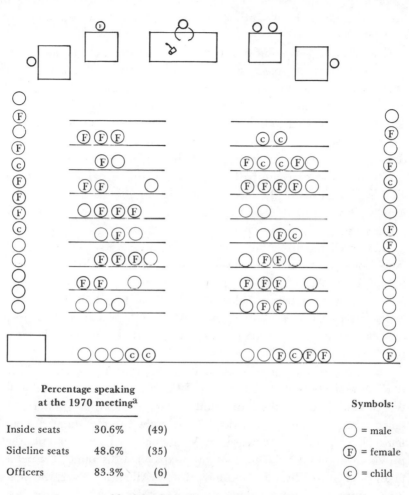

Percentage speaking at the 1970 meeting[a]		
Inside seats	30.6%	(49)
Sideline seats	48.6%	(35)
Officers	83.3%	(6)

Symbols:

◯ = male

Ⓕ = female

ⓒ = child

90 adults, 84 registered to vote in Selby

[a] In the 1970 morning session, 16 percent of those in the inside seats spoke, compared to 23 percent of those on the sidelines. In the afternoon session, 18 percent of those from the inside seats spoke, compared to 37 percent of those on the sidelines. In the 1971 morning session, 8 percent of those on inside seats spoke, compared to 20 percent on the sidelines, and in the afternoon session, 11 percent of those from the inside seats spoke, compared to 20 percent from the sidelines. While some of these differences are not statistically significant taken in isolation, the probability that the pattern would recur four times by chance is extremely low. An exact test is impossible because successive seating patterns are not fully independent.

rhinestone-studded glasses did not soften the severity of her demeanor, went quickly, with nominations, seconds, and unanimous voice vote. In equally quick succession, the town voted to accept the minutes of the last meeting and to authorize the selectmen to appoint a road commissioner.

Each year, at this point in the meeting, the town elects one of its three major executives, a selectman, who then serves for three years. Almost as quickly as the earlier votes, three nominations for selectman were made and seconded. Two of those nominated—moderator Homer Allen, selectman for the past eight years, and Frank Pate, who the next year was elected selectman—immediately requested that their names be withdrawn. A voice from the floor moved that the town meeting by voice vote ask the clerk to cast one ballot for the remaining nominee. The ensuing chorus of ayes made the election unanimous. By 10:20, one of the most important votes of the meeting had come and gone, with not a word of discussion.

Homer Allen, still moderator but now no longer selectman, asked for a voice vote to set the town officers' salaries at the level they had been the year before. Wallace Tyson, round-faced and corpulent, his blue shirt and dark trousers barely held in by his long thin belt, joked about the "huge" salary of $600 allotted his wife, the dour-looking clerk up on the dais, and the citizens unanimously voted to retain the salaries at the previous year's level.

The meeting had now reached item eight on the agenda: "To set a date for collection of Real Estate and Personal Property taxes and to vote whether with or without discount." "Mr. Moderator," asked a female voice from the back, "what does it mean, 'with or without discount'?" I learned later, from a treatise on Vermont town government, that this provision allows a town to give any taxpayer a discount of 2 percent on taxes paid in full by the deadline. Homer Allen, however, did not know its meaning. As he bent down to confer with a friend on the floor, the townspeople consulted their town reports, until finally a voice from the floor broke the impasse by calling out a motion that "we have the collection of taxes *same as in the past!*" This and the next item passed quickly with unanimous aye votes.

Homer Allen was then nominated moderator for the annual vote on one of three school directors. I did not realize until after the meeting that it was a Selby tradition to interrupt the "town meeting" at this point, begin a legally separate "school district meeting" to vote the school budget, then return to the "town meeting" to vote the taxes. While I leafed through the town report trying to make sense out of it, a unanimous aye vote elected Homer Allen moderator of the "school district meeting," and from around me voices made and seconded nominations for school director. I watched Samuel Holt, an older farmer with a gentle face, circulate through the hall giving each person who asked a slip of paper to use as a ballot. With the growing noise of scraping chairs, shuffling feet, hellos, jokes, and courtesies, most of the people in the meeting filed down each side of the hall to deposit their ballots with the ballot counters at the front. For ten minutes, the meeting became a party; the volume of sound quadrupled; old friends gathered to pass the time while they waited. It was then 10:30, and I counted seventy-five people in the meeting hall, including myself. Among those who came in late were two young men whose hair and dress marked them as "longhairs" (members of Vermont's counterculture) and with them a young woman, wrapped in a peasant shawl and carrying a tiny baby who screamed at intervals until she had to take it out.

A few minutes after the last voter had handed in his ballot, the moderator announced the vote. It was divided among four candidates—12, 20, 15, and 13—and to win, I found, a candidate needed a majority of the votes cast—in this case, 31 out of 60. None of the candidates withdrew; again the voters lined up on the sides of the room to hand in, one by one, their folded slips of paper. On this second ballot, one candidate succeeded in collecting 31 votes, but now 67 had voted, requiring a new majority of 34. For the third time, Samuel Holt handed out slips of paper, and the townspeople made their way to the front of the room, laughing or groaning at how the time was passing. While the votes were being counted, a woman on the sideline stood to read a citation to Homer Allen, now replaced as selectman by younger blood. As she read from her notes the words, "his face an epitome of New England virtue," she stopped and grinned. "That's Mrs. Cornford's phrase; I couldn't have thought that up!" The two had gotten together during one of the earlier votes to compose these comments, which now provoked a round of applause.

In a few minutes, Homer Allen leaned forward to announce that on this third ballot the leading candidate had managed to acquire 34 votes. Unfortunately, one new voter had now joined the lists, making the total voting 68 and the number of votes needed to win 35. At that announcement, the meeting burst into comments and laughter, taking the fiasco, it seemed, with fine good humor.

Before the fourth vote was taken, one of the long-haired young men asked if the candidates for school director could stand to identify themselves and briefly to explain their candidacies. This appeared never to have happened before. Most of the candidates turned out not to be at the meeting, but the incumbent, a friendly looking, redfaced man dressed in a suit and open-collared shirt, got up to mumble some words I could not hear, ending with something that sounded like "I'm not running." Who was he? My neighbor whispered, "Harvey Simonds." His share of the vote had fluctuated from 13 to 7 to 16 votes, but in each of the three ballots, he had been last or next to last. Later in the year, in my interviews, I was to hear him described by a newcomer as a "laborer," unfit therefore to help run "the biggest budget in town." His soft-spoken speech must have contained his withdrawal, for the next ballot omitted his name, allowing the leading candidate finally to poll 42 votes, a majority of the 71 people now voting. It was 11:40.

After Homer Allen reported the result of the last ballot, one of the townspeople stood to ask a question about the school budget, but Wallace Tyson jumped up shouting, "No, that's number twelve!" and people fumbled through their town reports to determine the difference between item eleven, on which Wallace Tyson argued we ought to be, and item twelve, on which he argued we ought not to be. Homer Allen looked confused. A voice from the floor moved quickly that number eleven be accepted and whatever it was passed unanimously by voice vote. I had a hard time keeping up, as the town began in earnest its discussion of the school budget, with a short speech full of facts and numbers from an articulate man in suit and tie, who had come in late and was, I learned, the superintendent of a state-created district that included six schools, among them Selby's. The burden of his message was that a recent state law now made further expenses mandatory. After the set talk, he answered questions about the cost of tuition for Selby students in the neighboring high schools, about transportation, and about whether a vocational high school diploma allows a student to go on to college.

Mrs. Carnahan, a school director with a kind, thin face, looking jaunty in her plaid jumper and holding a clipboard, got up to try to defend the budget. Wally Tyson took some pleasure in blasting away at her with ammunition from the newspaper and the town report. "I read in the *Free Press* the other night . . ." he began, then challenged her on the numbers in the town report. "Where does the $34,000 come in?" Mrs. Carnahan glanced down at her clipboard in alarm. The superintendent stepped in with precise figures. Tyson and the superintendent argued over the numbers while bored murmurs and subconversations filled the room. I overheard a young man with sideburns comment to the older man next to him, "If they spent the time in school that they spend in buses, they'd be educated," and his friend, contradicting him, "You ask the kids; they're a lot better informed than we are." Mary Carnahan long ago had moved that the budget be accepted, so finally, as the moderator forced quiet in the room, the issue came to a voice vote, loud ayes and nays sounding no consensus. As this meant another secret ballot, immediately a welcome motion boomed out that we adjourn for dinner.

Still reeling slightly from the confusion, I walked slowly over to the church basement, where town meeting dinner brings those who can afford the $1.75 price of admission a traditional and filling meal. Of the 81 adults and 9 children I had counted at the morning session of the meeting, 65 came to the dinner. The kitchen burst with women preparing their own recipes of home-baked beans and franks, brown bread and cornbread, apple and mince pie. Amid gestures and calls to pass the milk, the butter, the pot of beans, the plates of bread, I heard angry comments about the budget. The farmer to my right explained between mouthfuls that construction workers from the interstate highway had picked Selby to live in because the town had no zoning, and they could live inexpensively on rented land in a trailer park, paying no direct property tax and sending their children free to the Selby school.

In three years, the number of children in Selby's elementary and high school programs had increased by 38 children, from 123 to 161. Substitute teachers were hired, new books bought, transportation expanded, and more tuition paid to the neighboring high schools at a price that rose in this short period from $450 to $800 a head. Independently, the cost of all schooling rose to the point where, in these three years, school expenses had doubled. Since school expenses made up 70 percent of the town's budget, the town tax rate doubled as well. A farmer who in 1967 paid $6.40 in taxes for every $1,000 of his property found himself in 1970 paying $14.00. The increased property tax put further pressure on poor farmers already strained to the breaking point by state regulations requiring expensive concrete floors in dairy barns and by the milk companies, now collecting milk in tank trucks, that required each farmer to buy compatible, electronically controlled bulk storage tanks. The very next year after the taxes doubled, state aid to Selby schools fell drastically. This required another full dollar rise on the tax rate, a rise that would have to be voted in this years' town meeting. But my neighbor at the dinner saw the main problem as the newcomers: "One fellow moved into Lyford's [Trailer Park] down there had *twelve* children!"

The year before, in two tumultuous meetings, the increased school budget had passed. This year, the school directors insisted that the budget could not be cut. The town could eliminate the existing choice between the two neighboring high schools and insist that all parents send their children to the cheaper of the two, or it could make parents pay for their children's busing since transportation cost the school $17,000. Or the town could simply go into debt at 5 percent with the First National Bank, a suggestion Wallace Tyson kept making. These were the choices batted about at dinner.

By one o'clock, we straggled back to the meeting hall to plunge into full discussion of the school budget. The school superintendent had gone on to one of the other five town meetings he was to visit that day. My count of men in the hall remained the same as before lunch, but ten more women had joined them. Some had simply come late; others had spent the morning preparing the noontime dinner served at the church.

Predictably, Wallace Tyson began by asking about the school bills. Mary Carnahan, looking through the papers on her clipboard, could not find the answer. A woman in a red dress suggested that Harvey Simonds, the recently defeated school director, must have the bills with him. Mildred Tyson, town clerk, read aloud the figures in the town report. People shifted in their seats, flipped through their town reports, started conversations among themselves. A woman called out in the hubbub, "Mildred, what are you reading?" Another asked the former school director if his figures compared with the ones Mildred had. Tyson and others stood to make unrelated comments. The first questioner asked again, "Doesn't Harvey have his figures with him so that he can check them against Mildred's?"

Harvey, even redder in the face than he had been, stood and read inaudibly: "[mumble] . . . first of December. . . . Still don't see. . . . After all. . . ." Mildred Tyson continued to read from the town report. Mildred and Harvey finally huddled at the front, trying to get the figures straight. Others asked questions of no one in particular. Wallace Tyson repeated, "I still don't think this town should go over a fourteen dollar tax rate. We can go into deficit at five percent." He was now answered by a woman's, "Isn't that what got us into all the trouble last year, borrowing money that we can't pay off?"

A few people came in the front door, voices buzzed around the hall. Finally, Samuel Holt suggested a vote. Ralph Holt, his son, a plumber and one of the school directors, countered from across the hall: "Let's set the vote over till Harvey checks his figures out with Mildred." "Good idea, Ralph!" came a voice from the back. "Let's go on with other business!" The moderator, looking down into his town report, came up with item twenty-three, an appropriation of $457.50 to the Caledonia County Mental Health Service.

Now, a minute into the discussion, a tough-faced, gray-haired woman bustled in, apologized for being late because of helping over at the dining hall, passed out a report, and gave a little speech about the importance of mental health. This was Olive Pierce, who had lived in Selby for thirty-three years and for six of them had been the town's representative to the state legislature. Her stand on mental health now found support in a testimonial from one of the three young teachers in the Selby school: "I'm always running into problems I can't deal with. I wish I could carry Miss Pickett [the mental health nurse] around in my suitcase. It's our sort of right arm in trying to deal with the whole child." More arguments about the cost from Wallace Tyson, but the voice vote produced only two or three nays, Wallace's among them.

Item twenty-four seemed innocuous enough: "To see if the town will vote to empower and authorize the Selectmen to appropriate $.50 per capita to the Regional Planning and Development Commission." A fellow in an Ivy League jacket, one of the few people there who had seemed out of place, now stood to reveal himself as the executive director of the state-sponsored Regional Planning Commission. I learned that he was Robert Gretsch, a lawyer who had moved there nine years earlier, built a resort condominium near the state forest, and thereby become one of the richest men in town. He and other entrepreneurs who have bene-fited from the quality tourist trade have an investment in preserving Selby's rural atmosphere. The poorer farmers, on the other hand, have as great an interest in being able to sell their land in small parcels, unim-peded by zoning.

Gretsch gestured toward a bushy-sideburned younger lawyer who busily set up a stand of maps in front of the hall and launched into a presentation designed to convince the town to appropriate money for the commission, and eventually to zone. "Ladies and gentlemen of Selby, I'll try to be brief with your time. The future of Selby. . . . Look at this land-use patterns map. . . . Are the towns going to be prepared for this? *Our* work is so *they* can prepare *themselves*." As the presentation finally plodded to its end, one of the town's longhairs snapped out, "Who wrote that up for you?" The young lawyer's hesitant beginning, "Our staff . . ." met the booming interruption of a heavyset farmer on the sidelines: "That takes away part of the *right* of the man who owns the property! It takes away his *rights!*"

The next ten minutes produced angry debate. Farmer Clayton Bedell argued that "there's no sense in fighting communism if your neighbor or your selectman can come in and tell you what to do with your property! What are we fighting communism for?" The lawyer responded coolly, "That's a very good and very pertinent question," and swept on to de-scribe again, in terms understandable to a six-year-old, the advantages neighboring towns had realized from the work of the zoning commission. "Langford *has* such dreaded things as zoning. *They* know that there are going to be gasoline stations, and *they* want to prepare themselves." He suggested that right must be balanced against right and that in town meeting everyone could have his say. Red-faced, Bedell exploded, "If I got any say, it'd be the first time I *ever* had a say!"

Now the longhairs brought Bedell some aid. One argued that the Planning Commission would not be effective anyway: "What good does your zoning do if it allows a Howard Johnson to move in?" Another raised the issue of existing state zoning under the environmental control laws. "Is there any authority now like Clayton says?" When the young lawyer, Bill, said there was *no* such authority, Wallace Tyson took notice: "Hey, Bill, what about environmental control? Doesn't the state come in?" This brought an exultant cry from Bedell: "You're absolutely *right*, Wally!" A longhair pointed out, "You take money from the state, and they tell you what to do!" and a woman in the back shouted, "Right!" The lawyer began to answer, "The state has told the town that if it doesn't zone, the state will. So the towns should do it."

"What if it doesn't satisfy the state?"

"That's what we [the commission] are here for!"

At this reply, the hall broke into pandemonium. The antizoning forces had been trying to prove just that—the Planning Commission was only there to satisfy the *state*, not the town. In the free-for-all that followed, Bedell called the director of the Planning Commission a "con man." Gretsch, to whom this epithet was addressed, turned, stood, and as we all stared walked deliberately up the aisle to the farmer's seat. In the concentrated quiet, he looked down at Bedell: "You keep your mouth shut, Clayton, or you and I'll be in court."

Later, when the discussion seemed to go against the prozoning group, Gretsch implicitly threatened some of the others there. Leaving his seat for a second time, he strode up to the front of the hall and announced deliberately, "We are missing that Selby has a pollution problem. At least *fifteen* people are now running their *effluent directly* into the Annamnac River or a tributary. These people are now *against the law*. *We* did not have anything to do, Clayton—I mean *Mister* Bedell—with causing this pollution. *We* did not have anything to do with the fact that the town dump is now *illegal*. But we can give you help. . . ."

Ed Holt, Samuel's youngest son, jumped up, flustered: "You know you're talking so sweet, but the federal government's getting us under control! You say you're just doing it for the town. . . ."

Gretsch interrupted: "I don't suppose anyone can believe people do things for *charity*."

"No, I don't!"

"So," shouted Gretsch angrily, "I'll say I'm not going to live forever. I'll want to retire, and I'll want the highest price!"

Young Holt, angry, made a motion to vote, by ballot—a secret ballot that would protect the poorer farmers and others in the antizoning group from having to declare their position in public.

Samuel Holt passed out the ballot slips. The voices of the little group of longhairs in front of me grew louder and louder, as a quarrel emerged between the "environmentalists" and those who disliked the state, or Gretsch, or the fifty-cent levy. Furious, one young man yelled at another in a voice that carried to all corners of the meeting house: "You are an *ass!* You are an *absolute ass!*" The tension of the meeting, waiting for the vote, broke into laughter. Older people grinned to one another: "Ah hah, they fight against each other!"

After the count, the moderator announced that the vote had gone against the Planning Commission, 32 to 37 (69 people voting). But from the back of the room near the door, Manfred Krauer shouted, "Let's have a recount on that!" Someone turned to face him: "What do you want a recount for, to waste time?" Krauer sat there stubbornly: "I asked for a recount." Now Ed Holt stood again, his face tight. "You didn't ask for recounts on the other votes!" But the motion held for a revote as well as a recount, and this second ballot, with one more person voting, reversed the result and *favored* the Planning Commission, 36 to 34. Eddie Holt, not to be beaten, demanded a second revote, and Olive Pierce, the former representative, cautioned, "If there's a recount and a revote, we should do it by the voter checklist." The previous votes, in the heat of the moment, had been counted by simply collecting the ballots. Now all the voters, as they handed in their ballots, would be checked off on the voter checklist to prevent double votes. When the voters had returned to their seats and the votes were counted for a third time, the Planning Commission had lost, in a second dramatic reversal, 35 to 37. The final contest collected 72 votes. Perhaps one side or the other had rushed out to recruit people between votes; I had been too caught up in the drama to keep an eye on the door.

The fight over, everything afterward seemed anticlimactic. The school budget was approved, although Bedell moved to reduce it by $1,500 and was met only with mutters of, "For heaven's sake!" An appropriation for a kindergarten, put on the "warning" by state law, was voted down as usual. Olive Pierce read a piece in praise of Harvey Simonds, the red-faced school director just voted out. ("Thankless public office. . . . For twelve years, braved weather. . . . Sane, sound Yankee good sense. . . . Thank you.") The volunteer fire department got an increased appropriation.

By 3:45, many had left. In the discussion of the appropriation for roads, Bedell's demand, "Why do we need money for roads if everyone has to build their own culverts like I do?" brought general groans. The road commissioner began to argue with him, and when Bedell quoted Vermont Statute Title 19, Section 34, from his notes, the commissioner broke in: "I've got something I want to say, Clayton. Apparently the selectmen don't want to say it, but I will. You've got no business running your manure spreader up and down the road."

"You're trying to tell me how to run my business like these zoning people?"

"*Somebody* ought to because you're letting manure fall all over the road!" Delighted laughter greeted the road commissioner's last sally, and Bedell fell silent. The last few items passed unanimously with little discussion, and by 4:30 the meeting had adjourned.

The town meeting was over. A selectman had been elected with no opposition. An increased school budget, which would bear heavily on the poorer farmers, had been voted in by a nearly unanimous voice vote. A Planning Commission headed by one of the richest and most politically experienced men in town had lost its funding. The ninety town residents who had showed up for the meeting—the legislators of the town—returned to their homes.

Chapter 6

Unitary Forces in a Face-to-Face Assembly

> Wrath and love came up to
> town meeting in company.
>
> —EMERSON

I LEFT the town meeting grinning. This meeting, unlike the ones I had attended in other states, had finally fitted my fantasy of what a town meeting should be, and perhaps had been when Tocqueville and Emerson described them. These people had debated energetically the practical and the ideological sides of issues vital to their town. They had taken responsibility for the decisions they would have to live with. Votes had been close. Farmers and workers had spoken out often and strong. The town had no obvious "power elite."

In the interviews later, I intended to pursue the question of class—that is, whether some economic groups in the town participated more in town meeting and felt more powerful than others. I had not intended to ask questions about the forces that promote consensus in the face-to-face democracy of a town meeting. Yet talking with the townspeople six months after the meeting, I discovered that face-to-face conflict in town meeting creates fears of which I had not been sufficiently aware. These fears made the town meeting act more like a unitary democracy than it would otherwise have done. Several years later, when I had finished interviewing the workers at Helpline and had thought through the implications of my research, I realized that friendship as well as fear pushed Selby toward unitary democracy. But it was the fears I noticed first.

Young James Pedley, for example, had recently been appointed to the small town job of Viewer of Wood and Lumber. This office requires its incumbent on rare occasions to examine and classify the quality of lumber sold in the town. Primarily, however, it served to show Jamie Pedley that the townspeople he respects recognize his continuing interest in town affairs. Pedley, like one or two of Selby's other poorer farmers, does speak out in town meeting. But even he hesitates to pit what he calls the "public speaking and parliamentary rule" he learned back in high school from the Future Farmers of America against the greater verbal and legal skills of others at the meeting. For him, the psychic costs of town meeting have a simple physical manifestation. "I kinda dread going," he told me, "because I know when I come home I'm going to have the worst headache I ever had, a splitting headache."

A year before, Jamie Pedley was partially blinded in one eye when a piece flew off his old harvester. He concluded then that he was "not even a good farmer." Yet he has to master these feelings of failure in order to go to, and talk at, town meeings:

> There's a few people who really are brave enough to get up and say what they think in town meetings in this day and age. They'd sit back and say, "Well, it don't make any difference whether I go or not; they're going to get what they want." They're afraid to get up and say what they want.
>
> 'Cause it does take a little bit of courage. 'Specially if you get up and make a boo-boo. I mean you make a mistake and say something, then people would never get up and say anything again. They feel themselves inferior.
>
> Now, I guess when you basically put down a person, now myself, I feel inferior, in ways, to other people. I mean, at times I'll tell anybody no, it doesn't bother me, when it does, and I won't let anybody know that it bothers me. And in the end, I'm damn glad I didn't. Well you got—oh, let's see, forty percent of the people on this road that don't show up for town meeting—a lot of them feel that way.

Clayton Bedell is one of those who does not usually show up. Before the town meeting in 1970, he had not attended a meeting in ten years. In the end, his vote and one other could be considered the deciding two that deprived the Regional Planning Commission of its funding. Yet Bedell's arguments had met patronizing explanations, and his anger had evoked the threat of a lawsuit that he had neither the expertise nor the money to meet. Although he spoke a great deal at the meeting, he left convinced that, as he put it, "If I got any say, it'd be the first time I *ever* had a say!"

In the town meeting, people had laughed at Bedell when the road commissioner took him to task for letting manure fall off his spreader onto the road. Months after the meeting, as I talked with people in town, some were still laughing or even sneering:

Clayton Bedell is just an ordinary farmer, that's all he is.

We had an occasion this last spring, and it got to a, well, it got to a personal conflict, and the person that got up and made a perfect fool of himself and insulted this taxpayer, it should have been stopped right there and it wasn't.

When people get out of place—I say "people" but I really mean one man— when they're disagreeable and insult everyone, or actually insult just one man, I don't like it. Of course, he's definitely from the lower strata of society, if you have to say "higher" or "lower," you know.

Some people make a lot of noise, but they aren't the people who ought to control things, and they don't.

Some of the poorer and less-educated people in town are intimidated when someone like Clayton Bedell gets treated this way. Edith Hurley, living in a tiny apartment over the general store and just barely managing never to go on welfare, sides with her more affluent neighbors in laughing at Bedell. Yet she quietly draws a lesson for herself. She has not attended a town meeting in the last ten years:

I don't care to—well, to tell my part, you know, right agin a whole mess of people. . . . I don't know, I don't like to get up in town meeting and say, well, this and that . . . well, everybody's looking, or doing something, and they'll say [whisper], "She's a fool!" There's one man in particular [Bedell], that's up on this road here, boy oh boy, he's into hot water all the time. [He talks up in town meetings?] Oh! Gracious to Betsy, I guess he did. [Do people pay attention to him?] Hah, hah, no they don't, boy, we just, ah. . . .

Florence Johnson, who cleans house on a weekly basis for people in Selby and in the next town, lives with her five children in a trailer off one of the town's dirt back-hill roads. She sympathizes with Bedell but draws the same practical conclusion from what she has heard of the incident. She has never gone to a town meeting. Asked why she thinks so few people go, she answers:

I don't know. If you go there, and you speak up, they make fun of you for speaking up and so on, and I guess people just don't want to go and be made fun of. Why, I don't say anything so they don't just laugh it off anyway.

I mean we have some friends [Bedell] that went last year, and the guy stood up, and he said some things about a few issues . . . and they just laughed at him. So what good did it do him to open his mouth? I mean, he'd have been better off if he had stayed home.

Like Edith Hurley, she too has a vivid picture of what would happen if she spoke:

They all sit there, and they listen while you're talking, but the minute you leave the room or something, they laugh behind your back and poke fun at it because you did open your mouth.

The fear of being made to seem a fool is compounded by the fear of losing one's self-control. People who do not like to speak in public often hold back their ideas and feelings until their pent-up anger breaks down the barriers of reticence. In the 1940s, Granville Hicks contended that the typical "native" in a small town in New York avoided talking until he was almost out of control.

Even with his feeling that the majority are behind him, he has to work himself up to the point of self-expression, and he usually talks wildly. If, on the other hand, he thinks he is in the minority, a still greater emotional pressure is necessary to bring him to his feet, and when he gets there, he usually explodes.[1]

In Selby, even a retired businessman whose job required speaking says he would only speak up at town meeting if he got mad:

Some people are eloquent and can make others feel inferior. They can shut them down. I wouldn't say a word at town meetings unless they got me madder'n hell.

His wife, too, has only spoken at a town meeting once, and again it was when she was angry. A young truck driver would only think of speaking at the meeting if he "got mad enough." Edith Hurley, who is afraid that people might whisper, "She's a fool," decided she might speak in the town meeting if she got mad. "Unless I get mad," she says, "[then] I'm going to tell you about it. Unless I get mad, [then] I can tell them off."

But the loss of control that can accompany anger produces problems of its own. One old farmer, for instance, who never finished elementary school, is restrained from speaking by believing, like Hurley and Johnson, that if he did get up at a town meeting and say something, "Why, they'd all laugh at me." "I did speak once," he says, "and pretty near got throwed out. Got to speaking too loud. I get to swearing." He imagines that things were different before women's suffrage. Now "you got to hold your temper." The meeting is "not like it used to be. No, [then] you could shake your fist in the other's face!"

To counter the anxiety of speaking in public, groups will sometimes caucus before they anticipate a major conflict, delegate some of their number to speak, and rev up the motors of self-confidence by assuring one another that they are right. In another town about the size of Selby, I witnessed such a ritual among a small group of partisans who met the night before town meeting to discuss a major issue that was coming up the next day. They collected at the house of one of the participants for a strategy session after supper; went over the issue, the personalities of their opponents, and the major points in their argument; and bolstered one another's courage against the coming ordeal.

They needed this support because face-to-face contact, along with exposing one publicly to being a fool, makes the disagreements people voice seem more like personal criticism. Even in the abstract and intellectual pages of a journal, ideas can rarely be divorced from the personalities of their advocates. Face-to-face contact reinforces this identification. Points of information reach the floor of town meeting dressed in the personality of particular human beings. Citizens at the meeting dismiss what Clayton Bedell says because his speech and tumbledown farm place him in "the lower strata of society." Bedell knows this. Robert Gretsch too knows that people—ironically often the same people who deride Bedell—vote against his Planning Commission because they find him abrasive and condescending or because he dresses, speaks, and lives in a style more cosmopolitan than they.

Nor can differing opinions be dissociated from bitter personal disputes among individuals. Gretsch's debate with Bedell on zoning in 1970 was in many ways a private war, not eased by the complicated history, known to many at the meeting, of Gretsch's broken fences and Bedell's foraging cows. When I asked one of the selectmen, a taciturn master carpenter, if he found anything frustrating about town meetings, he looked at the ground and grit out the words: "Too much personalities involved." Phyllis Gunn, who became active in town affairs soon after she moved in twenty-one years before, told me bitterly, "They get so darned *personal* at town meeting!" A more recent newcomer attended one Selby town meeting and concluded: "No one *likes* each other!"

Afraid of the enemies they will make, some townspeople in Selby hesitate not only to speak in town meeting but also to accept town office. One newcomer's husband took time from running their antique business to be selectman six years before, but quit the job because, as she explains stiffly, "My husband is the kind that doesn't like to have disagreements." An older farmer, poor enough to have to work out in the winter for twenty-three dollars a day, held the job of Lister, or property appraiser, for seven years. For his wife, it was a difficult experience. "Now a number of farmers do take office occasionally," she says, "but Lord, there's so much criticism and so little pay!" One woman who fought for the increased school budget in 1969 feels that "there are several people in town who've held it against me ever since." Another comments drily, "You make a few enemies." Phyllis Gunn, when asked if she ever speaks at meetings, lets loose her sarcasm: "Oh, yes, often—it makes me *very* popular!" And another newcomer answers the same question: "Speak? All the time. That's how I got so many enemies." When his wife suggests that town meetings give people a chance to say what they think, he shakes his head and snorts, "Well, you make a lot of enemies, that's all I know."

In a town this small, your enemies are also your neighbors for life, so, as Phyllis Gunn says, "People are reluctant to be counted. If my neighbor's for it and I'm against it, there'll be trouble." An old-timer points out that local intermarriage makes it worse: "People are afraid to oppose each other in a small town. It's family relationships. You can't say anything because you might be talking about their own relatives."

For an official, criticism can make even the town meeting dinner unpleasant. In 1969, says one young schoolteacher, the teachers were

> put on the spot. We just sat and people got on each side, and we had to be right in the middle of the table. And so it seemed like you were getting pro and con all the way around you—so as delicious a dinner as it was, it didn't digest that easily.

Another town official describes giving a report in town meeting: "You felt as though you were in the spotlight, you know, and they were going to nail you."

Time and again in the interviews, the townspeople gave as a major reason people don't speak up their fear of criticism. "They're just scared," "scared to death . . . petrified," "afraid to open up," "afraid . . . fear or something . . . no courage." "Some people are afraid to get up and say anything." "They're afraid that others won't like it." Or as Lena Thresher has it, "Everybody's pussy!"

Physical proximity in a dispute can even induce unconscious fears of violence. The sight and sound of anger can trigger "flight or fight" mechanisms—sweating hands, adrenalin pumped into the bloodstream, and a quickened heartbeat. These effects may be pleasant in some contexts, but in a dispute in town meeting, most people do not relish the excitement.

When communication is overloaded and the signals people give touch emotions in untried ways, the outcome is sometimes unpredictable, so the participant is likely to feel that the meeting is never completely under control. The group has a life of its own; the individual is always outnumbered. Consequently, the tension in a direct democracy some-times has within it an element of physical fear. Phyllis Gunn gets excited herself as she describes how, whenever someone takes a controversial stand at town meeting, people at the meeting become "very frightened of what you think. Their anxiety level goes SWOOOSH!"—she sweeps her arm violently up above her head—"*Way* up!"

Three people in town say they actually like the "fights" in town meeting, but many more are upset by them. One young woman, living in a neat, new trailer along the state highway, has never been to a town meeting. But she says, "Well, to me, all it is is more or less a fight . . . a big argument." In a trailer half a mile away, a factory worker who has also never attended, agrees: "Myself, I just get sick of, uh, get sick of it, I say . . . [to] sit and listen to 'em argue and wrangle for four or five hours." A farmer's wife says that she goes to town meeting sometimes, "but after they get to arguing about so much and it doesn't amount to anything, I get sick of it." Edith Hurley has never gone to a town meeting, but still reports with distaste that "you get in a lot of hubbub . . . people get quarreling." Others describe the meeting as "this bickering back and forth," "petty quarrels," a "nasty argument," and "a big fight." Lena Thresher says that she does not like "the way people knowingly go against one another." Even one of the three who rather enjoy the fights agrees that many are put off by them. Many will not go to the meeting, she says, and when you ask them why, "they'll say, 'Too damn many arguments!'" An older woman sums it up—"I just don't like disagreeable situations."

Even in a representative democracy, many nonvoters avoid politics because it involves conflict.[2] Face-to-face confrontation increases the tension dramatically: Jamie Pedley acquires a splitting headache. An older man claims he stopped going because he is afraid for his heart. A man in the next town tells how his hands shake for hours after the meeting. Altogether more than a quarter of the people I talked to suggested without prompting that the conflictual character of the town meeting in some way upset them.

The Consequences of Fear

After Selby's 1970 meeting, I heard many criticisms of Homer Allen, the moderator. This was not because he had not known the difference between "with and without discount," because he had not made clear which item in the agenda was being discussed, or because he had wasted time over the discrepancy between Harvey's and Mildred's accounts. People criticized him for not having stopped the fight between Gretsch and Bedell. The moderator's main job, people feel, is to keep the peace. He should quash the first sign of anger or quickly expel the perpetrator. Roberts' Rules of Order, the gavel, the constable—all the trappings of formal procedure—should save the townspeople from the explosions that can build up face to face. The title of "moderator" is well chosen.

Yet relaxing the rules of order helps quiet other fears. It diffuses the formality of the meeting, substitutes a private or familial atmosphere for a public one, and lets friendly as well as unfriendly feelings come out. Lapses from parliamentary rule can make the townspeople feel more at home.

Because the moderator is only Homer Allen, who does not know the meaning of "with or without discount" any more than most other people at the meeting, those who can follow the meeting in their town reports are also likely to take some responsibility for its progress. In 1970, when Allen could not answer the question about discounts, someone else solved his problem by calling out from the floor the suggestion that "we have the collection of taxes *same as in the past!*" Later in the meeting, a woman in the back helped out by asking: "Doesn't Harvey have his figures with him so he can check them against Mildred's?" Ralph Holt suggested from ·the floor: "Let's put the vote over till Harvey checks his figures out with Mildred," while another man was prompted to add: "Good idea, Ralph. Let's go on with other business!" Without going so far as to praise disasters for their laudable propensity to bring people together in mutual aid, I would argue that the intermittent disorder in this meeting served to spread responsibility. In the interviews, the people who said they generally did not talk in town meeting also seemed to take pride in mentioning that they sometimes spoke, "just to second a nomination or make a motion— help the meeting along."

The informality in Selby's meeting includes using first names and joking. Wallace Tyson makes a sally about his wife's "huge" salary, calls out a comment on Harvey Simonds ("If his figures aren't right, I'll get him later!"), or, in another town meeting, jokes about the three women who had been town auditors for years ("I nominate Leona Bussiere because if Leona didn't do it, Ada Mosher wouldn't do it, and if Ada Mosher didn't do it, Ethel Quimby would be out in the cold!"). These witticisms, not very funny to an outsider, relieve the tension and remind the townspeople that they are all friends, all in on the joke.[3]

The feeling of friendship extends beyond joking and first names to a form of mutual protection. In public, Selby's townspeople are usually careful of one another's feelings. Why are the same people returned to office time after time? "They don't want to hurt anyone's feelings." A newcomer finds that an incompetent school bus driver cannot be fired because "He's a nice guy." In town meeting itself, whenever any incumbent is voted out of office, Dora Brumell always finds a moment to read a citation she and another woman have composed on the virtues of the former official. In one recent town meeting, after Selectman Coffrin had sold some land to a nonprofit developer, made a large profit himself, and deprived the town permanently of taxes from that land, he received only one vote when the ballots were counted. Yet no one at the meeting mentioned his misdeeds. The meeting elected another selectman with no discussion, and after the election, Dora Brumell read, to great applause, a testimonial to Coffrin that ended, "We gratefully allow him this brief vacation before putting him in harness again."

In the same way, selectmen and townspeople sometimes conspire—consciously and unconsciously—to prevent controversial matters like a road commissioner's illegal work with the town's backhoe from ever coming up at town meeting. If the road commissioner has to be punished, or even fired, they would prefer not to have it done publicly.

To avoid the kind of open fight in town meeting that might hurt feelings, the selectmen and school directors do some groundwork beforehand, finding candidates who are acceptable to everyone and will agree to take office. They ask around, get suggestions, and sound out likely prospects. The night before a meeting, a selectman gets on the phone to make sure the candidates come to the meeting. At the meeting itself, the election usually goes off routinely. In 1970, for instance, the grapevine had reported to Homer Allen that some felt he was getting too old for the job, and he had made it clear in return that he no longer cared to be selectman. Yet at the town meeting, someone nominated him anyway, an arrangement that allowed him to withdraw with good grace. A friend nominated Frank Pate, but Frank knew that someone else had informally agreed to take the job, so he too withdrew his name in order to make the vote for the remaining candidate unanimous.

The elected officer was thereby spared a fight and at the same time was allowed to feel he had the full support of the town. Without such protection against public defeat and open hostility, many townspeople would be unwilling to run for office at all.

Elections in a town meeting, like those in a football team, an academic department, or most other groups that value unity, tend to proceed this way from informal negotiation to formal unanimity. The disguise is most easily penetrated when, as in American presidential conventions, a formal unity succeeds bitter rivalry. But the pattern is often the same, although less obvious, in smaller groups.

Town meetings will try to reach unanimity even on substantive issues.

The religious towns of seventeenth-century New England actively pursued the ideal of harmony. Few town decisions were made by majority vote. The town clerk recorded in the minutes only that "the town decided," "agreed," or "voted" a certain policy. The desire for unity was so great that when an issue did create two seemingly irreconcilable factions, a town might deal with the problem by dividing in two rather than deciding by majority vote.[4] Although New England towns today are no longer bound by a religious conviction that prescribes unity among the people of God, they still, like other unitary groups, committees, or tribes, prefer to make decisions unanimously. When agreement seems impossible, they usually still strive to minimize conflict. Town meeting government for the same reasons is likely to be nonpartisan. Factions are thought to turn neighbor against neighbor in daily lives.

In any given instance, it is often difficult to separate the yearning for harmony from the desire to avoid conflict or from the simple dislike of not having one's own way. All these motives may have prompted one older woman to remark wistfully at the end of a partisan, conflict-torn meeting in another small town in Vermont:

> It's always been such a peaceful town. But now these people come in—they say they want to live here because it *is* peaceful—and then they just argue and won't trust anyone.

As she turned to go home, she concluded, "I feel tired. I don't think people will come if they know they'll get too tired." The town meeting was no longer her own; it had lost its qualities of friendship.

For those who are full members of a community, the friendly joking and informality, the attempts to cover up embarrassing incidents, and the unanimous votes make a potentially frightening situation bearable. Each of these actions eases tension, dissipates friction, and allows the shier members of the community to participate more fully. For the "in-group," these devices make the difference between a welcoming friendship to which they belong and a self-interested competition to which they would be uneasy spectators.

Unfortunately, the very devices that make participation easier for established members of the community make it harder for newcomers. The same procedure that spares Homer Allen the shame of being voted out of office leads the stranger quite rightly to suspect that the entire story behind the vote for selectman is not being told. As the vote for selectman takes less than ten minutes, all the nominees but one withdraw, and the voters are asked to participate in a unanimous aye vote, those not in the know can only be convinced that they have been had. Jamie Pedley says:

Sometimes a few people get together, and they'll sort of cut and dry things. Somebody will get up and make a nomination, someone second it, and someone else get right up and move the nominations cease. It's very cut and dried.

Lena Thresher describes another town meeting on the school budget:

This small group had gotten together first, and everyone had learned their part, what they were supposed to say, and they swept the budget through the meeting.

A farmer who holds a set of small town offices and feels impervious to group pressure explains the coercive effect on others of a voice vote instead of a secret ballot:

If you say, "Those in favor say aye," they'll vote aye. I call 'em so many sheep following the goats. People should have the courage to vote no if they mean no.

Another town officer who opposed the school budget at the 1969 special meeting points out angrily that a voice vote made it more difficult for the townspeople to vote against that budget:

You're looked down on if you say no to anything the school director wants. If anyone thought quickly enough, they could say they want to do it by ballot.

To people not familiar with the town meeting, these practices can be more than a source of irritation: they can be totally discouraging. A retired road worker who never finished elementary school says:

Probably a lot feel same as I do. They don't get a chance to speak their piece. If you get up and say your piece, they'll call you out of order whether you are or not.
It's all cut and dried before the town meeting. They'll pass right over you if you get up to nominate. It's organized their way before the meeting. No, I never speak. I've seen so many called out of order.

Phyllis Gunn tells me that "If you don't say what they want to hear you're not even acknowledged. I had to ask four times on a question about the budget, but they'd rather not talk about it. If you don't agree with them, they don't want to hear you."
In a town meeting, each decision to resolve a matter beforehand to avoid hurt feelings becomes simultaneously a decision to withhold in-

formation from those who need it most. The informality and occasional confusion also make it harder for the uninitiated to understand the issues. Even a resident of twenty-one years' standing like Phyllis Gunn can sometimes suspect that there are habitual, deliberate attempts to keep outsiders from understanding what is going on." The confusing thing about it," she says, "is that no one knows what they're voting for. I'm sure this is *deliberate!*" When I looked surprised, she added, "Actually, it probably isn't, but that is the way it comes across."

The informality that lets some townspeople feel that they are part of an intimate community also emphasizes to outsiders that they are not. They may not even know who "Mildred" and "Harvey" are, and it will take years before some of them will dare to call the stern, white-haired town clerk by her first name. Most newcomers will never feel easy about laughing at one of Wally Tyson's jokes. They will be confused by conventions like the one that puts the school meeting in the middle of the town meeting. In a system based on informal knowledge, they may find themselves asking "stupid" questions, like the young woman in Selby's meeting the following year who asked about allocating money for a kindergarten, when "everyone" knew that this item, only on the warning by state law, was always unanimously voted down.

Outsiders will also see the protection that the selectmen extend to their erring road commissioner as corruption. Such outsiders often press for formal, universalistic, public standards, and as they do so, they tear away the web of informal protection that the community extends to its own. The young newcomer who was confused with the procedure and, meaning no harm, asked the candidates for school director to identify themselves and to say a few words about their candidacy, forced Harvey Simonds, a laborer, to speak in public and expose himself to the risk of ridicule. Worse, the demand came at a moment when the three votes for school director had placed him at the bottom of a field of four, and he might well at that point have wanted to vanish. Not surprisingly, hidden in his mumbles was a withdrawal from the race. Mrs. Thresher told me afterward that Harvey Simonds had decided not to continue to be active in town affairs: "He's given up."

In this town meeting, as in many face-to-face democracies, the fears of making a fool of oneself, of losing control, of criticism, and of making enemies all contribute to the tension that arises in the settlement of disputes. The informal arrangements for the suppression of conflict that result tyrannize as well as protect. To preserve an atmosphere of agreement, the more powerful participants are likely to withhold information and to exert subtle pressures that often work ultimately to the disadvantage of the least powerful.

Such tyranny is not usually deliberate. Nor, although it generally works against the interests of the least powerful, is it always the tyranny of one stable group over another. For although insiders generally benefit from these arrangements, most participants in the town meeting are neither entirely insiders nor entirely outsiders. Most of the participants benefit in some way from the meeting's informality and from its efforts to prevent embarrassment and open conflict. At the same time, most participants also feel that they do not always know what is going on. Lena Thresher can be angry at the way the outsiders embarrassed Harvey Simonds and at the same time complain about how the insiders sweep decisions through a meeting. The ways she wants the meeting to manage conflict also in the long run increase her own feelings of powerlessness.

Repressing conflict therefore has its uses. Participation in face-to-face democracies is not automatically therapeutic: it can make participants feel humiliated, frightened, and even more powerless than before. Joking, informality, avoiding public embarrassment, and downplaying disruptive issues help assuage these fears, but while setting an emotional tone conducive to democracy as friendship, these soothing measures further isolate the powerless.

Wanting to Be Friends

The notes from my first town meeting in Selby reflect, for the most part, its adversary aspects. When I discovered the extent of the fears that people revealed to me in subsequent interviews, I attributed most of the unanimity in the town meeting to fear of conflict. Only after spending time in the more unitary crisis center did I realize that Selby could not be fully understood with the categories of traditional adversary analysis. Only then did I begin paying retrospective attention to the unitary side of Selby's political life. This evolution in my methods means that my investigation of the disadvantages of unitary behavior in Selby has more depth and detail than my investigation of its advantages.

My emphasis on the pitfalls of unitary democracy in Selby derives from both substantive and methodological considerations. Substantively, the citizens of Selby do have many conflicting interests, and the town is consequently closer to the adversary end of the political spectrum than is my second case, the worker-controlled crisis center. When Selby put unitary procedures into practice, those procedures came under greater strain than they did in the crisis center and more frequently worked against the already disadvantaged. For these reasons Selby gave me an excellent opportunity to document the problems of unitary democracy.

Yet my emphasis on the negative side of unitary democracy is also related to the way I went about studying the town. Trained in the adversary discipline of political science, I had begun by looking for a town where serious issues closely divided the populace. I decided to study Selby in large part because Selby had such a conflict while most other towns did not. I did not include in my questionnaire any items on perception of common interest. And when someone made a comment like "We're all friends here" or "They're just like I am" in an interview, I did not usually ask what they meant or seem interested.

It was only when I looked back at Selby after completing my study of the crisis center that I began to see the positive forces making for genuine consensus in the town. There are three routes to genuine consensus in any group: overlapping private interests, individuals adopting the good of others as their own, and individuals making the good of the whole their own. All three routes are easier to follow in Selby than in most communities. Thus, while there are major conflicts of interest in Selby, it is still a far more unitary polity than, say, the United States.

The unanimous vote in Selby's 1970 town meeting approving the budget for the town's volunteer fire department, for example, need not have resulted from fear of conflict. It may instead have reflected something close to a genuine common interest. The homogeneity of the town's population meant that risk from fire did not vary enough among the individuals at town meeting to give them substantially different needs for fire protection. The implicit questions before the meeting therefore became administrative: "What is the appropriate level of fire protection for everyone?" and "Is this level being delivered for the lowest cost?" These were technical problems, not matters of differing interest; in theory, questions like these could have correct answers. In fact, because it would have cost too much to collect sufficient information to answer these questions even approximately correctly, the town meeting accepted the judgment of its technical experts, the men of the volunteer fire department. This decision was probably in the interest of everyone at the meeting. Administrative questions like these appear often enough in town meeting for Selby's citizens to grow accustomed to having common rather than conflicting interests.

Selby's citizens also create common interest when they adopt as their own the interests of fellow citizens. They do not call Harvey or Mildred on the carpet for not having the figures right in the town report because they are likely to think: "What if I were in their shoes?" The conspiracy of silence around former Selectman Coffrin's misdeeds, the kind encomium after any official is voted out of office, and the efforts to prevent open disagreement in electing the town's officials all protect those who expose themselves by taking office. This empathetic protection is a general predisposition in town meeting, although it admits of exceptions: the Clayton Bedells and Robert Gretschs of the system are less carefully protected than others. Bedell is poor and Gretsch a newcomer, their personal styles are different from the rest, and their outspokenness makes others think they are thick-skinned, not needing the protection that the community customarily extends to is own. The townspeople then, do not distribute their empathy equally. Yet their ability to understand and respect their neighbors' needs still seems to generate a good part of the common interest of the town.

In addition to overlapping private interests and empathy, another source of harmony in Selby's is that some people—possibly a good many —have made the good of the whole town their own. Some of these people told me in the interviews that they generally went to town meeting out of "duty" or spoke "just to help the meeting along." One farmer contributed land for the dump because it was "for the town," while many gave their time to the volunteer fire department, the library, or the Old Home Day celebration. Some of those who had had to "go on the town" for support during hard times paid the town back when their fortunes improved. Others would will money to the library when they died, just as the original donor of the building had done. In their interviews, such people said they did these things because "It's for our town."

While self-interest no doubt enters into this altruism, it still means that Selby can rely on voluntary gifts of time and money to an extent that towns with a less unitary tradition cannot. Towns larger than Selby, and towns that do not bring their citizens together once a year in town meeting, seem more often to have a "free rider" problem: their members are willing to accept the benefits of contributions from others without contributing anything themselves. Such towns have fewer informal social pressures to take the place of formal coercion, but in addition, their population seems to get less positive satisfaction out of helping the town.

In Selby, the people who volunteer their time, money, or land for town projects talk about "the town" almost as if it were part of their family.

At one point in the 1970 Selby meeting, Ed Holt taunted Robert Gretsch by challenging his motives: "You say you're just doing it for the town"; Gretsch countered with a sarcastic: "I don't suppose anyone can believe people do things for *charity*," and Holt retorted, "No, I don't!" The interchange illuminates how subtly unitary and adversary assumptions intertwine in Selby's democracy. Gretsch in the end was able to trap Holt into the adversary claim that Selby's citizens only acted out of self-interest. In a more unitary polity, Holt would never have agreed with Gretsch, even in a confused debate where he meant to attack only Gretsch's motives, not those of the other Selby citizens. But on the unitary side, Holt had lived in Selby all his life, and he knew what it meant to do things "for the town." Gretsch's translation of this idea into a diffuse, undirected "do things for charity" betrayed his big city origins. He found it hard to understand or to imitate the personal terms in which some of Selby's citizens thought of their town. Holt's "town" was a real, living entity, with interests of its own, just like a person. Thinking of the town like this made it easier for Holt and others like him to adopt its interests as their own.

Selby's citizens thus have three potential strands of common interest— interest in technically correct solutions, empathy with others, and the possibility of adopting the good of the whole as their own. The face-to-face character of the town meeting deepens the ties that bind members of the town together. Citizens who see one another at a meeting realize that their opponents are human. Warmth creeps into their voices when they tell me even about someone like Bedell: "Well, I suppose he has to have his say." While an abrasive personality may turn the townspeople away from some proposal, a friendly explanation of why the books are not balanced can meet with sympathy. Moreover, the citizen who manages to attend town meeting year after year will collect a set of memories— sitting down to the home-cooked dinner, laughing or wondering at Wally Tyson's jokes, watching the mother of the family down the road try to keep her young son quiet and follow the town report at the same time, walking up to deliver a ballot and getting a smile from the ballot counter, voting the appropriation for Old Home Day with a unanimous chorus of ayes, learning the ins and outs of the meeting, and perhaps even helping it along by seconding a nomination. One day, such a citizen is likely to look around and think: "These are my neighbors," and "This is our town." The face-to-face quality of town meeting has helped bring about a feeling touched with love. When the townspeople of Selby search for unanimity, it is not only because they fear conflict but also because they want to be friends. As Emerson says, both wrath and love come up to town meeting in company.

Unitary versus Adversary Democracy

When Selby's townspeople have similar interests on questions of policy, they can act like a unitary democracy. But they also face conflicts of interest, and when that happens, they must shift from the harmonious consensus they prefer into the adversary mode: one-citizen/one-vote, majority rule.

The Selby townspeople encounter at least three problems when they try to do this. First, since they are not entirely comfortable with the adversary process, their fear of argument and desire to remain friends make them try to avoid conflict in the meeting itself. The present chapter has documented this effect of face-to-face assembly. In Selby's 1970 town meeting, it is true, an argument did arise over zoning between the poorer, older farmers and the richer newcomers, but the meeting's gentle conspiracy to dampen disputes prevented other potential conflicts from emerging. The divergent views of old and young, high and low taxpayers, and villagers and nonvillagers on the issue of school expenses and transportation never surfaced, for example. Not bringing conflicts into the open like this usually gives more power to the members of whatever inside group settles things informally before or after the meeting.

Second, although it is relatively easy in principle for a meeting to shift from consensual decision making to majority rule, one-citizen/one-vote, it is harder to make the shift from unitary to adversary assumptions in selecting town officers. As the next chapter will show, Selby's townspeople by and large consider themselves friends with common interests. They therefore tend to select leaders primarily on the basis of presumed competence, assuming those they select will use their greater competence in common affairs for the good of the whole. Selby's citizens do not try to select leaders who will represent their individual interests when these interests conflict with those of other citizens. As a result, when interests do conflict, the town's officers are not representative of the citizenry and may have both interests and preferences at odds with those of the majority. This elite is also likely, consciously or unconsciously, to prevent some decisions from reaching the policy arena at all.

Third, while these two problems arise because it is difficult to shift from the unitary to the adversary mode, even implementing adversary ideals poses a problem. As later chapters will indicate, some groups in Selby are more likely than others to attend the town meeting. The mechanism of one-citizen/one-vote, majority rule in an open assembly therefore consistently overrepresents certain interests. This pattern persists even when overt conflict erupts.

I will argue that any democracy that incorporates the elements of face-to-face assembly in its local institutions should address itself to these three problems. It must learn how to make the switch from unitary to adversary procedures in its meetings, and it should learn to consider both common and conflicting interests in selecting its leaders. It should also design adversary procedures that protect interests as equally as possible.

Unfortunately, using Selby as I do in the following chapters to point out the problems of the unitary mode runs the risk of making it seem all problems and no joy. When a French-Canadian farmer tells me, "Anybody in this town, we're all friends. You can stop and talk to anyone," I use his words only to suggest how little he realizes that in moments of conflict his "friends" do not necessarily represent his interests.[5] In my concentration on the problems of unitary democracy, I do not stress the benefits in mutual warmth that he reaps from a community where social and political life is indeed very like a friendship. In the second study, of a worker-managed urban crisis center, I discuss the benefits of unitary democracy in more detail.

Chapter 7

The Common Interest

In these assemblies, the public
weal, the call of . . . duty, [and]
religion, were heard. . . .

—Emerson

THE SELBY townspeople generally explain political conflict in their town as resulting not from conflicting interests but from conflicting estimates of who can best pursue the common good. Most of the townspeople think that taking the job of selectman is an unselfish gesture, made for the good of the town. The town officials, even in moments of bitter conflict, see themselves as responsible for the good of all, not just one group. A school director who worked hard to push through the controversial increase in the school budget, sending notes out with all the children to get their parents to come to the meeting and to outvote their opponents, nevertheless reflects afterward on the "terrible burden" the higher taxes would place on the very people he had tried so hard to defeat. Seeing no contradiction, he mixes within one sentence thanks that his own side had won and genuine sympathy for the side that lost: "It was very gratifying. The parents came out, and we . . . got an overwhelming vote, and they raised the tax, and it was really a burden on everyone."

This way of looking at the town assumes that in most, or at least many, cases, there is a public weal, a common good. Sometimes the common good involves no more than finding a technical solution to a problem. In one town meeting that raised the question of how to garage the town equipment, for instance, several men in the assembly came up with suggestions for discounts and other savings opportunities that they themselves had used in building their own garages. Their technical know-how furthered the common good. Frequently, however, the process involves what citizens in another era would have called "reasoning together," which includes coming to understand the needs of other people, as Selby's school director tried to do when he expressed concern for people on whom the school taxes would be a burden. Part of this process may also require thinking of particular issues in a larger context than the one in which they originally appeared. On an everyday level, for example, even a childless citizen, whose taxes would rise with a higher school budget, might decide that it was bad for "the town" or for "the children" to pare school outlays and on these grounds would vote for a tax increase.

Political theorists in the adversary tradition have tended to downplay the idea of a common good. But despite the frequent recurrence of real conflict, the ideal finds ample support in Selby, whose residents disapprove of "factions," "cliques," and "special groups." When they talk about the town, Selby's citizens seem not only to hope but to expect that the town meeting will make policy and the townspeople elect officers on the grounds of common interest, not according to which faction had the most votes. That conviction lies behind the strong preference for nonpartisan local government in Vermont.

If Selby has a public weal, or a common good, it follows that the job of the town meeting and the town officials must be to find that good and to pursue policies that will promote it. Political issues thus often turn on the questions of which people's insights into the common good are most to be trusted and which people have the skills to promote that good most effectively.

Judging by the way town offices are distributed, those who vote at town meeting believe that almost all of Selby's old-timers but only the upper-middle- and middle-class newcomers are competent to promote the common good. As Figure 2 indicates, on a socioeconomic scale it is the highest three quarters of the old-timers (arbitrarily defined here as those who had lived in town more than twelve years) and the highest one quarter of the newcomers (those who had been in Selby twelve years or less) who can successfully contend for a major town office. Some of the poorest old-timers and working-class newcomers even acquiesce in the dominant feeling that they are not suited for leadership or possibly for any political activity.

The class lines in Figure 2 may, however, be somewhat misleading. While it is true that old-timers who own a general store, a garage, or a

FIGURE 2

Class, Officeholding, and Political Alienation among Old-timers and Newcomers

Old-timers	Newcomers	Class	Coding

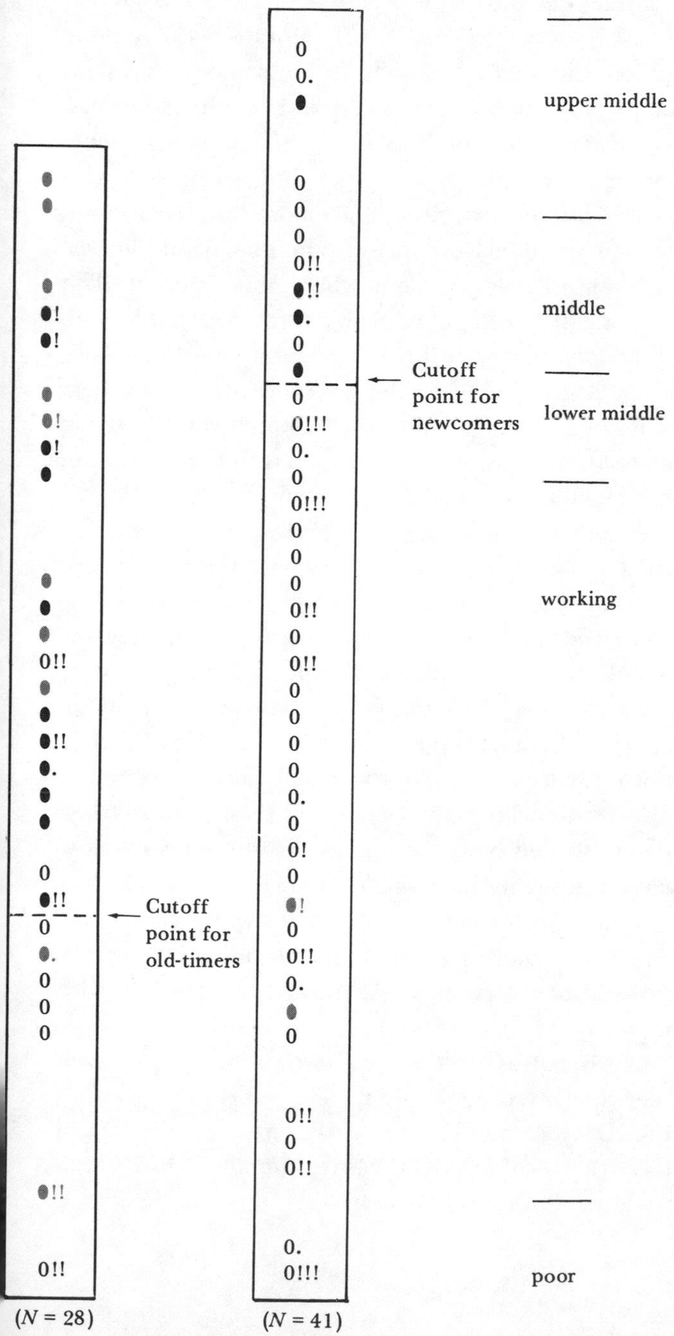

Socioeconomic status:

Individuals are arranged vertically according to their scores on my composite index of socioeconomic status (see Appendix B).

The dividing lines between "classes" are based on my subjective judgment, which depended primarily on occupation.

Officeholding:

Selectman or school director in family = ●

Lesser offices in family = ◐

No town office in family = 0

Dashed line indicates lowest socioeconomic level holding office of selectman or school director.

Political alienation:

Little expressed alienation from the town = blank

Some alienation = .

Greater alienation = !

Strong alienation = !!

Extreme alienation = !!!

Scores based on my composite index of political alienation (see Appendix B).

Classes (from top to bottom): upper middle, middle, lower middle, working, poor

Cutoff point for newcomers

Cutoff point for old-timers

(N = 28)   (N = 41)

cabinetmaking shop tend to have slightly more education and income than most farmers and most of those who work for others, even those who work for others tend to own a truck, the tools of their trade, or a small farm, and often derive part of their income from self-employment. All these old-timers talk and think much alike, intermarry, and treat one another as social equals. They would have deferred to Horace Fletcher, who owned the town's last big sawmill, but "Uncle Horace," as everyone called him, is now dead and the sawmill closed. They also perceive themselves as being more competent than the town's very old people, alcoholics, and welfare recipients. They distribute the major town offices freely within their middle- and upper-working-class group, but not outside it.

Among newcomers, class differences follow lines more familiar to non-Vermonters. The differences in education and income among the upper-middle, middle, and working classes are somewhat more marked. The upper-middle class is generally college educated, and people in the working class usually take jobs that give them less autonomy than those of working-class old-timers. Thus, excluding the less successful newcomers involves excluding culturally distinct groups, even though their position on my composite index of socioeconomic status is similar to that of certain old-timers who have held major town offices.

As long as interests are similar, it makes sense to let the more competent have more power. Both the large upper stratum of old-timers and the small upper stratum of newcomers can claim a better than average perception of the common good and better than average capacities for bringing it about. They both therefore feel that they have a claim to more than equal power in town affairs. The old-timers base their claim on tradition and on their greater-than-average knowledge of the town; they also expect power because townspeople like them have always exercised it. Newcomers in the top stratum base their claim on their greater-than-average competence, demonstrated by success in the world outside Selby. They too expect power because in the non-Vermont world people like them exercise power. Neither group usually articulates these claims, for an overt claim to more than equal power would seem undemocratic. Both nevertheless believe strongly that they should be entrusted with leadership in the town.

Unfortunately, the town is not as unitary as it would like to be. And neither the old-timers nor the newcomers fully recognize the other group's claims. They also harbor different perceptions of the grounds of political legitimacy in Selby, with the result that otherwise mundane town conflicts often take on the character of moral crusades.

Old-timers and Newcomers

In Selby's days of declining population, the town was short on middle-class leaders, and intermarriage gave most of the less prosperous old-timers ties of kinship to more "respectable citizens." Even a laborer like Harvey Simonds could hold an important town office. The community was also generally attentive to the lessons of farming life. It saw economic success as the result of a combination of foresight, prudence, intelligence, and hard work, for which an individual was responsible, and good land, for which he was not. By and large, townspeople judged their fellows on what they had made out of what they originally had, rather than on their absolute economic standing. As a result, the poor but hardworking Harvey Simonds received more respect than the slightly less poor Clayton Bedell, who let the paint peel off his barns.

Many of the poorer old-timers still hold town office in Selby. Joe Aseltine, who owns a small carpentry shop and lives in a trailer next door, was one of the selectmen in 1970. Frank Pate, a repairman at the state park, was to become selectman the year after. Mrs. Carnahan, the wife of a road foreman, who herself works part time at the Country Store, was a school director, along with Harvey Simonds, a laborer, and Ralph Holt, a plumber. Samuel Holt, another of the town's poorer farmers, made a dignified justice of the peace Even Curtis Munzel, who never finished elementary school and whose parents had been poor enough to receive regular Christmas baskets from the town, was related by blood to two town officials.

Jamie Pedley's partial blindness has not made it easier for him to feed his four small children from the poor and rocky farm he inherited when his parents died. He would not rank high on any socioeconomic scale, but in 1970, he was Selby's Viewer of Wood and Lumber, and he hopes one day to play an even greater role in town affairs. In a rare moment of self-confidence, he told me that in Selby political influence derives from a reputation for hard work:

If you are industrious, you can be heard. In a small town, they know a person is working hard. They can see this. And if they see him working hard, they know a person is trying to get ahead, and they know he is going to have a clear head about him.

Jamie's claim to power rests on his having known the town intimately since childhood. Old-timers like him feel that they understand the needs of their town better than a stranger ever could, and have an investment in the way it is run. They have struggled with its problems and have come up with solutions of which they are proud. They have mixed their labor with the town; it is theirs.

But the advent of middle-class newcomers has begun to make these old-timers feel less sure of their claim. Jamie now worries over the ease with which some of the newcomers are slipping into positions of power: "I don't think that some of them who just come in," he says, "just 'cause he fits into a social pattern, should be put right into a town office."

The "social pattern" that worries him includes professional expertise, ease with words, and a ready assumption of authority, a pattern characteristic of the top stratum of newcomers, and based largely on many years of formal schooling—"education." One older farmer, who in the past held a number of town offices, now feels that his lack of education makes him look foolish at the meeting. In the village one day, he gestures at one of the town's old one-room schoolhouses and explains bitterly:

I didn't even have high school. This little box was my main form of education.
I don't care how smart a fellow may be. We have so many today moving in here—they may be lawyers, professional men, or anything. They can outtalk a native so much that he feels he might as well stay at home.

In the old days, he says, people did not go to town meetings because it "used to be, a lot couldn't read and write. Today there's none of that, but you will find class distinction has a great deal to do with it." He has stopped going to the meeting, and is convinced that "if I should go down there today, nine out of ten of 'em would laugh in my face!"

Another old-timer is still angry over the consolidation of the town's one-room schools. Their closing makes clear to her what people think of the education she received. Her talk bristles with references to the governor, "with all his education"; to the school superintendent, "with his educated airs"; and to Gretsch, "who makes people feel inferior." She believes that everybody has something to contribute and that each person, no matter who, has something he or she is good at and can teach others —"unlike some people, especially nowadays, who think that education's so important!" She rubs her hands angrily on her apron:

They think the people around here don't know anything! That Gretsch thinks they need to get out a brochure because no one knows anything about Selby. Well, Selby's been here a good long time and a lot of people know a lot about it!

Both she and her husband are irritated at the newcomers' facility with words. "Mr. Bedell is quite high strung. He makes one or two good points, but he's no good at *expressing* them." Her husband, thinking perhaps of Gretsch, asks angrily,

> We have our natural born orators, don't we? I think we do. It's just the same as anything else. They carry more than their share of the weight. These people who come in, they're all right, but if they would only keep their mouths shut for one or two, or three or four years—or maybe ten!

To combat the educated newcomers' eloquence and the professional expertise that overawes the natives at town meeting ("You keep your mouth shut, Clayton, or you and I'll be in court"), the old-timers are tightening their hold on many of the town's institutions. When they need it, they gleefully wheel out their major weapon of legitimacy—they are native-born. Newcomers pass around stories like this one: "A lady was nominated for office at a town meeting once a couple of years ago—she had lived here for twenty-five years and before that lived in Langford [a neighboring town]—and someone there said right out, 'No, she's an outsider!'" Once, when Mr. Gretsch met opposition to one of his proposals, he faced the town meeting and demanded, "Just how long does it take to get accepted around here?"—to which, the story goes, Frank Pate shouted out from the back of the room, "For you? Never!"

Selby's upper-middle-class newcomers usually have the status and expertise to gain office despite this opposition. Yet below this class, among the newcomers whose socio-economic status roughly parallels that of most of the old-timers who held offices in Selby, the chances of having major influence in the town are poor indeed. Of the three respondents who are most bitter about their lack of power, two hold social and economic positions just under those of the newcomers who have "made it." Their marginal status may make them particularly sensitive to the exercise of power by old-timers of possibly lower status.

Sam Michalski, for instance, has recently moved from New Jersey to open his own television repair service. A union man back in New Jersey, with some college education but not enough to earn a degree, his class position is marginal. He has come almost to hate the town:

> I don't think they accomplish anything. If you've been here forty years, you get what you want; if you ain't, you don't get nothin', that's all, that's the type of thing it is.
>
> [So you never go to town meetings?] Went to one, found out it was a waste of time. Everybody gets up and talks about everybody else and—ah—

this one wants that one, and somebody moved in, and town taxes are coming up in the school, and—uh—it's just a lot of baloney as far as I'm concerned.

Later he expanded on his anger:

No, anyone who wasn't born and bred in Vermont, they really don't have much say. It's a community thing—the brother's the storekeeper, and the wife is the town clerk, and the brother-in-law runs the gravel truck, and Uncle Joe works on the roads. They're not open to new suggestions, they can't afford it, you know: "It's worked fine all these years, and I can't see why it ain't gonna work now. . . ."

In face of what he called a "closed-circuit" system, where "you have no say about anything," his pride had prevented him from ever actually making a suggestion. When I asked why he thought the same people were elected year after year, he snorted:

Who wants it? Who'd run it? I wouldn't waste my time. My wife went to the, what is it, PTA—no the PTC—every time she suggested something, it was turned down by the people who had been there for years.
[Do you see any chance that that'll change?] Yeah, sure, when all the Vermonters die up here—and you can quote me on that!

A friend who was browsing in the back of Michalski's repair shop came over to be introduced.

This gentleman moves in with twelve children, taxes went up. He's a bastard, you see, 'cause he had twelve children and taxes went up. It's idiotic. The old-timers who've raised their children, everybody else paid for them, see, and this is how they feel. So it's a real tough thing, to the point where I wouldn't care if the town of Selby burned down!

In the questionnaire and interview items on national politics, Michalski appears competent, politically efficacious, and a high participant; he distrusts politicians but believes in the system. "Thing is," he told me, "that when you write to your congressman and stuff you don't believe that your little voice will be heard. But if enough people do it, then it is heard. You know how this country's run; I don't have to tell you. If you want to get somewhere, all you have to do is picket."

On the local level, however, his underlying energy as a self-made man meets a system that he is just marginally too low on the totem pole to crack. He therefore rejects the town he sees as rejecting him. When I asked what he would do if the town were considering an unjust regulation, he answered first with enthusiasm, then denial: "I'd be the first one up there, believe me!—if I was interested! But like me, I don't care if the town burned down! . . . Don't care, don't care," he repeated. "Told you, the town could burn down; it wouldn't bother me in the least!"

Another recent newcomer, a registered nurse in St. Johnsbury, again with "some" college education, feels she cannot take town meeting day off from work, and has never been to the meeting: "But from what I hear around here, most things are settled before you even *get* to a town meeting! They usually meet in someone's home the day before. Most of it's pretty cut and dried before you get there." She has no interest in the meeting since "a lot of them feel it's useless—they don't do anything." Nor does she mind not going: "It wouldn't make any difference at all one way or the other."

Although she is not generally well informed on town activities, she had heard of the recent attempt by Gretsch and the prozoning forces to get the town selectmen to adopt an interim zoning law. This law would have stopped her neighbor half a mile away from selling used and broken tools and furniture from his porch:

They have a *very simple* zoning law to stop things like those horrendous trailers and the guy down the road with all that junk, who're just mushrooming! Mr. Cargil told me—the man who worked on it—that there's a very, very simple law that could be used in a town like this. Well, he gave it to the selectmen, and they just *dropped* it! That was the end of it!

Only obstinacy or stupidity, she implied, kept the selectmen from instituting, "well, some *small* laws to regulate, to keep things clean, like this junk down the road." Like Michalski, she concluded, "Believe me, they don't want any suggestions, I can tell you!"

She, too, participates actively in national politics and feels that she can influence the national government, expressing the self-confidence and competence normally associated with the middle class. Yet she, Michalski, and Florence Johnson were the only three people in my sample who strongly agreed with the questionnaire statement: "In this town, people like me don't have any say in what the town does." The extreme disaffection of these two seemed to me to stem from their having less power in Selby than they felt their education, political acumen, and self-confidence deserved.

The pattern of greatest bitterness at exclusion extends even into the officeholding middle class when the class position of the officeholder is in some way marginal. When Phyllis and Calvin Gunn moved to Selby in 1949, they bought the big Texaco station in the village and began to get involved in town politics. Within seven years, Calvin was voted a lister and later a selectman, while his wife was elected school director for a term and became a trustee of the town library. In the last ten years, Phyllis Gunn has attended ten of the twelve town meetings. A young newcomer who lives next door sums up their political power succinctly: "The Gunns there, really, they got the town of Selby right in their hand."

Yet Phyllis Gunn concludes that for her the town meetings are "a waste of time." "The biggest part of town meeting," she tells me, "is before and after. It's all done the way they're going to do it anyway." Like the television repairman and the registered nurse, Mrs. Gunn has some college education but not a degree, and like them, she feels hurt that her advice has been, or could be, rejected: "If you're not born here, you're a nice fellow, but you're not accepted. But I pay *three times* more in taxes than the people who accuse me of not belonging!"

Since she has held a position of considerably more than average power in the town, Mrs. Gunn's anger cannot be explained as the resentment of a permanent minority. Rather, it may come from feeling that, as a member of the middle class, she should have even greater power than she does. When she read a statement that "The meetings are just run by a bunch of important people anyway," she exploded: "Huh! By a few *un*important people! So many people are just a big splash in a little puddle!"

Newcomers tend to think that, because of their demonstrated competence outside Selby, "important" people—with education, money, experience in management—should run things. Unimportant people—small farmers, laborers, blue-collar workers—should not. One newcomer, active in town meeting, makes explicit the class dimension of the old-timer–newcomer controversy:

> You see, the thing with this town, they've got a laborer and a plumber and a housewife for running the biggest budget in town. And I don't think they're qualified to do it. But all your *wheels* are from out of town. You know, I mean people from out of state there, who moved in here. And they don't like them, so they don't want them on here.

Robert Gretsch, owner of Metterling Condominium and leader of the prozoning forces in the town, is one of the important people, the "wheels" who these newcomers think ought to exercise power. While an old-timer may say that Gretsch's advantages derive from his "education," a newcomer will call it his "intelligence." One newcomer, a woman who four years ago opened a small mail-order cheese business in Selby, concluded: "They're class conscious here. They hate Gretsch because he's intelligent." A construction foreman echoes her sentiments: "Gretsch, he's sharp. He's more intelligent than they are, so they don't trust him."

In this way, most of the old-timers and the elite among the newcomers compete for legitimacy. The old-timers can claim that they are best for the town on the grounds that they know it well and have always run it; the elite newcomers can claim that they are best for it on the grounds of their status or abilities.

The other two groups—the very poorest old-timers and the lower-middle- or working-class newcomers—are not even in the running. In Weberian terms they have neither the "traditional" claims to legitimacy of the old-timers nor the "rational-legal" claims of the newcomers. Because the poorest old-timers and working-class newcomers often assume both that the town has a common good and that others are more capable of determining and acting on that good than they are, many of them willingly accept their less than average power. A machinist who moved to Selby twenty years before and has never been to town meeting says, "I figure to let the people who know more about it run it." A house painter who moved in seven years before tells me, "I let smarter men than I get the headaches," while his wife exclaims, "Myself, I'd throw up my hands in despair!" A woman who works on an assembly line in St. Johnsbury, has lived in town for four years, and has never gone to town meeting says people like her do not usually go:

A lot of people are not educated enough to understand it . . . like which I am. I mean, I'm too shy to get mixed into a lot of stuff like this, and I haven't got the education to decide on this stuff like my husband has, and I think that is a lot of it.

Of the four poorest people in my sample, one, an old-timer, expressed the same acquiescence. Edith Hurley believes that if she spoke in town meeting people would call her a fool. When I asked why only a qurater of the voters went to town meeting, she volunteered, "Well, I've heard a lot of people—most generally people say, 'the main ones that's right at town meeting, it always goes the way they want it.'" Looking at a list of reasons that people give for not going, she pointed to one that read, "They would make the same decisions whether I went or not." "That's it right there. You read this one right here—ain't that right, right there." Her daughter read it aloud, agreeing, "Yes, that's true. Yes, that's true."

Edith Hurley has never gone to town meeting, although she lives right over the store and could easily attend. "No," she says, "I stay right 'round home." I asked whether she was more interested in national politics or local affairs. "Anything like that, I don't stick my nose much into. A lot of times I listen and things like that, keep it to myself, but. . . ." Her sentence trailed off.

What if the town were considering an unjust regulation? "Probably not me alone could do anything." "What about you *with* someone?" And as she said nothing, I asked again, "Would you think about getting together with some people about it?" "No," she concluded slowly, "I ain't much of a hand at doing anything like that. No, I'm not."

I asked, then, what she thought she could do about a law she thought unjust or harmful that was being considered by Congress. She looked at me and burst out in astonishment, "ME? They'd say 'AAAAGH! She ain't nothing!'" I was sure, from the way she said it, that at least in the political arena this was also her judgment on herself.

If the interests of Selby's citizens are generally similar—and the residents of Selby usually seem to think they are—then the present distribution of power is perfectly consistent with the unitary democratic ideal. When interests are similar, citizens do not need equal power to protect their individual interests; they only need to persuade their wisest, cleverest, most virtuous, and most experienced citizens to spend their time solving town problems in the best interests of everyone. The regular town meeting attenders and the town officeholders may not be the best possible people for the job, but they include most of those to whom the citizens of Selby would want to entrust their affairs.

The question, then, is whether Selby's citizens really do have similar interests. If interests are the choices people would make with perfect information, no one can know with certainty what choices Selby's citizens would make on the issues that come before the town. Nonetheless, one must make assumptions about people's interests. If Selby's citizens had perfect information about building a town garage or deciding whether to buy a new backhoe they would probably all choose the same policy. On such issues, there is usually one solution that is best for all, and everyone benefits from giving a more capable subgroup, whether the old-timers or the elite newcomers, greater power than others.

Yet the interests of Selby's citizens are not always the same. Even if a particular policy helped everyone, it might help some groups more than others, so that the citizens' material interests would be advanced unequally. Moreover, individual interests are not all material. Unequal power can injure the self-esteem of the less powerful, diminish the social basis of equal respect, or deprive the less powerful of the opportunity to become more politically capable and more aware of their own and others' needs. If an unequal allocation of power makes the less powerful feel about themselves, as Edith Hurley does, "AAAAGH! She ain't nothing!" few would say that this system was in their interest.

Chapter 8

Conflicting Interests

In these assemblies . . . the
call of interest [was also]
heard. . . .

—EMERSON

GROUPS that have more than their
share of power in Selby often have what one must assume to be different
interests, both material and broadly psychological, from groups that have
less power. The groups with the most power in Selby are the old-timers,
those who live in the village, the middle classes, the men, and the old. To
the extent that newcomers, nonvillagers, the working class, the women, and
the young do not participate in town politics, their interests are less likely
to be protected in moments of conflict.

In Selby, one obvious cleavage is between newcomers and old-timers.
Their interests differ on taxes, schools, zoning, and corruption. Newcomers, particularly former city dwellers, expect more government services
than do old-timers. They also tend to live on smaller tracts of land and to
pay less property tax. Because the benefits to them are higher and the
costs are lower, newcomers generally demand more services, even if this
means higher taxes for the town.

The old-timers are likely to hold large tracts of land and are therefore
more vulnerable to the property tax that pays for town services. More
of them are farmers, squeezed by mounting capital costs.[1] As the cost of
town services goes up, the tax burden on the landed old-timers grows.
Short of selling their land, they cannot get the cash to pay those taxes, but
the more land they sell, the less economical it is to farm. One old farmer

explodes, "These people [the newcomers] think that money grows on bushes! Huh! Those bushes were winterkilled a long time ago!" Along with his livelihood, the newcomers threaten his sense of self. "Wasn't too many years ago," he muses, "that I knew most everyone in this town. But now, we don't fit. Our thinking doesn't fit. We'll be driven right off our land by taxes."

Even those old-timers who hold wage-paying jobs—working on the roads, maintaining the state forests, driving a school bus—still have roots in a noncash economy. They heat their houses with home-grown wood, raise chickens and a calf or two, and spend the fall canning enough of their garden produce to last them through the winter. They resent the newcomers' easy access to cash. The poorer newcomers who live in old trailers in Lyford's Trailer Park and hold down two badly paying jobs can sometimes buy things for which farmers, with most of their capital tied up in land and farm machinery, can only long. Lourena Bartlett, married to one of the town's poor farmers, says wistfully over her kitchen table:

> Those trailer parks with hundreds of trailers—if two are working, they have a good income. I know a fellow—he's moved now—if he wanted to get his wife a car for a birthday present, he didn't think twice!

The Bartletts live back in the hills where long winters often bring isolation, family quarrels, and alcoholism, and where the snowmobile has become the greatest liberator since television. The Bartletts do not have the cash to buy one, but when they drive down along the state highway, they see two or even three snowmobiles parked behind some of the mobile homes. When the Bartletts see in the town's public tax record that they pay ten times as much taxes as many of the snowmobile owners, they become bitter. They try to keep both services and taxes down.

Along with finding it more difficult to pay taxes, the old-timers place less value on the services those taxes buy. Their attitude toward the schools, which take 70 percent of the town's budget, is an example. Selby's newcomers, whether working or middle class, are usually tied to a technological, mobile economy. They feel that success or failure is determined by how people do in school. For them, school provides the entrée into the world beyond the town; it gives a child a transferable credential. Since newcomers do not usually expect their children to stay in Selby after they are grown, they want to send them into the world with an arsenal of skills and diplomas as good as the ones that other children acquire elsewhere.

Old-timers, whose livelihoods derive from a rural economy, feel that success depends more on self-discipline, good management, and native shrewdness than on schooling. They are more likely than newcomers to be self-employed.[2] They expect to leave their land or businesses to at least one of their children, and they expect the rest to be self-employed in other ways. The goodwill a child inherits from his or her family, the network of acquaintances, and the family reputation for reliability all seem more important to old-timers for a future as an independent carpenter or garage owner than does an academic credential.

The old-timers also have a more abstract interest in spending less on the school. Mrs. Bartlett, for instance, remarks of the newcomers, "A certain group just wants material things. There are too many that like material things and 'show.' *We* like basic education." By this, I think she means more than that her family wants to avoid higher taxes. The farmers' frugal, low cash flow, self-sufficient budgets for the school resemble their family budgets. And "basic education" in their minds produces self-reliance, independence from a technological economy, and rejection of the subtle manipulations of social studies, learning resources and progressive teachers. If the school only teaches reading, writing, and arithmetic, rewards only hard work and reliable attendance, and punishes transgressions openly, even physically, children will return home in the same psychic condition as when they left it. Some old-timers probably feel also that the new demands "for all this education" devalue the kind of education they received. When old Curtis Munzel says that "the worst thing they ever done was get rid of the rural schools," part of what I think he means is that people like him are as good as everyone else. He tells me proudly that he got his expertise outside of school, by becoming "the best sawyer there was in Selby—and people knew it too! You have to do a lot of figuring in your head to get the best out of a log!"

Even regarding their children's recreation, newcomers and old-timers differ. Newcomers have no farm work to keep their children busy; they are likely to live in trailers or small houses clustered along the state highway, where their children visit one another, create a peer culture, and get into mischief. So they are concerned with supervision. Sam Michalski, the owner of the television repair service, suggested that "the school could be turned into an after-hours place for the children, put a pool table in and different things, and give them an area of recreation." Although it met Michalski's children's needs, such a suggestion would have shocked the older residents; their response would have been not to build a pool table but to put the child to work. On the farm, a child is safely out of contact with others: "If you have an unruly dog, you keep it close to home. Kids are the same. Let 'em hang around together, and they get like a dog pack."

Along with taxes, schools, and recreation, another major point of difference is zoning. Old-timers with large tracts of land are usually still marginally engaged in farming. If they have to sell their land, they prefer to sell it free of zoning, in small enough parcels to meet taxes or to support themselves while they retain enough to live on and to farm. Newcomers with large tracts of land either are refugees from city living who want zoning to protect the undeveloped rural charm they came for or are entrepreneurs who have a stake in the tourist industry, like Gretsch with his condominiums or the Kepplers with their Country Mill. Zoning ordinances that make land salable only in large lots and for restricted uses maintain the value of their investment.

The conflict over zoning is exacerbated by the zoning regulations themselves, most of which are merely guidelines that leave enforcement to an appointed board. The old-timers might feel comfortable if the board were made up of people like themselves, who share their daily problems, but zoning and land-planning commissions at the state and regional levels consist almost entirely of wealthy, college-educated, recently arrived volunteers, who never seem to need to add a mobile home out back, who see a nonfunctioning automobile as "horrendous junk" rather than as a storehouse of spare parts, and who might deprive some old-timers' homes of heat by making wood burning illegal.

Differences over styles of living exacerbate the conflicts over zoning as they do those over education. The isolation of the hill farm, the comparative self-sufficiency of small-scale agriculture, and the independence of self-employment lead old-timers to resent social regulations like zoning, while newcomers from more populated areas are more apt to accept regulation as part of life.

Finally, different ideas about what constitutes "corruption" divide newcomers from old-timers. All three of the poorest male old-timers have worked in some capacity for the town, usually on the roads. Many manual workers among the old-timers belong to the volunteer fire department. The propertied old-timers invariably have close relatives in some town office. Thus, two years before, when the road commissioner was caught doing a little work with Selby's town backhoe for extra money, the selectmen worried because they had appointed him, his friends in the volunteer fire department supported him, and the men who worked under him on the roads, in spite of their glee that he had been caught, wanted to head off any major investigation of road maintenance efficiency. To avoid the disruptive effects of public exposure, the old-timers simply waited for the incident to blow over. The newcomers, hearing of what had happened, knowing they were excluded from the protective network, and being used to the enforcement of formal standards, added this irritation to their growing list of grudges.

This does not mean that newcomers and old-timers invariably find themselves lined up on opposite sides. In many cases, their interests coincide—for example, the interests of the long-haired newcomers and the poorer farmers, both engaged in marginal agriculture, often come together on zoning decisions. But when differences in interest do divide the old-timers from the newcomers, the attempt to find a common good can cloud whatever is at issue.

The town of Selby shows other cleavages as well. The interests of villagers and nonvillagers often diverge. The $17,000 that the town spends annually for school transportation benefits only the people who live outside the central village. And because the villagers live on the state highway, where the road is repaired and plowed by the state, they vote money for town roads with less enthusiasm than do people who live on town roads back in the hills. A few years before, when the villagers proposed that the town install a municipal sewer system that would serve only houses in the village, the nonvillagers fought the measure.

The young in Selby have markedly different interests from the old in health, recreation, and employment. The young also have more "modern" ideas about schooling. They are less attached to the traditions of the town and less enthusiastic about appropriating money for the town's annual Old Home Day. The central difference, however, in a town where 70 percent of the budget is spent on schools, is that young people tend to have children in school, and are therefore the major clients for the most expensive service the town provides. Because, at the same time, they do not own as much property, the same young on whom the town spends the most money pay the least in taxes.[3]

The interests of Selby's male and female citizens do not differ so markedly. It would no doubt be to the women's interest to establish a kindergarten or day-care center, and increased school spending might also serve their interests more. Women are more likely than men to want to keep the town "dry." If the town had to choose among industries to invite in or among skills in which to offer training, the choices it made might well benefit one of the sexes more than the other. But within the spectrum of issues traditionally decided by the town, few divide women from men as clearly as they divide old-timers from newcomers, old from young, rich from poor. On issues like the schools, zoning, or roads, most often it is an entire family that either benefits or suffers.

Even in the tiny confines of Selby, however, the exercise of governmental power affects one's long-run psychic and economic interests as well as one's immediate concerns. The distribution of power reinforces patterns of social domination and subordination that influence both one's potential economic status and one's deepest sense of self. Women in Selby, like women everywhere, are expected to take care of their children. They are only part-time or sporadic breadwinners, and the reduced economic power that results translates into reduced political power. The expectation that women will not be leaders in the town then translates back into reduced expectations for power in the home or on the job. To the extent that the men of Selby benefit psychically and economically from traditional sex roles, they have an interest (although they would probably not formulate it that way) in maintaining patterns of political power that reinforce these roles. To the extent that these roles put women at a disadvantage, women have an interest in breaking down the supportive political patterns.

Class differences produce the most obvious forms of conflict in material interest, even though the property tax bears heavily on all large landholders, including the poor farmers. The poor generally have an interest in replacing the town's property tax with a progressive income tax, although no one from Selby has ever urged the state to make this a possibility. Moreover, the issues that do come to the town meeting usually place in opposition the interests, excepting the poor farmers, of the more and the less wealthy. In its most obvious and perennial form, each year's decisions on taxes and expenditures affect differently the taxpaying and the service-receiving classes. In 1969, for example, one solution almost used to resolve the town's budgetary crisis was to make the parents of schoolchildren pay individually for the school bus on a per-child basis. The next year, the town almost authorized a commission to zone the town to exclude most forms of low-income housing, an exclusion that would eventually have forced more poor people to live elsewhere, even if they worked or had grown up in Selby. These were both issues where class lines clearly divided the voters.

Many other issues could be raised that would place in open opposition the interests of the poorer residents and those who pay most of the taxes. Day care, remedial reading classes, free breakfasts, and hot lunches all help working-class children more than they do middle-class children, whose parents can afford to pay for them privately. Prepaid group medical care, hospital insurance, and public housing also help the poor more than they do the affluent. Increases in salaries for town employees put more money into working-class pockets. These are all within the town's power to provide, but they all would cost large taxpayers more than they would small ones. As far as I know, no one has suggested at town meeting that the town provide any of these services except a kindergarten, and even that has never been seriously debated.

Like the differences in interest between men and women, class differences in interest can also have a psychological component. When machinists, carpenters, and factory operatives decide not to exercise political power because they are not smart enough or educated enough, they acquiesce in a pattern of domination that undermines their self-esteem. When the economic system directs them to jobs with little control over their work, this deprives them of skills they need to take responsibility in the political world. The economic system convinces them that they have no influence; the political system reinforces that message.

These conflicts of interest—between newcomer and old-timer, villager and nonvillager, young and old, male and female, rich and poor—clearly exist in Selby. Yet few people mentioned conflicting interests when I asked them to explain the political conflicts that came up in town meeting. Instead, they portrayed the town's political conflicts as differences of opinion over who could best represent the interests of all.

One reason for the infrequent mention of conflicting interests may have arisen from my low-key interview technique: I did not urge people to explore specific conflicts of interest in the town. Class conflicts are further confused by the fact that the property tax bears heavily on all large landholders, rich or poor; because the town economy is no longer based on land, this tax is not strictly divided along class lines.

Yet a more fundamental reason behind the lack of comment on conflicts of interest is that admitting such conflicts would call into question the neighborliness and consensual unity of the community. One of the town's poorest farmers, for instance, is a French-Canadian who never goes to town meeting. He believes that he does not need to go and, as I noted earlier, explains the reason in what initially struck me as a nonsequitur: "Anybody in this town, we're all friends. You can stop and talk to anyone."[4]

If your interests are the same as your neighbor's, your neighbor can represent those interests as well as you can. A machinist who has "never participated in any part of it" can tell me in one breath that he could do nothing about an unjust town regulation because "Like I say, they been in it. These people that go every year, they just know how to outtalk you. And they can come up with some arguments you'd never dream of," and in another breath that he figures he should "let the people that know more about it run it." He reconciles these contradictory statements by saying that the few people who run the town represent him in an almost literal way: they make him "present" at the meeting by being so much like himself. "Why, if it wasn't all right, I'd have to only go to the meeting and change it, wouldn't I?" he says. "They're just like I am." When conflicts of interest are not immediately apparent, the warmth of a unitary polity makes it easy for the powerless to believe that the people who make decisions make them in the interest of all.

Chapter 9

Political Inequality: Selby

In a town-meeting [was] the problem solved,
how to give every individual his fair
weight in the government. . . .

—EMERSON

SELBY'S POLITICS illustrate the problems of combining adversary and unitary democracy. In the minds of most of Selby's townspeople, the goal of town meeting is to find the best solution to problems that affect everyone. Yet irreconcilable conflicts of interest do exist in Selby, and the political process must handle them. The citizens in Selby's town meeting shift back and forth between the unanimous voice vote, which they use for most of the issues before the town, and the secret ballot with majority rule, which they employ in moments of conflict.

Traditionally, adversary democracies have handled irreconcilable conflicts by giving each interested individual a vote of equal weight. Over time, Locke's right to a "fair and equal Representative"[1] has become the doctrine of one-person/one-vote, and then the principle that each person's vote should "be given as much weight as any other vote."[2]

In Selby, the town forms one political district. All adult residents can attend the town meeting, and all votes are of equal weight. Yet not all groups have a "fair and equal Representative" in town meeting. Different groups incur different immediate costs when they attend the meeting, and they get different immediate satisfactions. As a consequence, some groups are more likely than others to attend. Whenever interests in Selby conflict, the interests of the old-timers, the villagers, the old, and the wealthy are better represented.

I did not try to measure the power of these groups in Selby. Even if I had been able to come to a provisional understanding of what I ought to measure, the methods I used—a combination of survey-research items and a probing of the feelings that town meeting evoked—were not suitable for following decisions in detail or for asking about the power of specific persons.[3] Consequently, I measured only participation, as reported in the town records and in interviews, and the amount of power the people I interviewed estimated that they, and people like them, had.

Table 2 summarizes the results, and the rest of this chapter discusses them in more detail. The first two rows of Table 2 cover attendance at town meetings and holding town office. These data are available for most residents of the town. The remaining three rows cover contacting town officers, speaking at town meetings, and self-estimated power. These data are only available for the sixty-nine adults whom I interviewed and include those not registered. Because most of these numbers are based on very small samples, they are subject to large random sampling errors. Since both the numbers that fit my expectations and those that did not were not always statistically significant—that is, could in principle be due to chance—I have often given greater weight to those that are consistent with my theoretical expectations or with other evidence. The data are not definitive and should be interpreted cautiously.

As Table 2 shows, people who have lived in town a long time are more likely to attend town meeting and to have held office than are the more recently arrived. They are more likely to have contacted a town officer. They are also likely to estimate their own power as high and slightly less likely to say that they speak at town meeting, but these differences could well be due to chance.

Village dwellers are very slightly more likely than those outside to have held town office. They also estimate their power higher than do the non-villagers. These differences are probably not due to chance and are consistent with frequent complaints by nonvillagers about the villagers' power. Villagers are also slightly more likely to have contacted a town officer and to have attended town meeting and are less likely to speak in town meeting, but these differences are more likely to be due to chance.

The old participate in town affairs quite a bit more often than do the young. The old people in my sample were slightly less likely to speak in the meeting, but this difference is not significant.

At least with these crude measures of participation and power, Selby's men are no more likely to participate or to feel powerful than are its women, although, for reasons I discuss later, they seem to have a greater impact on the town.

TABLE 2

Participation and Sense of Efficacy by
Individual Characteristics in Selby[a]

	Length of time in town	Living in village	Age	Gender[b]	Socioeconomic status
Attendance at town meeting	.31**	.10	.36**	.02	.25***[c]
Holding town office	.34**	.12*	.36***	.04	.12[c]
Contacting town officer	.24*	.16	.27*	.05	.11
Speaking at town meeting	−.16	−.05	−.12	−.08[d]	.26
Self-estimated power[e]	.17	.27*	.14	.01	.35**

[a]All correlations are based on the interview sample (N ≤ 69) except those of attendance at town meeting and holding town office with living in village, gender and socioeconomic status. The correlations of attendance with living in the village and gender are based on data covering all registered voters (N=300). The correlations of holding town office with living in the village and gender are based on data covering all residents (N=379). The correlation of attendance with socioeconomic status is based on registered voters who are also taxpayers (N=176). The correlation of holding town office with socioeconomic status is based on all taxpayers (N=197).

The numbers shown are zero-order product-moment correlation coefficients. If every man spoke once but no women spoke, this perfect correlation would be represented by +1.00. If men and women were equally likely to speak, this absence of any correlation would be represented by .00. (The correlation between education and income in the United States is about .40.) As many of these variables are noninterval and some may have nonlinear relationships, the correlations should be understood as approximations. They are presented here and in subsequent tables only to facilitate comparisons of the strength of relationships.

Statistical significance is indicated by asterisks. If the observed association between the two variables would appear by chance in less than 5 percent of all samples of this size (p < .05), one asterisk follows the correlation. If p < .01, two asterisks appear. If p < .001, three asterisks appear. All tests are one-tailed. See Appendix A, "Key to Tables" for further discussion of significance.

In computing these correlations, I treated "Attendance at town meeting," "Speaking at town meeting," "Self-estimated power," "Length of time in town," "Age," and "Socioeconomic status" as continuous variables. Appendix A provides tables in which the same variables appear in dichotomized form. Appendix B gives the wording of the variables, their marginals, the composition of the indexes, the intercorrelations of the index components, and the intercorrelations of the major independent variables.

[b]Coded females = 0, males = 1; positive correlations thus indicate higher male participation.

[c]Based on assessed valuation of home, with renters (40 percent of population) excluded.

[d]Not consistent with observed data in 1970-72. See p. 106.

[e]"Self-estimated power" is another name for the index of "local political efficacy" (see Appendix A).

Selby's large property owners are more likely to attend town meeting than are small ones. The higher a citizen's socioeconomic status, the less likely that citizen is to indicate that he or she feels powerless in town. The other measures of participation—holding town office, contacting a town officer, and speaking in town meeting—are also positively correlated with socioeconomic status, but the relationships are not strong enough to rule out the possibility that they are due to chance.

The differences in participation levels revealed in Table 2 are not usually large. When a vote is close, however, even a small difference in participation can produce a major difference in policy. Moreover, as will become clear, these small differences have appreciable effects on the feelings of Selby's citizens.

Opening up the doors to participation in a direct, face-to-face democracy does not guarantee equal participation, let alone equal power, at least not in Selby. Without comparative data, however, one cannot tell whether the situation is worse or better than it would be in a representative, secret ballot democracy. The Selby data suggests only that in a classic face-to-face democracy of the kind that has been the model for so much political theory participation is unequal, and that these inequalities follow quite predictable patterns. Since participation is unequal, power is probably even more so.

Length of Residence

Newcomers are at a disadvantage in Selby's political life, just as they are elsewhere.[4] Because of their shorter time in town, newcomers have obviously had less chance to hold a town office or to contact a town officer. But newcomers are also less likely to have attended the town meetings held since they first registered to vote.

So why, then, do old-timers think that the newcomers have more than their share of power? One reason may be that the newcomers who *do* attend town meeting participate quite actively. Take speaking in public: the average newcomer is no more talkative than anyone else, but those who go to town meeting appear more talkative than those who stay away.[5] Among old-timers, in contrast, those who attend town meeting seem *less* at ease with words than do those who stay away, although this could be due to chance.[6] In the rural culture that produced Calvin Coolidge, the most taciturn citizens are often believed to be the most knowledgeable and virtuous. Such suspicion of good talkers is another reason why old-timers prefer to settle thorny problems before the meeting starts so that their less fluent members can exert influence more nearly proportionate to their standing in their neighbors' eyes.

Selective participation may also make the older residents misjudge the newcomers' class. Selby's newcomers, many of whom are construction workers, are not much more likely to be middle class than are the old-timers. Nor are the middle-class newcomers in my sample much more likely than the working-class newcomers to attend town meeting. But the newcomers who *speak* in town meeting are very likely to be middle class, at least in my sample,[7] so if old-timers judge the newcomers by those who speak, as they probably do, they are likely to conclude that they are mostly middle class as well as fluent.

For most newcomers, however, participation is even more difficult than it is for old-timers. The newcomers are no more at ease with words than are the old-timers, are less likely to know other participants personally, and have fewer close friends in town, in part because they less often have jobs in Selby itself (see Appendix A, Table A.1). In addition, they have fewer relatives in Selby, and those in my sample spend more time with their immediate families. The old-timers, in contrast, have both family and friendship ties to town government. Only a fifth of the town's residents have lived there all their lives, but this group is heavily intermarried. Members of three extended families run the general store, the town clerk's office, the Church Ladies' Guild, the Parent-Teachers Club, the post office, and the town's only real estate office. Their names appear every year in some town office, large or small. In fact, of the fourteen people in my sample of sixty-nine who had lived in town all their lives, ten held, or had very recently held, or had a close relative who had held a town office. This pattern recurs in many other Vermont towns.

The old-timers are further drawn together by the remnants of the town's traditional social life—the Parent-Teachers Club, the volunteer fire department, the Grange before it closed, the Church Ladies' Guild, and the now-dying "Home Dem" Club. Several of the men worked together in Horace Fletcher's sawmill before it shut down. These long-term ties create a fund of politically useful information. The old-timers are likely to know the names of the town selectmen. They may also be more likely than the newcomers to remember when town meeting is and to have a good idea of what will be discussed there, although these relationships were not statistically significant in my sample (see Appendix A, Table A.1).

Their deeper social ties and readier information make it easier for

Selby's old-timers to act in town politics.[8] Their immediate costs are fewer: they need to learn less, exert themselves less, and face fewer strangers in order to understand an issue and change others' minds about it. Their immediate benefits are greater: in town meeting, they see their friends, understand the jokes, and enjoy a long gossip at the noontime dinner. For the newcomers, however, the costs are often heavy. Vermont's history of declining population, its isolating climate and terrain, and, until recently, its farm economy do not generate a culture of welcome. As one Selby-born woman, now friends with some newcomers, says, "the out-of-staters are treated just like they were Communists or foreigners or something, coming from an altogether different country, and they really are put down upon!"

The newcomers are less likely than the old-timers to feel powerful in the town, but the difference here is smaller than the difference in actual participation: it does not even reach statistical significance. This may be the effect of a belief in equal opportunity; although they do not in fact participate, many newcomers feel they could exercise power if they tried.

Living in the Village

The same pattern emerges between the villagers and the nonvillagers in Selby, but it is a great deal less pronounced (see Appendix A, Table A.2).

Low participation among nonvillagers is partly a matter of convenience. Those who live back in the hills along unpaved roads find it harder to get to the meeting. But distance is not the main obstacle. In a small-scale, nonpartisan direct democracy, candidates for office seldom make speeches, send out newsletters, or even stress the ways in which they differ from other candidates. People run for office not on the basis of specific adversary issues but on their personal reputations for competence. Without a party system that schematizes town issues along adversary lines and gets the news out to its supporters, information must travel informal routes.[9] Lew Nye, the talkative postmaster, spreads information in the course of his daily delivery. A newcomer like Judy Saxman, living several miles from the village on an unpaved hill road, depends on Mr. Nye for her news. Asked what she would do if the town were considering an unjust regulation, her first thought is, "I'd talk to the mailman or the people at the store in the village." Explaining how she came to know of

Clayton Bedell's fight with the selectmen over road repairs, she says, "I got this from Henry, the garbageman."[10]

Itinerant town criers like the mailman and garbageman bring the news to the people back in the hills only sporadically, while villagers hear it every day. The lunch counter, the store, the town clerk's office, the gas pump are all centers of information and political excitement. As one village wife reminded her husband: "You go over to the lunch counter every day, so you can get all the local news and gossip and so on and so forth." [JM to the husband: Do you ever talk local politics?] "Yeah, all the time at the counter!"

Even Edith Hurley, who does not go to town meeting, sees and talks with others in the village every day:

Yeah, it's Ma Elton, or the schoolteacher, Miss Lettie Boardman, or the people that run the garage. I go down almost every day to the store, where somebody is, and I talk with the postmaster. Ma Elton or Lettie, we always get together on the back porch if it's a nice day.

Villagers say of a local political question that they "discussed it down at the store." Villagers do not make appointments with town officials; they just "run into them down at the store."

As in other small New England towns, the physical closeness of neighbors in Selby's village center has produced a distinctive culture of gossip and frequent social contact. The backroaders recognize this culture and dislike it. Mrs. Waite, wife of a foreman in a St. Johnsbury trucking firm, says of the village:

Down there they buzz buzz all the time. I wouldn't live down there for anything because I don't think everybody's business is everybody's business, and I don't go along with that. Every little thing makes a lot of—what I call gossip!

I don't like it. I wouldn't like it. I wouldn't live there for nothing! If there's something up here I heard, or something somebody heard, if it's a newsy thing, okay, fine. I like to know what's going on, but otherwise I like to mind my own business. And this is the way we like it. But see, down there everybody's business is everybody's.

It's just so different. They live a different life, let's face it.

Farther up the road from the Waites, a part-time farmer who holds a small town office complains that:

There's too much that goes on before town meeting that we don't know about unless we're part of it. They're slack in presenting all the information you need to function completely.

His wife adds scornfully, "Of course, these groups constantly on the telephone for an hour every morning find out, but *we* don't do that." Mr. Waite thinks a more detailed town report would help, but most of the more interesting information he needs to help him make his decisions is not likely to appear in any official report, especially in a community anxious to protect its members from public criticism.

Differences in culture between village and outback produce measurable differences in social connections and level of information. Selby's villagers are more likely to spend their free time outside their families and more likely to know accurately the day of town meeting. They are also more likely to work in town, recognize their fellow citizens, know the names of the selectmen, and feel they understand local issues, although these differences are not statistically significant[11] (see Appendix A, Table A.2).

Some time ago, a study of a university housing project where students had been assigned randomly to their rooms demonstrated that the accident of being put in a room at the bottom of a stairwell or some other point of physical communication increased a student's chances of becoming involved in the internal politics of the project.[12] In Selby, the some forces operate, but the assignment is not random. While a few residents were born in the village, most actively chose to live there. These people are more likely than are the nonvillagers to call thmselves "outgoing" and to participate in any kind of election.[13] Village culture no doubt encourages political participation, but outgoing, participating people may also choose to live in the village, while those who keep to themselves "wouldn't live down there for anything!" Older people, who are more active than the young in town politics, also congregate in the village, where life is not so arduous and the roads are less often impassable. The combination of age, the social disposition of the villagers, and an information-disseminating culture more than accounts for the slightly greater political activity of villagers in my sample.[14]

Whenever the interests of villagers and nonvillagers conflict, the villagers have a slight edge. Nonvillagers realize this and resent it. A machinist outside the village says that decisions in Selby are "like a local affair," while Mr. Waite, who wanted a better town report, says of town meeting, "The people in the village, they get together and hash it all out. They have their minds made up." His wife is even more vehement:

> I don't know why, it's just that a certain few in this town want to run it. And that's the way. And no one in the back roads has anything to say.
> It isn't just in the town meeting. It's in the church or the school, or whatever. They'll call you as a parent if they need something, but if you speak up at a

meeting and say something, they're all against you, and you're out of line, so you just back off and say, "Run it, then."

And that's the way it is. We all up here on this road feel the same—"Well, let them run it." We just set back here, and when they want me, they'll call us for help on this or that, and we always do. It's our town, but it's where really joining in is just not possible. I found it very difficult.

Age

More than a quarter of Selby's adult citizens were thirty or under in 1970. These young people had seldom had the kinds of responsibilities that make one contact a town officer, and for some of this time, they had not been eligible to hold town office. But age also affected town meeting attendance. Only 20 percent of those thirty or under had attended a quarter or more of the meetings for which they were eligible, compared to 58 percent of those over thirty (see Appendix A, Table A.3.).

Age seems to improve the cost/benefit ratio in attending town meeting. Growing older increases the contacts and information that make political activity possible. Although the older people in my sample were no more likely than the young to spend their free time outside the family, they were otherwise more connected socially in the town and possessed a good deal more basic information on the town's politics. These advantages explain some of their more frequent town meeting attendance.[15]

Gender

American women won the vote in 1920. Since that time, they have become most politically active in areas in which they are presumed to have special competence—child care, education, and sometimes health. Both men and women also believe that interest in local government is more consonant with a woman's traditional role than is interest in national or international affairs.[16] As a consequence of this sexual division of political labor, women in the United States are more likely to be involved in local school politics than in any other arena.

Selby is no exception to this rule. The town has never once elected a woman to the crucial town offices of selectman, moderator, or lister,[17] but women are as likely as men to be school directors. If one also takes account of minor town offices, women constitute 40 percent of all Selby's officeholders,[18] but again, these are without exception school-related or secretarial offices. Finally, although the women I interviewed were as likely as the men to say that they had contacted a town official, almost all the women had made their contacts on issues involving their children or the school.

Selby women also attend town meeting as often as the men, but they say much less. In the three town meetings I attended, for example, 49 percent of those who attended were women, but only 29 percent of those who spoke.[19] This difference is accentuated when one looks at what was said. In the 1970 meeting, for example, 24 percent of the speakers were women, but even those who spoke confined themselves largely to giving reports and asking questions. They made only 8 percent of the major statements of opinion and initiated none of the ten controversial exchanges.[20]

Nonetheless, the women I interviewed reported speaking as often as the men in town meeting (see Appendix A, Table A.4). This means either that I had an unrepresentative sample or that the discrepancy between actual and self-reported behavior varies by gender.[21] Thus, it seems doubly significant that even the women in my sample reported that the other women they knew were more nervous than the men about speaking in public.[22] A woman official told me that, while men do not go to town meeting because they have to work, "the women don't like to go because they don't want to get involved in the discussions." Another woman official explained that Selby women are cautious about expressing an opinion in town meeting: "Oh, there's certain ones that'll make motions and that, but to actually get up and express themselves, there's very few that do." A woman newcomer told me with irritation that "the women just sit there and don't say a word."

Some of the women in Selby still see politics as basically immoral and therefore inappropriate for women. Mr. Tyson's mother, who had been elected to the state legislature after her husband had held the office, reportedly decided to quit "because of the logrolling." Olive Pierce, another former state representative, tells me, "I've lost my zest" for politics because she has concluded that "we don't have that much right to influence each other." Mrs. Shetler, whose house painter husband has held a small town office for several years, strongly disapproves of women mixing in the political realm. "*I'm* not politically minded at all," she says. "There are other things on my mind, and I let the men take care of that." Politics for her smacks of the disreputable. She tells me with a stern look that people do not go to town meeting because "they've got other things on their mind, which they should have maybe." When I probe further, she concedes, "Well, if there's something that my husband thinks we should hold up and vote for, well, I would possibly go and vote, you know, to help out some good cause." Old Mrs. Toby refused to talk to me at all about town politics and even about town meeting, repeating, whenever I broached the subject, that women "should leave things like that up to the men."

In my interviewing, I had to be careful not to upset the older women of the town by paying more attention to their views than to those of their husbands, even when the woman was the nominal respondent. On my last day in town, one older woman refused to return her questionnaire and told a friend not to return hers because in my interview with her I had consistently talked with her instead of with her husband. Yet I had been bending over backward not to make that mistake, as I had made it in one of my first interviews. When I had gone to pick up the questionnaire of another older woman, the wife of a town official, she happened to mention as she handed it back to me that "My husband filled it out, but he put my age instead of his." Making as much of a joke of it as I could, I asked, "Did he put his opinions instead of yours?" I had to ask, in order to know whether or not to scrap the questionnaire, but I understood as I said it that the question was a mistake. Her eyes snapped, her thin lips pressed together, and she dismissed me coldly: "I looked it over, and we pretty much have the same opinions."[23]

Newcomers are sometimes exasperated by the political effect of these attitudes. A hospital cafeteria worker told me that "For four years I fought to get guardrails on the road. Maybe the reasons they gave me were right, but I think personally it was because I was a *woman* fighting for it!" Even a college-educated newcomer hesitates at the idea of trying to exercise political influence: "This is a very segregated society around here, with the women in the kitchen, so being a female, I might have a hard time getting anyone to take me seriously."

Class

Selby's richer neighbors consider the town "red-neck" and unprogressive. Half of the town's adults are working class,[24] and a third have never finished high school. When I arrived, the town's school board consisted of a housewife, a laborer, and a plumber. Yet blue-collar workers and poor farmers do not have the impact on Selby's politics that their numbers would suggest. In Selby, as elsewhere in the United States, class (a term I use here interchangeably with socioeconomic status) affects both political activity and the amount of power one feels one has.

My sample of Selby's residents probably underestimates the relationship between class and voting,[25] but even in my sample, 38 percent of the blue-collar workers have never once attended town meeting, compared to only 12 percent of their white-collar neighbors. One reason for this discrepancy is the higher price that workers on hourly wages must pay for their attendance. Small towns like Selby that conduct most of their business in town meeting usually hold that meeting during the day because it takes at least four hours. The state legislature has made it illegal to keep an employee at work on town meeting day but has never voted to make the day a legal holiday. Businesses remain open, and anyone paid by the hour or the day who goes to town meeting therefore loses that day's wages. As soon as I indicated an interest in town meetings, Frank Pate, a manual worker and Selby's most recently elected selectman, protested that "it should be a legal holiday. That's the first thing that I've got to say. I've said it for a good many years." Before the sawmill closed for good, Pate had persuaded Horace Fletcher, the owner, to close it on town meeting day: "So this is what he did, shut the mill right down, and you'd be surprised at the number of those people at the town meeting." When I asked other townspeople why so few voters go to town meeting, by far the most frequent explanation they volunteered was that people had to be at work.[26] "It's without pay, so I've never taken it. I can't see losing a day's pay, not when you have children to feed."

Ironically, although town meeting day is not a legal holiday, the schools are closed. Thus, women with young children have to find and pay a babysitter in order to attend the meeting. This cost, too, is proportionately greater for the poor families in town.

Yet even when no monetary cost is involved, as in contacting town officials, townspeople in the lower socioeconomic brackets may still be less likely than their neighbors to take political action. The low status people in my sample must need town services at least as often as their more prosperous and educated neighbors. They can contact a town official in the evening, and those with phones can do so quite easily. But at least in my sample, fewer of the townspeople with below average socioeconomic status (measured by combining education, occupational prestige, income, and the assessed value of the home) report actually making such a contact. They also report having spoken less in town meeting, although they talked equally long in my interview and seemed as likely as other townspeople to think of themselves as good talkers[27] (see Appendix A, Table A.5). While none of these relationships quite reaches statistical significance, my own observations suggest a relationship at least between class and speaking at town meeting.

These patterns imply that the psychic costs of participation are greater and the benefits fewer for lower status citizens. In contacting town officials, for instance, they feel more defensive beforehand and are less likely to get results afterward. In speaking at meetings, they feel more subject to ridicule (remember the comments, "They'll say 'She's a fool!' "; "I haven't got the education to decide on that stuff"; "If you go there and speak up, they make fun of you") and are less likely to convince anyone. Each act of participation not only costs them more but also usually produces less. Although it is hard to measure "power," it seems likely that lower status people gain less actual power from their participation than do their higher status neighbors. At the moment of a vote, each individual "counts for one and none for more than one," but this is not true in the many moments before, between, and after votes.

Certainly, lower status people are less able to bring to the town's decisions any forms of explicit or implicit coercion. A lawyer and major property owner like Robert Gretsch can threaten individuals in town meeting ("You keep your mouth shut, Clayton, or you and I'll be in court"), threaten particular groups ("At least *fifteen* people are now running their effluent directly into the Annamnac River or a tributary. These people are now *against the law*"), threaten the town itself ("The town dump is now *illegal*"), and implicitly threaten to remove himself and his taxpaying, employment-producing enterprise from the town. That Gretsch was a big taxpayer was not lost on the citizens attending the 1970 meeting, one of whom commented to me on the Bedell incident, "the *person* that . . . insulted that *taxpayer*, it should have been stopped right there . . ." (my emphasis).

For all these reasons, the poorer, less-educated townspeople not only participate less than the rich but also are significantly less likely to feel that they have any say in the town (see Appendix A, Table A.5). Their low participation and even lower perceived power seem not to be due to great differences in social ties or information. Although the poorer, less-educated people are less likely to work in the town, they are no less likely to be active socially. And although they are less likely to know the exact day of town meeting, those in my sample are more likely than are the better educated and more affluent sample members to know the names of two of the selectmen. The greater costs that the disadvantaged must incur to participate appear to be economic and emotional, not informational and social.

"Personality": Attitudes toward Self and the World

Responses to questions about politics often depend as much on the way people feel about themselves and about how the world works as on the actual political situation, which is often difficult to assess. In the absence of reliable information or personal experience, for example, those whose upbringing, experience, and underlying personality have taught them to trust others will also be likely to trust the political system in which they live. Mr. Kitteridge, a retired lawyer, moved to Selby only recently, has never attended a town meeting, and cannot give the name of one of the three selectmen. Yet he confidently marks "strongly disagree" on the questionnaire item: "The selectmen do not care much what people like me think." He simply assumes that the selectmen pay attention to what people like him think.

Mr. Kitteridge also reports that he feels people generally can be trusted to be fair and will try to be helpful. His life has led him to expect benefit rather than harm from the social system, and he seems to have applied this expectation to Selby. Mr. Kitteridge is typical of those whose experiences have led them to hold benign expectations of others. Such people feel relatively powerful in the political system and are somewhat more likely than are others to take action in town politics (see Appendix A, Table A.6). Because they expect fewer reprisals, they can act politically at lower psychic cost. When a contrary experience teaches people that others will try to take advantage of them, they are more reluctant to make themselves vulnerable by speaking at town meeting, taking office, consulting an officer, or in any way trying to influence town politics.

The same pattern prevails in regard to feeling in control of important events in one's life. Those whose experiences lead them to feel that they often have to change their plans, that events they hope for do not come about, and that they have more than their share of bad luck may be wary of trying to get their way politically. The same circumstances that put such people at the mercy of economic and social forces tend also to put the political realm beyond their control (see Appendix A, Table A.6).[28]

Those low on the socioeconomic ladder are, not surprisingly, somewhat more likely than are others to feel that people will not try to be helpful and that their plans will not work out according to their hopes (see Appendix A, Table A.6). Such feelings of distrust and pessimism about the future may have contributed to the low social and economic status of those who hold them. In most cases, however, their class position has probably created situations in which distrust and pessimism were realistic. Working-class citizens in Selby avoid town meeting not only because they need the day's pay but also because their experience outside town meeting leads them to assume they will not be able to influence what goes on at the meeting.

Political Inequality in Practice: Two 1969 Town Meetings

In spite of the theoretically open character of the town meeting, the costs and benefits of attending are distributed in such a way that the old-timers, the villagers, the elderly, the middle class, and the self-confident are somewhat more likely to attend than are their neighbors. This means that when an issue comes to a vote these groups will have slightly more than their proportionate share of the votes. Since in addition, they are more likely to be elected to town office, they will also be able to exercise disproportionate influence before and after the vote.

I could not measure the policy effects of group differences in holding town office, but Selby's 1969 town meeting demonstrated the effect of differences in attendance. The influx of construction workers, including Mr. Michalski's friend with twelve children, had begun in 1966. The school budget had doubled, and it looked as if the tax load would double as well. Panicked, some older taxpayers and farmers came to town meeting with a proposal that parents of schoolchildren individually pay for the school bus taking the children to and from school, a measure that would have reduced the school budget by $17,000. With an agenda promising either doubled taxes or a radical increase in costs to the parents, 66 percent of the adult population attended the March town meeting.

Yet while the turnout was twice as high as usual, the composition of the town meeting remained the same: old-timers, villagers, the old, and the rich were overrepresented. This unrepresentative sample of the citizenry rejected the proposed increase in the tax load and sent the school budget back to the school directors with recommendations for drastic cuts, particularly in the cost of transportation.

Throughout the rest of March and April, the school directors worked on both their budget and their political strategy. In May, they called a special meeting of the town, as happens roughly every other year in Selby. Town officials can call a special meeting when the yearly meeting in March does not finish transacting its business, and 5 percent of the registered voters (in Selby, this means fifteen people) can also call a special meeting. This year, the school board prepared for the special meeting by sending a note home with every Selby schoolchild stressing the importance of the decisions to be made. A school director described the result:

> The parents came out, and we were all ready with facts and figures of tuition costs and enrollment and backed and got an overwhelming vote, and they raised the tax. . . . It showed that if an issue came up that was a big money issue, they really came out . . . the parents with the children came out in force.

The opposition, quite naturally, felt that the May meeting had been "packed." My sample indicates that they may have been right. While overall attendance was far lower than in March, parents were almost as likely to have attended this meeting as the earlier one. Now a majority, they were able to control the meeting. The initial school budget passed, the town continued to pay for transportation, and taxes were increased to cover the costs.

From another point of view, however, it is the yearly meetings of the town that are "packed," for the body that year after year makes decisions for the town is even less representative of the town as a whole. Using the network of schoolchildren to spread news about the meeting simply produced a lopsided effect different from that caused by the more usual social networks, for the school's efforts to get out the vote for this meeting was sufficient to offset the ordinarily higher costs of attendance for young people with children. Only half as many people showed up for the special May meeting, but in all respects except having school-age children, this meeting, which finally voted through the double budget, was more representative of the town as a whole than was the larger March meeting, which had rejected it (see Table 3).

In the regular March meeting, many groups who were numerically a majority in the town were underrepresented, and so lost the vote. In the special May meeting, the newcomers (who wanted school services), the

TABLE 3

Two 1969 Town Meetings

(The majority is indicated by a circle)

Interest group	Number in group	1969 March meeting		1969 May special meeting	
		Number of attenders	Percentage of interest group attending	Number of attenders	Percentage of interest group attending
Newcomers	(29)	15	52%	⑩	35%
Old-timers	(25)	⑰	68%	8	32%
Far[a]	(28)	14	50%	⑩	36%
Near	(26)	⑱	69%	8	31%
Low Socio-economic status	(30)	14	47%	⑩	33%
High Socio-economic status	(24)	⑱	75%	8	33%
Low Tax[b]	(24)	13	54%	⑨	38%
High Tax	(16)	13	81%	6	38%
Parents of Schoolchildren[c]	(19)	11	58%	⑩	53%
Nonparents	(21)	⑮	71%	6	29%
Younger[d]	(27)	14	52%	⑩	37%
Older	(27)	⑱	67%	8	29%

[a]"Far" = more than two miles from town meeting hall.
[b]Calculated only on those who paid a property tax.
[c]Calculated only on those who reported the number of their children on the questionnaire.
[d]"Younger" = under forty-four.

people who lived at a distance (who did not want to pay for their children's school bus), the lower socioeconomic groups, and the low taxpayers all turned out in proportion to their numbers, and won.

Selby's townspeople occasionally indicate that they realize how their varying degrees of activity affect the political process. The school director, without speculating on the representative quality of either body, knew that in the second school meeting the parents "turned out in force." A nonvillager, knowing that nonvillagers actually have a decisive majority in the town, says, "We went down and tried our best, but those in the village, they outvoted us three to one." One newcomer is convinced that a town meeting that represented all groups in proportion to their number would legislate zoning: "I think if you could get everyone in the town out, maybe the majority would win. But the majority of people who go out to these meetings is a majority of the ones, the old natives, who will not change their ways."

Very rarely, as in the May 1969 meeting, an almost representative body may gather in town meeting to make decisions for the town, but such equal representation is achieved only by an extraordinary effort to offset the effects of the usual communications networks and the usual disparate balance of incentives. Otherwise, year in and year out, the decisions of the town are made by a body that in moments of conflict systematically misrepresents the conflicting interests of the townspeople.

Without comparative data and a careful analysis of outcomes, it is impossible to say whether Selby's mixed unitary-adversary form of government is more or is less effective in protecting the interests of its less influential citizens than would be a form of government more toward the adversary end of the spectrum—for example, a representative legislature organized along party lines. It is clear, however, that even when Selby's town meeting shifts into the adversary mode, brings fundamental conflict into the open, and decides issues on the basis of one-citizen/one-vote, it is still not protecting the interests of all its citizens equally.

Chapter 10

Free Choice in Selby

In this open democracy, every
opinion had an utterance; every
objection, every fact, every acre
of land, every bushel of rye, its
entire weight. . . .

—EMERSON

ALTHOUGH in practice the costs
and benefits of political activity in Selby serve to discourage some
groups and to encourage others, the absence of legal barriers leads most
Selby citizens to look on participation or nonparticipation as only a matter
of choice. Many townspeople believe, for instance, that holding town
office depends primarily on one's willingness to take the job. To my question on why year after year the same people were elected to town office
in Selby, 45 percent of the sample answered that these people were
simply willing to accept the office. Over and over again, people told me:
"Nobody wants the job." Jamie Pedley, for instance, shakes his head:
"Some of these jobs, now, like selectman, probably they lose ten days'
work a year. Some people, selfishly, due to their pockets, would not take
it."

These remarks are true of a certain group of "eligibles"—males who
have been born in the town and whose reputations have not been
muddied by histories of alcoholism or joblessness. Among those who are
unlikely to be elected—newcomers, women, or the young—it is not true
that "nobody wants the job." One of the male newcomers told me explicitly that he would like to be selectman. Most of those not likely to be
elected, however, never consider the question at all. They eliminate

themselves from the running in anticipation of failure. When the towns-people summarize this pattern as "nobody wants the job," they capture part of the truth but ignore the situation of a large majority of their adult population.

The townspeople also believe that anyone can easily speak in town meeting:

This way, you can go to a town meeting; you can voice your opinion, right or wrong.

At least you can get up and give your opinion.

The average person has a chance to say what he thinks.

People certainly can voice their opinions if they want to be heard.[1]

The belief in free speech at the town meeting does make it possible for inarticulate citizens to speak at the meeting without severer sanctions than they now suffer. Even the highway foreman who greatly respects a "sharp" businessman like Gretsch can say magnanimously of the less than sharp speakers at the meeting, "They don't know what they're talking about once in a while, but you have that in anything." A young woman denigrates Bedell as "an alcoholic," but then she adds that, "seeing as how it's only once a year, a person can put up with it." Right after the husband of one couple labeled Bedell "just an ignorant farmer," his wife chimed in apologetically, "I know, but he likes to get up in town meeting and have his say. That's the only time, I guess, he has to voice his say."

However, this conviction that freedom of speech extends to everyone the opportunity to speak up in town meeting blinds many to the disadvantages of those who find speaking out difficult. The belief in "openness" then ironically closes any avenue of complaint and soothes the consciences of the privileged. In the words of one town official: "There's no reason to complain about it, because anyone can voice their opinion."

In the same way, the idea that anyone "can" go to town meeting undermines the legitimacy of any protest on the part of nonattenders. When I first asked why turnout at town meeting was so low, only 22 percent of my sample attributed it to not "wanting" to go. Instead, they explained it by the need to work on town meeting day, or shyness, or the unlikelihood of accomplishing anything if one did go. Yet twelve of those who gave these explanations in response to a direct question, later in the interview revealed how much they saw failure to attend as implying failure of concern. Mrs. Sampson is typical. To the direct question, she answered, "Well, a lot just can't get away. Poor people just have to count their pennies, you know." But later she said that the nonattenders "don't come because they don't care," and concluded, as if she had never discussed the various reasons for nonattendance, "By gosh, you have no right to gripe if you don't go to town meeting!"

Officeholders, as one might expect, are often self-righteous in their condemnation of the nonparticipants: "Most just don't have that much interest, I guess. They would rather just sit back the rest of the year and complain."[2] Yet even those who feel powerless or who do not attend at all take the same, now self-disparaging, line. One truck driver who occasionally works for the town has gone to fully half of the last twelve town meetings, and is convinced from what he has seen that people like him have no say in the decisions. "Just a few run the town anyway," he told me. "What the others say don't amount to much." But in spite of this conviction, later in the interview he blamed himself for not attending more often: "Don't take no interest in it. Should, I suppose. Those that don't go do a lot of hollering after." A young working-class woman with two young children who lives outside the village has, not surprisingly, never gone to the meeting, but again the "sit back and complain" formula directs her to look for causation only in her own lack of concern. She begins with a general formulation: "Most of the people don't bother to go, and they gripe all the rest of the year. They are, well, uninterested, really—until it comes time for them to dish out money, and then they gripe!" She then turns this formulation against herself: "People like me don't get their opinions voiced . . . mainly because I don't go about seeing that my voice is heard." Another young woman with three children, also working class and living outside the village, is the one who told me that she has never gone because of her lack of "education." Like the others, however, she concludes by lumping herself with the people who "sit back": "Like my husband says, if more people would get together, if they had the time, and go, it would help. You know, instead of sitting back and bitching, go and. . . ." Here she trails off, unable perhaps to visualize what someone with as few skills as she sees herself as having would actually do if she did attend.

This widely accepted analysis defuses criticism. When I asked if a few people run the town, for example, the highway foreman piped up, "If they do, it's the *people's* fault. If you have a legitimate complaint and they don't pay any attention, when it comes time for town meeting you can ask them why!" Or as one town official puts it triumphantly, "If they do kick, you can say, 'Why weren't *you* at the meeting?'"

There is much truth in this way of thinking. Just as one theory of property holds that the fruits of the land should belong to those who have invested their labor in cultivating it, so those people who have invested time and energy in trying to solve a problem have a claim to greater weight in its final determination than do those who have spent their time and energy elsewhere. Yet the idea that participation creates entitlement ignores the problem of representation. When interests differ, the underlying principles of adversary democracy require that the interests of the citizens be represented in proportion to their number. If social and economic systems produce disparities in representation, a polity whose goal is "a fair and equal representative" for each individual must strive to correct those disparities. In Selby, this could mean declaring town meeting day a legal holiday, providing day care for families with children, or even, as in ancient Athens, paying citizens to attend the meeting. But because Selby's citizens have a hard time recognizing conflicts of interest and therefore shy away from the adversary model, they make no conscious effort to reduce disparities in representation. As a consequence, a person with every sociological strike against her—a young, recently arrived, poor woman with children, living outside the village—has vitually no chance of having her interests equally protected. This would remain true even if she herself attended, since others with similar interests still would not.

Should Florence Johnson Vote?

Florence Johnson works on a daily basis cleaning house for some of the more wealthy citizens in towns adjoining Selby. Her husband deserted her in 1967 and sends her no money. On the $400 or so she earns each month, she raises her four children in an old trailer up on the land of one of the poorer backhill farmers. She is young, a recent newcomer, lives several miles up in the "outback," and is poor. These characteristics would lead one to expect her not to have attended any town meetings, and indeed she has not.

This woman stands out among the poorest residents in my sample in one respect. She is articulate in her stand against the town's power structure. But her problems with the town are not unique. I heard similar stories in the small house of the woman factory operative and in the trailer of the nurse's aide.

When I walked up to her trailer on a late summer afternoon, Florence Johnson invited me to sit with her on a wooden bench she had placed out under a tree, where a light wind cut the sticky heat of the day. In her floppy housedress, she held her youngest child in her lap, brushing off the yellowjackets that settled on our arms, our legs, and on the patches of jam that spotted the child's chubby cheeks and lips. Following her example, I too shrugged off the more persistent of those bees that hovered around my face.

Like many other women, Mrs. Johnson's most important problems concern the town's school and her children's transportation to school. Several times her son's teacher had slapped him, and once the school bus driver had gotten stuck and, although two hours late, had neither notified the parents nor made any particular effort to take the children home some other way. In each of these incidents, Mrs. Johnson was outraged but made no official complaint. She felt that she had no hope of redress. Whenever she had to communicate with the town, she did so cautiously, through the mediation of the farmer from whom she rented her land. There was also another obstacle to her contacting town officials. When I asked her if she had ever contacted an official, she answered, "No, I've never called them myself, no. I've never had a telephone."

For Florence Johnson, Selby's open, decentralized democracy is no better than the national political system. Along with the television repair service owner and the registered nurse, she is the third person in my sample to "strongly agree" with the questionnaire statement that in Selby people like her have no say in the town. In the interview, she tells me that "It's them rich ones and the head ones of the town that make all the decisions, and you have to live by them." Even the plumber, laborer, and housewife, who run the school board in Selby, are part of a social system that Florence Johnson feels to be far above her. "Well, they're awful stuck up," she explains. "I mean, they don't even talk to you, let alone anything else. High society guys and stuff like that."

One would not expect this woman to feel powerful in national politics. In her national political world, "they" elect presidents to office. "They" turn and go wherever they want. "We" accidentally got one good president, but "of course," he was assassinated:

I think the war in Vietnam is a bunch of hogwash, and I think there should be a stop put to it. I don't agree with a lot of President Nixon's ideas, and I think they elected the worst president this country ever had when they put him in office. The best president we ever had was Kennedy, and of course, he was assassinated. And then they started from there out, and I think they've turned and gone toward the worse end instead of the better since Kennedy.

She sees the state government, which she knows more intimately than the national, as very like the town:

I think that some of the head ones are like the head ones in town. If you want something done for you or something done about some of the problems in the state, they just laugh at your ideas about it. They just listen to the high ups, and that's it.

Florence Johnson is not one of the people in my sample who acquiesce in their political lot. Along with five others in the sample who answered the questionnaire, she agrees strongly with the statements: "Both major parties in this country are controlled by the wealthy and are run for their benefit" and "The laws of this country are supposed to benefit all of us equally, but the fact is that they're almost all 'rich-man's laws.'" She believes that she has no political power and writes in the margin of her questionnaire that "the poor person is seldom heard." In the economic realm, too, her world is divided into the rich and the poor, with the rich getting the breaks. "Poor people," she writes, "try to help others. Rich people take advantage of the poor."

Florence Johnson is still under the impression that she needs to pay a poll tax before she can vote in town meeting, although since 1968 all residents can vote in town meeting whether or not they have paid their poll tax. There are, however, other "taxes." She thinks of her friend Clayton Bedell's experience: "What good did it do him to open his mouth? I mean, he'd have been better off if he had stayed home." She thinks of the "high society guys" who run the town. And if she knew firsthand of the irritation of people like Mrs. Nye, who told me, "People who don't own any property—sometimes they just take it on themselves to talk about things they don't know anything about!" she would be even less likely to exercise her theoretical right to vote.

Should Florence Johnson vote? Should she attend town meeting? Should she speak? Should anyone pay attention? Should she hold town office? Should she be selectman? It might be good for Florence Johnson if we were to design a democracy in which she would vote, speak, and hold office, but would it be good for us?

Take the hardest case first: Should she be a selectman? It is not a difficult job; almost every male born in Selby either has been a selectman, believes that he could be selectman, or is related to a selectman. But individuals are not all equal in administrative ability, and there is no reason to suppose that everyone, including Florence Johnson, is even minimally qualified. In the small amount of time I spent with her, I came to respect Mrs. Johnson's energy, her self-reliance, the care and love she gave her children, and her common sense. I was grateful for the goodwill she extended to me, and I felt close to her as one woman to another. However, I also noticed that she seemed disorganized, had a simplistic conception of how the town worked, and was both quick to anger and sensitive to criticism. None of these qualities makes a good town administrator although in her case many of them may derive from having never had any power at all. It would probably be a mistake, both for her and for the town, to make Florence Johnson a selectman tomorrow.

It would not be hard, however, to conceive of the selectman's job, not to mention the smaller offices, as being distributed more widely. Such a system would give Florence Johnson the experience of some public trust. It might allow her to take responsibility both for herself and for others and to give what she could to the polity. Among the people born in Selby, 71 percent of whom have had at least one small town office in their family over the past decade, this kind of process has already taken place. A unitary society should balance the good to the whole in encouraging all its citizens to take some responsibility against the harm that can be done if incompetent people are given responsibilities that they cannot handle.

As for speaking in town meeting, the townspeople will always want to set limits on the time spent listening to others and will want both to entertain themselves and to learn as much useful, logical, factual, and emotional information as possible in the time they spend there. If Florence Johnson has not informed herself or thought carefully about the town's problems, or if she rambles on and on, the townspeople will be bored. These problems might decrease as she gained experience, but inequalities in articulateness can remain a problem, even after long experience. Nonetheless, the town may not be well served by her silence. Where one correct answer exists and the job of a group is to find it, groups that conscientiously solicit minority opinion are more likely to arrive at the answer, even though it takes longer and elicits some ideas that are, indeed, "boring." In Selby, for instance, the debate on zoning embraced disagreements over the proper role of the state, points of law and history, and different estimates of Selby's probable growth. No one raised the issue of low-cost housing. Because so few people of Florence Johnson's class spoke at the meeting, the minds of Selby's citizens were never invited to deliberate on that issue. The deference accorded the expert, articulate, or even majority opinion often leads to premature closure.[3]

Should Florence Johnson vote? Some political scientists have argued that she should not. They would not deprive her of the vote, but praise the forces that discourage her. Their case is not hard to argue. Florence Johnson is neither well informed nor deeply committed to the rules of the game. Like eleven others in my sample, she does not know that Franklin Delano Roosevelt was a Democrat. She is not able to name any of the state senators, or say how many Justices sit on the U.S. Supreme

Court. She agrees with the statement: "I don't mind a politician's methods if he manages to get the right things done." She strongly agrees both that "there are times when things get so bad that people have to take the law into their own hands to protect their way of life" and that "if someone is suspected of committing a crime, the police should be allowed to search his house even though the police don't have a search warrant."

If people believe, as Florence Johnson does, that they have no political power, the incentive to pay attention to the doings of political figures is diminished, as is the incentive for commitment to liberal procedural rules. It is unclear whether Florence Johnson has more or less to gain than others in society from politicians doing the right thing by wrong methods, by people taking the law into their own hands, and by police not having to get a search warrant. The police are more likely to search her trailer than the houses of the middle-class newcomers in Selby, and in the short run, she is more likely than they to be the victim when "people take the law into their own hands," for instance, when her former husband refuses to support their children or returns one night to beat her up. In a revolution, however, she might well have more to gain than the middle class has from the "people" taking the law into their own hands. Certainly, current rules do not provide Florence Johnson with what she needs to live a decent life, so she is not likely on that account to cherish them. Nor has she had the kinds of education and jobs that teach others to give "liberal" answers to questions about civil liberties.

The argument runs that democracies are fortunate when, as in the United States, their economic and political systems are so structured that those who are less informed and less committed to democratic procedures are also less likely to vote. But the argument that Florence Johnson does not vote today does not permit us to predict that she will not vote tomorrow (or find other ways to express her potential power). If she ever does enter the political process, she is likely to do so suddenly and to bring her lack of information with her, along with her lack of interest in procedural niceties. If political participation has any educative effect, the long-term interest even of those most concerned with stability may be better served by beginning Mrs. Johnson's education early than by risking the possibility that she will become active at some later date. Those who are interested in education for other reasons, such as improving the general well-being of the community by increasing the responsibility, the capability, and the largeness of view of its citizenry, will want to include Mrs. Johnson in their plan. Finally, finding ways of encouraging Mrs. Johnson to attend town meeting, possibly to speak in town meeting, and even to hold a small town office reinforces those bonds of community that depend on roughly equal status. It allows the members of the community to act toward one another as friends rather than as superiors and subordinates.

These considerations are all appropriate to a unitary democracy; they all refer to the good of the whole. They suggest that, although equal power is not necessary in a unitary democracy, widespread participation can contribute to the general good.

If interests conflict, there is a quite different reason for Florence Johnson to vote. Adversary democracy requires the equal representation of interests. If people in Florence Johnson's position do not attend town meeting in proportion to their numbers, the town is more likely to adopt policies harmful to their interests. If they do not speak in town meeting or are not listened to when they do speak, their interests are correspondingly less likely to be taken into account. If they do not hold office, it is less likely that policies will be implemented with their interests in mind.

Florence Johnson has psychological as well as material interests. In many ways, she is in the position of Edith Hurley, who never goes to town meeting and concludes of herself in national politics, "AAAAGH! She ain't nothing!" A town officer told me how important she thought the meetings were for the poorer citizens' sense of belonging to the town:

> I'd hate to see the town meeting go out of existence because there are a lot of old-timers that would come, and they never utter a word, but when they go up to cast a ballot for town officer, you can almost see them strut, you know, they feel just as proud. It may be some poor farmer from way back in the hills, but they feel definite pride that they are part of that town meeting.

This is an experience that Mrs. Johnson has never had. She could use it. Deserted by her husband, unable on $400 a month to care for her four children as well as she would like, recognizing the scorn of the "high society guys" in the village, she sometimes finds it difficult to maintain her self-esteem. She tells me on the questionnaire that she is not sure her life will work out the way she wants, that she has had her share of bad luck, that she often feels she does not have much to be proud of, and that sometimes she thinks she is no good at all. People, she reports, are often quite critical of her and seldom either respect her opinion or understand how she feels.

She is not so depressed that she has no interest in participating in the town's political life. But her youthful energy and determination have been sapped by the realities of Selby. In a number of questions about the town, she began with enthusiasm but soon remembered the spectacle she would present to the people who laughed at her friend Bedell:

JM: If the town were considering a regulation—maybe something about the taxes or the schools—that you thought was unfair or unjust, do you think there is anything you could do about it?
Mrs. Johnson: I'd try!
JM: What do you think you could do?
Mrs. Johnson: Well, I don't know. I think the first thing I'd do would be to get some of my friends together, and they could have another town meeting or whatever you want to call it, and then we'd try to fight it.
JM: How many people do you think you could get together or get in touch with?
Mrs. Johnson: Not many in Selby because most of the people in Selby have lived here all of their lives, and they're pretty high up in society, you know.
JM: Maybe four or five?
Mrs. Johnson: Probably four or five, but not many more than that. And then we'd probably get laughed at. . . .

At this, she hesitated and stopped. We talked on about the town, until I asked a similar question about an unjust law in Congress. Uncertain, she did not tell me then what she would do but what "you" could do. Nevertheless, she brightened up, and her next response told me how crucial her political role could be to her self-esteem:

Mrs. Johnson: Well, you could write your congressman a letter, anyway, and say that you didn't consider the law a right one, and if that didn't do any good, you could get quite a few people who could chip in and write a letter and have everybody sign it.
JM: Have you ever done anything like that?
Mrs. Johnson: No—I have gone to a school board in St. Johnsbury once, but that's all. We had a lot of trouble, not only me, but about eight or nine other people that I know in St. Johnsbury. We was all friends, and we lived in these block buildings, like, and our kids used to go on the school bus, and the bigger kids used to beat them up, and the bus driver used to just sit there and laugh about it. So we went up and barged in on the school meeting one night; that's what we done. Yeah, we got darn good results. We had two patrolmen put on each bus, and we had patrols on each bus corner where the stops were made and everything else, so it really came off. And there were patrols put in the halls at school, and everything.

As she talked about her triumph in St. Johnsbury, a town more than five times the size of Selby but still small enough so that a bunch of house-wives could barge in on the school meeting one night, her voice picked up, and she lifted her head. At the end of the story, she squeezed her child closer to her, looked at me, and smiled: "Yeah, we got darn good results."

That experience took her beyond her individual benefit and the pleasure she might have gotten from an adversary victory into the unitary realm of the common good, of right and wrong. It was immediately after this that I asked a standard question on interest in local or national politics, and she responded, proudly and with energy, "I'm not too interested in politics, but I mean, I like to stick up for what I feel is right. And what I don't feel is right, I'd like to see to it that I help push it under."

Although like all polities Selby lies somewhere between identity and pure conflict of interest and must therefore strike some balance between unitary and adversary democracy, in both situations there are arguments for encouraging Florence Johnson to participate more than she does now. When interests are similar, her greater participation would probably contribute in a number of ways to the collective good. When interests are in conflict, she would need either equal power or the equal representation of all her interests for the outcome to live up to the adversary ideal. In either case, Selby's experience indicates that the open door does not guarantee Florence Johnson and people like her their full say. Removing the legal barriers to influence, even in an open town meeting democracy, will not by itself produce either the political equality theoretically required by adversary democracy or the widespread participation and equal respect that sustains a unitary democracy.

Chapter 11

Was There a Golden Era?

A general contentment is the result.

—EMERSON

EMERSON, who voices the myths of America better than anyone, had this to say about his own town meeting:

For the first time, the ideal social compact was real. . . . In a town-meeting, the great secret of political science was uncovered, and the problem solved, how to give every individual his fair weight in the government, without any disorder from numbers. In a town-meeting, the roots of society were reached. Here the rich gave counsel, but the poor also, and moreover, the just and the unjust. . . . In this open democracy, every opinion had an utterance; every objection, every fact, every acre of land, every bushel of rye, its entire weight. . . . In these assemblies, the public weal, the call of interest, duty, religion, were heard; and every local feeling, every private grudge, every suggestion of petulance and ignorance, were not less faithfully produced. Wrath and love came up to town-meeting in company.

It is the consequence of this institution, that not a school house, a public pew, a bridge, a pound, a mill-dam, hath been set up, or pulled down, or altered, or bought, or sold, without the whole population of this town having a voice in the affair. A general contentment is the result. And the people truly feel that they are lords of the soil. In every winding road, in every stone fence, in the smokes of the poor-house chimney, in the clock on the church, they read their own power, and consider, at leisure, the wisdom and error of their judgment.[1]

Yet everything in Selby's experience points to one conclusion: radical democracy in its classic form—opening the marketplace or town hall to the citizens to gather, debate, and make their own laws—does not guarantee the realization of Emerson's vision that every individual have "his fair weight in the government," that "every opinion [have] an utterance," and that all "the people truly feel that they are lords of the soil." Probably no political system can ever fully overcome the patterns of advantage and disadvantage generated by its social and economic systems; certainly, the laissez-faire, voluntarist model of direct democracy—the open door—can only reflect their persistent patterns.

Some argue that the town meeting today is only a degenerate form of the once-vital institution and that observations about it cannot form the basis for valid conclusions about the optimal operation of small-scale face-to-face democracy. The town meeting has certainly lost a great deal of the power it once had, and attendance has declined. I would respond, however, that both lost power and declining attendance have had less effect than one might expect on the way the meeting works, on the fear of conflict it engenders, and on inequalities in participation. The greatest change is perhaps that, with increasing mobility and hetero-geneity in its population, democracies like Selby's have become less unitary.

This chapter tries to document the change and the lack of change by looking at former town power, town meeting attendance, inequalities in participation, and what little we know of the quality of interaction in early town meetings.

The Diminishing Power of the Vermont Town

Vermont towns have a unique history, being the only towns in the United States with both town meetings and a period of frontier inde-pendence in which the citizens were in a virtual state of nature. In all the other New England states, settlement took place under the auspices of a larger, central government. In Vermont, because New Hampshire and New York were fighting for control of the land that would eventually become the state, the settlers were for a long time subject to no superior authority.[2] When the independent towns in the area decided that it was to their advantage to join the Union, they themselves took the initiative to federate in a state government. In the constitution they drew up, they gave each town one seat in the State House of Representatives "forever."[3]

From this independent beginning, Vermont towns guarded their autonomy jealously. As late as 1958, they continued to "think of their

Representatives [to the Vermont legislature] as if they had a function like that of delegates to the United Nations."[4] The state's early frontier history, the constitutional predominance of the towns in the state legislature, and the lax party discipline of a one-party state all helped protect town autonomy.

Yet even in Vermont, state government slowly encroached on the town's traditional power over roads, schools, police, welfare, and zoning. The pace of this encroachment accelerated in the late 1960s, after the U.S. Supreme Court's reapportionment decision required a drastic reorganization of the Vermont State House of Representatives.[5] Before that year, Selby had its own representative to the legislature—the representation in theory guaranteed "forever" by the Vermont constitution. Selby's representative was a neighbor, physically available. But since 1965, Selby has been combined with four other towns in a district of 5,000 people. Its representatives come from and live in the largest town in their district.[6] They see themselves no longer as envoys of the town but as representing the diverse interests of the 5,000 individuals in their district. This constitutional change, combined with changes in the economy, in population patterns, and in mores, produced, along with a shift of power toward the larger cities, a revolutionary centralization of traditional town powers.

Vermont had, until the second half of the twentieth century, maintained a town school system relatively free from state interference.[7] As late as 1962, Vermont retained seventy-one functioning one-room schoolhouses, while the rest of New England combined had only sixty-seven.[8] This pattern began to change in 1969, when the newly reapportioned legislature for the first time required towns to meet state standards on instruction, faculty, and physical facility.[9] At the same time, more of the school budget slipped out of the hands of most towns because the amount of state aid available to the town became contingent on state estimates of local property values, which could change greatly from year to year.

The reapportioned legislature also produced a dramatic change in Vermont's welfare system. Until 1967, the state's welfare system still distinctly resembled its direct ancestor, the Elizabethan Poor Law of 1601, which made the town solely responsible for the poor.[10] Although from the 1930s on, federal and state governments had taken more and more of the burden—with old age and unemployment assistance, aid to the blind and disabled, and aid to dependent children—the towns retained responsibility for general relief under their locally elected Overseers of the Poor. In 1967, however, the state absorbed the entire local welfare system, and for good or ill, the standards of a paid state bureaucracy replaced personal and local responsibility.[11]

Traditionally, the state government of sparsely populated Vermont had seen little need to encroach on town powers over pollution, garbage, and zoning. Most Vermont towns had no zoning, no garbage collections or repositories other than open fields, no town water, and no sewage systems. In the 1940s, the state government did make it illegal to discharge raw sewage directly into streams, rivers, and large lakes,[12] but mindful of strong local feelings, it never enforced the law in small towns like Selby. In 1967, however, the newly reapportioned legislature banned open burning in town public dumps,[13] required towns to replace their open dumps with sanitary landfills,[14] made it illegal to deposit junk (including old automobiles and automobile parts) within 300 feet of one's property line or within view of a public highway, and gave town selectmen the independent power to adopt emergency zoning plans and regional planning commissions.[15] Finally, in 1970, the state legislature passed one of the strongest state land-use laws in the country, requiring every property owner to get a state permit before developing any land of an acre or more in most areas of Vermont.[16]

The 1960s, then, saw the towns lose control of the legislature, the welfare system, much of the education system, and the environment. At the same time, the state legislators began to build legal uniformity throughout the state at the expense of local discretion, for example, in 1971 exempting farm animals from town property tax rather than leaving this exemption to the discretion of the town. Taking these discretionary powers from the town reduced the number of important issues decided at town meeting.

Behind these changes in town control over the legislature, the schools, welfare, and the environment lie changes in the national economy. These larger changes have everywhere encouraged interdependence, expanding scale, and the triumph of universalistic over particularistic procedures. Each stage in expanding networks of transportation has created systems —railroads, airports, freeways—whose cost and administration cannot be borne entirely by the small towns whose land they happen to use, since the benefits do not accrue primarily to those towns. Each higher level of schooling has required facilities, equipment, and trained teachers increasingly beyond the resources of small towns to provide. Each stage of national concern with the poor has made it harder to accept a system in which the poor receive help only if they are longtime residents of a community that feels moved to help them and has enough money to do so. Each stage in the use of natural resources, which once seemed infinite, has entailed a growing ecological interdependence and further expenses for environmental protection.

The diminishing power of the town has inevitably had an effect on town meeting attendance. Citizens are not likely to "fly to the assemblies" when the decisions they make in those assemblies are trivial.

Still, some decisions the townspeople make at town meeting are not at all trivial. They include important matters like zoning, school expenditures, and road repairs that can be resolved, depending on the circumstances, in a unitary or an adversary manner. The combination of adversary and unitary incentives seems to have been strong enough to prevent a serious decline in town meeting attendance in Selby. The surprise is that the effect of declining town powers on attendance has not been greater.

Attendance in Early Town Meetings

No representative data are available on attendance at early town meetings. The fragmentary and possibly unrepresentative data I have located imply that from 20 to 60 percent of the potential voters attended town meetings in eighteenth-century Massachusetts. The nineteenth-century Massachusetts figures are similar, except in years of intense political controversy, when attendance sometimes reached 75 percent. In nineteenth-century Selby, average attendance at town meetings seems to have been between 30 percent and 35 percent. In recent years, Selby's attendance has been around 25 percent but has risen as high as 66 percent in moments of crisis.

When better historical data are collected, these eighteenth- and nineteenth-century attendance estimates may have to be revised. The information is not easily available, however, for in the interest of harmony and unanimity early town meetings rarely called for a "division." The votes were "aye" or "nay" and were recorded simply as "the town decided. . . ." Even when a division was called for, town clerks rarely recorded the exact vote, a tabulation that would have given later scholars the approximate number of citizens attending a meeting.

The town of Dedham, Massachusetts, founded in 1636, is one of the few that has preserved extensive records of its earliest years. In its first years, the town was more than a place to live; it was a spiritual community. The first settlers decided that no new family could take up residence in Dedham without getting the prior permission of the adult male householders gathered in town meeting, and the meeting could also expel from the town those it found unfit to be "admitted into society of such as seek peace." The town meeting created principles to regulate taxation and land distribution; it bought land for town use and forbade the use of it forever to those who could not pay their share within a month; it decided the number of pines each family could cut from the swamp and which families could cover their houses with clapboard. The men who went to that town meeting hammered out the abstract principles under which they would live and regulated the most minute details of their lives; the decisions they made then affected the lives of their children and grandchildren.

Yet in order to prevent "the discouragement of such as give better attendance," Dedham had to establish fines both for lateness and for failure to attend the meeting.[17] Even though no more than fifty-eight men were eligible to come to the Dedham town meeting and to make the decisions for the town, even though the decisions to which they addressed themselves were vital to their existence, even though every inhabitant was required to live within one mile of the meeting place, even though each absence from the meeting brought a fine, and even though a town crier personally visited the house of every latecomer half an hour after the meeting had begun, only 74 percent of those eligible actually showed up at the typical town meeting between 1636 and 1644.[18] This must come close to the highest attendance one can expect, on the average, in a geographically based direct democracy. Ten years later (1651–56) in Sudbury, a new settlement that did not impose fines, attendance at crucial town meetings averaged 46 percent.[19]

Eighteenth-century records of town meeting attendance give much the same picture as seventeenth-century Sudbury. In eighteenth-century Dorchester, attendance averaged about 38 percent, while in Concord, attendance averaged about 46 percent. These figures parallel those from Andover in 1708 (49 percent); Barnstable in 1715 (26 percent); Dedham in 1731 (28 percent); Manchester in 1737 (37 percent); and Watertown in 1736, 1742, and 1781 (50, 27, and 23 percent, respectively).[20]

By the mid-nineteenth century, in the era of Tocqueville's and Emerson's praises of town meeting democracy, turnout seems to have been somewhat higher. In 1834, anti-Masonic candidates tossed out Concord's longtime town clerk and other leaders of the town in a bitter political conflict. This controversy lured 52 percent of Concord's adult male taxpayers to the meeting. Six years later, with controversy still sweeping Concord, as many as 70 percent of the adult male taxpayers attended town meeting. Yet the average turnout in Concord between 1826 and 1840 was only 42 percent.[21] Emerson's picture of "the whole population of the town having a voice in the affair" was therefore somewhat exaggerated. In Bedford, also torn with local controversy in this period, turnout soared to 74 percent in 1834 and to 75 percent in 1843, averaging 63 percent in the twelve contested meetings between 1833 and 1846. But in towns where there were no bitter controversies, like Lincoln, Acton, Carlyle, and Lexington, turnout averaged 30 percent to 43 percent in the period 1821–40.[22] Fitchburg, a town larger than the others, had an attendance of only 18 percent in its one recorded division.[23]

In our town of Selby, the first records that can be used to calculate attendance come from a vote taken in the 1854 town meeting in response to the Vermont State Legislature's request that towns elect their county commissioner in town meeting. The division, 59 to 53, suggests that at least 112 men—39 percent of the town's male population over twenty-one—attended the meeting that year. A month later, the April election for state governor drew 73 percent of Selby's male population over twenty-one, while the previous year the election for governor had drawn 78 percent.

Only two other contests for county commissioner (1857 and 1858) were close enough to consider the vote an accurate assessment of the number of voters at the Selby town meeting. Average attendance for these two years was 32 percent, less than half the 67 percent turnout for the gubernatorial elections in the same years and considerably less than half the turnout of 74 percent in 1856 for the Buchanan–Fremont presidential election.[24]

Political Equality in Early Town Meetings

In early seventeenth-century New England towns, the right to vote at meetings was generally restricted to males over twenty-four who were church members and held property. In the eighteenth century, increased property restrictions eliminated from eligibility the poorest 20 to 25 percent of the adult male population.[25] Finally, even among the eligible, the poor attended the meetings less often. In Dedham's earliest meetings from 1636 to 1644, where recent settlement, geographic proximity, fines, and the personal promptings of the crier ought to have militated against it, the poorer eligible voters were less likely than the wealthy to attend the meeting.[26] So, too, in seventeenth-century Sudbury. This small town had a bitter fight over whether to divide the common lands so that each male householder received an equal share or so that the large landholders got proportionately larger shares. Here again the small property holders, who had most to gain from the equal division and who were in a majority in the town, did not attend the crucial meeting in proportion to their numbers:

> There were at least thirty-seven men who did not show up at the meeting, twenty of whom had been given no meadow grants, and the rest of them with an average of 12 acres apiece [compared to an average of 17 acres for the town as a whole]. Had all the men who still lacked meadow grants from the town come to oppose the order which denied them access to the town commons, the elder statesmen and their sizing party would have been completely overwhelmed.[27]

Two hundred years later, when Emerson wrote of every individual in Concord having "his fair weight in the government," the poorest of the eligible voters were still less likely than the wealthy to attend.[28]

In New England towns of the past, just as today, class had an even greater effect in determining who held town office than in determining who attended town meeting. Dedham's seventeenth-century selectmen, particularly those elected again and again for ten or twenty years, owned considerably more land than the average citizen. Between 1640 and 1740, "the selectmen almost without exception were in the most wealthy 20 percent of the town. Often, a majority of a particular board would be found in the top 10 percent."[29] Even in more egalitarian Watertown, not one of the poorest 40 percent of the taxpayers became a selectman in this period.[30] The nineteenth-century town of Concord also saw a strong association between class and officeholding.[31]

Distance from the central village probably also determined who would tend to exercise political power. In the frontier town of Kent, Connecticut, for example, the citizens who lived farthest from the Kent meeting house were the least likely to become "freemen," the eighteenth-century equivalent of registering to vote.[32] Although Concord's central village contained only about one-third of its population between 1765 and 1774, about two-thirds of the selectmen lived within one mile of the village center. In the following decade, this percentage was still a little over half.[33] It seems reasonable to assume that age and length of residence in the town also played an important role in earlier times, but the data needed to test that hypothesis have not been collected.

The Quality of Interaction in Early Town Meetings

If the relations of human beings with their neighbors are reflected and shaped by their institutions, we must assume that citizens of New England towns in the seventeenth century tried harder to treat one another with loving friendship than they do today. The settlers of seventeenth-century Dedham wanted to call their town "Contentment."[34] Each male householder signed a covenant to bar from the town "all such as are contrary-minded" and to admit only those who would "walk in a peaceable conversation," give "mutual encouragement," and seek "the good of each other out of which may be derived true peace."[35] Believing that they had a common good, they eschewed appeals to law and submitted all disputes between them to arbitration.[36] If they cared enough about mutual harmony to do all this, if they always relied on unanimity rather than on majority vote to make decisions, if like the members of the early Swiss communes they worked together on the roads, filling in the swamp, and building the meeting house, then they must have been brought in some way more closely together by their ideals and institutions than are the residents of present-day Selby.

Yet even in the seventeenth-century town, all was not communitarian bliss. The men of Dedham found it necessary to institute fines against those caught borrowing another's canoe without permission or cutting down the trees on common land.[37] The men in Sudbury fought bitterly over property allocation. By the nineteenth century, although communities were more highly integrated than they are today, descriptions of the meeting suggest that feelings of duty and concern for the public weal were mixed with the call of private interest. Even Emerson's romance with the meeting included the notion that it embodied "every local feeling, every private grudge, every suggestion of petulance and ignorance." Another writer, while rhapsodizing on the democracy of a town meeting around 1860, nevertheless took for granted the predominance of the rich, the parsimony of the taxpayers, and the battling of factions. He catalogued as typical that "the richest man in town [was] at the same time town treasurer" and smiled fondly at "important projects . . . stinted by miserly appropriations," "the intrigue of a certain few to oust the ministers from the school committee," or "the maneuvering of the factions to get hold of the German colony, a body of immigrants lately imported into the factory village to the North."[38]

We cannot assume, therefore, that there was ever a golden era when towns like Selby could act as pure unitary democracies. In order to achieve a satisfying unanimity, these towns were likely to have suppressed the interests of the least powerful and to have put their trust in the kinds of men who had always held power in the town. Yet their high and conscious aspirations make it likely that the citizens of these early towns experienced more pervasive feelings of unity with one another than do the citizens of Selby today. Selby, in spite of its continuing face-to-face tradition and in spite of its straining toward unity, has probably moved toward an adversary system.

The question remains as to whether or not any segment of modern industrial society can recreate the conditions necessary for unitary democracy. The next section suggests that a small-scale, worker-controlled enterprise, organized as a "participatory democracy" and staffed by young idealists of the New Left, can approximate those conditions.

III

A Participatory Workplace

Chapter 12

Helpline: A Crisis Center

THE WORKPLACE DEMOCRACY I chose to study could not meet the criterion of identity of interests required by a pure unitary democracy. Nor, in moments of conflict, could it provide its members with the political equality that pure adversary theory demands. It did, however, come closer to both these goals than did Selby.

There are several reasons for this relative success: the workplace had more favorable conditions, and it tried harder. Selby had a citizenry of 350; the workplace had forty-one. Selby's government shared its powers with a state and a federal government that dwarfed the town, and its citizens looked elsewhere for much of their work, pleasure, and political participation; the workplace commanded its members' concentrated attention. In a workplace, the relevance of decisions to every member's life is usually more obvious that it is in a town. Workers spend half their waking hours on the job. They have to know more about their work than about their town just to accomplish the task. They can be lured into participation by the interdependence of the work and by the knots of friendship formed on the job. They are paid to attend meetings held during the workday, rather than losing a day's pay each time they attend.

In this particular workplace, moreover, ideology was as responsible as were the conditions of interaction for the members' feelings that they had common interests and for their unusual degree of political equality. Selby's citizens, although by and large decent, kind, and generous people, were not deeply concerned with the quality or justice of their form of local government, while the members of this workplace, like members of virtually all radical collectives in the early 1970s, had spent a good deal of time and energy agonizing over questions of governance.

The workplace I selected was, on its face, as successful an example of workplace democracy as Selby had been of the town meeting. Compared to the other radical collectives with which I had come in contact, it was relatively egalitarian, communal, and able to do its job.[1] Helpline, Inc., as I shall call it, was located in a major American city, a city not necessarily in the forefront of the New Left but not far behind. The cosmopolitan, youth-oriented parts of this city and their adjoining interracial, ethnic, and working-class areas had spawned a variety of women's centers, underground papers, legal collectives, health clinics, food co-ops, free schools, and experimental universities—most of these attempting to govern themselves as radical "participatory" democracies.

Helpline, Inc., a "crisis center," had found quarters in an interracial neighborhood now slowly being settled by young people from the middle class. It was housed in an old brick schoolhouse across from a housing project and down a side street from a thoroughfare of fast-food carryouts and bars. It advertised in the local underground paper:

DO YOU WANT HELP?

The HELPLINE, INC., hot line is this city's 24-hour crisis intervention center, providing counseling and referral information for people with emotional, legal, medical, drug, or life-support problems, plus access to ambulance services, emergency shelters, short- and long-term counseling, special programs for teenagers. Services are free of charge and completely confidential. If you want help, don't wait until it's too late. Call 555-HELP. We can't help everyone, but maybe we can help you.

In the early 1970s, every large American city had such a crisis center. Many depended on only one source of funding, but Helpline, Inc., got grants from several local philanthropic and religious organizations and from the federal government. The organization also sold its services to city departments, to other cities and towns trying to set up similar centers, and, with some services, to individuals on a sliding scale. It had built up a full-time paid staff of forty-one. It was one of the largest workplace collectives I knew.

I saw Helpline first as anyone would who came for help to the drop-in center on the first floor. The battered front door opened right into a big first-floor room, where two volunteers on the Switchboard answered phone calls. They chatted with lonely alcoholics, referred pregnant teenagers to a testing and counseling service, talked acidheads down off bad trips, told caller after caller where they could find what they needed free or cheap, and gave advice to couples fighting, teenagers running from home, and potential suicides.

When I first came into the room, a couple of adolescents were talking agitatedly together on a broken-down sofa, while another wandered around the room looking at the pamphlets and posters: "Speed Kills," "Keep on Truckin'." They were waiting for appointments with their counselors or had just dropped in off the street. In the back of the room, screens divided the space into two counseling areas—no more than two beat-up, overstuffed chairs and an old rug—and a dark corner where a kid off the street had collapsed on a pile of mattresses to sleep something off.

As I came to know the premises, I learned that on the same floor, in another large open room, the Helpline community met in general assembly for the town meeting-like sessions that had come to be called Community Days. Encounter groups also used this room. So did the commune placement service, which twice a week brought together students, divorced housewives, newcomers to the city, and other people making a break with their past to look for communes to live in, to set up communes, or to get counseling on their communes' problems. On the same floor, in the back of the building, in a little room filled with mattresses, spreads, pillows, and posters, lit by a few rays filtering through its purple curtains, the drivers of the Emergency Van met, slept between shifts, and discussed the revolution. They kept their door locked.

Up the staircase, the second floor held the business phones, the counseling rooms, and the offices of the Switchboard staff. On that first day, I went directly to the third floor, a labyrinth of little cubbyholes for the administrative staff (fund raisers, public relations people, the lawyer) to a meeting of the Community Planning Council. Later, I discovered that even the fourth floor, the attic of this old building, had been pressed into service as sleeping quarters for some of the volunteers.

This organization, which I had heard of only as a hot line and drop-in center, was more ambitious than I had thought. When I began to study their organization, in 1973, Helpline, Inc., had evolved six distinct administrative sections: the *Switchboard*, a "hot-line" emergency service for drug calls, suicide calls, and information; the *Shelter*, a temporary shelter for runaways under eighteen years old; the *Emergency Van*, a twenty-four-hour patroling medical van staffed by paramedics and counselors; and the *Center for Community Counseling* (CCC), a resource bureau for communes. They had also bought a farm (the *Farm*) in a neighboring rural area, as a retreat that they hoped would be self-supporting and that could be used for community weekends. The staff grouped under the title of *Administrative Backup* raised funds and provided legal advice, publicity, and administration for the four major service groups and for the farm. Several hundred volunteers a year staffed the services of Helpline, Inc. They answered the phones at the Switch-board, accompanied the driver of the Emergency Van, helped at the Shelter, and worked with the CCC in its group counseling and commune-support programs. The paid staff provided continuity in counseling and an infrastructure for the volunteers.

From its inception, Helpline had always had the characteristics of a unitary democracy. It was dedicated to the common interest; it made its decisions by consensus, face-to-face; and it affirmed equal respect among its members. Yet its formal structure and the degree of political equality among its members had changed considerably through the years.

The organization had begun as a literal friendship in 1967, when Peter Danforth and his roommate, both seminary students, began to try to help neighborhood "street kids" who that year had started experimenting seriously with psychedelic and heavy drugs. When they saw the depth of the need, they began counseling in earnest, let some of the kids who had nowhere else to go "crash" in their apartment overnight, enlisted the help of other seminary students, and persuaded the seminary to give credit for the work as field experience. In less than one year, the operation could no longer be contained in their apartment. The group incorporated, got a small grant from one of the city churches, moved into a decaying building in an interracial neighborhood, and opened its doors to the runaways and street kids who had begun to flock into the city. In the summer of 1968, when the drug scene hit with full force and the city was inundated with several thousand flower children, Helpline, Inc., was the only group in the city that had any experience in helping them.

With the incorporation in 1967, Helpline began its search for a mode of governance that would satisfy its staff. For the first three years, Peter Danforth and an informal group of his friends acted as a board of directors and made the decisions for Helpline as a whole, although even then the need to rely on young and impatient volunteers assured that each work group ran its immediate affairs as it chose. The informal hierarchy with Peter at the head produced a series of conflicts between the board and the different work groups, and a parallel series of reorganizations, culminating in the Shelter's calling for a meeting of the entire Helpline community.

That meeting, a four-day weekend at the Farm in 1971, was the single most dramatic event in Helpline's history. Four consultants trained in organizational development and group process presided over encounters among the staff members, volunteers, and Peter and his friends. At the same time, groups meeting on the problems of organization devised an entirely new system of governance, referring all policy decisions to the Helpline community as a whole. The entire community, composed of all the volunteers and all the staff, was to meet together in assembly once a month or more often at the Farm, and all decisions would be made by "consensus"—a procedure in which any member could exercise a veto by refusing to go along with the others, but was expected not to veto except when the issue became too important to let pass.

The new town meeting form of organization ran into two problems. First, not everyone liked spending their weekends at the Farm, and these differences coincided with differences in interest. The "countercultural" members of Helpline, particularly represented in the Center for Community Counseling (CCC) and in Peter's closest circle, wanted Helpline both to encourage and to exemplify radical alternatives to existing forms of social, economic, and political organization. These people enjoyed the Farm, seeing its meetings and the backrubs they gave one another as part of the model they were developing for future society. Another group, particularly represented in the Shelter, wanted Helpline to assist people who were suffering and to do it as quickly and efficiently as possible. While the countercultural CCC and Peter's friends were soon overrepresented at the meetings on the Farm, the service-conscious Shelter counselors, exhausted after their week's work, were seriously underrepresented. Second, even with a meeting every month, the assembly form of democracy still left a vacuum in long-range planning that was again filled by Peter and his circle.

Consequently, in March 1972 an organizational task force suggested that Helpline scrap the pure town meeting system and put in its place a representative Community Planning Council (CPC) for long-range planning and a second representative group (DPW, meaning "Daily, Personnel, and Weekly") for short-range and maintenance issues. Each service group designated a member to work full or part time on funding in what became the Funding Office. These funders joined the others doing administrative work (the lawyer; the "office manager" or secretary; the carpenter-janitor; the "coordinator" or director; the treasurer; and three others responsible for public relations, research, and relations with the ministries) to form Administrative Backup, a group with the same status as the other service groups, sending one representative to the weekly meetings of the CPC and the DPW. The representatives to the CPC became the legal board of directors. To complete the transformation, Danforth left the organization in August 1972.

When I arrived in January 1973 to study the way Helpline made its decisions, the organizational structure set up in early 1972 was still in effect (Figure 3). Each member of the forty-one person paid staff belonged to a service group, the largest of which numbered twelve (the Shelter) and the smallest two (the Farm). Each service group established its own procedures, but all worked within a presumption of equality and attempted, more or less, to make decisions by consensus.

The entire organization still functioned primarily as a direct democracy. Each service group sent a representative to the long-range community policymaking body (CPC) and to the second committee on personnel and daily policy (DPW), both of which meet once a week. Yet these representatives were delegated little power. They made decisions by consensus, and, in theory, had to report all questions on which they suspected there might not be complete communitywide unanimity back to their service groups for final determination. Moreover, any interested member could participate in either CPC or DPW deliberations. At any stage, a community member could demand a full community meeting (called a Community Day), either for a day or for a weekend, to discuss and to decide on any issue collectively. All major policy decisions were to be made by the entire staff assembled at Community Day.

The volunteers had a parallel egalitarian and consensual organization, but because of the many problems of interpreting the meaning of participation in a voluntary association,[2] my analysis considered only the participation in decisions of the forty-one full-time paid staff.

The five months in which I sat in on meetings of the Community Planning Council (CPC) soon introduced me to Kaye, the tall, energetic vice-coordinator ("the queen of CPC," as someone called her); Tom, the coordinator; and Leon, the lawyer, a rougish, good-humored man with a thick black mustache, who hooked a red and black rug during the meetings. These three had independent positions on the CPC. Eben, the representative from the Farm, made a three-hour drive into the city almost every week for CPC meetings. Alex came upstairs from the Van, and first Greg, then Ken—a young lawyer new to Helpline—came from the Center for Community Counciling (CCC). Pamela, a quiet woman whom everyone considered "the mother" at the Shelter, walked over from their building five blocks away. Clarence, one of the few black members of Helpline, came up from the Switchboard. Nate, Switchboard's contribution to the Funding Office, also served as the representative of Administrative Backup to CPC.

DPW and CPC met once a week; each of the service groups met together at least once a week; and the whole community met together once every several months. Staff members reported that they spent an average of seven hours a week at meetings.

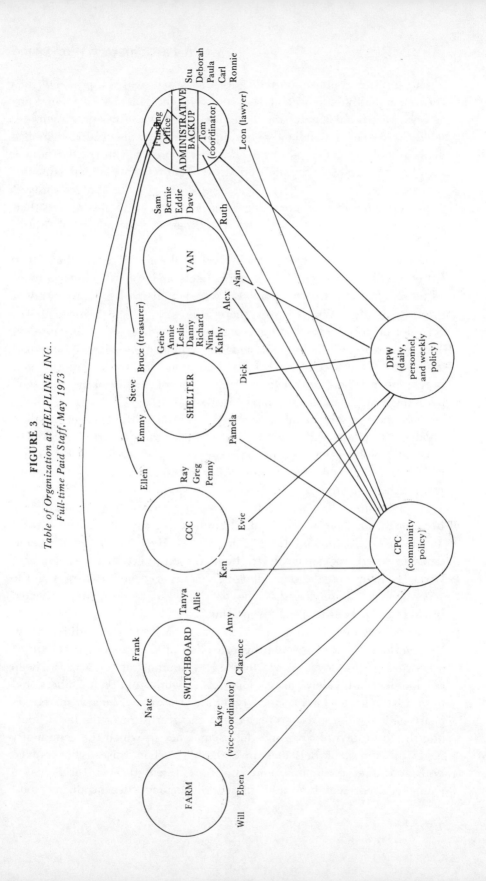

FIGURE 3

Table of Organization at HELPLINE, INC.
Full-time Paid Staff, May 1973

This form of organization indicates how strong was the practical concern for equality of power at Helpline. The individual veto under consensus created an irreducible minimum of power for every member, while the system of mandated representatives and frequent full assemblies made it difficult for a powerful elite to impose its will on the others. Helpline's staff was also intellectually committed to political equality. On the questionnaire I gave them, 63 percent of the staff considered "equality of power in internal decisions" very crucial to making Helpline what they wanted it to be; another 26 percent considered it "fairly crucial."

Salaries at Helpline were equal. Every full-time staff member made $5,000 a year, with increases for dependents and special grants in cases of need. Theoretically, the jobs also were equal, both in status and in intrinsic interest. While I was there, the job of "office manager," a euphemism for administrative secretary, was dismantled because its occupant, responsible for the general organization of Helpline, had gotten stuck with weeks of what was known as "shit work"—routine and boring labor. When she left to go back to school, each staff member took over the typing, mimeographing, and photocopying related to his or her job and the staff members using the central Bartlett Street building divided the phone shifts among them. This move left the division of labor at Helpline, with the possible exceptions of the job of carpenter-janitor and the night shift at the Shelter, as equal in fact as it was supposed to be in theory.

Helpline, Inc., had a director, according to some apologists, only because the outside world required someone of this title to sign leases and to talk with potential contributors. Yet Helpline also had an undeniable need for someone to take responsibility for coordination. Given Helpline's egalitarian ideology, the staff called this person the "coordinator," although legally he or she was not only the "director" but also the "president of the corporation."

The organization of Helpline, Inc., was typical of large radical collectives in the early 1970s. Similar histories had produced similar structures: a first period of innovation was marked by administrative chaos, by deep commitment but widely varying amounts of work from the members, and often by the leadership of one or two hard-working, visionary, sometimes charismatic figures. A second period saw the overthrow of the few leaders and the institution of town meeting democracy in which the community made all important decisions in assembly. When this system proved both too time consuming and too unrepresentative, a third period combined representation and direct democracy—decentralizing most decisions to small groups of six to twelve people, arranging some form of representation to a coordinating committee, and meeting in assembly periodically to hash out difficult problems and to reaffirm a sense of community.

I doubt that this form of organization could work in every community. The staff at Helpline, Inc., did not have personal histories of major political commitment. Probably no one had read the *Grundrisse*. Their parents had been, by and large, middle class. Several had applied to work at Helpline without even knowing beforehand that every staff member would be considered equal. Yet to be willing to do the emotionally exhausting work of short-term personal counseling and of administering an organization like Helpline, under conditions of low pay and marginal job security, the staff members had to be motivated at least in part by their ideals. Although few of the staff came to work at Helpline primarily because of its decision-making structure, and some of them had no idea of the way decisions were made until after they had been hired, all knew about the equal salary distribution and would have been surprised if decision making had not followed relatively egalitarian lines. The most important function of the time-consuming democratic procedures established at Helpline was, therefore, to meet the staff's ideals of the way their world should work. This idealism makes Helpline, Inc., a dubious prototype for the worker-controlled organization of the future.

Helpline was atypical in other ways as well. Of the paid staff at Helpline, 90 percent were under thirty years old. Of forty-one staff members, only three described their parents as "working class." These three and two others were the only staff at Helpline with no college education. More than half the staff had parents with incomes over $25,000 a year, and 81 percent had fathers whom they described as pretty independent or fairly independent in their jobs. Every person on the staff had participated in at least one political demonstration; half had participated in at least ten. In spite of their youth, 75 percent of the staff had at one point written to a public official (compared to, say, 38 percent of Selby's citizenry).

Institutionally, Helpline, Inc., was also atypical. It depended heavily on the unpaid work of more than a hundred volunteers a year. It produced services, not material goods,[3] and thus required a higher initial level of interpersonal competence than do most factory jobs. Helpline was basically a dispenser of counseling services, so that the job itself placed a premium on being able to understand other people. Helpline also provided constant on-the-job training in dealing with people. Because the staff members' education and middle-class status made it easy for them to find jobs elsewhere and because they were also adventurous, young, and undecided in their career plans, turnover was high. To survive without raising salaries or losing its staff and volunteers, the organization had to try to live up to the ideals of service, community, and democracy.

These atypical members, job requirements, and functional constraints reduce Helpline's use as a practical model for other worker-controlled organizations, but they make it useful for studying the internal tensions of a democracy. Except for their youth, almost all members of the Helpline staff had the ideal requirements for democratic citizenship. They were educated, practical, and communicated well with one another. They were committed to democratic ideals, and could afford to sacrifice other values to attain those ideals. Their attempts to put those ideals into practice thus brought into high relief the tension in any democracy between conflict and common interest.

Helpline, Inc., was small enough to allow strong bonds of friendship to develop between members, and it had more moments of truly common interest than did the town of Selby. Helpline was therefore closer than Selby to the unitary end of a spectrum between common and conflicting interests. Yet it had its moments of conflict. It was not a "pure" unitary democracy. Interestingly, in those moments of conflict, Helpline also approached the ideal of adversary democracy more closely than did Selby because at Helpline inequalities in political power between groups of conflicting interest were smaller. In Helpline, as in Selby, the newcomers, the geographically and socially isolated, the women, and the working class had less than equal power, at least in part because they did not participate in proportion to their numbers: the correlations between characteristics like being a newcomer and individual power were in fact as great or greater in Helpline than they were in Selby. But the absolute difference in power and participation between groups was much smaller. While inequality of power and participation had not been eliminated at Helpline, it had been significantly reduced.

Because its members tried harder than did the citizens of Selby to bring about a perfect democracy here on earth, and because the conditions under which they labored were more favorable, Helpline was able to generate both a strong sense of common interest and considerable political equality. Their individualist upbringing and the inescapable individuality of the human condition prevented the staff from joining indissolubly in a single unity. Nor did they know, philosophically, exactly what they wanted from their democracy. But as they struggled to act as one, as they tried not to compromise on any of the ideals of liberty, equality, or solidarity, they revealed important tensions in the concept of democracy itself.

Chapter 13

Fears of Conflict in a Face-to-Face Assembly

I N HELPLINE, as in Selby, face-to-face meetings were better at developing community than at dealing with conflict. The meetings reminded the staff of its solidarity and allowed people who rarely saw one another to take in the others' points of view. But Helpline's meetings also suppressed conflict. Helpline had fewer participants than Selby did, and its members were better trained to handle conflict. Yet when real conflicts of interest arose, responses in large face-to-face meetings at Helpline resembled in some ways those at Selby's town meeting: people held back their anger until they were about to explode; factions whipped up the courage of their supporters in pre-meeting caucuses; and those who attended the meeting were afraid of being ridiculed, having others take personally what they said, and making enemies. As a consequence, many in the group engaged in a collective effort to dampen hostilities. Crucial questions were often decided informally outside the public meeting, and avoiding the unpleasantness of conflict in itself provided a spur toward reaching unanimity.

Because some of the Helpline staff consciously tried to face up to conflict, these patterns were weaker than they were in Selby's town meeting. But each fear and each form of avoidance that I saw in Selby's meetings also appeared in Helpline's Community Days.

The first full assembly that I attended at Helpline was called at a time when a deepening economic depression had cut Helpline's income by a third. Since overhead costs were already minimal, this meant cutting staff by a third. Everyone at Helpline dreaded the coming "bloodbath." The members had agreed, through their representatives on CPC, that each service group would bring to the Community Day a plan to cut its own staff to fit within the new budget. Yet it became clear, as each group evolved its plan, that some service groups were cutting less than a third.

Tensions built before the meeting. The two most "service-oriented" groups, the Shelter and the Emergency Van, felt that they already could hardly provide decent services even with the staff they had. The Shelter proposed instead to increase its income by undertaking to care for more state-supported young adolescents on their way to placement in foster homes, even though it was afraid that taking more state wards might endanger the class and racial mix of tenants at the Shelter and might add too many people with serious emotional disturbances. The state, however, paid well. The Shelter also proposed cutting two of its staff, thereby paring to what they felt was below the bone. The Emergency Van decided simply that it could not cut any staff, and would face the community with that fact.

Both the Shelter and the Van nursed a long-standing grudge against the Center for Community Counseling (CCC). Although they were occasionally convinced that CCC's services (commune placement and counseling) were useful, they more often saw the group as providing luxuries for middle-class people who were neither in desperate need of services nor too poor to pay for them. Having discussed the subject carefully in their own service group meetings, they came to the Community Day hoping to make CCC cut drastically and determined to see it cut at least to the one-third guideline.

The Center for Community Counseling staff, however, did not propose to cut one-third. Instead, they prepared a complicated proposal that, of their six and one-half person staff, cut only the one who was working half time, cut out one salary, and shared the five remaining salaries among the six staff who were left; they also suggested that these six take occasional unpaid vacations. This package added up to a reduction of considerably less than one-third, as well as leaving those on reduced salaries or unpaid vacations with all the fringe benefits of the organization, like the health plan, potential claims regarding need, and equal power in community decision making.

Aware of the tensions that were growing, the agenda committee of the representative body, the Community Planning Council (CPC), had divided up the Community Day into eight parts. In each of the first six parts, one of the six service groups would report its plans for cutting back to the full assembly, the community in assembly would ask informational questions only, and the assembly would then divide up into four seven- to twelve-person groups. These four small groups, each designed to include a member of every service group, would discuss the plan just presented in the assembly. Members of the service group that had just presented its plan for cuts in the full assembly would defend that plan in the small group and would explain what their service group was doing, while others in the group asked questions, criticized, and spoke their minds. Finally, after the meeting had come together and had broken down six times for each of the service groups' proposals, the service groups themselves would meet separately to talk over what their members had learned. At 3:45 in the afternoon, the full meeting would come together for the final discussion.

On the Community Day itself, the somewhat nervous staff gathered in a large empty room on the bottom floor of the Bartlett Street building. As we milled around drinking orange juice and coffee from paper cups, the members of CCC organized us into doing physical exercises, and we settled into a circle on the floor or in the surrounding dilapidated chairs and sofas only fifteen minutes behind schedule.

The Shelter went first. One of their staff stood and spoke briefly and intensely, letting everyone understand how tortured the staff felt over its proposal for two cuts and for more foster home children. The meeting dispersed to small groups in the rooms upstairs, the groups discussed the Shelter's proposal, and everyone returned nervously to hear CCC, next on the agenda.

Cross-legged on the floor at the far end of the circle, CCC's first speaker shifted his position and began: "I feel a little defensive right now." (Nate, from Switchboard, whispered loud enough for me to hear, "As well you might!") "And I want to share it with people. I think it comes from coming after the Shelter, which is doing concrete things and seeing results." "Louder!" came a yell from the other side of the circle. "I'd rather talk softly," he pleaded, then raised his voice to a shout: "I'm feeling DEFENSIVE!" He concluded in a few words that CCC's goal was to "help people change their lives." A smiling fellow in an embroidered Indian shirt then continued CCC's presentation, telling how he was "getting off on the life of our collective," and a third, Ken, a young lawyer serious about his politics, who had joined Helpline only recently and who had soon become CCC's representative to the CPC, took up the rambling narrative. He, too, was "excited by the numbers wanting to make changes." "We need to ask questions," he expostulated. "What is community? Ignoring Third World people, ignoring the war. . . . There's something wrong with you if you're happy all the time with all this repression!" A woman from Switchboard cut this short: "What about *cutting back?*"

Ken was silent. Ellen, sitting next to him, explained CCC's one half-time job, one salary, and unpaid vacation package, all of which would result in a 23 percent cut. Pamela, the Shelter's representative to the CPC, raised her hand and pointed out that in a CPC meeting the CCC representative had said that they could cut to four people. Ellen was surprised at this news. Unthinkingly, she answered that "with four of us, we'd just be maintaining what we're doing!" "Yeah," Pamela snapped. "Well, that's where it's at!" Tom, chairing the meeting, broke in immediately: "The questions in this period should be only clarification; keep the criticisms to the small groups!"

This time, when the meeting broke up into groups, people lagged behind, whispering and talking with their friends. But eventually, the fifty or so people at the meeting traipsed upstairs to one of four small offices on the second and third floors. In the small group I had chosen to attend, Ken, who seemed more given to long-winded explanations than did anyone else at Helpline, took up the task of explaining to the others why CCC should not cut a full third. Among the twelve people in our group, he had no one else from CCC to support him, but he faced two staffers and one volunteer from the Shelter. Although Nate, from Switchboard, mediated and added his own analysis, the major confrontation took place between Ken and a staffer from the Shelter named Steve.

"Maybe my priorities are different from CCC's," Steve began. "I know there aren't any Third World people and people hurting desperately being helped by CCC: there's so much energy concerned with *self*-service at CCC." Ken answered that it depended on one's political analysis and asked, with an earnest look, "Do you read *Communities* magazine?" "Listen," Steve interjected angrily, "I *work* in a community!" Ken, unfazed, explained that he had written an article on the work that CCC was doing in *Communities* magazine, that he had worked for civil rights in the South and with Third World groups, that he took Marx very seriously, and that he thought the revolutionary strategy ought to be what CCC was doing—encouraging people to relate to their own oppression directly: "as the old-time Marxists would say, to the 'primary contradictions.' " Steve looked up impatiently, ready to interrupt. "Let me finish," urged Ken, "because this is the answer." As he went on, at length, I looked around the group. One man held his head in his hands, gazing morbidly at the floor; another looked blankly across the room away from the speaker. A third leaned his head heavily against his hand. A woman slouched down in her chair, eyes drifting around the group. Another stretched out on the floor in the back. Repressed, the tensions I knew were there were emerging as boredom.

Steve made a visible effort to control himself. Finally, a volunteer from the Shelter interrupted: "I have a need to cut you off, if you don't mind. I understand your answer and agree with a lot of it. But you don't understand what everyone else says—*we're* cutting back. I don't see how you've responded in an *economic* way, in proportion—now maybe you don't agree with proportion?—to what the Shelter is doing." Ken then pointed out that if the Shelter went through with its state-supported program the percentage cut in both the Shelter and the CCC would be about the same. When he concluded, "I think the issues are really trust issues," Steve nodded, and another Shelter member commented, "That's true," adding that the CCC program still remained "amorphous" to him. "It is harder for me to hear that," said Ken, "because I explained the things we're doing. " "I can hear that and take some responsibility for it," answered the member from the Shelter. And Ken echoed, "I hear that very clearly. I'm not doing a whitewash; I want to be straight."

After a while, Steven summed up the past fifteen minutes: "The discussion has cleared my head about some things—that the need is there and your program is directed toward it. But it seems like a high level to me—five salary slots." A few more questions, one still quite hostile ("You say you work hard, but your people just took four-week vacations!") from Steve, and someone in the group pointed out that the time was up.

Throughout the day in that small group, the discussions—of the Van, the Administrative Backup, and the Farm reports—took much the same path. Ken, always the serious radical, asked the broader "political" questions: why the Switchboard and the Van thought one-to-one counseling was better than group counseling, whether or not the Van was doing any political work around methadone, and why Administrative Backup always gave the office manager job to a woman. Steve asked pointed, service-related questions: how hard members of a group were working, whether or not they did follow-ups to evaluate their service, and, persistently, how groups could cut back further on staff. Nate, his smile, fuzzy hair, and loose soft shirt broadcasting the message that it was all not so important as it seemed, asked questions about the harmony within the groups and played a joking, mediating role: "I hate to sound like the dude with the meat cleaver, but the reality of the situation might be that we may not be able to afford it!" By the end of the day, Nate had spoken seventy-three times, Ken had spoken fifty-nine times, Steve had spoken fifty-six times, and the eight others had ranged themselves from thirty-two times to zero. The one person who never spoke at all was a young woman volunteer from Switchboard.

At three o'clock, the members joined their own service groups to discuss their reactions to the reports and to the small group discussions. When I joined the Shelter meeting, squirming into a corner on the floor a few minutes late, Steve was arguing that "we should take a stand that we think will pass and stick to it. Personally, I'd like to see CCC *go*. But in terms of a proposal that has some chance of *passing*, I'd like to see them cut to four, with one a funding person." Several Shelter members brought up the arrogance or insensitivity of CCC staff in their small groups. They concluded that, of all the service groups at Helpline, CCC was the only one "not willing to pay the price."

One man told the group that "our major war is with CCC." Another said that in the upcoming final assembly the Shelter should "make a strong statement just to make sure a strong statement is made." While four people actually defended CCC on the basis of what they had learned in their different small groups, even these four agreed that the Shelter should ask CCC to cut by a full third, not 23 percent. Almost everyone who spoke in that brief Shelter meeting brought in information learned in a small discussion group, but the meeting served as much to steel the nerves of the Shelter members before the final assembly as it did to assimilate new information. Looking at his watch, one man summed up the meeting: "Okay! We go to *confrontation* on the Farm and CCC, and say we'd *really* like to question the Van on whether they can cut more!"

The moment of the final assembly had arrived. Staff members clustered around the floor, whispering, joking, lighting cigarettes. Into the settling voices, someone made an announcement. Then the Shelter began: rent the Farm for a year; we can't get away from the upcoming $70,000 deficit; everyone else is making cuts. "We feel, and *feel very strongly* that CCC should cut by one-third!" Their curt, strongly stated report took two minutes. It focused on CCC.

Tom, as chair of the meeting, turned toward where the people from CCC were sitting, laughed in acknowledgment of the tension, and simply asked "CCC?" Ken glared around the circle, angry at a violation of what he thought were the ground rules: "*Our* assumption about this meeting was that we wouldn't have an 'evaluative' procedure! The point for us was to trust each service group! We felt a lot of trust in each service group's *self*-assessment!" But Ellen interjected that in the future CCC would work more seriously on fund raising, and Nate, sitting on the floor next to me, muttered, "That's fair."

Switchboard came next and also said that the CCC proposal was not acceptable to them. Then Nan, in a purple T-shirt with the words "I'm agin it!" across the front, stood to give the Van's report. Keeping her eyes on her notes, she read that the Van still planned to cut no staff, but had agreed to cut a salary and to share the loss among them. Looking up then, and over to where the group from CCC sat in the circle opposite, she flushed and stated boldly:

It seems to us important to look at the organization as a whole and how it serves people as a whole. We see a political question here. . . . Given Nixon's budget cuts, the institutions that serve people who are [the worst off] are the most important—and this means *Switchboard*, the *Shelter* and the *Van*! . . . we essentially feel that the Farm and CCC are extravagances at this point!

Recommending that CCC be cut by one-third, she sat down.

Administrative Backup made a brief, noncommittal statement, and the service groups' final reports were over. The chair asked for comments. He got total silence. No one from CCC spoke. After seconds of impasse, a man from the Shelter snapped out in the direction of CCC, "The Shelter is really committed to the statement we made. We really do expect you to cut by one-third. And we're *not* really negotiable on that!" People from the other service groups began to chime in with their criticisms of CCC, and two of the CCC staff, flustered, answered simply that they would try harder. But Ruth, who worked on the Van and rarely spoke at meetings, raised her voice: "The Van's statement came out pretty hard against CCC, and I'd like to hear an answer to that!"

With the gauntlet thus thrown down, two CCC men jumped in at once. The first shouted, "*We* think *we're* the most political group!" while the other, Ken, launched a discourse on how useless individual service projects, like those of the Van and the Shelter, were in a capitalist system. He argued that the United States was entering into "a period of armed struggle which requires great support" and that this support would come primarily from CCC's countercultural middle-class constituency or, "as Marx would say, from 'déclassé' or 'declassed' communities."

Around me, several people scowled at the rhetoric. Eddie, a working-class black on the Van, interrupted with a loud "What are you doing in Carlton Gardens?" To this question about the mostly black community near Helpline, the CCC lawyer took a calm breath and replied, "According to what *Brother Malcolm* said, we don't belong there!"

Eddie was floored. From around the room arose angry murmurs (presumably prompted as much by Ken's calling Malcolm X a "brother" as by his using the black leader's writings against Eddie). But before anything gelled, someone called out, "Wait a minute! Before we start slinging mud. . . !" Several people hastened to put in good words for CCC. When others renewed the attack, a man from Administrative Backup cut in: "People are counting coups right now. The points are all made. I'm not hearing new ones!" Someone recommended that CCC work up a plan taking the suggestions they had heard into account. The chair reminded everyone that they had not intended to come to a final decision in one day. Within minutes, the group reached a consensus, accepting the other four service groups' revised plans and asking CCC to submit a revised plan to the CPC by the following week.

Turning to the Farm, which the Shelter and the Van wanted to sell but were willing to rent, a brief flurry of discussion allowed the remaining participants to decide to discontinue the Farm's programs and to rent the buildings and land. The meeting adjourned just before six o'clock, with a couple of people shouting announcements into the air and the rest straggling wearily or rushing without ceremony toward the door.

The meeting had been relatively subdued. The strategies of not requiring a final decision at the meeting and relegating most of the criticisms to small group discussion had served the agenda committee's purpose of bringing conflicts into the open but not allowing them to get out of hand. Yet the criticism that did surface in the larger assembly left many participants shaken. A month later, Dave, on the Van, remembered vividly the moment when the Van made its final statement in the full assembly:

We were all just sitting there, kind of—whew—wow. . . . We were all super-nervous; we knew that it meant people's feelings. [JM: People in CCC?] Yeah.

We made a statement. And we were all pretty relieved when Monty [a volunteer from the Shelter] stood up and said what he said about cutbacks—you know, like he said that they [the Shelter] were making a demand that CCC cut back. And boy, was that a relief!

But it wasn't enough because when it was Nan's turn [to make the Van statement]—like Ruth, I had my eye on Ruth, and I had Susan down around my leg, and I had somebody beside me, and we were all holding each other, and we could all feel the weird vibes. I'm looking at Alex, and my eyes were bloodshot—I mean it was really heavy. It was like World War II in your living room! [laugh] Eddie was way across the other side of the room, and he was *bullshit!* He was absolutely bullshit! And I was real struck. I mean, we were communicating nonverbally, and we were all really scared, and when Nan stood up, I was looking at her, right at her eyes as hard as I could to see what was there, and I chanced to look away, and I saw that everybody else was doing it. Then when Stu shifted to look at the people at CCC, so did Eddie and so did Alex and so did Ruth and so did Susan [all members of the Van]. It was really heavy. And Bernie was there, and Bernie is happy-go-lucky, and it's the first time I've ever seen Bernie concerned about what was going to happen.

We thought it was like dropping a bomb. And it was; it really was. It was like saying, what we were saying in essence was that we're getting blown out of what we're doing, and we don't feel *you* are! . . .

That's really heavy—dropping a bomb and hurting people's feelings—

confronting them as a whole, saying that your projects aren't very valuable to Helpline. What we were saying is that "We don't want you. Not that we don't like you as people—we *don't!*" [laugh] It's not that bad, but there are individuals within that group that I just can't deal with!

[JM: How did you feel afterward?] Relieved that it was over. Like I was hallucinating. [laugh] At that point I was so tired. My mind couldn't even stay on. I was falling asleep on the floor. . . . Other people pretty much felt that too. I had been up for forty-eight hours. I wasn't eating well. Feeling . . . a lot of anxiety about people being stubborn.

That's the heaviest thing that I have ever gone through, at Helpline. The meeting and the head changes I was going through, and then going home and finding I was alone, that I really needed them. I cried.

Ruth, who worked on the Van, lived in a communal house with Ellen from CCC. They were good friends, although they disagreed on the value of the services that CCC provided. In the final assembly, Ruth had demanded that CCC answer the Van's criticism; afterward, she had to live with the consequences. "It was very strange for me," Ruth told me. "Kids on CCC are my *roommates!* One of them wasn't speaking to me!"

I just felt scared about Ellen—whether she would ever speak to me again. [laugh] That's been a contention thing ever since we both started working at Helpline. The Shelter and Van have *never* dug CCC. So when that started to come up, we just entirely cut that out of our relationship. We never talked about it.

But on this, she said I was taking her job away, her salary away, and *I* said that I wasn't doing anything to *her!*

I didn't know what to do. Because I felt that I was absolutely right in principle, and that's really how I believed it should be, and I felt like I had to say it. And I didn't want that to come between us personally, because we *knew* that that was there all along, that we disagreed on that. I don't know— I still don't.

People from the Shelter, who also had to take the position of attack, reported feeling "sick," "a wreck," and "so tired . . . drained physically . . . so blown away!"

If the meeting was tense for the staff from the Van and the Shelter, it was all the more so for the CCC staff. Ellen, from CCC, felt "terrible! I walked into that meeting, and I had been away for six weeks, and it seemed like the sky had fallen in! I cried a lot. I was really shocked." Ellen's colleagues on CCC felt "wasted," "angry," "real horror," and "hurt." One went home afterward and simply cried. Staff members who sympathized with CCC also felt "horrible," "awful," "frustrated and down," "upset over the backbiting," or had headaches. It had been one new member's first Community Day. When the meeting got "malicious" and "turned into a barbecue of CCC," he told me, it "ruined the whole thing for me!"

Dividing most of the Community Day into small groups had allowed the aggrieved to criticize and the attacked to respond in a situation that gave each individual more time and greater control over the outcome, and where people were not so likely to see requests for information as public criticism or criticism itself as humiliation. As a consequence, the memories of what happened in the small groups were somewhat brighter. A shy woman from the Shelter reported, "I got angry at —— in my small group, but I really felt good about the process, that there was a way to release that anger." A woman from CCC, which had received most of the criticism, agreed: "I liked my small group; I felt that at least there people were trying to listen to one another."

In a large assembly like Helpline's Community Day or Selby's town meeting, people generally have to plan what they want to say beforehand, work up the courage to speak, then spit it out. In the meantime, their anger collects and helps escalate conflict. A large group seems to provide only two alternatives—suppress what one wants to say or exacerbate the conflict. One man from the Shelter described how differently he had acted in the two situations:

In my small group things were much more friendly and supportive. People were much more antagonistic in the large group [and] things seemed more out of hand. I really didn't like to see CCC get slashed like that, although I got my digs in too. I didn't feel good about what I said; I said it in a very nasty way. I felt like I was attacking CCC, and I didn't want to do that.[1]

Yet even in the small groups anger surfaced, and people avoided saying what they believed. When they thought it might lead to a personal confrontation, a good many preferred to slouch down in their chairs and wish they were somewhere else.

The Fears

Many others would agree with the staff member who told me, "I've never gotten so angry as I have at meetings at Helpline." As in the Selby town meeting, face-to-face contact at Helpline makes conflict "more exposed, with all the anger out in the open," and everyone "super hepped up to everybody's vibes."

Even among the confident, therapeutically trained staff at Helpline, some people feared public ridicule. Danny, one of the working-class members of Helpline, put it best: "I've just seen people do numbers on people. It's a waste; it doesn't make anybody feel good. Humiliation is the word!"

As in Selby, the issues became confused with the personalities of the participants. Several people told me that "people take decisions very personally,"[2] and even the most articulate staff sometimes suppressed what they wanted to say because it would open them to personal attack.

People knew, too, that voicing a controversial opinion would make them enemies. Ruth, on the Van, found her best friend not speaking to her. The woman who made the Van statement that Community Day had similar fears:

I felt really weird standing up there and saying that all by myself. Just because I don't like to have people dislike me. And I know this is not going to make me too popular with the CCC people, and probably with a number of other people. And I faltered to some extent. I didn't say it as rationally as I had when I had been in the Van meeting and we were all "Yeah, yeah. give 'em hell!" (laugh) . . . [How did you feel after saying it?] I just felt very blown away. I was shaking.

Friendships that cut across service groups increase this difficulty because, like the Selby townspeople, the staff at Helpline will have to live and work with people they make their enemies.[3]

In fact, the very closeness of the friendships at Helpline made conflict harder to endure. When Helpline's office manager reflected on the battle she had fought to have her job abolished after she left, she concluded that she had actually been less able to stand up for herself at Helpline than she had in her former less attractive jobs:

Let's say I'm working at —— and making two dollars an hour and being pushed around a lot by a lot of schmucky people I don't really like, whose political leanings make me quite ill, and let's say they make some comment and I retort, "I don't like what you said." Well, I don't feel that I was threatened in that situation very much because I didn't have much to lose if they fired me. Whereas here I was so comfortable . . . everyone's so nice and friendly and some people come up and give you a back rub . . . it's kind of intimidating to be in that position.

Another staff member once worried that a meeting would attack his project:

I felt alone. Part of the fear was losing that group of people and being alone and not having them. A very large part of my life was involved in Helpline. I really didn't have anything else.

And after this Community Day, a member of CCC, afraid that his laggard performance had helped contribute to the wrath against the group, met with the others to make sure that they too would not turn against him. "It was important for me," he said, "to hear them say that they were not going to drive me into the wilderness!"

These fears mean that some people never speak out until they are "provided." At that point, they report, "I'm so angry that I get very frustrated, and I can't say what I think." The fears lead to groups' giving each other pep talks before a meeting, picking the hardest liners to make the statement, as the Shelter did at this Community Day, or, like the Van, developing a spirit of "Yeah, yeah, give 'em hell!"

Avoiding Conflict

The staff members at Helpline were young, daring, strong, competent, empathetic, and skilled in therapy. It would have gone against both their training and their natural inclinations to respond to the threat of open conflict by suppressing it or by pretending that it did not exist. They were likely to tell me that "conflict doesn't bother me, frankly," "I like controversy, I thrive on it," or "I'm a firm believer in creative conflict."

Some of the staff at Helpline even consciously tried to fight what they saw as a group tendency to avoid conflict. On this Community Day, Kaye insisted on written reports so that the details of each service group's plan could not be conveniently forgotten or misunderstood, and she and others also deliberately built a moment for criticism into the agenda. Yet half a dozen staff members told me, in virtually identical words, that even at Helpline "We have a nonconfronting system, a system that tries as much as possible to eliminate conflict. . . . People avoid dealing with things altogether."

To reassure themselves in a big meeting, the members of Helpline emphasize informality. In planning the meeting, written reports or other formal procedures that seem stuffy and uptight are suspect. On the day itself, people joke and banter; meetings may even begin with physical exercises intended to establish feelings of community among the participants. Members use therapy or counseling language to create rapport ("I feel a little defensive right now and I want to share it with people"; or "I can hear that and take some responsibility for it"). At tense moments, the chair laughs, and the members try to lard unpalatable messages with funny phrases ("I hate to sound like the dude with the meat cleaver, but. . . .”). When open, angry conflict does burst out at a meeting, people generally jump in to smooth it over. When Eddie might have turned in real anger on Ken, the CCC lawyer, someone called out quickly, “Wait a minute!” and others hurried to smooth over the waters. These procedures work. After this Community Day, one person from the Shelter commented in some disgust, “What we heard from other groups in private was not at all what came out here. What I heard at the meeting was much more muted!”

Because several CPC members had wanted this Community Day to bring out underlying conflicts, very few informal decisions were made beforehand. But in the second Community Day I attended, the before-hand meeting was the principal method used to avoid public conflict. Both of the major items on the agenda, the election of a new coordinator and the institution of a new legal service group, had been worked out with most of the competing parties before the meeting. Neither candidate for the position of coordinator had to feel defeated, nor did the new members of the legal service group have to face in public the strong suspicions of the Shelter and the Van. Both issues were decided by consensus, without stressing potential conflicts.

As in the town meeting, the protective devices of joking, informality, dampened conflict, prearrangement, and unanimity had the positive function of assuaging the fears of many of the members. Yet they also had the side effect of further alienating newcomers and those not tightly connected to the informal decision-making networks. Abbreviated names, therapy language, and in-jokes reassured the older members but, like any set of family traditions, made the newcomers feel out of the picture. Helpline's informality eliminated any procedure for explaining the staff's cozy abbreviations, jargon, or rules of the game. Staff members remembered that “it took me about six months just to find out what people were talking about! Like, what's ‘CCC’?” “They talked a different language—‘I hear you’ and ‘the consensus is.’ ” “Somehow the letters got garbaged in my mind.”

Even physical exercises, deliberately instituted to induce feelings of closeness by moving in concert with others—stretching, touching, making physical contact—only further alienated those who had not come with those feelings to begin with. For more than one Shelter member, the budget-cutting Community Day started off on a bad note:

[Someone from CCC] was doing this “reach for grapes” stuff—everyone had to do that. I was more relaxed just sitting down and drinking my coffee than getting up and doing all these hippie exercises. It just didn't make sense to me. It just wasn't the setting for it.

Leslie, a black woman from the Shelter, told me that her first reaction to the same Community Day was:

Yuk! I felt really pissed off because I wanted to spend my Saturday with my kid watching cartoons and didn't want to be there! I was hung over, and I was missing a day with my kid. I walk in and people are picking grapes and twisting their heads, being elephants. (laugh) I just thought, "What's the matter with you? What's wrong with you?"

Exercises designed to relax the participants thus succeeded only in further alienating those who felt already on foreign turf.

In spite of their training in group process, other ways in which the staff at Helpline tried to deal with or to avoid conflict also backfired in a way that further estranged those peripheral to the group. The informal negotiations that often went on before public meetings, the "groundwork" whereby staff members would "cultivate, go around, and discuss with people" before a meeting, sometimes convinced the relative outsiders that the meeting itself was essentially ineffective. In the first Community Day, the decision on how CCC would actually cut its staff was put off until after the meeting. As a consequence, Danny, one of the least active members of the Shelter, commented on the eventual compromise: "I know the way they did this was with some heavy wheeling and dealing!" He pointed out that matters not brought up explicitly at Community Day could be "slipped right through":

They could do it! All this input was shit! I could be right there at the Community Day and the Shelter could be right there . . . and it just wouldn't be dealt with fairly, I don't think.

Other members of the Shelter, which as a group was the least connected to the informal decision networks at Helpline, sometimes concluded that by the time they got to a meeting the decision "had already been sort of set up."

Thus, in spite of being conscious of the problem of avoidance, in spite of training in group skills, and in spite of explicit techniques like breaking large meetings down into small groups, patterns of conflict avoidance continued to arise, not only on this Community Day but throughout the history of Helpline. Those patterns in turn were likely to work to the disadvantage of those not fully integrated into the organization's informal networks.

Chapter 14

Consensus and the Common Interest

ALTHOUGH having to reduce the budget by a third brought out many underlying conflicts at Helpline, the staff resolved even this issue by consensus. Eventually CCC brought the CPC a second budget, cut by a third; CPC representatives took that budget to the service groups; and although some people were not fully satisfied with all its provisions, every group finally agreed to the second budget. Conflict had surfaced in the face-to-face meeting, and people had taken measures to repress it, but the Community Day seems nevertheless to have helped the staff in both CCC and the other groups to understand one another's feelings and points of view.

This was the way members of Helpline wanted to make their decisions. Despite their divisions, they believed that they could and should reach unity on issues of this kind. Their ideal was a unitary democracy; and requiring consensus gave that ideal institutional form. According to Helpline's rules, no decision involving the organization as a whole could be taken without the agreement of every one of its members. Within most service groups the procedure was the same. The decision rule—which, following both Helpline and New Left usage, I will call consensus rather than unanimity—required a great deal of real unity in the organization but did not demand unanimous substantive agreement on every point. It required instead that dissenters' objections be sought out, heard, and taken into consideration, and that at the end of the process they agree they could "live with" the decision of the greater part of the group.

Helpline had introduced the idea of stating that one could "live with" a decision, creating what they called "second-order consensus," primarily as a time-saving device. At first, most members expected it to cover only minor disagreements and not to override the assumption that the members' interests were essentially the same. When I observed consensus in practice, however, some of the service groups applied the verbal formula of second-order consensus in a way that made it quite similar to conventional majority rule.

Indeed, consensus as practiced at Helpline—and I would guess consensus in every organization with a formal unanimity rule—differed from majority rule in degree rather than in kind. Every decision-making rule, including majority rule, assumes that the losers can in some way "live with" a decision. The losers always have the option of leaving the polity, if only, in the most extreme cases, by suicide. To stay in the polity is, therefore, to make a statement of the weakest sort that one can literally "live with" a decision. Beyond this, the successful use of majority rule also requires some large-scale agreement on the rules of the game.

The reverse is also true. In face-to-face organizations, the actual practice of formal majority rule often looks more like consensus. Fears of conflict and the desire for harmony generate informal pressures to achieve unanimity. To the extent that a group operates emotionally like a friendship, the serious discomfort of any member with a decision makes the others reluctant to press forward with that decision. Thus, no polity in fact ever institutes a purely unitary or purely adversary decision-rule.

The formal rule of consensus can best be understood as giving legal support to the drive for harmony that appears in most face-to-face groups. It accentuates, but does not change, the character of the unifying processes that arise even when the face-to-face organization has a formal majority rule. Its advantages and disadvantages are those of unitary democracy as a whole, which works better the more an organization approaches unity and worse the more it must handle insuperable conflicts.

Although spontaneous consensus arises frequently and unnoticed when there is no disagreement whatever on either ends or means, the consensual decisions I examine in this chapter all began with spontaneous disagreement, usually over ends, but occasionally over means. The consensual process was one of converting initial disagreement into agreement or at least into universal willingness to go along with the result. This process takes time, and it must be repeated whenever anyone changes his or her mind or a newcomer with different ideas joins the group. It can also result in unclear decisions. When interests are in conflict, requiring consensus will result either in deadlock or in social coercion.

When interests conflict, therefore, consensus usually benefits those whose interests lie with the status quo (with the exception that requiring consensus allows those who object to the status quo to keep bringing up their objections over and over; it thus prevents the majority from simply cutting off discussion). Consensus benefits those who can make things happen outside the consensual process and who therefore set the boundaries for the decision. It benefits those who have the inner strength to stand up to group pressure. It benefits those who have the resources to act in moments of inactivity. Finally, it benefits those who determine the definition and formulation of issues and the tone of discussion.

Yet in spite of the costs in time, repetition, occasional lack of clarity, and potential inequality, requiring consensus has significant advantages whenever interests can be reconciled. It directs members' attention to the common good. It intensifies the tendency of any face-to-face group to focus attention and communication on dissidents, trying to draw them into the group. It encourages people to listen carefully to both the emotional tone and the intellectual content of what the others say. It helps bring out information, forges commitment, discourages factions, and creates the morale-building sense that "we are all in this together."

In Helpline, as in Selby, the group's pressure for unanimity distracted individuals from their personal interests. In both cases, this was a mixed blessing. At Helpline, however, the members' interests were closer than they were in Selby. The benefits of assuming common interests were therefore greater and the costs less. At Helpline all were committed to a common task—giving therapeutic support to people in trouble, while criticizing the polity and economy from which that trouble derived. Individual members inevitably had different interpretations of what that task entailed, and each service group had also evolved its own distinctive collective interpretation, ranging from the Shelter's commitment to "good service" for the runaways, through the Van's fantasy of a street people's revolution, to CCC's vision of a humane reordering of relationships through counseling, communes, and personal growth. These differing interpretations of the common interest provided a major source of disunity in the organization, especially when they coincided with the distinctive interests of the various service groups. The differing private interests of individuals were a second source of conflict. But their common task of "critical" therapy and their common bourgeois capitalist enemy bound the members of Helpline together in a unity more firm than that of most geographical polities, and made the assumption that important interests were similar true more often in Helpline than in Selby.

This chapter documents the uneasy tension between the assumption of common interest and the forces that made for disunity at Helpline. It begins by looking closely at instances that illustrate the disadvantages and advantages of consensus.

The Disadvantages of Consensus

Achieving consensus requires time—time that most of Helpline's staff would have rather spent providing services than making decisions. Clarence was disgusted at the waste of time. Bruce muttered that it was a good thing Helpline did not have to compete on the market with an efficient enterprise. Everyone complained about the time. Blocked by the time it takes to get something done or by the specter of hours "wasted" on meetings, highly motivated workers can get frustrated, angry, and depressed.

Helpline tried to preserve the spirit and the form of consensus even in emergencies, but discussion was inevitably curtailed. People who wanted their proposals to pass without amendment were therefore tempted to wait until the last moment to bring them up. The two most obvious instances of manipulation at Helpline used the pressure of time in that way, both causing considerable bitterness.

A second problem of consensus is repetition. Decisions must be made and remade. Because Helpline's unanimity rule required the consent of each member, it opened all policies to review whenever one or two people changed their minds or a new member joined the staff. Old members then felt "really frustrated because I hear the same things brought up over and over again."

In the Shelter, for instance, new members challenged an old policy against contact with a local street gang, the Scorpions. One of the new members explained:

People who hadn't been around long—and I was one of them—felt that the Scorpions were telling us they had changed, they weren't the Scorpions anymore, and that their ways of crime and violence sort of thing, they weren't into that anymore, that they were peaceful people.

And from our experience that was the case. We heard histories of them invading the Shelter, using physical force, and causing all kinds of trouble. But that was from way back, considerably before we got there. And there just wasn't any evidence of it.

After a long discussion initiated by the newcomers, the Shelter decided to keep its old anti-Scorpion policy. This formally consensual decision masked an actual split of about eight to four. But some of the four dissenters found it difficult to implement a policy in which they did not believe. Their leniency undermined the policy in practice and several weeks later forced the Shelter to thrash the problem out again. At this point, feeling at the Shelter shifted, running about nine to three in favor of allowing contact with the Scorpions. This new policy of allowing contact was a disaster. The Scorpions terrorized the kids in the Shelter. The newcomers then asked for a return to the old policy, and the Shelter reinstated it, this time with unanimous, heartfelt consensus.

The final consensus on the Scorpions convinced at least one of the newcomers of the importance of genuine unanimity:

There has to be a really complete understanding among people, a common understanding. So that becomes one of the goals of the meeting—and not just the meeting—to get that common understanding.

The final consensus drew some newcomers closer to the Shelter, but the incident also pushed some older members farther away. Two of the three counselors who had consistently opposed any change in the Scorpion policy left the Shelter only two months later. Neither gave this event as a reason for leaving, but one decided to quit on the weekend of the pro-Scorpion decision, and the other came to the conclusion that "my opinions are a lot different than a lot of people's." The third, remaining at Helpline, told me ruefully about meetings at the Shelter:

Decisions are made, decisions are revised, four months later the same type of decision—and I find myself not participating in those. Now I'm not ready to give that energy; I don't have it.

Consensual decision making also generates imprecision. In order to reach unanimous agreement, groups formulate their collective decision so as to blur potential disagreements. Rotating responsibility for taking minutes, as Helpline did, exacerbated this tendency. Kaye pointed out that decisions on general policy were left fuzzy more often than were decisions to take action, which had an immediately visible effect:

We're clearly better at making decisions on financial matters. . . . do we apply for a grant or don't we? You can't just muddle along, so we make those decisions! A lot of decisions about the *content* of what we're doing get lost.

But even when a decision was to be implemented immediately, members grasped at verbal formulas that meant different things to different people. Helpline's decision on the way it would cut its budget and staff by a third is a perfect example of the misleading use of a verbal formula. Everyone expected that the vital decision of what, and whom, to cut would come before the entire staff in a Community Day. However, before the Community Day, the CPC had to set the ground rules. The choice was either to give each service group autonomous control over the amount it cut its staff, with the assembly serving only to inform everyone of each group's plan, or instead to allow the assembly to pressure the service groups to reduce further. Two meetings of the CPC and a separate committee addressed this problem, eventually reaching a consensus that the Community Day would be one of "information sharing." But several days later, at the Community Day itself, two groups put strong pressure on CCC to cut more drastically, and their severe criticism sent a couple of CCC's members home in tears.

Later Ken, CCC's representative to the CPC, told me that he was absolutely certain that the CPC had decided *not* to allow this kind of criticism:

I think, I know—myself, I couldn't have done anything more to make it clear. I'm satisfied that I said things as clearly as I can say them. I don't know what else I could do. . . . Both Nate and I made that position clear. I was even making it so clear that people were a little pissed about it in the agenda committee because they were saying, "We already understand that; we *understand* that!" I said that I really wanted to make sure that that was really clear. And it was!

However, Kaye, who had a strong interest in evaluating each service group, was equally certain that the CPC had made the opposite decision:

I *never* agreed to [a ban on criticism]. Clearly it wasn't done. Not in my mind. I know *very clearly* there wasn't [such a decision].

The CPC's formula of "information sharing" had served as a vehicle for false consensus. Everyone at the final meeting of the CPC had been able to agree that "information" should be "shared." Some of the members at that meeting, however, including Ken and Nate, genuinely believed that this formula banned criticism; others, including Kaye, genuinely believed that the information shared would include criticism. None of the people involved had, to my knowledge, consciously or manipulatively left the decision unclear.[1]

Majoritarian bodies do not all make clear decisions either. Arranging coalitions and attracting undecided votes into those coalitions is itself a consensual process that encourages ambiguity. In an adversary proceeding, however, opposing coalitions also have an interest in pointing out such ambiguities and in forcing their opponents to clarify them. Taking a vote therefore often involves a clear-cut choice between a number of relatively distinct alternatives. As one of Helpline's staff put it:

I think majority vote would make it more of a decision-making *policy*. Because of consensus, people talk about things, something will become a policy, and even the people in the room won't know about it. Because it's just sort of talked about. It's sort of like if everybody agrees, this is what we're going to do.

There's always this continual argument—"This is the policy!" "No, *this* is the policy!"—and nobody knows what it is!

Lack of clarity generally bedevils "less structured" alternatives to traditional forms of decision making.[2] A conscientious chairperson, writing decisions down, having "a central file of minutes for every meeting and [having] people who take those minutes really put them in the file—so that you can look back and *say* what was our decision October 2!" can help fight fuzzy decisions. But because spelling out disagreements often leads to trouble, even writing down a specific phrase, like "information sharing," will not prevent a group searching for consensus from unconsciously avoiding clarity.

If a group cannot reach even an ambiguous consensus, a consensus rule will produce either deadlock or social coercion. Deadlock either preserves the status quo or helps those willing and able to act independently. At Helpline, the Van group argued for months over whether and how to paint the Van vehicle. Bernie wanted it painted in psychedelic colors as a hippie emergency van; Dave and one of the vounteers wanted it a solid color with the simple identifying letters, "Helpline, Inc., Emergency Van." Alex wanted to leave it unpainted, incognito. They all advanced good reasons, but none convinced the others. As one Van member described it:

Alex was really against it. And Dave really felt it should be on. This had come up for discussion a few times, and each time it had just come to a standstill. Meanwhile it was unpainted. So in effect, it was Alex's decision that was being implemented.

And Dave finally challenged that by taking the Van out to a garage and painting it.

[Is that what you meant by a power play?] Yeah. Like who would actually do something to change the status quo. So that provoked a lot of hot feelings for a couple of weeks, but the Van remains painted to this day!

Problems of deadlock, repeating decisions, "wasted" time, and lack of clarity are all, in one sense, problems of efficiency. Such costs of a consensus rule must therefore be balanced against the gains in efficiency from ensuring coordination, individual commitment, and a more comprehensive, informed decision. Insofar as consensus helps to produce a more humane, more loving, less coercive environment, this too must be taken into account. But consensus can also have negative effects on the quality of life, endangering as well as protecting the liberty of minorities.

In a consensual system, the minority is, in a sense, eliminated. After it agrees to go along, it leaves no trace. Its objections go unrecorded. Indeed, if those in the minority are intimidated, cannot give their reasons convincingly, or do not care enough to make a scene, they may never voice their objections. Therefore, because the costs in time and in emotional energy are often not worth the benefits of making one's disagreement public, the final and major weakness of the consensual system is "people being bullied into consensus" and "just kind of going along with it." One rather shy young woman told me that at meetings:

I'll just say "yes." And I have felt myself very intimidated to say "no" at times when I felt everyone else would say "yes." For example, a couple of little things have come up where I really honestly did have questions about things, but I didn't say anything until later because everyone seemed to say, "Oh yeah, let's do that."

Nate, who loves to shock, put it dramatically:

What consensus means at Helpline is that if you disagree with something, with what a majority of people are saying, when you don't want to get out on a branch by yourself or with a small group of people, *you keep your mouth shut!*

In the second Community Day that I attended, for instance, the group was choosing the next year's coordinator. Twenty-five of the forty-one paid staff attended that meeting; eighteen spoke. The chair commented, "Some people haven't talked, specifically all the people around you, Bruce —Leslie, Pamela, Steve." This got the three named people to say part of what they had on their minds, but seven others at the meeting never spoke a word. Pamela therefore asked for a straw vote before a motion for consensus was made, "just to know what people prefer." "I don't see a vote as apart from consensus," she insisted. "I just thought of it as a way of hearing from other people without talking to everybody." The straw vote made her point, revealing that nine people, or 31 percent at the meeting, were against the emerging "consensus."

I would not have guessed from the discussion that had preceded the vote that the minority was anywhere near that large. Members of the minority were as likely to have spoken as were members of the majority, but they did not speak as often or voice their opposition strongly enough to make me aware of their numbers.[3] Pamela had wanted a vote precisely because she felt her constituency to be less eloquent. She no doubt also wanted to put on record in some way that the emerging "consensus" was not at all unanimous since, she told me later, she had objected "from the start" to what she perceived as a subtle railroading of opinion.

For some people, registering their contrary opinion as "loyal opposition" is crucial to their integrity. The Van's lack of unity made its members particularly aware of this point. One of them threw the DPW committee into an uproar by insisting, " 'Either do it by majority rule, in which case you win, or we do it by consensus, in which case nothing happens!' And it just blew people's minds!" Eddie, also on the Van, warned that instead of "struggling" with the issues people would often say, "Well, let's find a cool place that we both can agree on—which is compromising both positions. 'Cause they don't want to hurt each others' feelings."[4]

Neither of these Van members objected to struggling through to a true consensus, but both realized that pressures for compromise often produce weak decisions that satisfy no one. They also saw those pressures as threats to individual integrity. The norms of honest expression, emotional risk in a supportive environment, and soliciting dissent that are part of group training protected Helpline's members to some extent against this kind of subtle coercion. So did the members' strong commitments to political and social ideals. But even at Helpline, the counterforces were not always strong enough to help individuals resist the group.

The Advantages of Consensus

Helpline needed unity. In the draining work of counseling, Helpline staff members relied on one another for constant support. The rule of consensus gave tangible expression to this emotional need for unity. In particular, it helped prevent the splintering of the organization into factions. Helpline's staff disapproved of factions even more strongly than the townspeople of Selby. One of the people in Administrative Backup who had been at Helpline the longest spelled out this political philosophy with fervor:

Voting buys into blocs, setting up groups against one another, majority and minority, who wins and who loses—factions, backroom activities designed for the purpose of getting up enough votes for whatever reason. Consensual decision-making is much more oriented to the idea that we are all in this together!

Another argued that a consensual rule eliminated "political maneuvering to get your vote, which I know would happen! We have enough strong aggressive people who want to have their way, that they would lobby for whatever they wanted and try to get votes." People did, of course, work behind the scenes to persuade others of their point of view. There were also ideological factions of a sort, centering on the different perspectives of the service groups. Service groups were likely to caucus and plan their strategies before important meetings the way factions do in a Vermont town. But just as the drive for unanimity in Selby discouraged partisan politics, so the formal rule of consensus at Helpline encouraged individual members to reach out from their service groups and try to identify with the whole. When members found themselves speaking as "us" against "them," they often regretted it and tried to find contexts in which they could surmount those feelings. Without the formal rule of consensus, they believed, "there would be far more game playing than exists."

Because it was frequently possible to uncover a truly common interest, the consensus rule had the further practical advantage of increasing commitment. The difficult, decentralized, unregimented work of Helpline demanded that each member be self-motivated. And in Helpline's consensual system, every worker had at least formally agreed that the task at hand ought to be done. Kaye, easily irritated by slackness, praised consensus for generating commitment: "You have people doing things that they understand they should do, and have agreed to do. It's an internalized sort of discipline."

Arriving at consensus can also elicit more information than the process of majority rule. If, in order to make a decision satisfy everyone, everyone is encouraged to speak, the final decision will incorporate a more thorough assessment of each member's needs. The pressure for unanimity can also throttle dissent and suppress information. But because the Helpline staff's counseling training encouraged each individual to stand up to the group and because they had developed some skill in keeping in touch with their own feelings, the consensus rule at Helpline probably produced more information than it suppressed.

Ronnie in Administrative Backup, for example, once put together a grant proposal that, if it came through, would have brought Helpline $220,000 and made possible some badly needed evaluative research. The principal investigator, a young professor who had helped design the study, was to receive a full-time salary of $20,000. This was four times more than other staff members without dependents made at Helpline and clearly violated the organization's egalitarian guidelines. Ronnie brought the proposal to CPC for approval only two weeks before it was due in Washington.

Helpline's financial condition was so desperate that a few months later every service group would have to cut its staff by a third. Everyone in the CPC meeting knew how much they needed the money. But this was the first time the $20,000 salary had been mentioned, and everyone was upset. Eben, from the Farm, refused to go along: "I don't feel comfortable with that. I will not be able to be part of a consensus that says go ahead with it." Ronnie, getting more agitated by the miunte, pointed out shrilly that there were only two people on the Farm. Tom, as coordinator, rejoined, "We've said we work on consensual decision-making models, and if this were a minor matter, it'd be different. But one group will not go along." In the course of a heated discussion, a few others at the meeting supported Eben, and the group reached a consensus that, in spite of the time pressures, a committee would meet with the professor to work out some solution within the week, in time to send the question back to the service groups for final approval. The committee produced a compromise whereby the professor would get the salary, but would have an office at his university rather than at Helpline, would be paid by his university, would be considered a consultant and not a staff member, and would not participate in Helpline decisions. After the special committee presented its compromise to the CPC, the representatives took it back to the groups, who approved it. Ronnie sent in the grant proposal one day before the deadline. At the same time, the CPC resolved formally that future grant applications involving exceptions to Helpline regulations should be brought to CPC well ahead of time.

The consensus rule had forced a reformulation that, it turned out, met major needs within the organization. In the interviews, seventeen of the forty-one staff members volunteered that they would have been very disturbed if the professor had joined the Helpline staff with a $20,000 salary. Several had had a hard time even accepting the final compromise, and three still contended that the compromise violated Helpline's principle of equality.

The compromise was not costless. From the moment the decision was brought to the CPC to the day the proposal went into the mailbox, nine days had passed. Counting one and a half hours in the first CPC meeting, fifteen minutes in the second, four more people reading the proposal, an hour in the special committee with the researcher, and an average of fifteen minutes in each service group, achieving consensus had required more than forty-two person-hours—a week's work. Had the CPC made decisions by majority vote, it would probably have settled the matter in a quarter as much time by approving the $20,000 salary with no changes. But by spending another thirty hours on the decision, Helpline had produced a better informed decision and had made it acceptable to a significant minority who might otherwise have disowned it.

Any organization that values its internal unity, whether governed by consensus, majority rule, or dictatorship, would be likely to discover some solution like Helpline's final compromise on the professor's salary. While Ronnie's not bringing the matter up until quite late increased the chances that his proposal would pass unamended, the formal rule of consensus redressed the balance, making it more likely that other opinions would be taken into account, even under the pressure of time.

Of all the advantages of consensus, the one that made the most difference to the staff members was the kind of interaction it encouraged. Because the members expected discussions to produce eventual agreement, those discussions became less unsettling. Assuming a common interest made them colleagues in a joint search rather than opponents in a competitive struggle. The need to include everyone promoted caring and listening.

Both the aggressive and the shy appreciated this effect. One self-confident woman told me:

I have a tendency to think that there is a right way to do things and a wrong way to do things, and the consensus model really breaks that down for me. By sitting through a three-hour meeting, by the time I get out of it I feel that the other person *did* have something to say, even if I felt that my way was the right way.

Two others, both by disposition rather quiet, said, "It's very hard sometimes to say things; I tend to feel shy. . . . Consensus is helpful because I feel like my opinion is listened to," and "I like consensual things because everyone can be heard."

The consensual goal at Helpline promoted strategies like breaking down the Community Days into small groups, where people were more likely to listen to another. Moreover, not being able to override potential opposition with numbers made it necessary to find out what that opposition really wanted:

"[With consensus] we work a little harder, compromises are worked out to a greater length, individual feelings have to be taken care of more, and those are important things to make this operation run the way it does."

"In consensus, there is a greater sensitivity to people's feelings per se—that is, 'You're feeling bad or you're upset, and I'm *sorry*, what's upsetting you?' "

"If you couldn't state every single person's position in the room, as well and with as much feeling as your own, then you shouldn't be making consensual decisions!"

Functional Sources of Consensus

The rule of consensus encouraged but could not guarantee unity at Helpline. The service groups that achieved genuine consensus on most issues were those whose work organization produced strong ties of friendship among the members and those that needed unity to function effectively. The service groups that did not nourish strong friendships or need informal cohesion to do their job frequently resorted to a "second order consensus" that was hard to distinguish from majority rule.

Table 4 shows the relationship between friendship patterns and consensual decision making. The groups with the largest number of interlocking friendships were also those most likely to achieve a form of consensus that did not paper over an underlying divided vote.

The relationship between functional need and consensus is harder to document but equally strong. Administrative Backup was the least closely knit group in Helpline. Unlike the other groups, it did not interview and hire most of its members. The staff as a whole selected the coordinator and treasurer, and each service group selected one of its members to work in the funding office. The other members of Administrative Backup

TABLE 4

Unity in the Service Groups[a]

	Shelter	CCC	Switchboard	Van	Administrative Backup
How many people in your service group do you feel personally close to? One or more.	100% (12)	100% (6)	100% (7)	80% (5)	67% (6)
Who are your closest friends at Helpline? Names someone in same service group.	100% (10)	100% (6)	86% (7)	80% (6)	25% (4)
Observed likelihood of making decisions with genuine unanimity.	*high*	*high*	*medium*	*low*	*low*

[a]The number of cases used to calculate each percentage is shown in parentheses.

worked in separate offices on unrelated tasks. Ronnie jokingly put a sign on his door, "Ronnie Ratler: Research Empire"; Leon described his legal skills as giving him "a separate fief."

This lack of functional unity helps explain why Administrative Backup put less effort into achieving genuine unanimity than did the other service groups. When Deborah, the office manager, gave notice and recommended the abolition of her job, the only other woman in Administrative Backup and one of the five men strongly supported her in her stand, while two of the men opposed her. One of those most strongly opposed described the process:

I said that "I can't give my approval to it." I made a very clear strong statement on it. I guess I was making sure that people weren't thinking it was a consensus. 'Cause it certainly wasn't.

Another opponent explained what had happened in terms that would have applied well if Administrative Backup had had a formal majority rule:

If there is a clear majority, that usually prevails; and if there is a pretty evenly divided split, then it's usually stopped, and the status quo prevails.

I think there's a basic understanding that if you're working with a group of this many people you're not going to get your way all the time. So then you have to decide whether you can live with that, with the decision, or whether you really can't. [If you can't?] Then you have to disown that particular decision of the organization as something that you agree with and decide whether there's enough that you want to own to remain a part of it.

Although this decision had been far from unanimous, not one of the group indicated any "serious reservations" about the process used to reach it. In fact, one of those defeated considered this basically majoritarian process "just fine," although he was later to indicate on the questionnaire that consensus was "very crucial" to making Helpline what he wanted it to be.

The Emergency Van was the next least unified group. The Van's crew worked staggered shifts, in which a paid staff member was usually paired with a volunteer. This arrangement allowed for less interaction between paid staff members than in any other service group. As a result, the Van rarely reached genuine consensus about decisions. Indeed, it eventually made a unanimous decision to make future decisions by a two-thirds majority. That two-thirds majority would only be able to make decisions when the minority had had ample time to make its case: "Like what happens at the Van is that there is a vote taken and those opposed to it are given a couple of weeks to speak to other people and maybe to work it out." This procedure preserved the "listening" quality of consensus but allowed a group with little mutual commitment to function.

The Shelter was the most cohesive service group in Helpline. It occupied a building six or seven blocks from Helpline's main building. This isolation probably encouraged internal cohesion. More important, however, was the nature of its work. The Shelter provided lodging and counseling for runaways and increasingly also for poor kids between their own and a foster home, who came to the Shelter in moments of legal and emotional crisis. With thirteen distraught adolescents aged eleven to seventeen living together under one roof, new crises arose daily. Dealing with any one of these crises took all the efforts of those on duty and sometimes the combined efforts of the entire staff. The atmosphere at the Shelter often resembled that of a besieged outpost. Communications were brief and sometimes unspoken, with each staff member playing an understood role. Each gave a great deal when needed and understood when others had been pushed too far. In periods between bombardments, the warriors sat around in twos and threes, cracked jokes, shared comradely put-downs, and congratulated one another on having made it through:

You get high off the spirit of the crunches. I know these people; I know they are really going to be as crunched as I am, and they are really competent people. It's okay to be in a crunch with them.

After the crisis that finally reaffirmed the anti-Scorpion rule, one of the Shelter staff told me:

I think that one of the real high points in my life was that. . . . I felt really close to the other people—a real part of the community. In that week I was totally involved, every part of my being was involved. All of my emotions, the way I felt toward the kids, all of my inspirations—it was just really, really *beautiful!*

The work at the Shelter—interdependent, communal, ridden with crises, yet finite and well boundaried, allowing at times the sense of a task completed—thus strengthened ties between individuals, developed their attachment to the Shelter as a whole, and made it easier for them to adopt as their own the good of others and of the whole.

Unanimity at the Shelter was also a functional necessity. After the Scorpion crisis, for instance, a newcomer concluded:

If everyone isn't really agreed on some policy, it usually doesn't work. Because there's a lot of feeling required behind any of the things that you tell the kids. And the kids know whether it's there or not. They know whether you believe what you're saying. And a lot of times they'll really push you to the limits of justifying something or of explaining the sense of something.

And if it's just some policy that someone else has made—and sometimes I've been in that situation, where it was somebody else's policy and I didn't really agree with it and had real active doubts about it—it just doesn't work. You just can't get it across to a kid.

Knowing this, the Shelter worked harder to achieve consensus than did, say, Administrative Backup or the Van. The internal practice of consensus in the Shelter carried over to decisions they made regarding the organization as a whole. A Shelter member, who had been a delegate to the Helpline DPW committee, explained it this way:

The Shelter can work by consensus because we share a tremendously powerful central experience, which is dealing with the kids every day. When I work at Bartlett Street [where the rest of Helpline is located], we all speak as "the Shelter," whereas other groups say, "Well, it [the implicit vote] was two-four-three." We're very fortunate that way.

Just as the high morale at the Shelter made its staff more likely to adopt the good of the whole as their own, so the Shelter's very ability to achieve consensus helped maintain morale under difficult conditions. Even before I began my interviews, one Shelter member said to me, laughing but full of pride, "Well, obviously the Shelter is the *best* group!" In the interviews, two others said, quite simply, "I love the Shelter," and "My feeling for the Shelter is love." A fourth Shelter member at the end of our interview turned to me with genuine emotion and blurted, "We're wonderful, God bless us!"

Identity of Interests

The essential question in assessing the consensus rule both in the service groups and in Helpline as a whole is, I believe, to what extent the staff had similar interests. Individual interests were never identical either in the service groups or in the organization as a whole. Yet many minor decisions were made by consensus on the basis of underlying common interests. Even in major crises that potentially could split the organization into two conflicting camps, it frequently seemed possible to discern a common interest. All the advantages of consensus in this process appeared in Helpline's decision not to take a contract from the Air Force.

The issue arose when the Switchboard decided to take a $15,000 contract to work with some young Air Force recruits who had asked for help improving the hotline and drug counseling service they had set up at their base. Having reported their decision to the CPC almost as a matter of course, the Switchboard staff was surprised to find other members of the CPC questioning their judgment and sending the issue of "helping the military" back to all the service groups for discussion. Members of the Switchboard had made personal commitments to the young Air Force men, whom they had come to know and like. In spite of a position paper by some staff members opposing the contract and a week's discussion in the hallways, the members of Switchboard went into the second, decisive CPC meeting still believing that objections to the contract were no more than "Pavlovian radicalism."

Four of the seven Switchboard staffers attended the meeting. They argued that a hotline at the Air Force base already existed, that the volunteers who staffed it had no experience in counseling, that the adolescents in the Air Force who needed the counseling were suffering, and that they and their wives would be afraid to go to an "alternative" service off the base. They also argued that a hotline was not automatically a prop to the military and that taking money from the Defense Department was no worse than taking it from other conservative, capitalist departments of the government, as long as it had no strings.

The opponents of the project argued that despite the Air Force's assurances there was no way for Helpline, with its meager resources, to protect confidentiality or to determine how information collected on the hotline would be used. Moreover, if the program were a success, it would reduce discontent in the Air Force generally and at that base in particular. The base was one of the three North American support bases for the Vietnam-Cambodian bombing. When one of the Switchboard members asked where anyone could draw the line between the proposed program at the Air Force base and Helpline's other hotline programs that also took money from and helped support the government, Tom, who opposed the project, answered simply, "We draw the line at the purveyors of death and destruction."

The debate was often emotional, "even more emotional," one participant reported, "than the [professor's salary] thing!" Frank, on the Switchboard, spoke movingly of his own experience in the Army and begged the others to "talk about people, and people possibly in pain—*that's* what we ought to relate to!" Tanya, a member of Switchboard with deep motherly feelings, had come to feel responsible for the young men who were asking for counseling training. At one point in the debate, she blurted out that if Helpline would not help them she "would like to request that one of you tell them because I can't!" Her plea made Ken, violently in opposition, retort, "I'd be very happy to! I *like* to tell pigs where to get off!" Ken's words brought a deep flush to Tanya's face and cries from the others: "Ken, that's an *outrageous* statement!" and "They're *people*, Ken!"

Yet in spite of these extremes of anger and conviction, the participants did not become wholly partisan. In the heat of the debate, Tanya, sympathetic to the young Air Force men, turned to Ken, who considered them "pigs," and said quietly and, I believe, sincerely, "I want to learn from you." Kaye, who also had come in committed to the project, chaired the meeting with concern for both sides and ended by saying, "I love being chairperson at meetings like this." Even during the meeting, one of the participants commented, "This is one of the few good issues we've had in a long time. I'm interested and learning."

In the course of the discussion, the two points against the Air Force that began to tell more and more were Helpline's inability to guarantee absolute confidentiality to whomever used the hotline and the intimate connection of this particular base with the war in Vietnam. The Switchboard members were most moved by the argument about confidentiality; for the others, both points seemed equally troublesome. At the end of the meeting, a consensus was reached not to take the contract.

Afterward, all the major participants on both sides felt it had been a good meeting. The discussion had changed many people's minds.[5] Even the four members of the Switchboard, who had come into the meeting with strong feelings and had "lost," told me independently that they were pleased with how the meeting had gone. Tanya had been responsible for bringing the young enlisted men to Helpline in the first place and had been close to tears several times in the meeting, but when I asked what she thought about the decision, she answered:

I liked that. And I was the one who brought that in. That felt really fine to me. I liked the debate we got into in the CPC meeting.

See, a lot of things can come out of these issues, and if they're allowed to come out, I think it's really fine.

I mean, the Air Force Base I was *invested* in! Obviously, I wanted to do it! And it didn't work out, and I understand people's reasons why. And that was fine. I mean, I was negotiable on that. I accepted what the end result was. I liked the process.

Even Frank, who had made the most emotional plea for keeping the contract, said afterward, "I didn't feel that I had been manipulated or overwhelmed or bludgeoned into a situation. It was a very touchy issue, one that I even had questions about myself." Kaye told me that the "Air Force Base [decision] is the first time that something has been sensibly and clearly and cogently refused and rejected that made sense—to me."

Switchboard's fourth member at the meeting, Amy, actually gave this decision as an example of a "nice thing" about consensus. For her, the meeting had been "exciting and challenging," for it had asked her "to think about things on a lot of different levels, about why you choose to do things and what your reasons are for doing them":

It was stimulating to think about things on that sort of philosophical basis, and not just think, "Well, they would be giving us x amount of money and we should do it for practical reasons."

The interests of all the staff members in this decision may not have been entirely identical. The people on Switchboard had closer relationships with the young men who had come to them for help; others in Helpline had a greater stake in the antiwar movement. The decision, which required giving up a $15,000 contract in a period of financial stringency, eventually led to cutting three staff positions, and those members whose positions were later cut presumably had a greater interest than others in taking the contract. Finally, the working-class members of the organization might have benefited, both psychologically and in terms of the future direction of the group, from a contract that would have served primarily working-class clients.

Yet the three members whose jobs were later cut, the three working-class members, and even those involved with the young Air Force men never seemed to weigh their material, class, or personal interests as heavily as they did their interest in reaching the "right" decision for the organization. For various reasons, including the group's tacit assumption that only arguments addressed to the common good were legitimate, these members may not have realized that their individual interests were being sacrificed, or they may have underestimated the importance of these interests. But even with perfect information they might have judged such self-regarding interests less important to them than their interest in belonging to an organization that acted rightly. In this case all forty-one staff members would have a common interest, even in a conflict-ridden decision like that over the Air Force contract.

As an organization becomes larger and less self-selected, its members will be less likely to have identical views about what is "right." Even in Helpline, some thought that its size and the "pretty broad spectrum of what our activities are and what our goals are" had brought the organization to the limits of consensus:

If we were all Shelter workers or we were all Switchboard workers, consensus would be easier because our goals would be closer and more aligned. The more disparity you get among the groups that are working together and trying to make some kind of consensus, the harder it is. I think that it's push-ing it, having basically four different groups.

Yet because the members needed each other's support, because the work required a high degree of individual commitment, and because a unanimity rule in these circumstances encouraged the staff to listen more carefully to one another, Helpline continued to keep consensus as its formal decision rule. Making decisions this way corresponded to a model each member held of how human beings ought to act toward one another. The decision rule of consensus, which required considerable unity to begin with, helped them behave like friends.

Chapter 15

Political Inequality: Helpline

THE FACT that Helpline could operate for five years under a unanimity rule—albeit one modified to take account of being able to "live with" a decision—provides the most impressive evidence of the existence of a strong common interest.

If only a few members had had inside information on decisions or if only a few had participated actively in them, this evidence for a common interest would be suspect. In Selby, for instance, citizens at town meeting often voted unanimously for a selectman. Yet because pre-election activity in which only a few participated generally resulted in all but one candidate withdrawing from the race, the resulting unanimity does not constitute convincing evidence for a strong common interest. At Helpline, even a discussion as long and thorough as the discussion of the Air Force contract did not raise all the points of potential conflict. But the evidence that everyone understood and had personally confronted most of the issues is stronger here than in Selby. Helpline's being able to come to a consensual decision on a question as potentially troublesome as the Air Force contract suggests that its members did have strong common interests. In regard to the protection of interests, therefore, equality of power would not be so important at Helpline as in Selby.

To the extent that real conflicts in Helpline emerged, however, those with greater power unquestionably had an advantage over the others. By common agreement, power at Helpline was unequally distributed. At the end of the interview, I asked the forty staff members I spoke with to place the names of all the staff members in one of a series of concentric circles around a central point depicting "the center of power at Helpline."

No one who participated in the exercise put all the names in one place, thereby indicating an equal distribution of power. Seven declined the exercise on the grounds that for various reasons it did not reflect the reality at Helpline. Of these, one argued that the distribution of power at Helpline was in fact equal, one argued that it was unequal, and the others did not commit themselves on the question of overall distribution of power. All told, therefore, at least 85 percent of those asked to participate in the exercise indicated that central power at Helpline was not equally divided.

Moreover, as in Selby, some inequalities in power coincided with the lines between potential interest groups: again, newcomers, the geographically distant, the younger members, and the working-class members of Helpline were less likely to participate in Helpline decisions, to perceive themselves as powerful, and to be perceived as powerful by other members of the organization (see Table 5). In Helpline, the women participated almost as much as the men, and were ranked by other staff members as equal in power to the men, although they remained less confident about their participation. There were no black townspeople in Selby; at Helpline, the three black members seemed almost as likely as the whites to exercise power. Those interest groups at Helpline that for one reason or other had acquired more than equal power had, in adversary moments, an advantage over the others.

Helpline differed from Selby in two major respects. First, as I have already suggested, Helpline saw many fewer moments of conflict of interest than did Selby. It came closer than Selby to pure unitary democracy. As a consequence, some of these potential interest groups did not seem, in fact, to have actual conflicts of interest.

Second, although the members of Helpline differed in participation and power, those differences were not large. In the course of the power-ranking exercise, many members pointed out that the single center of power depicted in the exercise reflected only a small part of decision making at Helpline, first, because each service group had great autonomy and, second, because within the service group each staff member had great latitude in determining his or her working conditions. Most of the staff therefore had considerable influence over the decisions that affected them most—decision ranging from when to show up at work to hiring new colleagues.

Even when all forty-one members of the staff had to make a decision together, no one charismatic leader or set of leaders emerged. No one group dominated. Administrative Backup had no internal cohesion, nor did any tightly knit set of friends take its place.[1] In its formal and informal

Participation, Ranked Power, Sense of Efficacy and
Satisfaction by Individual Characteristic at Helpline[a]

Power and Participation	Length of time in organization	Physical proximity to social center	Age	Race[b] (Bl., Wh.)	Gender (F., M.)	Socioeconomic status	
						Parents' class (working class, other)[b]	Own education (controlled for age)
Speaking at meetings	.26*	.25	.20	.02	.11	.37**	.25
Attending meetings	.30*	.31*	.30*	.09	.17	.46**	.20
Ranked high in "power" by other staff	.28*	.34*	.22	.17	.06	.26	.35*
Efficacy and Satisfaction							
Reports self as high in "say" and "power"	.29*	.38**	.25	.11	.21	.36*	.17
Reports satisfaction with decisions	.17	.26	.17	.07	.25	.30*	.36*

[a]These calculations are product-moment correlation coefficients based on forty-one cases, with some variation for nonresponse (for explanation, see note to Table 2). As many of these variables are noninterval and some may have nonlinear relationships, the correlations should be understood as approximate. Because I surveyed the entire Helpline staff and not a sample, tests of statistical significance are useful primarily to indicate that the observed associations are due to some systematic causal relations among the variables under study, and not to chance alone (see Appendix A for further discussion of significance). In this and in subsequent tables, I have used asterisks or the notation .05, etc., to indicate conditions that would be significant if this were a random sample (* = < .05, ** = p < .01, one-tailed test).

"Speaking at meetings" combines a questionnaire report of how frequently one speaks at meetings with observed measures of speaking in the major representative committee and at Community Days. "Attending meetings" combines three questionnaire reports of attendance with observed measures of attendance in four different forms over six months. "Ranked high in 'power'" derives from an exercise administered at the end of the interview. "Reports self as high in 'say' and 'power'" combines one's self-ranking on the power exercise with two questionnaire items reporting amount of "say," in decisions at Helpline. "Reports satisfaction with decisions" combines four questionnaire items reporting various forms of satisfaction. For complete description of indices and other variables, see Appendix B.

[b]There are only three blacks and three working-class members in Helpline. This places a severe upper limit on the likely correlations.

political structure, Helpline therefore seemed in many ways to follow the pluralist ideal. Different groups of individuals exercised influence on different issues. More than three quarters of the staff reported that "decisions around Helpline are made by a process of give and take among a number of groups and individuals" in differing combinations, as opposed to being made "by a small group of people."[2] My own observations confirmed this general perception. Of the six major decisions I studied closely, one person figured prominently in three. Not surprisingly, this was the coordinator. One figured prominently in two decisions. The nine remaining major actors appeared prominently in only one decision each.[3]

Almost everyone at Helpline participated extensively in making decisions. Only two of the forty-one staff members missed both of the full assemblies while I was at Helpline. Of those who attended, all but two or three spoke out. Of the staff who had been in the organization a year and a half, all but one had been a representative on one of the two major committees. The formal rule of consensus, moreover, gave every member the resources to deadlock the community for a while by refusing to go along.

During the six months I observed decisions at Helpline, I concluded that if the least powerful members of Helpline had made a great effort, they could have exercised as much power on any issue as the most powerful person did with little effort. This was not true in Selby. The differences in power at Helpline were not great enough to make anyone feel powerless, to destroy the equality of respect on which friendship rests, or to deprive anyone of either responsibility or the opportunity to discover real interests by participating in conflict. Although the association between participation and individual characteristics, like being a newcomer or working class, was as strong or stronger at Helpline than in Selby, everyone at Helpline was participating as much as Selby's most active tenth. As a consequence, the Helpline staff differed less from one another in the absolute amount they participated than did the people of Selby.[4]

Length of Time in the Organization

Like many organizations that employ only young people, Helpline, Inc., saw a rapid turnover among its staff. The average staff member had been at Helpline only one and three quarter years, and most expected to leave within two more years. When I returned to Helpline in January 1977, four years after my original observations, only six of the forty-one people I had known and interviewed in 1973 still worked there.

In such circumstances, longevity breeds power. While inequalities of power were much smaller in Helpline than in Selby, similar patterns of lack of confidence and information among the newcomers produced similar patterns of power and participation in both places (see Appendix A, Table A.7). Speaking at meetings, attending meetings, being thought to have power, and thinking oneself powerful were all distinctly related to the length of time a staff member had been at Helpline. In the case of reported attendance at Community Days, however, the relationship was negative because the great frequency of Community Days in the earliest era of participatory governance had led most older members to attend only some of those meetings. More recently, the community had called Community Days only when it had urgent issues to discuss, and the newcomers were therefore more likely to have attended all, or almost all, of the meetings held since their arrival. Satisfaction was also negatively related to longevity, perhaps because the old-timers, who joined Helpline in an era more attuned to their countercultural ideals, had grown increasingly frustrated with the impact such an organization could have. But although they were less satisfied than the newcomers, on every measure of participation and power those with a longer tenure in the organization showed an advantage.

The reasons for the old-timers' greater power and participation are not difficult to decipher. Newcomers took a while to become familiar with the system of making decisions, to gather the confidence to try to influence decisions, and to get to a point in their work where they had the time and interest to become involved in the larger process.

The names, initials, and jargon that the older participants tossed around often confused the newcomers. Deborah, the office manager and a member of Administrative Backup, described her first months:

I felt really intimidated for a while, but now I don't feel quite so intimidated. It would be easier now for me to take it.
[What made you feel intimidated?] Well, the first Administrative Backup meeting I went to people started talking, "Well, CPC has to do this," and "The Shelter is going to do this," and I said, "What the hell?" Nobody ever oriented me to what these facilities were; the way I found out was by typing a brochure! (laugh)
Well, you could say, "Well, you could have asked," and I could have, but I said, "Hey, wait a minute, what do these letters stand for?" and they kind of laughed—but the next time someone new came in they did the same thing! (laugh) By then I knew what the letters were, but that was intimidating. . . .
I had this strange idea that CPC [the long-range planning committee] was the

"outsiders," and had to do with the Center for Community Counseling, [CCC]. Somehow the letters got garbaged in my mind.

To a newcomer like Deborah, the significance of issues with a long organizational history remained a mystery for quite a while. She had already been at Helpline for more than six months when she attended the two crucial CPC meetings setting the agenda for the budget-cutting Community Day. But she completely missed the point of the discussion on whether the "information sharing" on that Community Day should include critical "evaluation":

I find myself really confused often by meetings, until recently. And even so, some of the things I couldn't follow what they were talking about. I'm sure it wasn't because I was too stupid to understand. But there seemed to be some kind of communication that just went beyond me.

Recently, we had a discussion about what the word "evaluation" means. To me what the word means is self-evident. I mean I don't have any problems with that at all. But that seemed to be a very big issue. [So] I have never really contributed that much.

The informal nature of Helpline's organization exacerbates the newcomers' uncertainties in the period in between meetings as well as within them. Deborah, for example, "continually had the feeling that I never knew what was going on. Things kept cropping up and surprising me. Sometimes you would get the minutes and sometimes you wouldn't." Those uncertainties were compounded when the newcomers were shy. Deborah again reported:

I really didn't realize that people were free to go [to CPC]. I know that sounds really silly, but I didn't understand it. And I did feel that CPC was some kind of special deal and you had to have some special status to belong.

The newest member of the Shelter had the same story:

I'm not sure where I fit in yet. I've never felt that I'm the downtrodden one, that I don't have any say at all, but I don't use it [my "say"] all the time. I don't feel comfortable about using it.

I'm the newest member here. I'm more hesitant to say something, or to try and control a business meeting, or try to lead the way in making a decision. I kind of rely on people who have been here longer. I feel sometimes like I should be taking on more responsibility in business meetings, but I've never been someone who speaks out actively in groups. I just don't. So I have a tendency to withdraw in those situations. I disagree if I need to, but I don't like to particularly.

[Have you ever thought of being in CPC or anything?] I'd have to force myself to go. I've sort of designated myself as the lowest on the rung. I feel a little hesitant. . . . I went to one CPC meeting, and I had just gotten into Helpline, and I was totally lost.

Political Inequality: Helpline

The newest member of Administrative Backup told me with slightly more bravado:

> The meetings I go to? I try *not* to go to them! Because I usually don't say anything. Because everyone else seems to have something they want to say. And maybe it's because I haven't been here that long. And I don't know that much about the organization itself—where their head is at. So I sort of keep my mouth shut at meetings—unless I feel it's necessary.

Familiarity with the organization gave old-timers at Helpline not only more courage than the newcomers but also the advantage of contacts and inside knowledge. They knew more people and were known by more.[5] They were more likely to know whom to contact on any problem and to be the one others contacted.[6] They had built up the social networks that, at Helpline as in Selby, made the process of mutual influence easier. When the staff members gave reasons behind the inequality they portrayed in the power-circle exercise, they cited longevity more than any other.

Geographical Centrality

Helpline was decentralized, in work, in decision making, and in emotional commitment. More than half the staff members' best friends at Helpline came from within their own service group. As one might expect, the number and intensity of these decentralized social contacts were uncorrelated with participation and power in Helpline as a whole. The number of close friends the staff had outside their work group, however, was related to their participation and power in central decisions.[7] Any circumstance that increased the members' chances of meeting other staff outside their own work group therefore seems to have increased their chances of participating and exercising power in the central organization. The staff who worked at the bottom of the stairwell, right by the front door, for instance, saw more people outside their own group every day, and on average, had more power than others at Helpline. The staff who worked away from the building usually participated less and exercised less power.

Of the five major service groups at Helpline, the Shelter was the most distant. Five blocks away from Bartlett Street, the main Helpline headquarters, the Runaway Shelter maintained a separate building. In this twelve-room, brick building, fitted out with accommodations for a maximum of twenty runaways, the Shelter staff members lived through the crises of the day or night, grabbed their lunch or breakfast, sought consolation from their friends, cried, slept, and hugged each other farewell at the end of a work shift. In the course of a week, most of them never had to "go over to Bartlett Street." They were the least likely of any of the five major service groups to feel close to people outside their own service group, and along with the two members of the Farm, which was even more distant, they were correspondingly less likely to attend communitywide meetings, speak at those meetings, rank themselves as powerful, or be ranked by others as powerful (see Appendix A, Table A.8).

At the other end of the spectrum, the Switchboard occupied a major part of the first floor of Bartlett Street, right at the front door, at the bottom of the stairs, where anyone going in or out could drop in, say a word, see and be seen. The Switchboard was the official welcoming arm of Helpline. Here anyone could come in from the street and hang around, check out the bulletin board, read a book, rap with the counselors on duty, or lie down on the mattresses at the back of the room. Here the Switchboard phones rang and counselors took calls. Here people always went to find anyone in the building. "Have you seen Ronnie?" "Yes, he went out with Ruth half an hour ago." "Oh, well, if you see him, will you tell him I thought we had an interview at three?"

Their respective physical positions undoubtedly accounted for part of the fact that members of the Switchboard were the most likely of the major service groups to feel close to people outside their own group, whereas members of the Shelter were the least.[8] Switchboard members were also, on the average, ranked the most powerful and were the most likely to participate in meetings of any of the groups at Helpline. If the causality is as I suggest, friendship contacts outside the group explain much of the effect of proximity to the social center on power.[9]

Age

Age had little salience at Helpline. No one in the interviews told me that he or she was older or younger than anyone else at Helpline or implied that any consequences for power or participation might follow from one's age. Although the ages of Helpline members ranged from nineteen to thirty-seven, I would often have been hard pressed to know which were young and which old. Certainly the members had no conscious respect for age. If anything, the premium was on youth, because the people who came to Helpline for counseling were usually young, and members tended to assume that they could be helped better by those who resembled them. Nonetheless, age was correlated with participation (see Appendix A, Table A.9). In another organization, this might have become an issue. In the heyday of participatory egalitarianism, stalwart egalitarians condemned as "ageism" any suggestion that being older ought to bring prerogatives. Because at Helpline every staff member did respected, important work and age commanded no visible respect, this problem did not arise. In fact, the greater participation of Helpline's older members can be explained almost entirely by their greater education,[10] but differences in education also did not appear to matter to most of the Helpline staff.

Gender

As in Selby, at Helpline being female limited one's power and participation in ways that are subtle and difficult to measure. Although the effects of class on participation were much stronger than those of gender, the staff at Helpline while I was there seemed more aware of women's problems in attempting to exercise power than they were of the problems of their working-class members.

Part of the explanation for the comparatively strong interest in women must have derived from the national strength of the women's liberation movement in 1973. As the struggle to eliminate the job of office manager demonstrated, the staff at Helpline had made distinct efforts to see that the women in the organization had as much power as the men. The men on the staff had become self-conscious about interrupting when women were talking at meetings and not expecting women to become fund raisers or coordinators. Partly as a result of this campaign against sexism and partly because one woman, Kaye, had extremely high scores on participation and power, the women at Helpline as a whole scored only slightly lower than the men on most of my measures of participation and power. Women tended to talk and to attend meetings slightly less often than the men, were less satisfied with the decisions at Helpline, and perceived their own power as lower. But they were as likely as the men to be chosen as someone whose judgment another would respect on an issue relating to Helpline, and their average power scores differed only marginally from those of the men (see Appendix A, Table A.10).

My own observations of decision making at Helpline also suggest that the women had as much "power" as the men. They seemed as able as the men to get the organization to do what they wanted. The women worked hard, had good ideas, and seemed to command considerable respect. Yet if they exercised equal power, all but Kaye did so behind the scenes. They did not take either of the two major leadership positions at Helpline —coordinator or treasurer. Only one woman had ever become a fund raiser. In the six decisions I studied closely, women took major initiating roles in only one, and that one (eliminating the job of office manager) was explicitly a woman's issue.

Why did most of the women at Helpline exercise their power behind the scenes? My data suggest that the women had lower verbal self-confidence, a weaker career orientation, greater interest in curing people than in administrating an organization, and no model for leadership other than that of the "pushy bitch."

On a checklist of traits, the women of Helpline were significantly more likely than the men to report that "articulate people intimidate me," and significantly less likely to report "I express myself well in words." They were somewhat less likely than the men to report that "people seem to respect my opinion about things," and more likely to report that "I don't like to 'operate.'" In general, female responses on this checklist were associated with the tendency not to take on leadership positions, but, except for the strong difference in verbal self-confidence, the differences should not be taken too seriously. The men, for example, tended to have more positive attitudes toward the exercise of power, but the differences were not large. Women were more likely than men to report, "I like taking responsibility," and there was no difference between men and women reporting, "I enjoy power."[11] It was the level of verbal self-confidence that most distinguished men from women. As one woman put it, "I often feel that I've got to hear everything before I can say something because I feel insecure about saying things. I am especially insecure if it's mostly males talking."

Women at Helpline also seemed less likely than the men to think of their work as part of a career. Only 15 percent of the women intended to stay at Helpline more than a year, compared to 53 percent of the men. Even among those who intended to stay the same length of time, as one woman said, "It's just a whole different headset the men are into, like it's their career." In the American economy, interrupted careers explain something like half the difference between men's and women's wages.[12] At Helpline, an "interruptible" career orientation may help explain some of the subtle differences in power and participation between men and women.

The product at Helpline is counseling. Most of the staff joined Helpline for the satisfaction of doing counseling. No one was particularly interested in administration, including the coordinator, who was a full-time administrator but considered it "shitwork." The men may, however, have been more likely to enjoy the power and status of administration. As one woman said of the coordinator-director, whom she liked:

> Like he realizes that the fact that he's director has nothing to do with what he does as a job and enjoys doing. It's the thing of "I'm the director; look at me!" And it's just very strange to me. I wouldn't do that for all the world! But somehow, to men there's a reward associated with it. You do the shitwork, but the title is a good enough reward!

If the men were more gratified by status and the women by providing nurturance, this would help explain why the men were slightly more likely to take administrative positions.

When I interviewed the women who did take leadership roles in Helpline, however, another potential barrier emerged. Everyone in this participatory democracy had trouble imagining what truly democratic leadership would look like. For the women, this problem was compounded. It was hard for women to visualize any female leadership that was not "bitchy." One woman who did not usually take on leadership but worked hard to push a controversial innovation, remembered: "I was afraid that I was coming on bitchy. . . . I feel that if I'm at all bitchy, they are going to use it against me." Another avoided bringing up issues because "I get all hostile and bitchy." A third woman refused after a while to go to any of the large Helpline meetings. She felt that even in the small meetings of her group, "They put me in this role—I took it myself, too—of house bitch."

The women were helped in the quest for equal participation by their numbers, for although three of the five service groups had all-male cliques (see Figure 4) there were enough women at Helpline so that if they could not join a mixed-sex clique, as in the Shelter, they could band together for support, as in the Switchboard. By contrast, only three staff members in 1973 were black, and only three had, according to their own description, working-class parents.

FIGURE 4
Friendship Choices within the Service Groups[a]

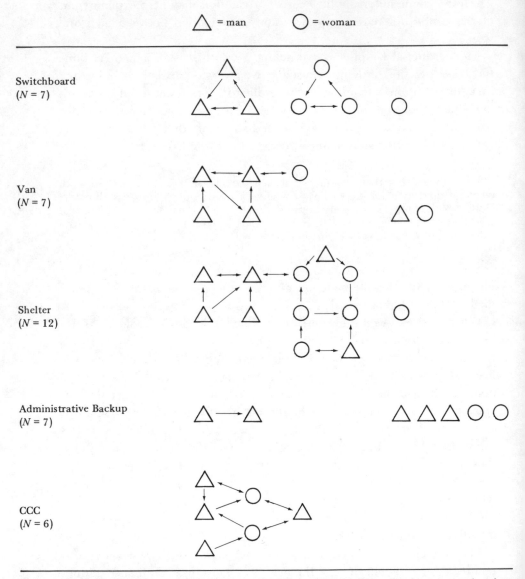

[a]I am indebted to Ron Breiger, Department of Sociology, Harvard University for constructing these diagrams and bringing this phenomenon to my attention.
Solitary individuals either did not answer this question or chose friends outside their service group.

Race

Although being a woman in Helpline in 1973 carried with it centuries of traditional inequality, being a black in Helpline in the same year brought with it an even more painful tradition and required that blacks participate in a workplace culture that often seemed to them irretrievably alien. Yet on the measures I collected in the course of my six months at Helpline, the three black staff members participated no less and were perceived as having no less power than the thirty-eight whites (see Appendix A, Table A.11). Like the women, their problems with Helpline were more subtle. Unlike the women, however, the three blacks were distinctly outnumbered. They were also scattered among the service groups—Leslie in the Shelter, Clarence on the Switchboard, and Eddie on the Van.

Even before I collected the quantitative data at Helpline, I knew of the relatively high participation of the three black staff members. I saw that they were socially integrated into their service groups. I felt Helpline to be "color-blind," and I believed the important disabilities in participation to derive from class, not from race. Moreover, I am not black, and I am a woman. For all these reasons, I did not use the interviews to probe Leslie, Clarence, or Eddie on the particular problems they might have had as blacks participating in Helpline governance. In spite of being aware of this issue in the larger society, I simply assumed that race was not a problem at Helpline, and in my first quantification of the data, I did not even create a variable for race. It was only later, when I realized what I had done, that I reread the interviews and telephoned Leslie, the one black staff member who remained in the city. Of the three black members of Helpline, Leslie had originally seemed to me so fully integrated into her service group that her race was truly incidental, never a cause of either nervousness or remark. The eleven other staff in the Shelter saw Leslie simply as a good counselor and friend. In the interviews, only one person mentioned her race. Leslie herself only mentioned race once, in a context that emphasized her integration rather than her alienation. She was comparing the Shelter favorably to the rest of Helpline:

> We have a real sense of social struggle, we have a real sense of human struggle—being middle class, being poor, being black, all of that sort of has effects. We are from totally different backgrounds in this group—some from Bedford-Stuyvesant (me), from California, from Newton.

Yet even Leslie, who had close friends and a roommate among her co-workers at the Shelter, found it harder than most of her co-workers to relate to Helpline as a whole. When I talked with her three years later, she reported:

> I needed help understanding Helpline. I didn't know what people were talking about half the time. I kept thinking, "Why do I have to talk with all these idiots?"
>
> [It was a cultural shock?] It was an *enormous* cultural shock! I mean, they talked a different language: "I hear you saying" and "The consensus is." Among blacks, if you had a problem, you dealt with your problem. Same conclusion, different process. It wearied me out at times. I'd say to myself, "What am I doing here? This place is *strange!*"

Leslie felt that the tight support structure of the Shelter protected her from the worst of the alien culture in the rest of Helpline. "When I joined the Shelter, they told me, 'You don't have to relate to the entire philosophy and Bartlett Street. We'll do that. You just do what you're good at.'" Three years later, there were many more black and minority staff members at Helpline than there were when she was there, but she reflected, "I still don't believe it will work out—you've got to buy into that [countercultural] philosophy, and most black folks and poor folks don't have that philosophy."

Eddie, on the Van, was not only black but working class. None of the six other members of Helpline mentioned Eddie's race in the interviews. He himself, however, described his frustration with Helpline's apparent inability to provide services for the racially mixed community in which it was located. He concluded:

> I'm not saying that the people at Helpline are pigs, but you can't come from a lot of shit and not have some of that on you. Like a lot of them are into chauvinism [and] racism, but it's very hard to do something that you've never done before.

When I asked, "Have you ever hated Helpline?" he answered:

> No. I think I've hated certain things within Helpline. Helpline is very racist. And they don't deal with that. There's one black person that works at the Van, me, and there's one paid person, black, that works at Switchboard, and there's one black person who works at the Shelter and gets paid. There's tokenism going on; it's obvious.

Leslie's reflections on the strangeness of Helpline made me realize, rereading the interviews, that Eddie had had much the same experience. He had felt the full, classic newcomer's response:

> It took me about six months just to find out what people were talking about! Like what's CCC? You know? And if you walked up to someone and said, "What's CCC?" they'd say, "What's wrong with you? (laugh) Get on the ball!"

He had then come to "feel close to most of the Van, I think. Like when you work with somebody you naturally get close." But even after a year on the Van, the chasm between him and the others, particularly outside his service group, still loomed large. He told me, with resignation:

You can't attack everything that you see as wrong because then all you become is an attacker. Things I feel about Helpline's direction, I get a lot of "What's with you? Off the wall!" kind of thing. (laugh) A lot of things I let go by that should be struggled with, but I don't have that much support in struggling with a lot of things. They say, "He's a revolutionary," like there's no reason to talk. . . .

Clarence, who came to the Switchboard under the auspices of a good friend of his (white) from grammar school, never found a niche for himself, sloughed off in his work, and when I interviewed him was planning to leave. He had, without success, spent much of his time at Helpline actively urging the hiring of other minority staff. Perhaps for this reason, four other members of Helpline mentioned Clarence's race in the interview with me. Particularly interested in funding, Clarence had found it hard to convince well-trained black people with sufficient background in fund raising to take a job for the pittance that Helpline paid. He had also found it difficult to convince Helpline to take the risk of hiring someone without a college degree or parallel experience and then train that person in fund raising.

Aside from his relationship with his childhood friend, there was little in the organization to generate any trust in Clarence for Helpline. Because his service group, the Switchboard, was so intimately associated with the larger organization, Clarence did not even have the support of a service group who also saw the rest of Helpline as "them." And like Leslie and Eddie, Clarence felt like a being from a different planet: "I know this is not my trip, okay? I'm not into the counterculture. I mean, I *have* a culture." He was impatient with what he thought of as Helpline's impractical idealism: "Egalitarianism?" I don't believe in egalitarianism because I don't believe it's an observable fact." In a determinedly anti-idealistic tone, he told me:

I'm working here for pretty much selfish reasons. The tasks that one does here vary, for one thing. And I'm interested in what's being done, at least to a certain point. I don't particularly care how it gets done, as long as it gets done.

Later, he returned to his anti-idealism: "I'm not really into subsystems being revolutionary. Maybe because that's not a choice I have to make. I don't want to give up my worldly stuff."

197

Having concluded that at Helpline if you want to get something done, "You ignore the consensual body and concentrate on the power sources, the high energy levels," Clarence was perplexed and irritated that the organization "doesn't acknowledge the existence of power." Clarence distrusted Helpline's egalitarian decision making as having only a tenuous connection with the reality of self-interest and could only conclude: "I don't trust a lot of what people say. It's very chic and very fashionable to say, okay? [But] I don't think that it's real." The key to his position in Helpline came out in one sentence: "I don't feel safe here."

Trust, in the most restricted sense of being able to predict behavior, is a necessary condition of social interchange. In a village, trust develops through knowing innumerable details about specific individuals and their relations with other individuals in that setting.[13] In a tightly knit traditional society, prescribed rules and relatively certain punishment for deviants facilitate this kind of predictive trust. When associations of human beings lose these bases of trust, they generally fall back on one predictor—self-interest. This is why arms-control theorists reason that, in the amoral war of all against all that comprises international relations, the only safe motive on which one country can base its perdictions about another country's behavior is self-interest. Adversary democracy, designed for communities where traditional ties have dissolved, attempts to build legitimate decisions on self-interest. Individuals who have few other bases for trust, like Clarence at Helpline, also must rely on the predictive power of self-interest. When self-interest is declared irrelevant, they feel confused and insecure.

The gap in bases for trust was one reason among many why Eddie never tried to take an active part in the governance of Helpline. It was the major reason why Leslie, although doing her part, attending Community Days and acting as a representative on committees, never wanted to be more involved. And it played a major part in making Clarence, for all his activism, withdraw from the direction of the organization. On the average, the three black members of Helpline had no fewer of the external signs of participation and power. But it is possible that maintaining this level of participation cost them a great deal more than it did the other members of the organization.

Class

In one sense, all the staff at Helpline might be said to have been of the same "class." They all did much the same work, and they received the same salary. Administrative Backup did not do direct counseling, and the fund raisers had the closest access to capital, but it would be difficult to say that any group at Helpline "controlled the means of production." The ostensible class of all the members was, therefore, the same. In background, however, they differed. In the future, they would also differ, for the staff had varying degrees of education, which when they left Helpline would greatly influence their socioeconomic status. Within Helpline, one's past and future socioeconomic status influenced one's participation, power, feelings of powerfulness, and satisfaction.[14]

Of the forty-one staff members at Helpline, three described their parents as "working class." These were Danny, who did not give either parent's occupation; Nina, daughter of a boilermaker and a part-time salesclerk; and Eddie, who simply described both his parents as "workers." I will call these three the "working-class members." Two other staff members, Frank and Nate, described their parents as "lower middle class." The rest ranged their parents among the categories of "middle-middle," "upper-middle," and "upper" class. The three staff members who had working-class parents also had no college education themselves. All but two of the other Helpline staff members had at least some college.

The working-class members were distinct from the other groups at Helpline, not only in the background of their parents and in their own education, but also in the way they came to work at Helpline. Danny and Nina, counselors at the Shelter, had themselves originally come to Helpline for help. Eddie had been hanging out on the street when he got to know the members of the Emergency Van. Although a few people in the middle-class group had first gotten in touch with Helpline because of their own problems, most of them had arrived at their jobs through a college internship, a conscientious objector's alternative service, or another self-assigned "helping" role. This difference in provenance undoubtedly accentuated class differences in participation and power. The three members of Helpline who had working-class parents were a great deal less likely than their co-workers to speak at meetings, attend meetings, be perceived as powerful, feel powerful, or feel satisfied with the decisions at Helpline (see Appendix A, Table A.12).

In particular, the three working-class members of Helpline—Danny, Eddie, and Nina—were put at a disadvantage by its highly verbal face-to-face democracy. Danny had decided that "the people who think Helpline is attractive are people with verbal skills." He believed that there was as much hierarchy at Helpline as in the last place he had worked but that the power came from "skills in persuasion." Finishing the power-circle exercise, Danny explained that some people got to be in the center because "they can verbalize; they twist things around."

When Nina did the power-circle exercise, she too explained that she put one staff member out on the edge because "He's . . . like I am, not very articulate." Of another, she said, "He's kind of thick, like me—he won't argue with their big words." When I asked what she meant by "like me," she answered, "He doesn't have a large vocabulary to explain exactly what—and the way things go at Bartlett Street, it's like meeting with an encyclopedia going to one of their meetings! The words they use!" Later, when I brought up the issue again, she told me that words have "a hell of a lot to do with" power:

> To me, that ties in with money. Most of the people you see up here had enough money to go to college for four years, or wherever they went, and learn how to use a lot of big words. (laugh) That has a lot to do with it! You really have to play word games! At CPC or wherever you go to. . . .

Nina told me that at one point she had considered going into politics but had concluded: "I couldn't do it. First, I'd have to go to school for twenty years to learn how to talk the way they talk, and by then, it wouldn't do any good."

Eddie felt the same way. When I asked if he had ever thought of going on the CPC, he answered:

> No. I never liked talking ideas. I really have a hard time. I can talk to you; you're only one person and I only have to deal with one head, but where there's a lot of people, like, I find myself repeating myself.

He also said he avoided Community Days:

> Some people don't *feel* like standing up in front of sixty people and saying things. Me too, so that's why it was good to get out of that [budget-cutting Community Day] meeting. (laugh) I find that with me there is a question of education involved. Like most people [here] come from an academic background; they feel confident with papers and pens.

According to Eddie, leadership in the organization should depend on how much work one does, rather than on how well one can talk:

> People are psyched out by people with a quick wit. If you can talk nice, and you have a lot of witty things to say, it goes over big, that shit. Kaye is a very articulate person. . . . She can rap very fast, and she can make it sound like

she knows what she's talking about. Kaye will hit 'em with a heavy rap, she'll use a lot of wall-to-wall words, and people don't know what she's talking about!

As he did the power-ranking exercise, Eddie mused, "I'll put the most talkative people [at the center of power]," and when I asked, after the exercise, why some people ended up in the center, he answered simply, "They know how to talk."

This low confidence in their verbal skills revealed itself not only in what these people told me in the interviews but in their questionnaire responses as well. Not one of Helpline's working-class members answered "seldom" or "never" to the statement, "Articulate people intimidate me," compared to 79 percent of the others at Helpline. Not one of the working-class members answered "Almost always" or "often" to the statement, "I express myself well in words," compared to 61 percent of the others at Helpline. This comparative lack of confidence in their verbal skills goes a long way toward explaining the tendency of the working-class members to attend fewer meetings, speak less frequently at meetings, and in other ways exercise less power in the organization as a whole.[15]

However, it was not only the verbal methods of the others that Danny, Nina, and Eddie felt were foreign; it was also the prevalent forms of manipulation. Danny objected to doing "ground work" before a meeting, "cultivating" the other members: "It's strange that you have to throw so much energy into dealing with this shit! It isn't *me*. I'm at Helpline, Inc., to *do* something!" Manipulators, he told me:

piss me off. Then again, I find myself doing it. And *that* pisses me off. And the reason that I do it is that I really feel as though I *have* to, to deal with the people that I have to deal with. When you manipulate, exert power, you miss a lot. You block off a lot. And that hinders your intake or absorption of what else is going on.

Nina also concluded that "it's all manipulation, who can manipulate better as far as the real inner circles." Doing the power-circle exercise, she commented, "I guess, except for the funders right in the middle, this is all based on how they manipulate—how high they got."

For Nina, the worst sort of manipulation was the interpersonal tugging at heartstrings that gained the sympathy of many middle-class members of Helpline. Indignant over one staff member's asking for a grant for a car, she exploded:

There was such incredible manipulating! I mean, coming to us at that Personnel [DPW] meeting and telling us this sob story of his life about how he's always been poor. I mean, I wanted to punch him out! Because that's shit! *Do* something about it! or endure it! But he really knew how to manipulate people!

I don't think there was anybody on that committee who had ever been poor. Except by choice. —— is poor because he chooses to be. Me, I had no choice. (laugh) I had to find money to go to school. I'll be poor until I get rich. Which will happen. But it won't happen because I go *crying*; it will happen because I work for it!

Eddie, from a slightly different perspective, also criticized the manipulative use of crying:

The heaviest meetings that I have been to have been about money! Where tears would flow, you know? . . . I went to one meeting where CCC was going to get severed from Helpline, and people were crying!

JM: The one [budget-cutting Community Day] last September?

EDDIE: Yeah. That was a big joke! If *I* ever cry about money—especially when we're supposed to be friends! . . .

JM: How does that make you feel when people start crying at meetings?

EDDIE: It depends on what they're crying over. If they're crying over a personal issue, . . . then that's cool. But to cry over somebody else's crumbs—if you're going to *cry* over them, why not just *fight* over them! Be real about it!

Eddie objected to this particular reason for crying but was also simply irritated at his co-workers using crying to influence their friends. His own method was more direct, and he would rather fight than cry.

All three of the working-class members despaired of being able to influence others. Perceiving himself as unwilling or unable to engage in emotional manipulation, Danny withdrew. "I guess what I usually do is let things take their course. . . . [I] just listen, man. (laugh) Listen to things that just freak me out." Eddie and Nina both spoke out bluntly, often getting angry, and found that the others simply stopped listening. I think that Eddie was correct in believing that the others pigeonholed him as a "revolutionary" and then discounted what he said. Nina too I think was not exaggerating when she perceived that her honest, but not subtly articulated, explosions earned her little attention:

When I speak out at a business meeting, I think that I was put in a role where *I* would voice the bitchiness and the anger that everyone in the Shelter had . . . so *they* would be very philosophical, and I would just say, "To hell with this, to hell with that!" and that was good for the Shelter, but not good as far as decision making went because any time I said anything negative (—and *sometimes* I really try and explain myself! I *usually* don't.), it was just negated because they were so used to me saying "To hell with this and that" that it didn't do any good.

Neither Danny nor Eddie nor Nina achieved the mix of emotional and verbal techniques that allowed the middle-class staff to influence their peers at Helpline with ease.

Eddie wanted Helpline to "develop some new class attitudes"; Nina "saw Helpline as a bunch of middle-class, white, mostly rich Jewish (laugh) people running Helpline, Inc."; Danny never mentioned class. But while they varied in class consciousness, the three working-class members shared some of the same class culture. They were deeply committed to their work, and they believed in Helpline's ideals only insofar as those ideals seemed useful and practical. They thought equal power in internal decisions crucial only because they believed an egalitarian system made them do better work, not because it was part of some larger ideal. When I asked Danny how he felt "about the whole idea of people being equal," he answered, "It doesn't mean anything to me because I don't think it's true. People aren't equal; they're not." Eddie told me that "There's no such thing as equality. . . . I don't believe there's any such thing as equality!" He thought it important to have equal power at Helpline but had "struggled" with the question of whether:

> if you had somebody to tell you to do something and if you didn't do it you would get fired, would it *get more done* if it were set up that way? Or is there a limitation to *that* structure itself? There are times when you can do a job and [just] get it done; and there are other times when [because you are not under someone's power] you can do that job and be very creative.

Nina too had a determinedly anti-idealistic streak: "I'm power hungry," she told me. "I have been for a long time. . . . I love to order people around. I love the feeling." But then she laughed and added, "I don't know if that's a true statement."

Danny, Eddie, and Nina saw themselves as realists. This perspective might have derived from a class culture that stresses practicality. It might have come from their need to preserve some strong identity in the face of an idealistic, middle-class organization and a middle-class interviewer. But it seemed to derive in large part from their commitment to good work. This led Nina to say of the new job for which she was applying:

> Maybe there will be some kind of director who will direct the program and do it right. Tell people what to do, and I'll enjoy that. (laugh) Maybe that way the work will be fun. John and Sally directed [a program outside Helpline and] felt really rotten about having to be directors and order people around, but that program did really good work because they had the guts to fire people.

At the time of the Scorpion crisis at the Shelter, she had thought:

> maybe having a director would maybe be a good idea [because] if someone said, "Look, *I'm* writing your paychecks out (laugh) and I think that *this* is the way it's going to be!" then . . . those kids . . . would be in a much better place.

Although many of the staff worried about the problems of inadequate self-discipline and although many did not do their share of the necessary boring, routine work, only the working-class staff actually blamed themselves in the interview. Eddie said right out, "I have a bad work attitude," and Nina, who had become demoralized before she quit at the time of the budget cuts, told me that "*I* wouldn't hire someone who worked the way I worked there the last few months!" Because my impression was that these two were not the worst offenders in slacking off, I concluded that the strength of their self-criticism might have come in part from their strong desire to see the work done and their impatience with the inefficient aspects of the Helpline ideals.

In the fact, but not in the content, of their anti-idealism, Danny, Eddie, and Nina resembled the lower-middle-class members of Helpline. Nate and Frank were the only staff at Helpline to characterize their parents as "lower-middle class." Clarence indicated that his parents were "middle-middle class," but he had grown up in the same neighborhood and milieu as Nate.[16] These three were the only other people at Helpline to take determinedly anti-idealistic stands. Their anti-idealism, however, included an explicit concern for money, which Eddie had disdained, Danny had never mentioned, and Nina had dismissed with the offhand, "I'll be poor until I get rich. Which will happen." Nate and Frank, who were close friends with Clarence and on the Switchboard with him, echoed his "I don't want to give up my worldly stuff." Nate told me:

My class, social background is very different than a lot of people here. Pretty poor, working class. My mother and father split when I was a kid, and my mother worked, and we made it on what my sister and her made, which was diddley-shit for a long time. Her class background was also poor. . . .
People from here come from the upper-middle class pretty much. . . . I don't feel guilty about money. I would like to have a lot of money. . . . I like things. I like to travel. A lot of people here, they've been to Europe. I've never traveled; I would like to do that.

He concluded, "I feel sometimes that people [here] are naive. And I'm not naive." Frank used much the same language:

I think I'm different in many ways from most people here. Because I'm from a very lower-middle-class background. Scarce childhood where material goods were always very chancy. Conflicts about spending money.
[How does that make you feel different from people here?] I think it makes me more pragmatic. More realistic. I'm more willing to sacrifice philosophical ideals for sometimes economic gains or political gains.

Because Frank, Nate, and Clarence were on the Switchboard, because they all felt upwardly mobile, and because they all had at least some college education, they participated actively in Helpline decisions, perceived themselves to have power, and were perceived by others as powerful in Helpline. Frank was elected coordinator of Helpline just before I left, and both Clarence and Nate were on the CPC. While these three were not quite so articulate as some of the upper-middle-class males at Helpline, none of them showed any hesitation about speaking. Their intense activity and upward mobility did not make them a reference group for the working-class members of Helpline.

In their isolation, Danny, Nina, and Eddie found themselves drawing closer to their service groups. Reflecting on the respect with which I knew he was held in the Shelter, Danny told me, "In the Shelter, I feel powerful." Nina concluded, "I love the Shelter," and Eddie told me, "I feel close to most of the Van." In the intimate setting of the work group, the other staff valued these people for what they did. The positions of these three therefore accentuated the tendency in decentralized systems toward hostility among the separate parts. Eddie explained the syndrome more clearly than anyone in the organization:

> I don't know how it got started, but I found myself, like, not diggin' people at Switchboard and having resentment toward ———— I found that I was adopted into it, 'cause I became part of the *Van*. I didn't become part of Helpline; I became part of the Van. Like when you join a club, you take on all the ———— without even understanding it! It was really weird. Like you don't spend time with the people, so you don't get to know them, and you go on with those things based on hearsay.

Danny and Nina were equally tied to the Shelter and hostile to the rest of Helpline. Danny told me that when he first joined Helpline:

> at that time, it was the Shelter versus Bartlett Street. And it's always been like that. And naturally, I fell right into it. Here was something in my life that had a lot to do with the direction of my life. And so, naturally, the Shelter were the "good guys." Bartlett Street was the "bad guys."

Nina's alienation from "Bartlett Street" was so great that, as she told me, "I just refused to go over there. I would do anything I could not to go over there."

For this reason, the three working-class people perceived themselves as having *chosen* not to exercise much power in central Helpline's decisions. Nina, doing the power-circle exercise, said, "————, Danny, and I are on the outside by choice." When I asked Eddie and Danny if they had ever thought of going on CPC, Eddie answered, "No. I never liked talking ideas," and Danny answered, "No. I'll be damned if I'm going to be drained any more than I already am. A lot of people ask me that, and my usual response is 'NO!'" He concluded that "the reason I don't know what they're doing [over at Bartlett Street] is that I'm not there. I *could* be."

Discriminating Among Inequalities

The differences in power attributable to length of membership, geographical distance, age and class proved difficult to eradicate at Helpline, even with the organization's elaborate set of procedures for spreading participation. Yet because the members' interests were more often congruent than in conflict, equal power was not as necessary to protect interests equally as it would have been in a more adversary situation.

For example, differences in interest between newcomers and old-timers and between young and old at Helpline were negligible. The long-established policy of equal salaries meant that pay and promotion could not depend on seniority or age. Contrary to organization theory, the longer tenured staff were not more interested in organizational maintenance than were the newcomers. The low material rewards guaranteed a staff devoted to the work itself, rather than to maintaining the organization, while the countercultural ideal demanded that as soon as Helpline stopped performing useful tasks it should go out of business.[17]

If there had been more variation in age at Helpline, this too could have made for differing interests among the members. In most alternative organizations, older members are more likely to have children and to have friends in jobs with higher pay. They are therefore more likely to press for across-the-board wage increases or wages graded by age.[18] They often support less "risky" policies. Yet at Helpline, the age variation (nineteen to thirty-seven) was so small, the turnover so great, and the original commitment to equal salaries so strong that those who desired higher salaries simply moved on to other jobs. Among those who stayed, the older members were actually more in favor of equal salaries than the younger.[19]

I discerned only one operative difference in interest between newcomers and old-timers, young and old. The newcomers, having joined the organization in the early 1970s rather than in the late 1960s, had ideas that were somewhat less "countercultural" and more "political" than those of the older staff.[20] Both the newcomers and the young had plenty of opportunities to take responsibility, participate in conflict, and grow. In regard to equal respect, the old-timers often did not want to go through the full explanations and the rehashing of past decisions that would have made the newcomers truly equal. The newcomers sometimes felt slightly crushed by the personal consequences of this, but since in any case they never remained in that state more than a few months, the consequences to their self-esteem were neither serious nor long-lasting.

Geographical centrality created more differences in interest than seniority or age. The Shelter, which was geographically isolated from the rest of Helpline, had a set of specific interests (preservation of the Shelter runaway program and staff) and a philosophical orientation (commitment to short-term "service" rather than to long-term "revolution") that differed slightly from the interests of the rest of the staff at Helpline. When it came time to select a new coordinator for Helpline, the Shelter also had its own candidate. Like the nonvillagers in Selby, the staff of the Shelter had a social interest in equal information and power; they did not want to feel cut off. They were not, however, deprived of respect or the opportunities for growth.

In all but the case of the eventually dismantled office manager job, work and salaries were so equally divided at Helpline that women differed little from men in their material interest. In another, less therapeutically inclined community, the women might have had different ideas from the men about the direction of the organization. At Helpline, this seemed true only in the Van, where the women complained about the erratic, "macho" style in which the men did their work, staying up for three days straight, then collapsing. The women at Helpline did, however, have an interest in maintaining their self-esteem, and because the women were members of a readily identifiable group with a history of oppression, they had a psychological interest in having equal power at Helpline. For example, to the extent that women habitually participated less than men in meetings at Helpline, this pattern would probably reinforce the women's acceptance of their subordinate position in the larger society.

I discovered no differences in individual power and participation between blacks and whites at Helpline. Had I discovered any such inequalities, they would have been important because the blacks' interests did differ from those of the whites. Like the women, the three blacks at Helpline belonged to an identifiable group with a subordinate position in the outside society. It was therefore pychologically important for the three black staff members at Helpline to exercise equal power in the organization. Moreover, other interests of the blacks differed from those of the whites. All three blacks at Helpline wanted the organization to become more involved with the partially black community in the area in which Helpline was located. This idea generally met resistance from the whites, who saw their programs as citywide. The three blacks also supported affirmative minority hiring, while the whites tended to choose from whoever happened to apply. Finally, two of the three blacks at Helpline were more concerned than most of the other members about the difficulty of raising a family on the salary available at Helpline.

Of all the readily identifiable groups with less than equal power at Helpline, the three members who described their parents as working class had interests that seemed to differ most from those of their fellow workers. They gave a distinctly higher value than the other members to efficiency and accountability within the organization.[21] They could quite reasonably have had a greater interest in higher salaries than members with middle-class parents, although they gave me no indication of this. They could also have had interests in Helpline's hiring more working-class people, trying to attract more working-class clients, instituting a high school and college equivalency program for its staff, or making it easier in other ways for its working-class members to get jobs after they left Helpline. Taking a more active part in the determination of central issues at Helpline might have made them more aware of these interests. Moreover, as members of a social group whose power in the outside society was lower than the average, these three were more likely than the other staff members to lose self-esteem through low participation in decisions since this would corroborate the external stereotype. They were respected at Helpline for their counseling skills, but their own comments on their verbal ability suggest that such respect may not have been enough to maintain their own self-esteem. Perhaps because of this they were more likely than others in the organization to place a high value on equal power and equal influence.[22]

Yet these differences in interest, while hardly trivial, add up to less than the differences between old-timer and newcomer, villager and non-villager, old and young, rich and poor in Selby. The staff at Helpline was also drawn together by stronger everyday bonds of common interest than were the citizens of Selby. The citizens of Selby and Helpline both believed in the common interest. But when people in Selby realized that their private interests differed from their neighbors', they tended to vote according to these private interests. This was less true at Helpline. The more educated staff members at Helpline, for instance, were perfectly aware that they would have benefited economically from a pay scale graduated on the basis of education, but this awareness did not lead them to favor such a pay scale. Indeed, the higher the staff members' academic credentials, the more likely they were to believe that *equal* salaries were crucial to making Helpline what they wanted it to be.[23]

In short, the interests of the staff at Helpline were not in great conflict. If Helpline were to have devoted even more of its scarce resources to promoting greater equality of power, this analysis suggests that it should have tried to increase the power of the working-class members, just as it had earlier focused on the special problems of women and possibly blacks. It might also have given attention to the slightly lower power of the most geographically distant work group. In both of these cases, the members' interests might not have been represented in proportion to their numbers.

Chapter 16

The Lust for Power

HELPLINE'S STAFF believed in equal salaries, equal respect, and equal power. But Helpline's division of labor precluded an equal distribution of power. Fund raising, representing one's service group at the CPC, or acting as coordinator, vice-coordinator, or treasurer provided individuals with resources that gave them greater than average power over the direction of the organization. These jobs required the incumbents to gather critical information, present that information in digested form to the community, and make small but far-reaching decisions along the way both as to which information to collect and how to present it to the others. The treasurer, the coordinator, the fund raisers, and the representatives to the CPC all knew more about the central organization than did the rest of the staff. They all consequently had the opportunity to make interstitial decisions that limited the decisions open to others. While Helpline had eliminated its separate funding staff and dispersed the chore of funding to members from the different groups, the members concerned with funding still had more power than others. Moreover, the staff had decided that the treasurer's job—which combined keeping the accounts, making budgetary predictions, and letting each service group know how much it could spend —had best not be divided. They had also decided against dividing the position of coordinator. Finally, having tried to make all decisions in assembly, they had decided to create a system of mandated representation.

Legally, there was no monopoly of information. The treasurer's books were publicly available, the coordinator could not make secret agreements, and the meetings of CPC representatives were open to anyone who wanted to attend. But no one in the organization could master all the information that the treasurer, coordinator, and CPC representatives acquired and still continue to do his or her own productive work. The community therefore had to trust the individuals who filled these positions to use their greater power and participation in the interests of the whole.[1]

In spite of its formal system of direct democracy and mandated representation, then, Helpline had created an informal system of nonmandated representation, in which members who filled positions of greater power represented the interests of the others without being formally accountable to them. As in any representative system, the question arose as to whether the very skills, desires, and personality characteristics that led some people to take on powerful positions might also lead them to develop different interests from the rest and to pursue those interests instead of representing the interests of the others.

Staff members worried particularly that their peers might be attracted to the central positions by a lust for power, a fascination with the joy of "seeing 'em jump."[2] They concentrated their fears on this personality trait rather than on other, more structural causes of differences in power because it was directly and obviously linked to the selection process for positions of power, because it seemed harder than other differences to control, and because it produced in them a deeper feeling of ideological and emotional revulsion.

The evidence justifies one part of this fear. Those who gave "propower" answers to questionnaire items such as "I enjoy power," "I enjoy planning things and taking charge," "I like competition," and "I like taking responsibility," were in fact more likely to be judged powerful both by themselves and by others. They were also more likely to attend meetings and speak at them (see Table 6). Those who gave "pro-power" answers to these and other questions were also more likely to be administrators or CPC representatives.[3] It is not clear, of course, what causes what. Those who had come to occupy positions of power might, over time, find themselves more comfortable with responsibility, planning things, taking charge, giving orders, and the general exercise of power. Still, it seems reasonable to suppose that those who enjoyed power would make more effort to exercise it than those who did not enjoy it.

One need not be power-hungry to want a position that provides the resources of power. Some staff members took administrative jobs because, as they stayed longer in the organization and were exposed to more of its different aspects, they came to care as much about the whole organization as they did about their own service group or set of clients. Some took up unpopular administrative burdens because they wanted to win the gratitude of their fellow workers or because their self-esteem depended on

TABLE 6

*Participation, Ranked Power, Sense of Efficacy and
Satisfaction by Liking Power and Responsibility
at Helpline*[a]

	Liking power and responsibility
Power and Participation	
Speaking at meetings	.60***
Attending meetings	.49**
Ranked high in "power" by other staff	.69***
Efficacy and Satisfaction	
Reports self as high in "say" and "power"	.52***
Reports satisfaction with decisions	.08

[a] The measures of participation, power, efficacy, and satisfaction in this table are the same as those in Table 5. The index of "Liking power and responsibility" combines answers to the questionnaire items, "I enjoy power," "I hate to tell others what to do," "I enjoy planning things and taking charge," "I like competition," "I like taking responsibility," "I don't like to 'operate,'" and "If you had your choice, would you rather have a job where you gave the orders or a job where somebody else told you what do do?"

not shirking the task. Some took the jobs because they preferred long-range work, with deferred gratification but permanent results and a tangible product like a new program or a grant. Others avoided these jobs because they preferred the immediate gratification but intangible results of person-to-person counseling. Some, like Bruce, the treasurer, took administrative jobs in order to expand their horizons:

> I felt I was playing out different sides of myself by getting involved in those different aspects. Treasurer of this organization?—that's not me! Treasurer! And yet I'm aware that those are skills that I see as important to have, and I feel that I chose to do that. I took responsibility, nobody pressured me to do this. . . . So I feel that Helpline has given me an opportunity to really develop my potential.

One or two men seem to have taken administrative positions because they believed that the experience and title would help them get good jobs after leaving Helpline. Some took the more powerful jobs in order, as one new representative to the DPW put it, "to know what's going on, be in touch with things." Finally, several counselors told me that certain of the administrative staff had not been good therapists, and one of the administrators himself gave this reason for his having moved into administration.

The purest motives, however, could not guarantee that those with administrative jobs at Helpline would perfectly represent the interests of the least powerful. Even in the formal representative structure of the CPC and DPW, I recorded several instances in which the representatives, with the best will in the world, did not adequately communicate both sides of an argument to the service groups or report all the dissents and positions in the service group back to the CPC or DPW.[4] Nina, from the Shelter, told me that she had stopped being a DPW representative because:

> at the meetings, the room fills with smoke for three hours, and it gets very emotional 'cause of how you feel. . . .
> I don't know if it's possible for [anyone] to go there and represent how the Shelter feels. . . . Pamela, you can't say she's going to CPC and representing the Shelter.
> And when *I* went to Bartlett Street [to DPW], I tried to represent the Shelter, but when it got down to the heated arguments, I couldn't. I tried to integrate what everybody had said at the [Shelter] meeting on whatever issue was being discussed, but I'm sure that's what happens in any legislature—you get down to your *own* interests; you get down to what *you* believe.

In positions of informal power, the disparities between the opinions of the more and less powerful were even stronger because the incumbents did not think of themselves as "representatives." In developing a course of action that they perceived as good for all, they would become engaged with their own plan and stop listening to objections.

Because it was crucial to Helpline that the staff in positions of greater power not lose sight of the common good, the other staff frequently scrutinized the motives of the most powerful. They worried about their colleagues' potentially stubborn investments in their own projects. They looked for positive signals from the powerful that they could be budged from their own ideas and made to see things another way. This was the reason why one woman staff member felt comfortable with the treasurer's power: "Bruce is powerful, but I think he's reasonable; you can change his mind. I trust him." Another woman criticized the men in her service group because instead of being "into hearing all the sides and then making the decisions, [they] often come in with an agenda of what they want and then try and convince people of it." Most staff disapproved of "people who consciously decide, 'I want this to happen, and I'm going to do whatever I need to do to make this happen.'" Indeed, most people gave this as their definition of a "power trip":

> When somebody throws a power trip, that means that a decision has already been made. And a power trip is just imposing that decision. The decision's been made in his mind.

The staff worried most about the motives that made people want power, in part because these motives seemed even harder to control than emotional or intellectual investment. Members of the Shelter, for example, were afraid that Frank, who wanted to be coordinator, might be on a "power trip," wanting "power for its own sake":

Let's say Frank didn't have the skills, but since it was a power thing, he'd show up and do it, even though he didn't have the skills.

That's always in my head—when someone volunteers for something, *why* did that person volunteer? Because the group is depending on you to represent them, and for the outcome to be a good one. So it is a powerful position, and you really should have the skills, not just the [desire for] power to accept it. [You shouldn't] do something just because it's an impressive role to be in at that time or because you need to be on the spot.

The lust for power also created real revulsion among the staff, particularly when they connected it with almost sexual, perhaps sadistic, pleasure. One staffer, remembering his own experience, told me that:

There is a certain thrill to being in a position of control. It made me feel bad. . . . I got carried away, however minimally. . . . Sometimes it picks you up and takes you someplace.

He therefore worried that Frank, who was running for coordinator and clearly enjoyed power, might be "in it because he gets a 'rush' from it. That it satisfies some unclean need that he has." Another of the staff used the word "unwholesome." And another felt the subject was "too personal" to say more than "I've had to confront myself on my own power trips—I've gone way back to LSD fantasies that I used to have. They really involve power."

If the nonpowerful staff worried about the motives of the powerful, so did the powerful themselves, and with twice the intensity. The staff who had taken positions of greater power in this egalitarian organization had to justify that choice to both themselves and others. They did so in three ways. Some, whom in the spirit of exaggeration I will call "the power-hungry," rejected part of the organization's egalitarian ideology. Others, whom I will call "the ambivalent," blamed the victims; they saw the apathy or unwillingness of others as forcing them to take on greater power. The third group, whom I will call "the facilitators," distanced their concepts of themselves from the powerful positions they held, going so far in two cases as to deny the extent of their power.

Helpline was a counseling center, and because its staff placed a premium on understanding their own emotions and communicating openly, they were more likely than most people to tell me as honestly as they could how they actually felt about power. Moreover, they were experimentalists, committed to equality but not to any particular ideological line. They wanted to be as searching as possible about how they felt, as part of their ongoing experimental interest in how to make democracy work. They therefore told me, frankly, of feelings about power that ranged from eager relish to abhorrence. The following analysis will concentrate on the experiences of the eight people who ranked highest on the power-ranking exercise (the top 20 percent), and two of the eight people in the lowest 20 percent.

The "Power-Hungry"

As I reread the Helpline interviews, I noticed that the most powerful staff at Helpline seemed to need to replay as adults their early parent-child struggles for control. Among the eight staff members who scored highest in the power ranking, 63 percent spontaneously mentioned their parents at some point in the interview, compared to only 9 percent among the rest of the staff. Moreover, within this top group of eight, everyone who told me outright that he or she liked power also at some point mentioned a parent, while those who appeared indifferent to power never referred to their parents.[5]

Several of the staff members in the most powerful group themselves brought up the issue of parent-child control. Frank had the fourth highest power score, wanted to become coordinator, and was described, not quite fairly, by one staff member as "just about the most power-hungry person I know." The first words in his interview were:

My father has a farm, and he's very much tied to the farm, which is a very hierarchical kind of structure—the father is head of the family—and he expected me to go into farm work with him, which was impossible because of my nature and a number of other things. I had a very strong father, and I rebelled against him.

Not long after this, he told me that Helpline had an "incredible mania for destroying what I call father figures," namely, people like himself. Later still, he added, "What's inherent in our culture is the destruction of the father, of the superego. It has a lot to do with age, I think—a need to destroy that kind of image."

For people who are still replaying the drama of parent against child in their own lives, the process of growing up, if successful, is one of moving to the top and of becoming the "parent" to someone else's "child." Frank accepted this model, asserting that "hierarchy is very natural in the way of human existence." In Frank's natural hierachy, "there is *a* person who is *the* leader" [emphasis mine]. Frank appreciated the unambiguous clarity of the model—father and son, master and apprentice—even when he was not on top:

> I was an apprentice when I came here. I was Chris Sandron's assistant. It was very simple for me to fit into that role. I was learning the task, and Chris definitely knew it—fund raising. Chris was definitely the master of it. And there was no doubt about it, our roles. I was his assistant. It was clear.

Frank's language reveals the quiet pleasure he took in being first:

> I sort of play the role of leadership. What that means is that I go first, sometimes. It doesn't necessarily mean that I do all the decision-making processes—which is not true; it's not a totalitarian situation—but just by the nature of my personality. . . . I may open discussion first, I may do a lot of thinking in terms of problems that we have, and I may lay out a whole agenda of things that have to be done. But I don't make the decisions on how they are to be carried out necessarily. I usually just do a lot of forethinking about it.

Among the most powerful eight members of Helpline, Frank was one of the three who most openly acknowledged a desire for power. Of these three, however, Frank was the most circumspect, saying that he was a leader "just by the nature of my personality" and that he would like to use the job of coordinator "to shift the thing back to more leadership—to at least a person who fills that leadership role."[6] Nate, Frank's close friend, was blunter but more casual about it, and less serious: "I'm interested in power; I'm mostly interested in power. . . . If I'm not on top, I don't want to be involved! (laugh)" Leon, in keeping with his position as Helpline lawyer, deployed his verbal skills on the subject:

> JM: You don't feel bad about the concept of power?
> LEON: No, not in the slightest. I'm sure trial law in a sense is an ego trip for me. Look at the power I have over years of a person's life, the power I have to cross-examine, the power I have to—all kinds of shit. One of the power trips of all time is the final summation to a jury. There's no one but you and those twelve people. The rest of the world just doesn't exist. You can use the whole courtroom as your stage; all the props are there—it's just neat! (laugh) It's just so intense.
> You either enjoy it or you don't enjoy it. Power is something that I enjoy. For a while, I was contemplating seeking political office, but political offices themselves are not that powerful.
> JM: How can someone who enjoys power enjoy an egalitarian organization?
> LEON: I have enough outlets. I have that courtroom. I also have another kind of power within the organization. Even though we defy professionalism, I have power because I am a professional, and I have a kind of knowledge

that few people have. So people come to me when they want help on a legal matter.

These men, in varying degrees, all recognized the personal gratifications of power, stressed the importance of personality in acquiring power, and made it clear that they occupied powerful positions not by accident but by the force of their own characters.

In order to take such a stance in an egalitarian organization, they had to reject at least part of the egalitarian ideology. Each of the three rather prided himself on having made that rejection. Nate told me, "I get angry at Helpline a lot . . . at what I see as naiveté. . . ." He called himself a "blasphemer" and made it clear early in the interview that he was "moving away from a kind of egalitarian view of the universe: everybody ain't the same, you know." Frank pointed out that:

inherently in any system you are going to come up with people who are suitable for carrying out one part of the task or another. So that your non-hierarchical, egalitarian, group-decision, consensual organization is really a— it's rhetoric.

Leon took the inside-dopester line:

I had some political skills that a lot of people [at Helpline] didn't have. It was pretty obvious to me that it would be very, very easy for me to figure out the internal power structure here—how things happened, what have you. . . . I could see what the decision-making process was. I could see what was really happening. I could see what the outcome of a controversy was going to be.

I'm really a believer that you either have a feel or you don't have a feel for those sorts of things. How you get that feel I have no idea. Maybe it's experience; maybe it's just something you're born with—just understanding how things within an organization are happening, how the power structure lies, who the people are that are influential, who the people are who are *not* influential. . . .

It was not that these three had rejected all egalitarian values. Frank declared that he had "always been drawn to the collective kind of ideal. . . . I guess it sort of comes from a childhood of scarcity." Leon was so impressed by the system of consensual decision making that he had begun to proselytize on the subject and was teaching it at a local law school. Nate still yearned for "revolutionary struggle," as long as it did not "confuse hope with reality." But it embarrassed Nate as much to admit idealism as it did others to admit to private motives.[7] Although the personalities of these three men were very different, they were all alike in combining, with relative ease, an overt desire for personal power with a continuing belief in some egalitarian values.

The Ambivalent

The same was not true of Kaye. As vice-coordinator of Helpline, she had the third highest power score in the organization, after Tom, the co-ordinator, and Bruce, the treasurer. She liked power and said so. Like Frank, she also raised parent-child issues within the first minute of the interview. She had come to Helpline, she said, because she had hated the parent-child roles in graduate school. "I had a couple of professors who played 'Daddy.' I mean, I have a Jewish daddy, and I know how to play that game!" When I asked about her emotional lows at Helpline, Kaye told me that she became discouraged when she had to "lecture and be 'Mommy.'" When I asked about highs, she described the "very, very up and very exhilarating" Community Day meetings right after Helpline's original founder—"Helpline's Daddy," as she put it—had left: "Daddy leaves, and are you going to establish a surrogate daddy? Are you going to set it up the way Daddy would have liked it done? And we didn't!"

But Kaye worried about liking power and sometimes disapproved of these feelings in herself. In her case, the tensions of having more than equal power in an egalitarian organization must have been exacerbated by being a woman. Energetic, intelligent, feisty, and decisive, Kaye did not have the usual women's problem of lacking verbal self-confidence—she had no trouble speaking up or getting angry. At the average CPC meeting, she spoke twice as often as any other woman and almost half again as much as any man. Her participation alone raised the average number of times women spoke in those meetings from 8.5 to 11.3 (the male average was 11.1). She also provided eight of the nine times women got angry in the meetings, creating an average score for anger among the women equal to that of the men. The same was true in Community Days. Without her activity, the women's participation scores would have been much lower than they were.[8] Kaye told me, "Conflict doesn't bother me, frankly. The model I set up for me does very well under conflict. I come out well enough personally to be very selfish about it—if it's really there, I prefer to deal with it honestly."

With these attitudes, Kaye was able to chair the Air Force contract meeting brilliantly, preventing interruptions, calming anxieties, and making sure that each quiet person had a chance to speak. At the end of the meeting, she exulted out loud, "I love being chairperson at meetings like this!"

As vice-coordinator of Helpline, Kaye kept a file of the minutes, and as one man who disliked her put it, "she has an encyclopedic memory for conversations and commitments that have been made." She liked to have things put in writing, pushed to have the minutes written up on time, and fought the fuzzy-edged decisions that tend to emerge in a consensual process. She was the organization's strongest advocate of formal evaluations. She used the anger that came so easily to her to chivy her colleagues into making their policies explicit and remembering what decisions had been made. One day, for instance, I overheard her in the corridor dressing down two of the staff members in her service group:

WOMAN: I didn't realize . . . (unintelligible).
KAYE: . . . and I'm upset about it. And if *you* want that policy changed, you bring it up!
WOMAN: Maybe it's time to clarify it [the policy]?
MAN (interjecting):   We've been gradually clarifying it. . . .
KAYE (to the man):   Speak for yourself! I've always been clear about what *I* was doing. . . . Read the damn training manual!

Soon after this, the woman postponed an appointment she had with me, saying, "I'd better not do the interview now, I'm pretty shaken up."

In one CPC meeting, before the budget-cutting Community Day, Kaye insisted, against considerable resistance, that the service groups give written as well as oral reports on the extent to which they would cut their staff. After much talk back and forth, she blew up: "It's not *reasonable* to present a comprehensive picture in ten minutes! There are six discrete things [reports], and we're talking about spending one or two minutes on each of them! I'm *tired* of making decisions on the basis of how mellow somebody's rap sounds!" The group agreed to written reports. The next week she had to repeat the act. A staff member who had not attended the previous meeting brought up the issue again, arguing that "position papers don't get read." Kaye snapped back: "If people don't read it, that's their lookout!" The response, "I don't want an organization based on position papers," made her hit the roof: "That's not what I said, and I resent that. It's something that meant a lot to me last week, and I'll repeat it!" Consensus was reached again on having written reports.

These bludgeoning tactics, although relatively successful in the short run, took their internal toll. A few minutes after the first of these meetings, I passed Kaye on the stairs, looking exhausted, depressed, and, I thought, on the verge of tears. To my expression of concern, she shook her head: "I'm afraid I did it again—really laid my rap on them. [pause] But I really *believe* that things should be written out!" Later, in the interviews, I asked Kaye about some of the highs and lows she had experienced working at Helpline. She had told me about some of the highs, and when I asked, "What about downs?" she responded:

Big downs? Yeah. Stuff like—do you remember the meeting before the Community Day, when people said they didn't want to do written stuff? And I got mad, and I hollered at people and lectured them? That was a down.

I did that because I felt that I *had* to do it. That is was an important thing, and it wasn't going to be done unless I said that it needed to be done. And that if I *said* it needed to be done and it still didn't get done, I'd have to lecture and be "Mommy," and scold people and make them feel guilty so they would do it.

It was a downer. It was a down that people just were unwilling to put in a little bit of work that could really make something like that [Community Day] a lot more positive.

JM: How did you feel?

KAYE: I was angry, I was frustrated, and I was pissed. I was pissed at myself for buying into that role. I don't like it. I was very, very angry.

JM: Do you ever feel physically nervous or sick after meetings?

KAYE: Sometimes I get a headache after meetings. (laugh) Yeah, I had a headache after that meeting. I work myself up, and my adrenalin comes pounding out, and I get it all out.

In her ambivalence, pride in the ends fought against anguish over the means.

I get people to do things. I'm very effective as a hatchet woman. I mean, when I want people to do things, they goddamn well do them! And I know that! Big power! That's the part that's an ego trip.

The other part is the part that makes me sad because people don't do things that it makes a lot of sense for them to do.

It makes me sad that I get off on being that sort of person—because I don't like being that kind of person. That makes me very, very angry.

Much of Kaye's ambivalence about getting people to do things stemmed from her sensitivity to what that position did to others and to what it did to her. She had been attracted to Helpline's egalitarian structure partly because "I would be a new person, and in the structured situation near the bottom," and partly because:

it's also crummy to be at the *top*! For me because I'm a fairly aggressive person, and I think that sets me up in a situation where it allows me to be too many things that I don't like being—if I'm at the top.

In the Peace Corps, Kaye felt that "it did bad things for me to have that ["top-dog" position], being really able to work hard and having *my* views important, *my* views accepted." But in graduate school afterward, she had felt it even worse to be "the flunky for all the professors, and they were God and I was shit."

At Helpline, Kaye continued her ambivalence. She had thought about, but decided against, taking the job of coordinator:

It's an administrative job. I get some of my rocks off, as they say, from pushing that whole list of things that I just talked about, that are strong—but it's not enough. And in the end, it's very frustrating.

I mean, it gives me pleasure, and makes me feel tough. It's nice, it fills a lot of my fantasy needs, but it doesn't leave the kind of pleasure and satisfaction—it doesn't give me a real up. It gives me a mean up, frankly—"Aaah, I got *that* bastard down"—rather than saying, "Wow. I did something, and it's cool, and I really dig it."

The "mean up" that can accompany an exercise of power worried several people at Helpline. But it particularly worried Kaye because, for her, the only way to overtly exercise power as a woman was to "bitch" and "make noise." About her crusade for evaluations, she said, "They know that Kaye will make a lot of noise and bitch if we try to make them a cursory thing." While doing the power-ranking exercise, she placed herself close to the center, commenting, "I think I have lots of power. *Isn't that terrible*? I make a lot of noise" (my emphasis).

Noise is contentless. The phrase "making a lot of noise" implies coercion, not rational persuasion. It is, moreover, coercion on a primitive scale; the screams of a baby irritate the adults within hearing until they try to supply what the baby wants. When Kaye described herself and other women exercising power at Helpline, she consistently used the works "making noise," but when she described men in the same context, she spoke instead of "influence."[9]

Thus, the one woman at Helpline powerful enough to raise the women's power and participation scores to almost equal those of the men could not freely enjoy her greater power. Nor did she fit happily into a back-stage facilitator role. She portrayed public responsibility and the gratifications it provided as male—"getting your rocks off." And she infantilized her own leadership actions, substituting "noise" for reason. Of the eight most powerful individuals at Helpline, Kaye was the only one who expressed any anxiety to me about the discrepancy between her egalitarian convictions and her greater power. Many things in her background must have combined to produce this anxiety, but one of these was surely the traditional conception of a woman's role. As another woman at Helpline told me:

I know that Kaye, for example, when they are deciding about coordinator, said that she didn't want to do it because she didn't think that a woman would be as good, relating to the outside world about Helpline, as a man would be. She thought that practically it made more sense to have a man there. The world would respect that more. So I don't think she feels it's her place, so to speak.

For people like Kaye, who have trouble reconciling their egalitarian values with the fact of their own greater power, one solution is to aspire to a world in which the inequality would not exist and in which everyone would voluntarily take on the power that they now bear alone.

Like Kaye, Dave, who was not among the top 20 percent but, as co-ordinator of the Van, had the highest power ranking in his service group, had taken it upon himself to improve the level of performance of his colleagues by anger and nagging. But like parents with unruly children, Kaye and Dave both longed for an end to their burden and blamed those they nagged for forcing them to act coercively. Kaye told me that she had acquired power:

> because I don't like what's going on, and I assume responsibility to change it. But a lot of my reaction why I don't like it is I wish I didn't have to do it. In my best of all possible worlds, it wouldn't be going on. . . . It wouldn't be going on at all.

After she had done the power-circle exercise, she concluded that she felt comfortable with the inequality she had depicted there but that it was still "sad," sad for the individuals and "sad for the organization if there are this many people like *this* [on the edge of the circle]. Most of *these* [center] people are there because they started putting in an effort in the organization."

Dave, whose "chewing asses" on the Van had led to considerable criticism for "megalomania," had a response like Kaye's, except that after finishing the power-ranking exercise he told me that he felt decidedly un-comfortable with the inequalities he had just portrayed. He agonized that "everybody should be in the center!" and like Kaye, tended to blame those with less power: "Perhaps it's me having too high expecta-tions of these other people. I don't think they're doing as much work as the rest of us."[10] With a flair for the dramatic, Dave began to explain what the power circle he had created meant and what it should mean:

> DAVE: Some people [in the center] are people working really hard and hoping that the rest of the people will fall into the center too, or these [center] people will be allowed to spread out. Spread out with those other people. In one ring. All doing the same thing. Because we're a community; it's supposed to have some common—
> JM: Do you wish they all were in one ring?
> DAVE: Yeah. I think there should be an equal distribution of power and commitment. And all those other things.
> JM: How would that make you feel, if they were?
> DAVE: *Great!* I could—ah, *whew*—it would be great. I wouldn't have to worry about what other people are doing. I wouldn't have to get pissed off at other people. (laugh) I wouldn't have to know; it just happens. I wouldn't have to get blown out. I wouldn't have to be so critical. Things like that.

But even more important than that is just to be unified. To be able to share in something that's a whole.[11]

He looked wistfully at the power circle: "I guess I wish that everybody was in the middle."

Kaye and Dave wanted power but felt ambivalent about this side of themselves, an ambivalence reinforced by Helpline's egalitarian norms. In order to explain the power they had actually acquired, they blamed the less powerful for personality deficiencies that made their own exercise of power necessary. But by injecting tensions from their own ambivalence into their relations with their less-powerful colleagues and by explaining differences in power as deriving primarily from a willingness to take responsibility rather than from the nature of one's job, seniority, centrality, or other structural factors, they exacerbated the bad feelings between themselves and those with less power.

The Facilitators

The staff with more than average power in this egalitarian organization had to discover some way of excusing their extra power to themselves. The "power-hungry" reacted by rejecting as unrealistic those parts of the ideology that required equality of verbal facility, personality, strength of ego, friends, energy, skill, or desire to work. They put it to themselves that they did not have to apologize for their desire for power and looked for opportunities in the interview to make this clear to me. The "ambivalent" liked power but did not like liking it, blamed the less powerful, and tortured themselves on the subject. The "facilitators" envisioned their power as at the service of the community, felt uncomfortable at the suggestion that power might have personal rewards, stressed the importance of the position rather than the individual who filled it, and even explicitly disassociated their persons from their positions. These were not random choices of strategies. Those who took up the different roles had personalities congruent with their choice.

Of the eight most powerful people at Helpline, measured by the power scores, four portrayed their positions only as ways of advancing the good of the community. Tom, the cooordinator, who had the highest power score in the organization, said of his role as chair on the budget-cutting Community Day, "What I should have been doing if I had been doing my job right on that day was to help create a climate in which good things could happen."[12]

The facilitators generally aroused no ill will within the community. As Tom himself pointed out:

I haven't experienced any anger toward me with a couple of really small exceptions in all the time I've been here. That's one of the reasons that I got to be the director—because everybody sort of felt okay about me. I don't know if that's a wonderful trait to cultivate, but. . . .

Others also volunteered about Tom that "he's acceptable to everybody." One explicitly contrasted Tom's style with Frank's:

Frank and Bruce . . . have their own ideas, and they are trying to bring them forth. But Tom, and oftentimes Bruce too, more set out what is possible, and the realities, and ask people to make their own decisions. . . .

As Nate, whom I have lumped with the "power-hungry," laughingly portrayed Helpline's dilemma:

Like if they could have a coordinator's position without any human being in it, it would be the ideal situation! So what it takes in general for people to be into that [coordinator job] is a kind of amorphousness. Because if they are etched too deeply, if their lines are too broad. . . .

He neglected to finish the sentence, leaving the unmistakable impression that such a job would be impossible for him.

There is something to this analysis. In their interviews, the four powerful facilitators used language noticeably more bland than either the three "power-hungry" men or Kaye, the ambivalent woman. They used fewer exclamations and "I"s.[13] The facilitators spoke faciliteze. It was not jargon, but generalities. The others threw vivid words at me, conjured up pictures, unleashed past emotions, made me laugh, made me like them and dislike them.

Nonetheless, Nate's portrait is exaggeration. The coordinator, Tom, took a strong, principled, and effective stand on both the Air Force contract and the office manager decisions. On the office manager job, he reported:

I had *no doubt* where I stood there, that we shouldn't have an office manager. . . . So I didn't make any effort at all to play my usual "director" role to try to keep things together; I was just pissed at people who didn't see what Deborah and Paula [who brought the matter up] were talking about.

Nor was Tom free from the desire for power. He told me:

There is a part of me that wants to be influential. I want to be in a position where I have some [read "more than average"] say in the future of the organization.

I feel both good and bad about that. I decided that I wanted to have an impact on things, and I have. I feel bad about the fact that I feel that I have to "make my mark" in order to establish the fact that I am a real person.

Yet by and large, Tom avoided exercising personal power, and when he did, he did not seem to glory in it. Unlike the "power-hungry," he saw power as accruing to particular positions rather than to people and saw the positions themselves as allocated according to differences in tastes, not differences in skill:

A lot of administrative chores are going to be taken over by a small number of people for a lot of reasons—maybe the administrators enjoy doing that sort of work, or service people, given the option . . . would rather not do that work.[14]

He worried that this was "natural, but unfortunate," and would like to have spread the responsibility even further:

Being in touch with what it means for the organization to survive is something that everyone ought to deal with, and that involves writing proposals, et cetera. Everyone ought to be involved as much as possible.

He concluded that "The best thing that I did in my job was to lessen the influence of the job, really. It's paradoxical—I used my influence in order to reduce the influence of the job."[15]

All four facilitators found ways of disassociating themselves from their powerful roles. Tom, the coordinator, told me, "I know that I don't want to be an administrator. I know that I have some skills that way, but it's not really what I'm about, I think." Bruce, the treasurer mused, "Treasurer of this organization?—that's not me! Treasurer!" Pamela, a quiet, savvy woman with a lot of determination, represented Helpline's largest service group, the Shelter, at the CPC. The job put her among the eight ranked most powerful, but when I asked if some people's willingness to do administrative work might create an "imbalance of power," she shrugged:

No. I mean we all have shit jobs. I mean if I go to the CPC, the decisions there affect us [the Shelter] a little bit, but it's not really a problem.

Amy did referrals on the Switchboard and ranked seventh highest in the power scores at Helpline. Yet she praised Helpline's democracy as someone of lower status might, saying, "I know that I'll be listened to, that I'm as important as anyone else here."[16] Amy and Pamela hardly ever mentioned their own actions in decisions. Instead, they described what "the Switchboard" and "the Shelter" had done. I asked Pamela, for example, which people had been most influential in the professor's salary decision. I knew that she had been among the two or three people at the CPC who delayed the decision by refusing to go along, and she had then joined the small committee that met with the professor and recommended the eventual compromise. Almost everyone else had responded to this question on influential "people" by naming specific individuals. Pamela just answered, "I think the Switchboard and the Shelter were very influential."

Pamela and Amy may have chosen a facilitator role because of women's tendency, as Amy put it, to "generally go for the influence rather than the title" and to see the exercise of power itself as evil. "I wouldn't be interested in those traditional roles of power," Amy declared, "because that would set up terrible conflicts for me, in terms of just my own moral principles."

For both men and women, however, the adoption of the facilitator role may also come from an egalitarian childhood or from a secure, upper-middle-class background. When I asked Amy why she felt comfortable with the inequalities she had just portrayed in her power-circle exercise, she answered for herself and the rest of Helpline:

Well, I think we're a fairly homogeneous group—white, upper-middle class, fairly well educated—[and] we've all probably been brought up believing that we all have a certain amount of power of our own. . . . We basically feel powerful.

This statement did not describe everyone at Helpline, but it suited the four powerful facilitators perfectly. Because they had gravitated to their positions of power easily, without competing actively for the job and without arousing antagonism, they underestimated the extent of their power even to themselves.

Escape from Power

When, as at Helpline, the more powerful act as unofficial representatives of the rest, the members of the community who are not particularly interested in power must exercise some power themselves in order to maintain accountability. The less powerful must try to restrain the more powerful when their interests begin to diverge.

Most of Helpline's staff could enter into a power struggle if it were necessary, but for two or three of the least powerful 20 percent at Help-line, such a struggle would be close to impossible. One of the women in this group, for example, insisted over and over that she found wanting power incomprehensible:

I don't have much sense of wanting power, the sense of wanting power at all. It's something I really don't understand. . . .

Power—it's really a strange concept to me. I don't understand why anyone would want it! (laugh) The concept of having power over other people's lives is something that I just don't understand. I don't understand why anyone would want to do it. . . .

I can't imagine myself ever having that kind of power, ever wanting to have that kind of power. I don't operate on that level. I can't understand the feelings that a person would have who wanted that. I know that people do, but it's something that's really foreign to me!

Her repetition and insistence suggest some inner turmoil. But whatever its source, an inability to comprehend why others act the way they do makes it difficult to monitor their behavior accurately or to understand to what extent their interests coincide with one's own.

Certain members of Helpline could not be called upon when a crisis touched on matters of power, whether the crisis was a major one like replacing a coordinator or a minor one like deciding a case of special need in the DPW. Leslie told me, "I personally can't handle power," and Danny said that he avoided it partly because of "things that I feel about my attaining power and what may happen to me as a result of it." While these two were not among the eight ranked least powerful, their feelings about power still made it hard for them, when interests began to conflict, to defend their own interests without anxiety.

Ruth, one of the least powerful 20 percent, had the strongest negative reactions. She did not do the power-circle exercise because "I could see that certain people would get off on that, and that's what bothers me. Like someone saying, 'Oh, I have a very clear picture of who has power here!'" Like most of the people at Helpline, Ruth did not like "power politics": "I'm turned off by it. It just doesn't interest me. It has nothing to do with the kinds of things I'm into." Unlike most of the others, how-ever, her revulsion against anything to do with power almost incapaci-tated her. When I asked her what she would do if she had to try to change the policy direction of the Van, on which she worked, she answered:

I wouldn't. I wouldn't enjoy it. 'Cause it starts getting into the power thing. I would do it as long as it was necessary. (laugh) But not beyond that because I just don't like that.

That's what happened [in an incident in which she tried to persevere against one of the Van's men's "filibustering"] because I couldn't stand that role. I was just overwhelmed by it. I felt ashamed of myself for as far as I went.

'Cause I think it's a horrible thing to do, to deal with people like that. Aggressive.

Not only could she hardly act in situations she saw as touching on power; she also could hardly bear to think about them:

> JM: What does the word "power" conjure up to you?
> RUTH: The strutting rooster! (laugh) It's like this *empty,* horrible thing to me! . . .
> JM: What do you think about wanting to be director?
> RUTH: Yuk!
> JM: It really turns you off?
> RUTH: Yeah. I don't want anything to do with that. I don't want to *know* about it!

Later, commenting on the coordinator, whom she knew well, she said, "Like he'll say, 'Oh, I know I can influence this or that,' and it sort of makes me sick to my stomach!"

Ruth's language is extreme. It suggests an inner battle against impulses she fears rather than concern with other people's possible misuse of power. Her reaction made it close to impossible for her to speak up in Van meetings or to act independently in her work when she encountered more than the mildest, most rational opposition to her will. When she interpreted her own perspective as moral and the perspective of those interested in power as too deeply disgusting to contemplate, she compounded the problem, for this interpretation often made understanding as well as action impossible.

Such reactions reflect, in exaggerated form, suspicions of the desire for power that are widespread in democracies near the unitary end of the spectrum. In small towns like Selby, candidates for office are expected to seem reluctant to take the job.[17] In hunter-gatherer bands and certain American Indian tribes, "the important element is . . . that the individual should not appear to *want to be a leader. . . .*"[18] Plato explained in *The Republic* that "the city in which those who are to rule are least eager to hold office must needs be best administered and most free from dissension."[19]

Someone who desires power for its own sake may flaunt that power after achieving it, thus upsetting the previous equality of status. But citizens of unitary polities distrust an overt desire for power primarily because it detracts from total dedication to the common good. Because more homogeneous societies have less structural differentiation to create conflicting interests, citizens are more likely to explain conflict in terms of will or personality. Particularly when there are no formal mechanisms of accountability, citizens are always on the watch for signs of corruption in the wills and personalities of their more powerful neighbors. By focusing on the corruption of personality as the single source of differing interests, such citizens often overlook more structural sources like social class, the division of labor,[20] longevity, and centrality within the organization.

In an adversary democracy, on the other hand, the motives of the more powerful are supposed to be irrelevant. In theory, the system will work on self-interest alone. Representatives, with more power than other citizens, are kept accountable to their constituencies because they must compete for votes in the political marketplace, not because they are personally dedicated to the common good. The adversary machinery is indifferent to the nature of the passion that drives a politician to want to accumulate votes; indeed, a "lust" for power might well breed a more competitive candidate.

Helpline, being neither a pure unitary nor a pure adversary democracy, relied on both unitary and adversary mechanisms to keep the small inequalities in power among its members from producing policy outcomes inimical to the majority of the staff. The high degree of genuine common interest in the group meant that most of the time the more powerful staff acted in the interests of the less powerful. At the same time, when interests came in conflict, the less powerful exercised considerable control over their informal representatives.

The Helpline staff who most liked power appeared to have values very similar to those of everyone else. The only exception, although a significant one, was that the staff who enjoyed power were not as likely as others to consider "equality of political power in internal decisions" a crucial value for the organization.[21] This difference of opinion may or may not indicate a difference in interest. The more powerful had thought more carefully about power than had the less powerful. They may thus simply have been more aware that power could not easily be more equally distributed in the organization. Let us assume, however, that those who most enjoyed power also wanted to increase the degree of inequality in the organization and that those who enjoyed power less had an interest in decreasing inequality. On issues related to inequalities of power, then, those groups would have conflicting interests and would have to move from the unitary to the adversary mode. On no other issue did the staff who most liked power reveal to me, either in the questionnaire or in the interview, a set of concerns that differed from those of the other Helpline staff.

Still, Helpline was not a perfect unitary democracy. Interests on occasion did diverge. In those moments, the staff who enjoyed the exercise of power may have had an extra impetus to advance their own interests at the expense of others', for along with benefiting from the dominance of their interests they enjoyed the very process of winning. In these moments, Helpline worked much like an adversary democracy. The more powerful functioned as representatives who were, in effect, accountable and subject to recall. The less powerful voted with their energies: when they perceived deviations from the policies they would like to see pursued, they would simply be uncooperative. Frank, for example, had concluded:

> One person can't do it by himself. You have to be able to get people to do things. I guess I spent the last couple of years learning to exercise power in the most nonoffensive manner. I mean, that's the way it works.

The constant face-to-face contact between the more and the less powerful at Helpline also served to make it likely that those with more power would effectively represent the interests of the others. These representatives did not separate themselves from their constituents for long or come to care more about one another's opinions than about the opinions of those who elected them. Indeed, at Helpline the more powerful did not even form an interconnected friendship group. The "significant others" they saw day to day and whose respect they wanted to keep were the less centrally powerful members of Helpline, those engaged in the tasks of counseling. The more powerful thus depended on the approval of the others, not only to get the work done, but for their own self-esteem and comfort in what they were doing. As Frank put it, after he had succumbed to criticism of his methods:

> I did a very good job for about six months, from September to January. I think I did a really effective job. Things ran on time, and pretty much through sheer personality I was able to force the thing to work.
> And so people raised the issue again of "Look, like you're really dictating the situation. We should go back to the old process."
> And it's hard for you to argue with that. And I didn't like it. I felt really badly. I sulked for about a week and realized that I had to do that. I didn't have to, but I had to.

Helpline's mixture of unitary trust and adversary watchfulness kept the actions of the more powerful congruent with the interests of everyone else in the organization. The unitary method worked because the more powerful had, by and large, the same interests as the others. The adversary method worked because the difference in power between the most and the least powerful was not great and because face-to-face contact made the sanctions the others could impose on the more powerful immediate and effective.

IV

Conclusion

Chapter 17

Equality

SINCE few of us will live in a community governed by a town meeting or will work in a small workplace that in any way resembles Helpline, we may ask what relevance the experiences reported here have for us. The answer is that these experiences serve as prisms—to reflect, separately and more distinctly than ordinary life, the internal structure of our ideals. In these atypical cases, people are forced to confront the ideals of democracy in a way that most of us never have to do. The town meeting's position, halfway between unitary and adversary democracy, obliged its citizens to piece together a political fabric out of two contradictory ideals. In the workplace, the confrontation was more conscious; the extraordinary efforts of the members to put their democratic ideals into practice had the effect of casting into relief the nature of the ideals themselves.

Most of us will go to some lengths to avoid living in states of emotional or philosophic tension. If our ideals conflict with the ways we feel we must act, or if one of our ideals clashes with another, we unconsciously modify the ideals or find ways to put the conflict out of our minds. Our compromised lives thus ensure cloudy understandings of the ideals we profess. In extraordinary circumstances, however, we may for one reason or another find ourselves committed to the uncompromising pursuit of an ideal. The clarification of our ideals that these experiences provoke has important—sometimes radical—implications for the theory and practice of democracy. This chapter illustrates the general argument by using Helpline as a touchstone for analyzing one of the central ideals of democratic theory, political equality.

What Happened at Helpline

Helpline posed a fundamental paradox. Its staff was committed to political equality. Helpline's numbers had spent seven years developing a decision-making process that satisfied their egalitarian convictions. As I noted earlier, 89 percent said that they thought "equality of political power in internal decisions" was "very crucial" or "fairly crucial" to making the service group what they wanted it to be, and they paid for this conviction by spending an average of seven hours a week at meetings. Many of Helpline's formal procedures (like breaking down into small discussion groups at some point every Community Day) and informal norms (like urging members to take advantage of free training in sensitivity to group process) had been developed with an eye toward eliminating patterns that usually maintain political inequality.

Nonetheless, as we have seen, Helpline did not achieve complete political equality. The inequalities that remained were also related to factors like class that have traditionally been salient to egalitarian re-formers. The paradox is that in spite of their strong commitment to equality the Helpline staff remained undisturbed by the inequalities they perceived. After each staff member had ranked the entire staff in the power-circle exercise, I asked if he or she felt comfortable or uncomfort-able with the inequality just portrayed. Eighty-five percent of those who did the exercise (72 percent of the total) said that they felt comfortable with that inequality.

Such a response might mean that these professed egalitarians were either morally or intellectually obtuse. Yet most of them had given some thought to the problem and in other respects seemed neither stupid nor insensitive.

Such a response might also mean that the inequalities were so small that the staff was willing to tolerate them in order not to have to pay the price required to eliminate them altogether. Yet these people did not talk or act as if they were simply putting up with inequality in order to attain other goals. They talked and acted as if they actually felt com-fortable with the inequalities, finding them inoffensive.

Some members dealt with the inequality they had depicted by suggest-ing that it obscured a more basic kind of political equality—the equal opportunity that each member had to exercise equal power. All the staff "could" have equal power "if they wanted to." This formulation implies that the barriers to participation were equal for each member or that, if all members had competing interests, they all would have an equal chance to move the organization in the direction of their preferences. However, given equal effort, barriers to participation were not in fact equal. But because the inequalities were relatively small, the least powerful person in the organization probably could, with unusual effort, exercise as much power as the most powerful habitually did. This fact allowed some members to convince themselves that everyone in the organization had equal "potential" power. These people were, I think, simply fooling themselves.

But neither self-deception, obtuseness, nor the willingness to accept some inequality as a necessary cost of procuring other values explains the ease with which most staff members accepted inequalities in their organization. As they talked with me, they suggested other reasons why the inequalities in power they had just depicted were genuinely irrelevant to their major concerns. The staff at Helpline did not worry greatly about unequal power leading to unequal protection of interests because they felt that on most matters those with more power had the same interests as those with less. In explaining why they felt comfortable placing others close to the center of power and themselves not so close, the less powerful told me, "I have a lot of trust for the people in the center"; "They are really good and dedicated people, with a lot of goodwill"; "I'm like everyone that's close to the center; I trust them"; and "If we weren't so homogeneous, it might be a bigger issue than it is."[1] Behind the ideas of "trust" and being "like" lay the assumption that at Helpline common interests eliminated the need for completely equal power.

In thinking about these responses, I realized that for the Helpline staff equal power was a means to other ends. Furthermore, means other than equal power sometimes promoted those ends more effectively or at less cost. Thus, there was no necessary conflict between Helpline's egalitarianism and its willingness to live with certain kinds of political inequality. In order to see why this is so, however, we must review the arguments for political equality.

Why Do We Need Equal Power?

Traditional arguments for equal power can be reduced to these three:

1. *Equal protection of interests.* When interests conflict irreconcilably, the only equitable way to make a decision is to weight each individual's interests equally, choosing that course which accumulates the most

235

weight. A vote, for example, derives its legitimacy from the equal weight of every individual in the outcome, but unless a vote represents equal power, voting does not protect everyone's interests equally.

2. *Equal respect.* Equal power helps create, maintain, and symbolize equality of respect, dignity, or status.

3. *Personal growth.* Equal power encourages universal participation in public affairs. Such participation is necessary for personal development, to make one fully human, broad in outlook, and conscious of one's own interests.

In all three cases, equal power is a means to some other end. Each of these ends can sometimes be achieved by other means. None necessarily requires complete equality of power.

1. A polity in which everyone had common interests would not require equal power to protect everyone's interests equally.

2. A polity in which respect derived from sources other than personal power would not require equal power to maintain equal respect.

3. A polity in which each member was taking as much responsibility and handling as much conflict as he or she could manage would not produce more personal growth by distributing power more equally.

The conditions in which equal power is unnecessary are thus: (1) common interests; (2) at least partial separation of respect from power; and (3) a surfeit of opportunities for the exercise of responsibility and participation in conflict. No polity can meet these three conditions fully. The more these conditions hold, however, the less important it becomes to reduce inequalities of power.

Consider once again, the nine old men on the U.S. Supreme Court. This analysis suggests that their power is most acceptable when the nation comes closest to having a genuine long-run common interest (as one might argue that it did in *Brown v. Board of Education*, the 1954 school desegregation case), when the Justices are least likely to acquire a status that sets them fundamentally apart from other citizens, and when the Court's role is least likely to allow citizens to escape responsibility for making their own decisions on matters of justice and conflicting ideals.

Conceiving political equality as a means to the three ends of equal protection of interests, equal respect, and personal growth thus allows us to move beyond the simple equation of democracy with equal power and the consequent condemnation of all political inequality. Instead, it forces us to ask more fundamental questions:

1. How frequently do interests conflict? When they do, to what extent is every citizen's interest represented equally? To the extent that individual

members have similar interests in a collective decision, they do not need to protect their own interests against those of others. However, when interests often conflict or when individuals do not have equal power in these conflicts, a polity whose goal is the equal protection of interests must redistribute power—by instituting referenda, for example, or by making representatives more fully accountable.

2. Does equal respect pervade the polity? If not, does respect or status derive from power? Often, when respect or status is unequal, a polity can generate more equality by bringing citizens together in situations where their resources are more equal or the usual inequalities are reversed. However, when unequal respect derives in large part from unequal power, a polity whose goal is equal status must redistribute power.

3. Would more equal power in the polity make the members grow in responsibility, breadth of view, and consciousness of interests? Often when some members seem to atrophy through limited responsibility, a polity can break this pattern by introducing systems that require greater individual political responsibility but that do not effect the central power structure. However, when such growth requires more equal participation in central decisions, a polity whose goal is a responsible, conscious citizenry must redistribute power.

The rest of this chapter will examine the three rationales for equal power in more detail.

Equal Protection of Interests

The protection of interests has served as the most important rationale for political equality since the seventeenth century. As I noted earlier, the Levellers argued for universal and equal manhood suffrage in part on the grounds that if poor men did not have equal votes the rich could "crush them."[2] Even John Locke, who did not advocate equality of power, implied that giving up one's right to defend one's rightful interests by force in the state of nature entitled one to a "fair and equal Representative" in civil society.[3] This argument, that an equal vote is necessary to protect interests equally, is easily extended to encompass demands for equal power. The resolution of conflict by majority rule seeks to give each citizen equal power at the moment of voting. If this is necessary, it must also be necessary for each citizen to have equal power at other stages of a decision-making process.

One obvious exception to this general rule is the case where individuals do not know their interests as clearly as someone else does. We habitually make this assumption, for example, about children and about the mentally ill. Another exception is when individuals know their interests but believe that someone else can protect those interests better than they can. Certain forms of representation fit this description. But as long as interests conflict, it is virtually impossible to ensure that one individual will protect another's as assiduously as his or her own. Unequal power is therefore compatible with equal protection only when two or more individuals have truly common interests. This holds regardless of whether we consider parents exercising power in behalf of their children, representatives exercising power in behalf of their constituents, or one member of a collective exercising power in behalf of another.

Plato, Aristotle, Rousseau, Hegel, and possibly Marx all seem to have believed that a large proportion of political relationships could and should take place in the unitary context of common interests.[4] Writers in the adversary tradition usually argue that such situations are impossible;[5] they may even *define* politics as conflict, thereby eliminating situations involving common interests from the political arena.[6] Yet while no two individuals' interests can be identical at every point both as to means and as to ends, all members of a small, voluntary polity may consistently have very similar interests on the issues confronting that polity. Our preoccupation with national political systems that emphasize, legitimate, and even glorify conflict has partially blinded us to this possibility.

Moments of similar interest occurred with some frequency at Helpline. Even the Air Force contract decision, which threw Helpline into turmoil for two weeks, was marked by a strong perception of common interests. Those two weeks of discussion and position papers finally produced a consensus not to help in any service sponsored by the military. In the process, some staff members were more able than others to move the organization in the direction they wanted it to go. The two men who wrote the decisive position paper were able to call on resources that others did not have—specialized information, experience in political organizing, writing skills, and, in the case of one of them, a history of having often helped the group find good solutions. As a consequence, these two men probably exercised more power than anyone else on this issue.

As I emphasized earlier, it is impossible to determine with certainty the true interests of all the staff members in this decision. The three staff members whose positions were later cut in order to meet a reduced budget presumably had a greater material interest than others in taking the contract. Yet only one of these three originally favored taking the contract, and she later changed her mind. The other two argued against

the contract from the beginning. If these three had had perfect information, I believe they would still have chosen to make the good of the whole
their own, interpret that good this way, and reject the contract. But their
true interests might have been other, and greater participation on their
part could have led them to recognize this fact.

In the same way, Helpline's working-class staff might have benefited
from a contract that served primarily working-class clients. Again, not one
of them felt this way. It was Frank, whose background was farming and
"lower-middle class," who brought up the class issue at the CPC. But if
the working-class staff had misunderstood their interests, greater power
could have directed them to a clearer understanding.

These two groups, then, might have had interests in this decision that
differed from the interests of the other staff. But if we assume for a
moment that all of these people correctly perceived their real interest as
belonging to an organization they thought acted rightly and that their
final convictions as to what was right in fact represented their enlightened
preferences, then the interests of those who exercised least power in the
organization—the working-class members, those most recently hired, the
shiest, and those most uncomfortable with power—were protected adequately by the most powerful. They would all then have had a common
interest in this decision, and when the less-powerful staff members said
that they felt comfortable with the inequalities in the power-circle
exercise because they could "trust" those in the center of power, they
would have been right.[7]

One problem with blithely forsaking political equality on the grounds
of similarity of interest is that power acquired in one decision inevitably
carries over to another. If one or two people consistently manage to get
the organization to do what they want, this inequality may not be
relevant when interests are similar, but it becomes relevant as soon as
interests diverge, which they are bound to do at some point. The community's reliance on these people then gives them even greater power
when interests diverge. Even if political equality is irrelevant over
long stretches, this argument runs, it must still be maintained against
the day when it will become essential. On an individual level, even
when two people assess their interests as identical, not only at present,
but for the foreseeable future, they may want to feel free to change in
unpredictable ways. When they do so, their interests may well begin to
diverge, and they will want to hedge against that eventuality by maintaining equal power between them.

This argument acquires additional force when having different amounts of power itself gives individuals different interests. In Helpline, for example, those who acquired more power in the central organization might for that very reason have wanted to keep the organization going in its existing form. If the question had then arisen of whether Helpline should split into autonomous separate groups or remain as one, this issue could have placed the interests of the more and less powerful in conflict.

The same argument suggests that unequal power leads to conflicting interests between representatives and their constituents. Once representatives are cut off from daily face-to-face interaction with their constituents and enter into face-to-face interaction with other legislators, they inevitably develop different interests from their constituents. They acquire a greater stake in maintaining the system that has given them power and their own position in that system. They develop personal friendships and enmities with other legislators that affect their behavior independent of their constituents' interests. They also become irrationally attached to bills they have worked on, solutions they have invented, even forms of organization they helped devise, regardless of how their constituents feel about these matters.[8]

On the basis of such arguments, a single-minded egalitarian might reject any political inequality as a preventive measure, even in moments of truly common interest. Most people, however, regard the equal protection of interests as only one objective among many. If the costs of further reductions in political inequality are likely to be high, they will want to weigh them against the likely benefits. My argument suggests that egalitarians should order situations along a spectrum ranging from complete identity of interest to complete conflict and should be willing to pay more to get equal power as interests diverge. Applying this analysis to Helpline suggests, for instance, that the organization should have paid particular attention to inequalities based on social class and geographical proximity, since the working-class members and the most distant service groups were especially likely to have interests that differed significantly from those of the more powerful staff.

Applying this same analysis to the nation-state suggests that democrats should be especially concerned with political inequalities between groups that have a long history of conflict, such as the rich and the poor; ethnic, religious, or linguistic groups; or regions of the country.

Equal Respect

In unitary communities, where interests are largely the same, the most important reason for trying to give the members equal power is to help institute or maintain equality of respect. This was true in the early lives of most small "participatory democracies" with which I came in contact. In one women's group in New York, each member took twelve disks as a meeting began, having to spend one each time she spoke. Most participatory collectives either asked a different person to chair each meeting or used a "rotating chair," by which each participant after speaking called on the next, thus avoiding the domination of one chairperson. To keep the media from making a "star" of any individual, no one in the women's movement gave a speech or went on television alone, and women refused to pose individually for cover photographs for *Time* and *Life*. In Vietnam Summer, a radical political group active in 1967, the staff tried to spread power equally in meetings:

> Individuals who were not informed about the issues were sometimes included in policy-making discussions; while the "natural" leaders with the greatest experience, the best ideas, and the surest grasp of the facts sometimes deliberately refrained from voicing their opinions lest they appear to dominate.[9]

These groups were all willing to pay an extraordinary price at least in part to keep from developing distinctions in status that would erode the bonds of friendship within the group.

Even institutions with no strong ideological commitment to equality may institute political equality as a mark of equal respect. This is the main reason an academic department extends the vote to its junior faculty. The vote may, of course, give junior faculty a weapon to protect their interests. And when interests are identical, it gives them an incentive to add their energies to the pursuit of the right decision. Participation may also help junior faculty to develop largeness of view by taking responsibility, or to understand their interests by participating in conflict. But while all these arguments support extending the franchise, they are not usually decisive. Both the junior faculty, who desire the vote, and the senior faculty, who wish to extend it, understand that by instituting equal votes the department makes a symbolic statement that its junior members have full and equal citizenship in the department. To the extent that the vote is unequally weighted, or to the extent that it is a sham because the context is coercive or key decisions are not made by voting, that symbolic statement has not been made.

These considerations are not wholly divorced from the "protection-of-interests" tradition. An equal vote indicates both that one's interests are entitled to be counted equally and that one is recognized as an adequate defender of those interests. But in a community where most important interests converge, the equal vote primarily symbolizes equality of respect. It indicates that the decision makers have admitted one to their deliberations as an equal. By asserting the fundamentally equal worth of each individual, political equality here lays the necessary basis for the politics of friendship.

Formal arrangements for sharing power equally, like the equal vote, create the expectation of equal status. They also reinforce or maintain equal status when it already exists. Conversely, when power is a source of status, allowing one person more power than another can itself bestow higher status on the more powerful. Any blanket exclusion from power of whole categories of persons like blacks or women furthers the process by which they are perceived as inferior, while including them begins or furthers the process of considering them equal.

But assuming that the goal of equal respect is good, political equality is still not the only, or best, means to this end. At Helpline, for example, standards of respect and status were largely independent of the distribution of power. Although the staff might end up thinking that one member was better at one job and another at another, they developed a roughly equal respect for one another's abilities. This was because, in the first place, the staff placed a high value on helping people directly, so they gave most respect to individuals who were good at helping others. When members took administrative positions that resulted in their acquiring more power, their greater power had little effect on Helpline's status system. In this regard, Helpline was like many academic departments, where respect depends on intellectual performance, not on the power the department's chair can wield in internal politics. In the second place, members of Helpline were able to hire fellow workers whom they generally respected. A pool of highly qualified applicants was attracted by the interesting, useful work among congenial peers, and because the material incentives for the work were low, those who found themselves without the respect of their colleagues usually left.

When roughly equal respect is not achieved by selection, a unitary organization has three choices. First, it can redistribute the personal characteristics that affect status (the "supply") by training those with low status characteristics or by urging those with high status characteristics to suppress them. Second, it can change the value the group places on certain characteristics (the "demand"). Third, it can try to minimize the consequences of unequal status ("manipulate prices"). Each of these routes has limitations. Some characteristics are hard to redistribute or should not be redistributed; some norms are hard to manipulate or should not be manipulated; some consequences of inequality are hard to stamp out or should not be stamped out.[10]

Nonetheless, an organization can reduce some of the sources of unequal status by training its members in relevant skills. It can provide multiple sources of status or reduce the importance of any one source. It can also try to ensure that the sources of status do not correlate highly one with another. It can downplay the importance of status distinctions generally, making much of the ways in which members of the community are equal. These efforts can be quite successful. Experience both at Helpline and in the Israeli kibbutzim suggests that decreasing the number and size of status inequalities does not necessarily lead to the magnification of trivial differences. Nor does decreasing material incentives necessarily create a greater emphasis on status inequalities as incentives.[11] Concern for status seemed no greater, and in some ways much less, in Helpline than in hierarchical organizations that had greater status differences and that reinforced their nonmaterial incentives with material ones.

Helpline employed all of these means for reducing the sources of unequal status. Everyone was trained for a position of responsibility; there were almost as many ways of being valuable to the group as there were individual members; those who acquired status through learning administration were not able to acquire it through developing their skills in therapy; and the group engaged in continued and effective reminders of how meaningless were traditional marks of status like professional degrees. (One piece of group lore was that a study exists, to which no one could give me a citation, showing that years of training as a therapist are negatively correlated with ability to produce measurable benefits for clients.)

Groups like Helpline can also deliberately foster emotional identification by stressing a shared past. They can consciously create a perception of mutual likeness by harnessing the known effects of experiences like working together under stress, a common "transcendant" experience, or self-revelation in consciousness-raising sessions and encounter groups. In political collectives, a sense of experimentation, of difference from the outside world, and even of struggle against that world often reinforces the members' points of common identity. In all small groups, small size allows an intense interaction that soon becomes a meaningful common history. Each of these mechanisms produces an experience of identification that is then a firm basis for equal respect.

These means for reducing status inequalities can be more effective than insisting on complete political equality, for the role of political equality in producing or symbolizing equal respect depends on the source of status in a society. To the extent that status derives from other sources, equal power becomes irrelevant to the pursuit of equal respect.

"Political Education," or "Individual Development"

No one in Helpline ever suggested that political participation had educative value, much less that equal power was essential to learning anything. They did not think of political participation or working on the central administration as an educational experience, or at least not as one that they desired. Most of them would rather have gained skills in therapy than in administration, partly because therapy was more interesting to them and partly because it had higher status in the organization. Nonetheless, the writers who inspired the politically egalitarian vision of the New Left and who provided its philosophical justification have, by and large, devoted their time to showing that we should pursue political equality because of what might loosely be termed its "educative" effects.

The content of this "education" varies from writer to writer. Arnold Kaufman argued that the effects of participation would be generally therapeutic, improving the participants' powers of "thought, feeling and action."[12] The Port Huron Statement, in 1962, developed the theme that participation would bring people "out of isolation and into community" and would encourage "independence, a respect for others, a sense of dignity and a willingness to accept social responsibility."[13] Carole Pateman wrote that the virtue to be developed was "political efficacy."[14] More recently, Peter Bachrach has argued that the educational effect of participation lies not in coming to value others' interests over one's own private interests, as J. S. Mill seemed to suggest, but in coming to see one's private interests more clearly.[15]

Earlier democratic theorists in this tradition stressed the egalitarian context of participation rather than political equality per se. Pateman finds in both Rousseau and G. D. H. Cole the argument that the equal distribution of power will produce an enlightened, responsible, and public-minded citizenry.[16] Yet neither Rousseau nor Cole gave great attention to equality of power; for their polities, widespread participation, backed up by relatively egalitarian status and economic systems, sufficed.

Nor, as Pateman herself points out, did J. S. Mill desire more than widespread participation. Mill's *Representative Government* argues that giving the vote to more people would extend the educational advantages of responsible citizenship, producing in more people a "largeness" of sentiment, defined as a concern for interests other than one's own. Yet Mill also explicitly stated that the educational effects of participation flow from "a" voice in the political process, not an "equal" voice. And he suggested as well that it is not so much the vote, equally weighted or not, that transforms the characters of the citizenry, as the widespread distribution of small official responsibilities. The extent to which other people depend on one's decision is more forcefully brought home in a small office like jury duty than in the casting of a ballot.[17] Mill seems to have concluded that individual growth depends on taking as much responsibility as one needs or can handle at a given moment, not on being given a quantitatively equal dollop of power all the time.

Mill's view strikes me as correct. While educative goals are clearly important and usually neglected, there is no compelling reason to suppose that complete political equality is the appropriate means to such goals. Indeed, few philosophical advocates of more participation in the political process argue for perfectly equal participation, much less for perfectly equal power.[18] Education, like medical care, is a realm in which one benefits from getting what one needs rather than some mathematical allocation. Particularly if resources are scarce, mathematical equality seems an unproductive way to distribute the means of human development.

Almost everyone at Helpline, for example, already had as much responsibility as he or she could stand. Pressing for an even greater equality of power in the organization would not have been likely to increase the members' largeness of view; their powers of thought, feeling, and action; their communal feelings, independence, respect for others; or their willingness to accept responsibility.

On the national level, concentration on increasing responsibility, efficacy, and self-awareness might lead in the opposite direction from a stress on political equality per se. A guideline like "maximum feasible participation" did not necessarily increase political equality in America. It may well have only substituted new local elites for old. But the conflict it generated seems to have spread political experience among both old and new elites, as well as among the people who struggled against them. In the same way, giving local governments real powers might exacerbate inequality. It might give local elites greater power compared to others in their communities, discourage universalism, and reinforce policies that discriminate against both minorities and the poor. It might also be inefficient. But it would increase opportunities to take public responsibility. Finally, many forms of workers' stockownership, job enrichment, and "pseudoparticipation" do not do anything to equalize power, but they seem to give more workers a stake in their work, the experience of responsibility, and training in making collective decisions.

Arguments that political education and the development of citizens' faculties require full political equality often start with a commitment to equality as a means and then try to invent an end that would justify it. Looking at the ends rather than at the means suggests that if the goal is education in public and political affairs there is potential in inequality as well as in equality. National leaders could use their greater power to act as teachers, both in precept and in deed. The major parties could use their power to educate the citizenry, instead of taking the basic preferences of the populace as fixed. Any political actor with more power than the average could use that power to awaken the citizenry to its real interests. Taking the goal of "political education" seriously would mean, first, specifying the content of that education and, second, pursuing the specified ends in many cases by nonegalitarian as well as egalitarian means.

Costs

Considerations of means and ends are necessary only when there are costs to making power more equal. The expense is not inevitable. Sometimes, when organizations are extremely hierarchical to begin with, promoting greater equality may reduce the resistance of those at the bottom to organizational policies, increase the extent to which they feel responsible for organizational commitments, and increase the organization's likelihood of developing and utilizing their special aptitudes. When flexibility and innovation are at a premium, egalitarian organizations are often more efficient than their hierarchical equivalents.[19]

At some point, however, further movement toward equality will always begin to incur major costs. Even in a small organization, making power more equal usually entails a less specialized division of labor. Each participant must give more time, energy, intellectual concentration, and emotional commitment to matters that affect the whole group, leaving fewer resources for specialized tasks, which thus get less expert attention.

Equalizing power requires a less centralized system of communications, and this slows down decision making. It also means diffusing responsibility, which makes it difficult to conduct both internal and external negotiations. In the absence of strong social controls, diffusing responsibility also decreases the chance that individuals will hold themselves responsible for following through on a task.

Equalizing power also often means not exploiting to the full the administrative skills of those who have a particular aptitude for organization and who are better at organizing activities than they are at teaching others to do so. It can mean devaluing administrative skills and so carefully controlling the people who possess those skills that good administrators end up feeling that competence is "no longer something you can go on feeling good about."[20] As in other forms of human endeavor, equality cannot always be achieved simply by giving more to those with less. It sometimes requires handicapping those who for whatever reasons start out with more. Finally, if for various reasons equal power cannot be achieved, an ideology of equality often results in covering up those inequalities that continue to exist, with a consequent loss in accountability.[21]

While in some hierarchical organizations the costs of equalizing power may be offset by the gains in flexibility, creativity, and innovation attendant on increased participation, the costs are almost unavoidable when organizations that are relatively egalitarian to begin with try to achieve complete equality. At this point, an organization must begin to think hard about how much it values political equality relative to its other objectives. Indeed, whenever further equality has costs—not only in efficiency but also in high standards or freedom—it becomes necessary to ask when that equality is most valuable. It is most valuable when a polity cannot achieve equal protection, equal status, or a high level of citizen awareness by other means.

Conclusion

The atypical situation at Helpline placed its staff in the position of having to think more about, and act daily upon, convictions that most of us arrange to take for granted or to ignore. The conclusions they reached in feeling comfortable with certain kinds of unequal power compel the more general conclusion that both they and we value power as a means rather than as an end. The ends that equal power has traditionally been thought to promote are the equal protection of interests generally and two rather special forms of interest, namely, the interest in equal respect and that in individual development. Other arguments for equal power, such as that it is a "check on dictatorship" or "the least bad of the alternatives," can be assimilated into this scheme by asking, for example, why a check on dictatorship is desirable or what ends "the alternatives" to political equality are expected to meet. These three ends certainly encompass the major goals that political equality has been thought to promote. When these three ends can be more effectively pursued by other means, further equalization of power becomes unnecessary.

The key to meeting a polity's real needs is to choose the means most appropriate to the chosen end. If the goal is primarily to promote equal respect among the members, equal political power in every decision will sometimes be less effective than shared experience and the members' coming to know one another on more than one functional level. If the goal is to promote the individual political growth of members of the group, distributing power and participation in conflict according to need will almost always be more effective than distributing them equally. The precisely equal distribution of power makes most sense as an ideal in an adversary polity like the nation-state, where individuals' interests are in conflict and it is assumed that the interests of those individuals ought to be protected equally.

The ideal of political equality should not, therefore, be equated with democracy. Rather, it must be understood as one possible means to a variety of democratic ends. Understanding political equality as a means makes it possible to accept unequal power in unitary situations as long as this is compatible with the equal status and individual development of all. In moments of conflict, when the goal is equal protection of interests, equalizing power will usually remain the ideal toward which a democratic polity must struggle.

A Note on Equal Opportunity and Representation

Until recently, theorists in the adversary tradition usually assumed that protecting interests equally required not equal power but only "equal access to power" or "equal opportunity to exercise power."[22] Even radical democrats have often accepted this view. In the 1960s, for example, when college students struck in opposition to the Vietnam war, occupied buildings, and tried to reorganize their colleges, they usually made decisions in meetings open to all. Those who came often knew that their views differed from the views of those who stayed away and that a campuswide referendum would yield different results from the meeting. They justified making decisions at public meetings on the grounds of equal opportunity: "The path is open to anyone who wants to come." Groups of all persuasions make the same argument when it works to their advantage.

If the interests of those who attend a meeting are the same as the interests of those who stay away, attenders will protect the interests of nonattenders. Usually, however, the interests of attenders and non-attenders differ. When this happens, a case can still be made for the "equal opportunity" formula, but only in the unusual situation where the immediate costs and benefits of participation are roughly equal for participants and nonparticipants. When immediate costs and benefits are roughly equal, those who participate are presumably those who feel most strongly about the issue to be decided. Allowing those who participate most actively to exercise disproportionate influence thus becomes a kind of weighted voting, in which votes are weighted by intensity of concern with an issue. Such a weighting scheme will often increase the probability that the resulting decision promotes the greatest good of the greatest number.

This argument only holds, however, as long as the immediate costs and benefits of participation remain equal for everyone involved. Attending a meeting, for example, must involve equal inconvenience to all before we can say with confidence that those who attend feel more strongly about the issue than those who do not attend. If some people enjoy attending meetings while others do not, those who dislike meetings will have to feel more strongly about the outcome in order to try to influence it.

In practice the immediate costs and benefits of political participation usually vary considerably from one individual to the next, depending on the individuals' other obligations, financial resources, verbal skills, social ties, and information about the problem at hand. Those for whom the immediate costs of participation are low and the immediate benefits high tend to participate more, even when they do not have any greater interest in the outcome.

Take, for example, democracies without strong working-class parties, where the middle classes are more likely to vote, write to public officials, campaign, and hold office than the working classes. It is hard to argue that these differences in participation arise because political decisions have more impact on the lives of the middle classes than on the lives of the working classes. Rather, it appears that the immediate costs of participation are lower and the immediate benefits higher for the middle classes. They find it easier to campaign, hold office, and write to public officials because they have money, contacts, and verbal skills. In the case of voting, the material costs to different classes do not differ much, but taking an interest in political affairs is still less immediately rewarding for working-class citizens, at least in America, because they are less likely to belong to organizations where politics is discussed, because no poltical party addresses itself explicitly to working-class concerns, and because the working class sees the middle class dominating both process and outcome. In countries where working-class parties provide greater opportunities for organizational involvement, raise more issues directed to working-class concerns, and give working-class citizens more tangible evidence of having an effect, the immediate benefits of working-class participation are greater and the costs lower. As a result, the class gap in participation is reduced or even eliminated.[23] But even in these countries, the immediate costs and benefits of participation remain unequal for other groups that have not been organized equally effectively. Thus, what passes for "equal opportunity" does not in fact make it equally easy for all groups to protect their interests.

Nonetheless, letting those who attend a meeting make decisions in the name of those who do not attend has obvious appeal since the only alternative in a direct democracy is an endless series of referenda, the wording of which would in any case have to be decided by those who attended one or more meetings. But while democratic polities will undoubtedly continue to let those who attend meetings make decisions, they need not justify this procedure on the grounds of "equal opportunity." If the aim is to protect all members' interests equally, as it should be when interests conflict, democratic groups might treat those who attend meetings as representatives of those who do not attend and enjoin these representatives to make decisions that will protect the interests of all members rather than just their own.

In trying to ensure that the "volunteers" who attend a meeting will try to represent the entire group, three specific strategies might be helpful. First, polities could constantly experiment with devices aimed at ensuring that all major conflicting groups are equally represented at meetings. Such devices include altering the time and duration of meetings, making meeting days legal holidays, paying members to attend meetings,[24] and providing child care and transportation. Second, these polities could establish a mechanism, such as occasional referenda, for holding those who attend a meeting accountable to the entire group on certain major issues. Third, and perhaps most important, these polities could abandon rhetorical exhortations to attend meetings as a civic obligation since exhortations of this kind legitimate the idea that those who do not attend have behaved badly and deserve whatever misfortune befalls them as a result of their sins. Instead, democratic polities should define attendance at decision-making meetings as a privilege, open to all but carrying with it certain obligations, notably the obligation to consider not only one's own interests but also the interests of those not present. Taken together, these three devices should allow small assembly democracies in moments of conflict to protect all citizens' interests much more equally than they now do.

The crucial step is, of course, recognizing the right of all citizens in a democracy to have their interests represented equally in the political process. In a small assembly democracy, this representation is informal, but it should still be recognized as such. In a larger polity, representation must become formal. In both cases, the polity gives up on the idea of providing each citizen with equal power, and allows representatives, whether self-selected or elected, more power than their constituents. In an assembly, the only ways to make the self-selected volunteers who attend meetings act as representatives are moral exhortation and the threat that the group as a whole will overturn their decisions if the interests of absent members are completely ignored. In a formal representative democracy, the aim must be to make sure important public decisions are made within the representative process, to give each member equal weight in selecting representatives, to distribute representatives in a way that reflects the relative weight of different interests in the population, and to give great attention to accountability, trying to ensure in various ways that the representatives in fact work to protect their constituents' interests.

Chapter 18

Consensus

J UST AS Helpline's attempt to practice an upcompromising equality revealed that we generally value equal power more as a means than as an end, so Helpline's and Selby's attempts to practice consensus reveal something of the nature of consensual and majoritarian rule. Again, consensus appears as a means to various ends. And again, it seems that at least one end can be best met by other means. The adversary end of equal protection, it turns out, is not best met by either of the usual forms of consensus, nor, surprisingly, even by majority rule, although this is the traditional adversary device. I will argue that interests are protected most equally when, as in European "consociational" theory, benefits are allocated in proportion to the numerical distribution of interests in the population.

Consensus as a Means to Both Unitary and Adversary Ends

Like many collectives that adopted consensus as a formal decision rule, Helpline used the rule for two conflicting ends. Most of the time, the staff at Helpline used the rule to help maintain their solidarity. But when the members' interests came in conflict, they used the same rule to protect each individual against the others.

In their more unitary moments, polities like Selby as well as Helpline prefer to make decisions by consensus. They resist adversary procedures because the underlying assumptions of the adversary mode threaten their unity.

This is why Mike, one of William Foote Whyte's "corner boys" in Boston's North End in the 1930s, concluded:

It is better not to have a constitution and vote on all these things. As soon as you begin deciding questions by taking a vote, you'll see that some fellows are for you and some are against you, and in that way factions develop. It's best to get everybody to agree first, and then you don't have to vote.[1]

And why an SDS article on draft resistance exhorted:

You are a serious resistance: don't vote on issues, discuss them until you can agree. All the pain of long meetings amounts to a group which knows itself well, [and] holds together with a serious, human spirit. . . .[2]

In their unitary moments, the members of a small collective assume that the group is latently of one mind and that differences can be worked out by rational discussion or emotional transcendence. Thus, in one food co-op I observed, a member suggested that the co-op solve its decision-making problems by putting "an ounce of grass in each order."[3]

When a group extends its boundaries and incorporates diverging interests, but still remains a small and relatively homogeneous community, it often retains the procedures of consensus in order to preserve its increasingly tenuous unity. This is the point at which consensus comes to protect the interests of the less aggressive, the less verbal, or any other minority by giving them a potential veto, making it more likely that others will listen to them and will try to understand their point of view. Thus, one radical democrat argued for a consensual rule in her organization on the grounds that:

minority groups get trashed* so easily. . . . One thing about consensus is that in order to reach it, you need to have discussion and really go over things so that people understand them. The trouble with majority rule is that it's so easy just to make the decision, and nobody understands.[4]

Consensus protects the minority from being "trashed" by allowing it to command sufficient attention from the majority to make its position understood. Consensus guarantees respect and listening, by right.

Finally, as important conflicts of interest develop, the *liberum veto* of consensus turns into a negative weapon, serving every member of the association as a bill of rights and guaranteeing a broad area of noninterference. As one radical constitution was hammered out, the argument for consensus that I heard most often was: "I don't trust anyone except

---

* "Trashing," which originally meant looting and breaking windows in a riot, involves hurting a person by treating him or her with disrespect. Here it refers to the way a dominant majority might ignore the interests and feelings of a minority.

myself!" This bitter, self-protective refusal to be coerced by a majority has the most force when the potential harm to the minority is most immediately obvious, as it would be if the group were going to take illegal action.[5] But within an organization, a specific subgroup may also fear the slow, subtle process of having its interests in that organization consistently weakened. Its members may see themselves in the position of the South before 1860, and like Calhoun, they may want a constitution that gives them a veto.

The schema advanced at the beginning of this book (Table 1, p. 5), which orders all democratic polities along a spectrum from the "unitary" to the "adversary," is therefore incomplete. It characterizes unitary polities as making decisions by consensus while adversary polities rely on majority rule. But there is a third point on the spectrum—the "state of nature," or the war of all against all (Figure 5), a point that is usually outside the bounds of an ongoing polity. At this extreme of mutual distrust, enemies or strangers adopt a de facto unanimity rule, for only by giving each potential participant a self-protective veto can a group induce hostile opponents to collaborate, even temporarily.

FIGURE 5
The Full Spectrum

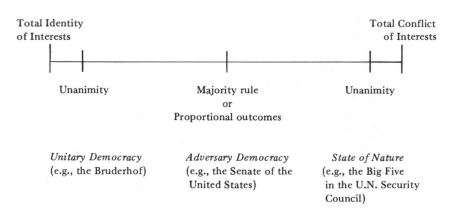

Total Identity of Interests		Total Conflict of Interests
Unanimity	Majority rule or Proportional outcomes	Unanimity
Unitary Democracy (e.g., the Bruderhof)	*Adversary Democracy* (e.g., the Senate of the United States)	*State of Nature* (e.g., the Big Five in the U.N. Security Council)

Forms of unanimity, then, appear at both ends of an extended spectrum from common to conflicting interests, with adversary democracy and majority rule in the middle. Most writers look at only part of this spectrum. Some focus on the more harmonious end of the spectrum, comparing consensus to majority rule. Others focus on the more conflict-ridden end of the spectrum, comparing unanimity-as-veto to majority rule. Once one makes the full spectrum explicit, however, a further paradox appears. Certain communities that make their decisions by consensus seem to lie at both ends of the spectrum, using consensus not only to affirm the existence of common interests but also to give every member a self-protective veto. This was the case with many small participatory collectives of the New Left. But when a democracy uses consensus in this dual role, it seldom achieves its intended purpose. In an ongoing polity, an explicit effort to achieve proportionate outcomes, or even majority rule, protects conflicting interests more effectively than the requirement of consensus, with its potential drawbacks of deadlock and social coercion.

Unanimity as a Unifier

Although Selby and Helpline demonstrate that when interests are in conflict consensus can suppress minority (and sometimes majority) interests, it is a mistake to assume that this will always happen. There are at least three possible reasons for genuine unanimity: the search for a correct solution (overlapping private interests), the independent value of unity (identifying one's own good with the good of the whole), and empathy (identifying one's own good with the good of other individual members).

First, some problems do have correct solutions. The unanimity rule in jury verdicts assumes, for example, that there is a truth about what happened, that the jury's job is to discover this truth, and that unanimity proves their success in this enterprise.[6] The relatively frequent unanimity on the Supreme Court of the United States (which has a formal majority rule) arises because the Justices often believe that they are addressing problems of interpretation that have a correct solution.[7] Experts in business management and organizational development actively promote consensual decisions in committees because they see these decisions as involving only technical solutions to common problems.[8] In a less technical realm, the Quakers believe that for every problem there is a will of God that all members of the congregation can eventually discover or understand.[9]

Second, a consensual decision reflects and creates emotional unity. Human beings appreciate unity with others of their kind, and when members of a group value unity, unanimity in decisions acquires symbolic value. In the fundamentalist Bruderhof, for example, political unanimity is the outward sign of the community's inner peace. The sect makes such unanimity a precondition for common prayer.[10] In many collectives, members report, on reaching a unanimous decision, satisfactions ranging from a quiet sense of oneness to a euphoric emotional high.[11]

Moreover, a consensual rule can actually create unity as well as reflcting it. At Helpline, the rule of consensus directed attention to the germs of potential agreement. The Quakers (who officially call themselves the Society of Friends) employ consensus in part to maintain their friendship: "Friends listen to other Friends views and try, when there is disagreement, to wait for the deeper understanding which they know from their experience they are justified in expecting."[12] Among the Bruderhof, consensus even helped generate unity in a paradoxical fashion: the rule created periodic deadlocks on important matters, and their eventual resolution produced tremendous joy. Zablocki speculates that "the function of these crises was undoubtedly at least as much to provide the impetus for a new wave of euphoria as to determine policy on any substantive issue."[13] He also reports that in nonreligious communes that made their decisions by consensus: "the more difficult the decision was to make, the closer together the discussion brought the community members."[14]

A third reason for adopting a consensual procedure is that empathy among members of the group has proceeded so far that the line between mine and thine has become indistinct, and each member feels the grief or joy of others in the body almost as if it were his or her own. Here, as in a loving family, no decision is easily taken that harms the interests of any one of the members. And here again, the rule of consensus seems not only to reflect empathy but to create it. At least at Helpline and among the Quakers, consensus encourages the members to listen carefully to one another and to respect the others' experience or point of view.

Non-Western thought easily accepts the idea that for any of these reasons a collectivity can often find solutions that genuinely accommodate the needs of all involved. The Japanese habitually try to uncover such solutions, many Japanese believing it "immoral" and "undemocratic" for a majority not to compromise with the minority.[15] In a philosophic vein, Jayaprakash Narayan writes:

Modern western democracy is based on a negation of the social nature of man and the true nature of human society. This democracy conceives of a society as an inorganic mass of separate grains of individuals: the conception is that of an atomized society. The brick with which the present edifice of democratic polity is constructed is the individual voter and the whole process of democracy rests on the arithmetic of votes. The individual casts his vote as an atom of society, not as a living cell in organic relationship with other living cells. It is not living together that is expressed and represented in the institutions and processes of democracy, but an abstracted individual. . . . [In contrast, historically] in the Indian village communities there were no elections to executive offices on the present majority-minority pattern, which is a divisive and disruptive process. Instead there was selection by general consensus of opinion, or sometimes by drawing lots.[16]

The sentiment against adversary democracy and majority rule was so strong in the Indian state of Rajastan that in 1960 the state legislature declared a special grant of close to ten cents a villager to those villages that elected their council chairman and at least 80 percent of their council members by unanimous vote.[17]

A modern Westerner may not believe that this desire for unity can encompass a genuine concern for the fate of the minority.[18] Yet at least in seventeenth-century New England, town meetings seem to have evidenced such concern. These towns went to great lengths to settle disputes amicably and unanimously, bringing issues up over and over again rather than allowing a majority to impose its opinion on the minority. A town clerk chronicled his town's "long debate and due consideration" in order "to accommodate the matters of dispute . . . to the end that they might be amicably adjusted."[19] In an account of this striving for unity (entitled *Peaceable Kingdoms*), Zuckerman reports that:

Framingham met ten different times between February 1725 and July 1726 to reconsider meetinghouse measures, and in its attempts to attain general acceptance the town gave countenance to almost any discontents. And in elections, town separations, and educational issues, there was the same necessity for a new determination when discontent came to the surface. The stated reason for reconsideration was always the same wish to clear up a residue of dissatisfaction. . . .[20]

In these towns, the idea that a polity should be based on friendship and amicability was seen as divinely ordained. Unanimity was part and parcel of this ideal.

Present-day Quakers also believe that "the members of a group always have something in common"[21] and that consensus can build on that commonality without endangering the rights of any individual. So, too, in my research at Helpline, I become convinced that the Air Force contract decision and the final decision at the Runaway Shelter to prohibit interaction with the Scorpion gang both ended in a recognition of genuine common interest. Those experiences lend credibility to Quaker reports that when a troubling question was decided by consensus "the members did not feel that weak compromise had been made but rather that the very best plan had been followed."[22]

Observers in the adversary tradition, however, find it hard to interpret consensus in a positive light. Vidich and Bensman have this difficulty in explaining the consensual politics of "Springdale," a town of about 3,000 in upstate New York. Unlike Selby, Springdale had no town meeting, so its citizens did not have the incentive of face-to-face contact in an assembly to lure them toward a unitary ideal of democracy. But the residents of Springdale did interact with many of their neighbors face to face. They often knew each other personally. Therefore, while the town's representative system might in a larger polity have encouraged conflict by delegating that conflict to those who minded it least, Springdale's representatives usually acted unanimously when they came together in their small assembly.

Vidich and Bensman report that on Springdale's village board "politics is conducted on the principle of unanimity of decision."[23] They also report their initial perplexity at the long process of discussion by which the village board of Springdale achieves unanimity:

> This discussion, which appears so strange to an outsider, takes place for the purpose of finding a common ground on which all can agree. . . . There is the continuous effort to seek the formula by which unanimity can be achieved. . . . [But] in no instance is a formula based on a recognition of conflicting interests which require balancing.[24]

Vidich and Bensman attribute this strange phenomenon of unanimity primarily to Springdale's village board members' being "relatively unsophisticated in the techniques of political analysis."[25] They argue that the experience of the board members:

> has been too narrow to encompass the range of political sentiment represented in the community. Hence, in calculating potential reactions to their actions, they think in personal rather than interest-group terms. They are not, then, able to assess their relationship to a constituency, and this lack of skill leads to the indecision which results in incompetence.[26]

In a later section, they further explain this outcome as resulting both from each board's having "neither skill nor knowledge nor a constituency to support him"[27] and from the board's desire to prevent a possible threat to its power from outside groups.[28]

But Springdale cannot be so different from Selby. If the two are at all alike, Springdale's consensual politics derives neither from its local elite's "lack of skill" nor from its conspiratorial designs but from the same two sources as in Selby and Helpline—a widespread desire to avoid conflict and a widespread willingness to make another person's good one's own.

258

The citizens of Springdale seem as anxious as the citizens of Selby not to engage in public disputes or public embarrassments:

When failures occur, when the play "was a flop," as of course must happen from time to time, one senses what is almost a communal conspiracy against any further public mention of it. So too with the successes of individuals. . . .[29]

When Springdale's citizens come together in moments of conflict, even some of the more powerful need to be prodded to speak, long awkward pauses appear in the discourse, and people are "afraid to speak up."[30] Even Vidich and Bensman admit, in one passage, that the members of the village board act as they do toward one another in part because each board member must continue to deal with the others "from month to month and in his daily living on a 'friendly' basis."[31]

In Springdale, as in Selby, the pressure for consensus suppresses information. More importantly, it suppresses information in a way that benefits the most powerful. Vidich and Bensman assume that the village board and the more prosperous farmers simply impose their political will on their neighbors. Yet I would guess that a very large proportion of Springdale's citizenry supports the ideals of peace and unity, even when some of their self-regarding or material interests suffer thereby. In this case, the desire to make decisions unanimously would become, like the desire not to embarrass one's neighbor, a "communal conspiracy."

If the strength of unitary democracy in Springdale derives at least in part from a deeply held ideal of friendship and the common good, then the village board members will often fail to "think . . . in interest-group terms" because to do so would be at odds with their ideal of community harmony. Many Springdalers would probably be repelled by the private-interest perspective that Vidich and Bensman propose. Take the farmer who, visiting a meeting of Springdale's town board, spoke for the first time when a possible conflict arose over whose roads should be fixed first. His one contribution to this moment of conflict was, as they report it, "No problem here. We're a peaceable bunch."[32] To be true to their argument, Vidich and Bensman should attribute the farmer's remark either to his lack of political understanding or to his desire, conscious or unconscious, to exclude outside groups, kill public interest in roads, or have certain roads (perhaps his own) repaired first. Yet I was struck by his use of the word "peaceable," which harks back to those seventeenth-century New England towns that Zuckerman describes as seeking to be "peaceable kingdoms."[33] Taking this farmer at his word, I interpreted him to mean that the ideals of peace, loving-kindness, harmony, unity, and friendship meant more to him and, he assumed, to his neighbors than the question of whose roads would be repaired first. In a town of this size, citizens may value more highly the social benefits to themselves of an atmosphere of harmony. They may also, on occasion, genuinely care for one another enough to make in some ways one another's good their own.

Unanimity as Self-Protective Veto

While unanimity in a collectivity like Helpline or even Selby can reflect a desire for unity, unanimity at the conflict end of the spectrum reflects the minimal conditions for "foreign relations" in the war of all against all. Some commentators—among them Georg Simmel, Robert Paul Wolff, and James Buchanan and Gordon Tullock—discuss the choice between unanimity and majority rule as if it arose only at this end of the spectrum. In their analyses, unanimity guarantees individual autonomy, while majority rule subsumes individuals into society. Like the writers from the unitary tradition who see unanimity only as the expression of a deep tribal or religious unity, these writers from the adversary tradition also have only one interpretation of the unanimity rule and only one explanation for its use.

Simmel attributes the unanimity rule to individualism and sees majority rule as a sign of unity. He argues that a unanimity rule derives from "a strong feeling of individuality on account of which one does not wish to yield to any decision without full consent,"[34] while majority rule marks the triumph of "the ideal that the unity of the whole must, under all circumstances, remain master over the antagonism of convictions and interests."[35] He adopts examples like the Polish Diet or the Aragonese Cortes, whose members have their primary bonds outside the group and who use a unanimity rule as a self-protective weapon. These examples then lead Simmel to conclude that "precisely where a super-individual unity . . . is *lacking*, it is necessary to have unanimity."[36]

Other commentators, less interested in describing social reality than in building an heuristic theory, advance equally individualistic schemes. Buchanan and Tullock, economists in the individualist tradition, also interpret the unanimity rule as appropriate in circumstances where "significant damage may be imposed on the individual."[37] Unlike Simmel, they are not particularly interested in describing the social circumstances that produce a unanimity rule. Like Simmel, however, they usually choose as examples associations whose members' primary bonds are outside the group.

Buchanan and Tullock begin their first chapter on politics with two quotations: "I do not, gentlemen, trust you" (Gunning Bedford of Delaware, Federal Convention of 1787) and ". . . free government is founded in jealousy and not in confidence" (Thomas Jefferson, in the Kentucky Resolution of 1798).[38] The theory they elaborate postulates that individual interests conflict[39] and that the individuals concerned are indifferent to the interests of other members in a decision-making body.[40] If these conditions held, they theorize, if there were no decision costs (and, I might add, if one were not concerned with redistribution), a unanimity rule with side payments would maximize the sum of individual benefits from any decision. Side payments are necessary to win the assent of those whose interests are not served by a given decision. Because the decision-costs of a unanimity rule are often high, they believe that the members of an organization will choose a unanimity rule only when their desire to protect themselves against the coercive power of others is particularly strong.

Wolff, writing in the neo-Kantian tradition, also values the unanimity rule only for the protection it affords individual autonomy. His approach is philosophical rather than sociological or economic, but he nevertheless sees unanimity only as a device for allowing individuals to fulfill their "duty" not to be swallowed up by the group.[41]

Each of these writers, so different in other respects, sees unanimity primarily as a weapon protecting full individuality. Simmel and Wolff do not ask how the unanimity rule will affect personal relations within the group. Buchanan and Tullock ask the question but conclude (preserving both their conflict framework and their unsullied individual goals) that it will encourage stubbornness, bluffing, and the pretense of unreasonableness.[42] Like other economists, they ignore the possibility that the way a group makes decisions can alter the members' goals. Thus, they never consider the possibility that a consensual form of the unanimity rule could encourage individuals to care for one another, as it seemed to me to do at Helpline. But economists are by no means unique in this respect. Modern citizens in an adversary world have seldom had the experience of a formal unitary democracy. As a consequence, their image of unanimity is the Big Five veto in the U.N. Security Council.

Unanimity as Both Unifier and Self-Protective Veto

Distinguishing the function of the unanimity rule when interests coincide from its function when they conflict allows us to describe reality better than if we assume that the rule serves only as a self-protective veto for those who anticipate extreme conflict. But real organizations seldom fit neatly on a spectrum running from total identity to total conflict of interest. Within any one organization, the members can use the unanimity rule in different ways on different issues. Moreover, even on a single issue, the group can simultaneously use the unanimity rule both as a unitary bond and as a self-protective weapon.

Writers like Narayan, for example, imply that the consensual tendencies of Indian villages derive from similarity of interests. Yet like the U.N. Security Council, the Indian village council may also have to seek consensus because its members have kept it too weak to enforce its will on a recalcitrant minority. F. G. Bailey, who observed consensus in a faction-ridden Indian village council, concluded that:

> some of the apparent anxiety to damp down dispute . . . springs from the fact that everyone knows that if the decision is not the result of an agreed compromise, then it cannot be implemented . . . the majority know that the minority must be carried with them on pain of taking no action at all.[43]

Anthropologists working in the less factional context of an African village have supported Bailey's conclusion. Adam Kuper tells of a water pump in one African village falling into terminal disrepair because the village could not reach consensus on who should run it. The pump's complex maintenance required monetary contributions from all its users. But because the village was divided on who should run the pump, a good number of users could always consider themselves exempt from payment on the ground that they opposed the choice of the pumper. In the absence of a full consensus, the village had no way of obliging those who did not go along with the choice of a pumper to contribute to the pump's upkeep.[44]

This incident could be interpreted, along Simmel's lines, as manifesting an individualism far beyond what most Westerners would consider practical. Consensual procedures seem in this case to have been used almost exclusively to protect each village group against coercion by their government. Yet several moments of discussion on that very issue in the village council seem to indicate that many members also had a sincere desire for unity.[45] If these sentiments can be accepted as genuine and if deadlock of this sort occurs infrequently, we can conclude that this African village used the procedure of consensus both to create genuine unity and to give each faction a self-protective veto over the polity. In this case, both Narayan and Simmel would be right. The village would experience a unity of interests stronger than most Westerners have felt outside their own families; yet in moments of relative conflict, a large minority would have more autonomy than most Westerners think practicable. Unanimity can serve both ends. Its functions can intertwine until, while analytically distinguishable, they become inseparable in practice.

Although the staff at Helpline used consensus primarily to unify the group, at times they too, like the Indian and African villagers, deliberately kept their government weak to protect themselves against possible coercion by their peers. Some of this weakness was intrinsic to the nature of the tasks the staff performed. Many tasks at Helpline required such strong commitment that they could not be done well under coercion. In these conditions, any government will be weak because it can only accomplish its ends with the active support of those who will perform the task.[46] Although no one at Helpline spoke of a desire to avoid coercion, I suspect that many relished the individual protection their veto gave them against their fellows. When this happens, the spectrum from common to conflicting interests becomes a circle. The individuals in the group use the rule of unanimity both to bring themselves closer to the group and to protect themselves from it.

Individual protection and group unity are not always at odds, for the individual protection afforded by the veto can sometimes reinforce group unity. In Helpline's Air Force contract decision, for instance, the members' willingness to listen with open minds to arguments from both sides might have derived in part from their knowing that if they or others desired they could block any decision. Then the unifying and the self-protective uses of the unanimity rule could work in tandem.[47] More frequently, however, using unanimity both as unifier and as protector is inefficient and in-egalitarian. It produces an impasse in which, when interests are in conflict, insistence on unanimity leads to conservative stalemate, unhappy compromise, or acquiescence under social pressure. These conditions usually benefit those who already have the advantage.

The Consensual Bargain

The adversary tradition suggests one use of unanimity that begins to resolve some of these problems. Buchanan and Tullock point out that when interests conflict a unanimity rule can be used to require sufficient side payments to bribe each party in the transaction to go along with the decision. This is the principle behind a bargain: both parties must be sufficiently satisfied to conclude the bargain (unanimously), but they need not be satisfied by the same good. Nor need the side payments be delivered at the same time, for, given sufficient trust between the partners, payments can take the form of taking turns. In a conflict of interest between two groups, some can have their way at one time and the others later.

Although the theoretical literature from the adversary tradition often stresses this use of unanimity, bargaining of this kind is rather rare at the unitary end of the spectrum. I witnessed no negotiations of this sort at Helpline, although I can imagine the staff deciding that a particular service group had been getting a relatively raw deal and leaning over backward to make up for it in some future decision. It is true that some small towns give half their committee posts to Republicans and half to Democrats[48] and that a tribe may feel that because one faction won the last time the opposing faction ought to win this time. But open bargaining is seldom legitimate in unitary groups. Indeed, the ideal of unity is usually taken so seriously that it bars even taking turns. The community must agree on each issue separately and without side payments before it can take action. This insistence that interests are ultimately the same on every issue precludes any satisfactory solution when in fact those interests conflict. Then the unanimity rule leads not to the development of greater trust but to the conviction that those who disagree with one's own position are opponents of the common good.

To express this dilemma, we can order situations not only as to whether interests are generally similar or in conflict (as in Figure 5), but also as to whether interests on the issue up for decision are similar or in conflict (see Table 7). If individual interests conflict (bottom row) and if side payments are legitimate, the members can negotiate a bargain (Cell IV). But if members usually perceive their interests as identical, side payments will probably not be acceptable, and no bargain can be struck. In theory, this should lead to deadlock (Cell III), but if deadlock threatens the organization, as it often does, minority views can simply be suppressed

TABLE 7

*Consequences of Unanimity and Conflict
on Specific Issues and Interests Generally*

	Interests generally similar	Interests generally in conflict
Interests on specific issues similar	Unitary democracy (I)	Temporary unanimity on one issue (II)
Interests on specific issues in conflict	Deadlock or social coercion (III)	Bargain (IV)

in the interests of a "managed" or coercive unanimity (Cell III). The greatest problem confronting a unitary democracy is its inability to resolve conflicts through bargaining, for then the group must resort either to inaction or to informal social coercion.

The Case for Proportional Outcomes

The inequity in a bargain, as in all solutions that depend on some form of unanimity-as-veto, is that it gives disproportionate weight to the status quo. If any one member holds out, the bargain cannot be struck, and the status quo prevails. There may be no objection to this in a traditional society where the citizenry wants to give the status quo extra weight. But one implication of what I have called the adversary revolution is precisely that interests consistent with the status quo should have no greater weight than any others. This is the underlying reason why majority rule has become the classic adversary method for making decisions whenever interests are both expected to conflict and do conflict on specific issues (see Table 7, Cell IV).

Yet majority rule, even with equal power among the participants, does not always result in the equal protection of interests. For this reason, very small groups, like couples (who have an obvious difficulty in making decisions by majority vote) and groups of three or four, usually achieve the goal of equal protection of interests not by majority vote but by arranging outcomes roughly in proportion to the number in the group preferring each outcome (proportional outcomes) or, when a good is indivisible, by taking turns. In taking turns, A wins today, B tomorrow, and C the next day—the victories being suitably balanced in intensity and other qualities. Because goods are so often indivisible, taking turns is the most common adversary procedure in very small groups. If individuals know and can communicate their interests equally with others, taking turns makes possible proportionality over time.

On its face, majority rule seems to protect interests equally because it gives each individual a vote of equal strength in the peaceful equivalent of a "fair fight." Yet despite the fairness implicit in tug-of-war and weights-in-the-scale analogies, majority rule does not always protect interests equally. As a winner-take-all system, it does not usually produce a proportional distribution of benefits, and it can create permanent minorities. If some one minority is always on the losing side in every collective decision, few would say that the minority's interests were being protected, let alone that they were being protected equally. Majority rule ensures equality only in the procedure, not in the result.[49]

None of the traditional arguments for majority rule either answers these criticisms or demonstrates its superiority to systems like taking turns that are specifically designed to produce proportional outcomes. Locke's argument for majority rule, that it duplicates peacefully the result that would obtain if the community fought the issue out[50] is an argument from expedience that has no normative weight. Rousseau argued for majority rule on the ground that in a good state it would tend to reflect the common good, but that argument applies only in a unitary democracy, where there is a common good.[51]

The most obvious argument for majority rule is that if people know and vote their own interests it will produce the greatest good for the greatest number. If a benefit must go in its entirety either to one group or to another, the greatest number will profit if the benefit goes to the most numerous group. This argument, however, holds only when every benefit is both indivisible and isolated. By the usual Benthamite calculus, those who have only a little of a divisible benefit are made happier by every addition than those who have a lot.[52] If this is true, it will produce more happiness to find ways of dividing a benefit equally among a population than to give it all, through majority rule, to a numerical majority. While not all benefits are divisible, indivisible benefits can usually be taken out of isolation and combined with other benefits in a divisible package, making possible an equal distribution rather than a system of winner-take-all. Under analysis, then, the argument from the greatest good for the greatest numbers turns out to favor proportional outcomes (distributing goods on the basis of the numerical strength of the competing factions) rather than majority rule.[53]

In Western democracies, majority rule has derived a good deal of its support from the fact that in some circumstances it produces much the same result as proportional distribution. When the cleavages in a society cut across one another (that is, when an individual's interests align on different issues with those of various other groups), most individuals find themselves aligned with a winning majority on some issues and with a losing minority on others. The result may approximate proportional outcomes, and in many Western democracies this happens frequently enough for majority rule not to be discredited.[54] However, when it does not happen (when, for example, whites in the southern states before the Civil War found themselves without cross-cutting interests and in a permanent minority vis-à-vis the North on all issues of major importance to them), support for majority rule is undermined. In such cases, majority rule does not protect interests equally.

Even in the United States, of course, social cleavages rarely cross-cut one another so randomly under a system of majority rule as to protect the interests of each individual equally. This is why when benefits are clearly divisible and of a "zero-sum" nature (one beneficiary must lose what the other gains), even U.S. legislatures will often distribute funds on a basis that approximates proportional outcomes. Federal formulas for allocating aid to states tend to be largely of this type, for example, with only minor adjustments to reflect political power. In other democratic nations, like Belgium, Switzerland, Austria, and the Netherlands, the populations are so segmented (on all major issues an individual aligns only with one group) that the consistent use of majority rule would create one or more permanent minorities. These nations approximate proportional outcomes by a system that has recently been labeled "consociational democracy."

In a consociational democracy, the elites of each major segment of the population arrange among themselves bargains, side payments, divisions of distributable goods, and turns in power that in theory reflect the distribution of interests in the population. The Netherlands, for example, has three major groups in its population—the Roman Catholics, the orthodox Calvinists, and the secularists. Each time the government subsidizes an activity, like social work, adult education, sport, libraries, or youth work, it divides the money proportionally: so much for the Roman Catholics, so much for the Calvinists, and so much for the secular group.[55] The rule of proportionality applies not only to government expenditures on schools, hospitals, and other welfare functions but also to network

time on state-owned radio and television stations, to civil service appointments both on the national and on the local level, to the staffing of public
corporations, and, of course, to parliamentary elections by proportional
representation.[56] When an issue cannot be divided, it is bargained, and
either substantial concessions are made to the losing groups or side
payments are made to them on other issues.[57] Some consociational democracies, like Switzerland, even substitute a council for a single head of
state; others rotate the executive office, taking turns.[58] Thus, the basic
characteristic of consociational theory is simply "that all groups influence
a decision in proportion to their numerical strength."[59]

No known political system or decision-rule can ensure that all groups
influence a decision in proportion to their numerical strength. The rule of
proportionality cannot, like majority rule, be applied easily to political
decisions,[60] and even consociational systems have structural features that
prevent them from producing fully proportional outcomes.[61] Yet my
analysis of the theoretical foundations of adversary democracy suggests
that proportionality is the normative standard we should use to judge the
results of any conflictual democratic system, whether majoritarian or consociational. If, over time, we find that a group involved in political conflict wins less frequently than its percentage in the population, we have
a *prima facie* case that its interests are not being protected equally.

The proportionality rule is a limited, adversary concept. It guarantees
neither justice nor even equal satisfaction.[62] Yet as a normative standard
it has radical implications: no major nation-state now comes close to
meeting the standard. When the interests of management and labor
conflict in America, for example, few would claim that in the political
outcome each group obtained benefits proportional to its numbers.

Conclusions

Helpline's attempt to apply the procedure of consensus in moments of
genuine conflict as well as in unity reveals the diverse ends consensus can
serve. When we view consensus as a means to other ends, two things
become apparent. First, groups like Helpline, with many common interests, can use consensus best to maintain unity, encourage a search
for the best possible solution, and nourish concern for the welfare of both
the group as a whole and its individual members. They should try to

avoid systematically using the same device to protect their interests against one another in moments of conflict.

Second, the adversary end of equal protection of interests is best met not by consensus, in either its unifying or protective incarnations, nor even by majority rule, the classic adversary device for protecting interests equally, but by some procedure for arranging proportional outcomes. To the extent that a nation-state, or any other polity, must act as an adversary democracy, this conclusion mandates a far greater equality in the proportional distribution of benefits than now prevails.

Chapter 19

Face-to-Face Assembly

O**N CLOSE INSPECTION,** it seems that small collectives like Helpline use not only equality and consensus but also face-to-face assemblies for both unitary and adversary ends. In its unitary incarnations, a small group gains much of its energy from the pleasure its members take in face-to-face contact. When its members' interests begin to diverge, the group may institute face-to-face meetings as a way to correct inaccuracies of perception, iron out differences, and create a spirit of community. The members then oppose referenda, for referenda do not allow the discussion that brings about a real consensus. They oppose representation, for representation deprives the member of the experience of citizenship. Finally, when major conflicts of interest develop, members demand face-to-face meetings as an adversary protection against the potential coercion of an elite. They now perceive referenda as giving them control only at the last stage of the process, when a question has already been formulated, discussed, worded, and placed, perhaps manipulatively, on the ballot. They now see representation as allowing a small group to make decisions in its own interest rather than in the interest of all the members.

Face-to-face contact works best for the unitary end of cementing friendship, and best in the most unitary context, the one closest to real friendship. In "The Face to Face Society," Peter Laslett argues, in fact, that political theorists have been led astray by not distinguishing the psychology of a "face to face [or unitary] society" from that of what he calls a "territorial [or adversary] society," in which the citizens will never meet and know one another.

The face-to-face society, as Laslett describes it, has two important characteristics: "first, that everyone in it *knows* everyone else in it," and "secondly, that all situations of crisis . . . are resolved by people meeting and talking."[1] The first of these conditions means that the members:

respond with their whole personality, conscious and unconscious, covert and overt, in all situations, and they behave with the knowledge that the other members do the same.[2]

The second means that:

the process of solving the crisis and making the decision will be to some extent one of ratiocination, analyzing the situation in terms of propositions, relating these propositions logically, and deciding to act in the way which logic lays down. But to a large degree it will be a matter of personal response, expressed not in propositions, but in exclamations, apostrophes, laughter and silence. . . . Once more it is a question of total intercourse between personalities, conscious or unconscious, and it may well be that the solution of the crisis takes place as much as a result of what is neither formulated nor expressed, as of what has been called ratiocination.[3]

These characteristics of mutual knowledge and subtle communication make fuller empathy possible so that each member can more easily make the other's interests his or her own. As Laslett writes, the members of a face-to-face society can "share enough of each other's experience"[4] to put themselves effectively in the other's place. He goes so far as to say that:

it is only under face to face conditions that such intuitive behavior—putting yourself in the position of the man you are face to face with—is both continuously possible, appropriate, and sufficient.[5]

While face-to-face contact is not logically related to the discovery of a common interest and can sometimes intensify conflict, it usually seems to encourage participants to find solutions they can all support. As Laslett puts it:

The interplay between the group of personalities in committee, in fact, can discover a consensus which all of them feel to be outside their own personalities, and after the decision is made it is remarkable how often it is accepted as if each personality had "willed" it for himself.[6]

Indeed, he argues that face-to-face interaction may make it difficult even to "conceive of separate interests and identities."[7]

Although we know little about the specific effects of face-to-face contact, it probably enhances concern for the common good both by fostering empathy and, as we have seen, by increasing the fear of conflict.

Face-to-Face Contact and the Generation of Common Interest

There is remarkably little evidence on the effect of face-to-face contact on feelings of empathy. In one of the few controlled experiments of which I am aware, Bibb Latané and John M. Darley tested the effect of a face-to-face meeting of less than one minute between the subject of their experiment and another person who feigned an epileptic seizure several minutes later in another room. All of the subjects who had met the "epileptic" face to face responded to his cries, compared to only 62 percent of those who had not had the same brief meeting. Moreover, those who had met the epileptic were more than twice as fast in responding with help. The subjects who had met the epileptic, and only they, "reported that when the victim began to have the fit, they could visualize him doing so. They could *picture* an actual individual in distress."[8] The face-to-face effect also emerges in one of Stanley Milgram's experiments, in which subjects were considerably less likely to give what they thought were possibly lethal electric shocks to a victim when they could see the victim in pain.[9]

Such evidence accords with the widespread assumption that it is more difficult for a ground soldier to kill another human being than it is for the bombing crew in a plane, and more difficult for someone with a contact weapon than with a gun. If face-to-face contact does promote empathy, citizens would be more likely to respond emphatically to fellow citizens' needs in a face-to-face meeting than in a referendum. Seeing another person's eyes, lips, tautness of cheek, and bearing probably makes it difficult to resist the impulse to empathy when the impulse is there, although the same stimuli may also make it difficult to resist the impulse to anger.

Because physical cues affect cognition as well as emotion and because nuances of facial expression and stature convey much that words do not, face-to-face contact also facilitates two-way communication. It allows people to communicate, subtly as well as directly, the questions that are bothering them and to receive responses tailored to their concerns. Face-to-face communication is therefore likely to increase accuracy of perception.[10] The speed and complexity of communication in face-to-face interchange also allow participants to enter a negotiation expecting that their positions will change. As one of Selby's townspeople told me:

I have to hear several people speak at town meeting before I understand who is behind which idea, the reason behind it, its desirability.

Even in a town as large as Springfield, Vermont (population, 11,000), an opinion poll conducted at the 1972 meeting indicated that 27 percent of the 875 citizens in attendance had changed their minds as a result of the meeting's debates.[11] For these reasons, the chances of two heads of state understanding each other and finding some common interest are usually improved by a face-to-face meeting. Difficult negotiations in any field are almost always conducted face to face.[12]

Face-to-face contact may also lead citizens to take a degree of responsibility for their vote that they do not take if they are not physically present at the time of the decision. Americans who make a decision publicly in a face-to-face group seem more likely to act on that decision than those who make the decision privately.[13] In a town meeting hall, too, responsibility for a decision devolves clearly on the people present. Anyone at the meeting can look around and see in the faces of neighbors the government of the town. The winner is more likely to recognize how his or her victory hurts the others, as Selby's school director did. As for losing, one farmer's wife told me, "You have a different feeling when you are there and outvoted from when you aren't there for the decision."

Face-to-Face Contact in Contexts of Conflict

Yet as we have seen, face-to-face assembly is hardly the perfect instrument for producing genuine cohesion. Whenever interests are in conflict, the greater publicity of one's own act and the greater sanction of one's neighbor's visible disapproval in a face-to-face situation can stimulate conformity to the majority against one's own real interests.[14]

In conditions of open conflict, the physical presence of one's opponent may also heighten anger, aggression, and feelings of competition. Athletes perform better in a meet, when the opponent is near by and the challenge immediate and personal, than they do racing against the clock. Consequently, among those trained to deal with face-to-face conflicts, hostility is usually restrained by a set of rules and courtesies designed to structure the adversary process and make it more formal. Among those without such training, the only solution is often to avoid the conflict altogether.

Face-to-face assemblies designed to produce feelings of community can thus backfire and intimidate the less self-reliant. At least in America, fear of open hostility is an important cause of nonparticipation in politics.[15] It can even provide a reason for abolishing face-to-face assembly. In a town five times the size of Selby, one citizen explained his town's changeover from a "talking town meeting" (face-to-face democracy) to an "Australian ballot" (referenda by secret ballot) as being at least in part the consequence of a particularly conflict-ridden meeting. "We 'divided the house' and exposed people," he said. "Friends and relatives got divided, and it was too much for them. [After that] the Australian ballot was pushed through. . . ."[16] Just as divorcing couples communicate through lawyers, so citizens may prefer to battle through representatives or referenda once the intensity of their conflict reaches a certain level.

This combination of effects makes face-to-face assembly a more effective means for promoting the unitary end of cohesion than the adversary end of self-protection. In moments of genuine common interest, the mutual understanding and warmth in a face-to-face assembly allow a group to discover and celebrate their common ground. The assembly is a much less effective guard against the domination of a few. As the experience of Selby and Helpline demonstrates, replacing representative with face-to-face democracy does not eliminate differences in power.

Nor does face-to-face democracy effectively protect a citizen's individuality. A high school student may argue that his school should be governed by a face-to-face assembly of all the students because "No one can represent me. I'm the only one who knows what I'm thinking and no one else can present my views."[17] He believes representation will force him into anonymity, identified only with an interest or set of interests. But for most people, the practical effect of a mass meeting is worse—it results in anonymity without even the guarantee of representation. In large assemblies, most people can contribute to the emotional tone of the discussion only by murmuring, cracking jokes with their neighbors, shuffling their feet, or in other ways indicating their approbation or discontent. As individuals, they are not likely to make an impression on the assembled body. Whenever a speaker adequately expresses the views of the silent, that speaker represents them. But the silent have no way of holding any speaker accountable, and no way of ensuring that anyone articulate will present their views at all.

In short, a face-to-face assembly lets those who have no trouble speaking in public defend their interests; it does not give the average citizen comparable protection. For most people, it is a more effective means to unitary than to adversary ends.

National Referenda, Representation, and
the Problems of Anonymous Contact

The more revolutionary democratic theorists have always had a soft spot for direct (as opposed to representative) democracy, whether in its face-to-face variant or in the more anonymous variant in which citizens make their decisions through referenda. But these theorists have not distinguished between the adversary and the unitary uses of direct democracy. In a unitary context, with face-to-face contact, direct democracy builds empathy and commitment to the common good (Helpline called its assemblies "Community Days"). In an adversary context, whether in face-to-face assembly or in referenda, direct democracy allows each individual to be present, in some sense, to protect his or her interests at the moment of decision.

This dual function persists unnoticed partly because the theorists of direct democracy rarely distinguish face-to-face meetings from referenda. Rousseau's vision of direct democracy conjures up Swiss peasants under an oak, drawing tighter the social bonds as they deliberate on the common good, or ancient Rome, whose citizens, flocking to the assembly, overflow the square and have to cast their votes from the rooftops.[18] But in spite of these vivid pictures of the face-to-face, unitary assembly, Rousseau grounded his argument for direct democracy on the logical proposition that citizens bound by laws to which they have not consented are not "free."[19] This argument makes no distinction between face-to-face meetings and referenda; consent does not demand face-to-face contact.

In contrast, present-day proponents of direct democracy usually assume that this would involve referenda and do not even consider the possibility of direct democracy in a face-to-face context. Neither proponents nor critics of referenda discuss the isolated and anonymous character of decisions made in a voting booth or how eliminating face-to-face contact among legislators might affect the relationship among citizens. Referenda provide the distance between opponents that the average citizen requires in moments of conflict, but unlike representation, which at least maintains face-to-face contact among the representatives, a referendum provides no opportunity for human contact or mutual persuasion.

Representation too eliminates citizen contact in times of conflict. In a representative democracy, citizens need not fight their battles themselves; they can send persons more temperamentally suited and trained for conflict out to fight for them. Usually representatives are able to handle conflicts better than their constituents. By running for office, they show themselves more willing than most to face both hostility and the humiliation of losing. By becoming politicians, they embark on a course of professional socialization that prescribes appropriate conduct for moments of conflict. Most important, they are accountable to their constituents, a major structural constraint that keeps them conscious of their adversary relation to one another.

Yet in the legislature, representatives do meet face to face. They are not immune to empathy, anger, and suppression of conflict. As a consequence, they also try to work in a unitary style, often assuming a common good and treating one another like friends. In doing so, they import the mutual respect, understanding, and willingness to compromise of unitary democracy into what is primarily an adversary relationship.

When citizens decide between referenda and representative systems on a national level, they must therefore ask to what extent they want to leaven their adversary relations with unitary elements. Neither referenda nor representation brings citizens together face to face, but when the referendum is truly a secret ballot, it is better defended than representation against the unitary tendencies of face-to-face interaction. Deciding the conflictual issues of national politics through the face-to-face interaction of representatives brings adversary and unitary modes together. One of a representative's most important skills is thus learning to recognize situations of common and conflicting interest and to shift from unitary to adversary procedures. The extent to which constituents feel their representatives have "sold out" depends both on the representatives' mastery of this task and on the constituents' understanding of the problem. Constituents might better understand the representatives' difficulty in selecting the right means to unitary and adversary ends if, on a more local level, they had themselves participated in small face-to-face assemblies.

Conclusion

Members of small participatory collectives often see face-to-face assemblies as the solution to both unitary and adversary problems—how to generate common interest and how to protect individual interests equally. Face-to-face democracy is, however, more suited to the first goal than to the second. In moments of genuine conflict, face-to-face contact among citizens encourages suppression of that conflict rather than settlements based on taking turns, proportional outcomes, or majority rule. It therefore accentuates rather than redressing the disadvantage of those with least power in a society. Here, as with equal power and consensus, the members of any democratic polity must ask themselves to what extent their interests in fact coincide. If their interests on an issue are similar, the face-to-face assembly of either citizens or representatives can help resolve misunderstandings and produce mutually beneficial solutions. If interests are strongly in conflict, face-to-face contact between citizens or their representatives will generate an equitable resolution only insofar as the citizens or representatives can withstand the face-to-face temptations to false unanimity.

Chapter 20

Size and the Two Forms of Democracy

EQUALITY, consensus, and face-to-face interaction turn out to have quite different functions when interests coincide and when interests conflict. Indeed, as I have argued, the kind of democracy appropriate in a context of common interests is qualitatively different from the kind of democracy appropriate when interests conflict. The question of when interests are most and least likely to conflict thus becomes central to democratic theory. This chapter will contend that, other things being equal, interests are least likely to conflict in very small polities.

The idea that "small is beautiful" won widespread support in America during the 1960s. As a result, there was considerable interest in decentralizing both government and workplaces so that more decisions could be made by local or shop floor groups. Many of those who advocated this kind of decentralization made their case on adversary grounds, claiming that conflicting interests were more equally protected in small units. As we shall see, the evidence for this claim was, and is, inconclusive. What is clear, however, is that decentralization makes sense from a unitary perspective. Both logic and experience suggest that it is easier to achieve a genuine common interest in a small group than in a large one. Thus, while decentralization to the level of the local workplace or neighborhood may not advance citizens' abilities to protect themselves against others, it does allow them to taste the delights and dangers of working for a common good.

Adversary Arguments for Decentralization

Adversary democrats who favor small workplaces and neighborhoods argue that small polities allow ordinary citizens to understand more precisely the problems that confront them, know their potential allies and opponents, see the impact of their actions on decisions, and exercise more control over events that will affect them. Giving individuals more control over their lives and making such control more visible have thus been among the main arguments for decentralization.

Unfortunately, decentralization poses a major dilemma regarding control. Small size does increase the average individual's power within his or her group, but it also reduces the group's power vis-à-vis the rest of the world. In a town like Selby, with 500 residents, only 80 of whom typically attend town meeting, Clayton Bedell will have a great deal of control. His vote, if he attends town meeting, will constitute 1/80th of a final decision. Yet that decision will affect only the 500 residents of Selby. When Bedell votes in the national presidential election, his vote will constitute only 1/86,000,000th of the final decision, but the decision will affect 200 million people in this country alone. At the same time, Bedell knows that the national government, which can declare war or restructure the economy, has more power over its citizens than any local government. Large governments usually exercise more power (that is, make more collective choices) than smaller units.[1] Thus, the paradox of decentralization is that while ordinary citizens feel better able to influence the government of a small polity than that of a large one, and are more likely to try to do so, they also feel that the governments of smaller units have less effect on their lives.[2]

Deliberate decentralization of political decisions to the smallest possible units would obviously increase the role of small polities in citizens' lives, but economic and ecological interdependence means that such decentralization is sometimes prohibitively costly. As a strategy for increasing citizens' chances of protecting and furthering their interests, decentralization works best when the scope of the decision need not be broad and when accuracy, speed, and adaptability are at a premium.[3]

When we turn from the average level of citizen control to the distribution of control among citizens, it is again unclear whether citizens' interests are protected more equally in small governments than in large. Theorists have taken both positions.

Grant McConnell, after studying the operation of interest groups, unions, and other private governments, concluded in 1966 that "the organization of political life by small constituencies tends . . . to discriminate in favor of elites" and that "decentralization will generally tend to accentuate any inequality in the distribution of power."[4]

Dennis Thompson, writing four years later during the wave of New Left enthusiasm for decentralization and community control, argued that the "dispersion of political power" to smaller units would benefit "those most disadvantaged in citizenship" since "persons of lower socio-economic status . . . are less likely to be outdone by higher status citizens in local politics than in national politics."[5]

The evidence on participation seems to support Thompson's hypothesis. Political participation seems to be more equally distributed in small political units than in large ones: speaking and leadership activities are more equally distributed in small groups than in large ones,[6] and town offices and political participation of all sorts are probably more equally distributed in small towns than in large ones.[7] Representatives from small constituencies are also more like their constituents, both in social characteristics and in policy preferences, than representatives from large constituencies.[8]

But while the participation gap between the economically advantaged and the economically disadvantaged is probably smaller in very small constituencies, it need not follow that the outcomes of participation are more equal in small constituencies. In Selby, for example, the participation gap between the rich and the poor was smaller in the local town meetings than in state and national elections. But when I asked both rich and poor whether people like them had a "say" in what various levels of government did, the class gap was larger when I asked about local government than when I asked about national government.[9] While we cannot be certain that citizens' perceptions about who controls various levels of government are accurate, large units do seem to be more redistributive than small ones. The federal government, for example, spends more per capita on programs directed specifically at the poor than state governments do, and state governments spend more than local governments.[10] Historical experience also indicates that when state governments intervene in local education and welfare programs, these programs tend to become more redistributive. The same pattern has usually held when the federal government intervened in state programs.

The evidence, then, points in two directions. The trappings of power appear to be more equally distributed between rich and poor in smaller units, suggesting that the interests of the poor should be more equally protected. But direct analysis of outcomes suggests that the interests of the poor are better protected in larger units. I can conclude only that if one judges on adversary grounds, the claim that small units protect individual interests more equally than large ones has not been proven.

The Unitary Argument: Size and Common Interests

The unitary case for greater common interest in smaller units is easier to make. Two people will usually have a harder time finding a policy that promotes both their interests than will one person, even someone locked in internal debate. Three people will have even greater difficulty, and so on.[11] This is the arithmetic basis of the relationship between size and common interests.

Real polities, moveover, are not random collections of individuals. Characteristics like ethnicity, language, religion, and socioeconomic status are unevenly distributed across the globe, so that any small geographically based political unit will tend to embrace people who are more alike in these respects than the members of the larger units.[12] The same logic usually holds for workplaces. Unless membership is based exclusively on common interests, a small group is always more likely to have common interests than a large one.

Self-selection can further increase the homogeneity of small groups when compared to large, because expanding the boundaries of the group reduces the saliency of common interests in recruitment. People want their closest acquaintances and colleagues to be quite similar to themselves.[13] Thus, if they are considering moving to a very small town or joining a very small workplace, they will try to find a town or a workplace whose members are like themselves since otherwise they will not have enough potential friends or colleagues. If they are considering moving to a big city or joining a big firm, they will be less concerned with the modal character of those already in the group because they can expect to find compatible friends or colleagues somewhere in the group even when the average member is very different from themselves.

Members of a polity may, of course, acquire common interests after joining the polity even though they did not have them when they entered. Those who moved to Selby, for example, acquired an interest in the town's share of state aid that they did not have before moving there, and members of Helpline acquired an interest in bringing in new money, promoting the organization's reputation, and seeing it do a good job. But the strength of these acquired common interests is again inversely related to size. The larger a geographic polity or workplace, the more salient will be conflicts among neighborhoods or small work units within the larger group, and the less salient will be their common interests vis-à-vis others. Robert Dahl and Edward Tufte suggest that natural limits on an organization or an effective polity's span of control lead most organizations and polities to break down into subunits as they grow in size. The proliferation of organized subunits in a large polity then stimulates greater diversity, as the subunits specialize and develop their own interests.[14]

Random and patterned similarity of interests, self-selection, and the absence of organized centrifugal forces help explain the greater coincidence of individual interest and thus help explain the greater degree of political unanimity in small communities. Dahl and Tufte, for example, report lower levels of party competition in the smaller political subdivisions of the Netherlands, Switzerland, and the United States,[15] while Seymour Martin Lipset, Martin Trow, and James Coleman find that printing shops with fewer than thirty union members are more likely than larger shops to approach voting unanimity in union elections.[16]

However, small groups achieve their greater degree of unanimity not only by reflecting a greater coincidence of previously recognized interests but also by producing changes in both perceived and actual interests among the individuals in a group. Thus, even when small groups find themselves in initial disagreeemnt, they are more likely than large groups to evolve toward consensus. Comparing Boy Scout groups of five and twelve members, for example, A. Paul Hare found that although the boys in both small and large groups had the same average amount of agreement before discussion, the boys in the small groups were significantly more likely than those in the large groups to agree after the discussion.[17]

Several different internal processes make it likely that individuals in a small group will either go along with the dominant opinion, although it is against their interests, or else come to recognize that in spite of initial disagreement they in fact have common interests. A small group can promote conformity and conflict avoidance, producing surface unanimity while masking a genuine opposition of interests. But the members of a small group can also gather more complete information about one another, so they are more likely to discover their common interests. Small groups foster the empathy and responsibility that lead some to adopt the good of others as their own; this in turn makes them more likely to develop a common interest. Finally, because members of small groups tend to place a higher value on the harmony of the whole, this shared value can become the basis for common interest. Although it is often hard to decide in practice which of these explanations may be operating, it is possible to distinguish most of them analytically.

First, there is no doubt that small size promotes conformity. If even one person supports a dissenter against a group, the chance of the dissenter's conforming drops drastically, and a dissenter is more likely in a large group to find someone to give such support.[18] A small setting also throws its members together in more frequent, varied, and intimate interaction. This makes it difficult for a dissenter to escape the sanctions of others by avoiding the others or confining interaction with them to an impersonal, single-faceted contact.

The characteristics of small size that promote conformity also suppress conflict, for members of small communities tend to avoid conflict[19] in part because of the greater sanctions their neighbors can wield. In Selby, the citizens knew that what they said at town meeting would affect the way others reacted to them as parents, neighbors, and frequenters of the local store and gas pump. Selby's townspeople worried about local "gossip," the most common social sanction. Similarly, at Helpline, Ruth found her friendship with her roommate imperiled by the conflict between their two service groups; she was afraid her friend would never speak to her again. In both cases, the small size of the setting and the resulting intimacy of interaction made each member more vulnerable to the others and more anxious not to bring up potential sources of conflict.

Next to the threat of sanctions, the least attractive method small groups employ for reaching consensus is to bribe their members into acquiescence. In smaller settings each member is more valuable to the others, and more likely to be recognized, understood, and valued. Members of smaller groups say they are more satisfied, laugh more, complain less, and look forward more to group meetings.[20] They feel included, needed, and accepted[21]—and not unreasonably so, because if a group is small, its identity becomes dependent on maintaining each one of its members, and each individual becomes more important to every other. But precisely because the group gives its members such rewards, the members' interests in preserving a positive relationship to the group become stronger relative to their interests in having their way or even asserting their unpopular views. Because the rewards are greater, the loss of those rewards would constitute a greater punishment.

Certainly small-town citizens, even when removed from small-town life, seem to continue to avoid conflict. James Barber writes that in the lower house of the 1969 Connecticut legislature, legislators from small towns tended to value "amicable" and "friendly" relations. They identified "politics," "political" things, and "politicians" with "haggling," "feuding," and "discontent," and often denied the existence of conflict in their towns:

> There is no politics in it at all in our town . . . no hagglings about whether they're Republican, Democrat, Socialist, or what they are. I don't think politically . . . there's been no, ah, feuding [laughs] among the two parties at all. They're very amicable in our town.[22]

These small-town legislators even managed to see the state legislature itself as harmonious. One commented that in the legislature "everybody seems to be amicable and sociable and happy and contented." Others expressed satisfaction that the committees they were on were "friendly," and remarked, "I haven't seen any of that, what-you-call political play. I haven't seen that." Another denied conflict by attributing disputes he could not ignore to quarrels between disputatious party leaders: "Of course, you know, it's like a couple of lawyers, the two leaders are going to get up and have controversies on things that are probably not important—I mean, the matters are not important."[23]

These legislators' amazing will to believe in harmony may have been a carry-over from the fear of sanctions they learned in their small towns.[24] But perhaps the greater possibility of actual common interest in the small communities from which they came made it more feasible for these legislators both to pursue harmony as an ideal and to adopt such personal strategies as interpreting events as harmonious in order to make them so. Indeed, small size does seem to make it easier for members of a community to reach common interest either by discovering that their interests coincide or by adopting the good of others as their own.

The greater information a small group can generate frequently helps its members uncover an underlying common interest. Small size lets the participants express nuances more fully and use the insight of the group to discover what they really want or need. Understanding what each member needs then lets the group work out a solution that can meet those needs. With each additional member, the possibilities for such in-depth understanding diminish. It becomes harder and harder, for example, to understand each member's relationship to the others, because the number of potential relationships in a group—between each individual and all other individuals, between each individual and all possible subgroups, and between each possible subgroup and all other possible subgroups—increases exponentially with the introduction of each new member into the group. By the time a group has seven members, it encompasses 966 such potential relationships.[25]

The lower level of conflict in smaller groups can also, by encouraging the exchange and assimilation of information, accelerate the process of finding a solution in the interest of all. Here lowered conflict helps reveal the truth rather than obscuring it.[26] On Helpline's stressful Community Day, when the organization had to cut its budget by a third, more useful information was exchanged in the calmer, less conflictual small groups than in the large mass meeting. In the small groups, the members were not looking for a fight. Because they did not have to work themselves up to face the "public," they could afford to listen and even to change their minds. They did not have to simplify their ideas to make them more efficient weapons. In this mood, facts could mean more than one thing, people could present themselves in some complexity, new interpretations were acceptable, and the members of a group could struggle toward a common goal.

Finally, small groups and small political units provide the conditions in which citizens are most likely to take responsibility for and empathize with others. They thus facilitate the creation of common interest through some members' making the good of others their own. An elaborate series of experiments in both natural and laboratory settings has demonstrated that the smaller the group, the more responsible each person in it feels for the good of the others.[27] Large groups diffuse responsibility; small ones focus it on the individual members. Moreover, like the effect of size on participation, the effect of size on taking responsibility for others seems to work most strongly on the potentially marginal members of a society.[28] Small settings may even have a long-term effect on one's tendency to make another's good one's own: in one experiment, people who had grown up in small towns were more likely than people from larger cities to respond to a stranger's cry for help.[29]

Small communities not only inhibit diffusion of responsibility in the social realm, but because they are understaffed and must press a greater proportion of their citizenry into office, they spread responsibility for others more widely in the public realm. Mill relied primarily on the responsibility engendered by widespread participation in small offices to develop the concern he wanted citizens to feel for others. Indeed, the vitality of Athenian democracy may have derived less from direct democracy in the assembly, which no more than 15 percent of the citizenry attended on any occasion, than from the constant involvement of the citizens in governing. In any year, as many as one out of six Athenian citizens had some governmental responsibility.[30]

We do not know whether members of small polities empathize more with one another than do members of large polities. Face-to-face contact probably stimulates empathy, and face-to-face contact among citizens decreases in proportion to a polity's size. Rousseau, for example, believed his democracy of common interest possible only in a polity in which everyone knew everyone else. In the modern era of geographical mobility and attenuated community, this places severe limits on size. Even in Selby, a town of 500, only one person among the sixty-nine I interviewed claimed to know everyone else, although nine others said they knew all but the newcomers. Thus, even if small size does promote empathy, the effect may well disappear by the time a political unit contains 1,000 people.

For all but the practiced orator, the upper limit of effective emotional communication may also be reached quite quickly as the numbers of people in a face-to-face assembly increase. In Selby's town meeting, the citizens sitting on the sidelines can shake their heads in disgust or nod wisely, knowing that they have communicated to anyone looking in their direction the general thrust of their sentiments. But when a town meeting has more than 200 participants, it usually installs a public address system. This means that instead of speaking from their seats, citizens must walk up the aisle, face a hall of people, and talk into a microphone. Then they can no longer raise a hand impetuously and be called on to speak their piece without rehearsing it mentally beforehand. They can no longer, without being called on, burst into an exclamation or a helpful suggestion: "Let's set the vote over till Harvey checks his figures with Mildred."

By the time a meeting includes 10,000 people, someone on the outskirts will be at least 120 feet away from a speaker at the center and will not be able to see whether the speaker's eyes are open or closed, let alone discern more subtle facial nuances.[31] Thus, although as many as 200,000 people can throng together in some of today's stadiums,[32] the emotional tenor of the resulting event is clearly different from that in a smaller meeting of even a few thousand. It is unlikely that any face-to-face democracy has ever encompassed more than 15,000 citizens.[33] In ancient Athens, 4,000 to 6,000 of the 40,000 eligible citizens usually gathered in the assembly;[34] and the Swiss cantons of Uri and Nidwalden each made room once, in the fields outside their capitals, for as many as 4,000 citizens in their annual Landesgemeinde.[35] In relatively huge assemblies like these, the pressures for conformity may become intense, but face-to-face contact probably does less to promote the greater communication, empathy, and sense of responsibility for others that help to generate a common interest.

It is hard to sort out the reasons that, at almost all levels of size, smaller political units generally have greater degrees of unanimity. The evidence we have on the effects of size is meager. Moreover, some evidence applies to differences among small groups of two to thirty members, some to differences among workplaces of thirty to 1,000 members, some to differences among cities, some to differences among states or provinces, some to differences among nations. Many effects of size undoubtedly have upper and lower boundaries beyond which the effect is sharply diminished or nonexistent; but here, too, we have little evidence. The only thing we can say with certainty, in the midst of this inconclusive evidence, is that at least one reason for greater unanimity in smaller groups, workplaces, and provinces is the actual greater coincidence of their members' interests. Small size may or many not promote the adversary goal of equal protection of interests, but it does make it easier to achieve the unitary goal of a common interest.

Conclusion

When the United States saw the beginnings of a movement toward decentralization, or "community control," in the 1960s, proponents of decentralization, at least on the Left, were bifurcated by professional discipline. While sociologists tended to take what I have labeled a unitary perspective, arguing that smaller units would engender feelings of community, political scientists generally took an adversary perspective, arguing that smaller units would give each individual greater control over policy.

Dahl and Tufte's *Size and Democracy* provides an admirable example of the political scientists' approach. The authors catalogue the pros and cons of units of different size with clarity and subtlety. Because small size is so intimately bound up with the possibilities for unitary democracy, they could hardly fail to notice and report on this potential. In chapter 1, "Size and Democracy in Political Thought," therefore, they report that in the unitary ideal of antiquity "citizens would all know each other and would be as friendly as possible toward one another," and "smallness made it possible for every citizen to know each other . . . to understand his problems, to develop friendly feelings toward him."[36] In the modern unitary ideal, also, the polity would be "small, cohesive, highly consensual . . . peopled by equal and substantially like-minded friends. . . . Friendliness and civic consensus all must decline as the population and the territory of the state increase."[37] They quote Montesquieu's conclusion that in a large republic "interests become particularized" and "the common good is sacrificed," whereas "in a small republic, the public good is more strongly felt, better known, and closer to each citizen."[38] Under the heading "On the Common Interest," they condense these conclusions into the claim that "smaller democracies make it easier for a citizen to perceive a relation between his own self-interest or understanding of the good and a public or general interest, the interests of others, or general conceptions of the good."[39]

This all comes in the first, historical chapter. Although the authors provide some evidence on consensus, there is no further discussion of the relation between size and friendliness or size and individual responsibility for the common good. The rest of the book addresses the adversary problem of whether large or small units are more likely to facilitate citizens' efforts to promote their interests.[40] Dahl and Tufte's "two criteria for the ideal democratic polity"—citizen effectiveness and system capacity—both have to do with policy outcomes. Neither criterion measures what happens to the citizens themselves—whether, for example, citizens of a small polity are more likely to direct themselves to a common good rather than to their separate self-regarding interests. The underlying assumption is that in judging how close a polity comes to the "ideal" only adversary criteria matter.

Dahl and Tufte conclude with a plea for a normative-empirical political theory that would offer useful guidance about the appropirate relations among units of different sizes. I would join in that plea. But the problem is much deeper than that of size. It is, in essence, the problem of the appropriate relations between unitary and aversary democracy. One cannot, like most contemporary political scientists, throw away the half of human experience that values unitary goods and judge a polity solely on adversary criteria. One must judge the pros and cons of sizes and forms of government according to the often competing claims of unitary and adversary democracy. Laslett was closer to the mark when he wrote that the problem facing political theory was how to articulate the face-to-face (and therefore unitary) society of legislators with the territorial (and therefore adversary) society of their constituents. I would go further and say that the problem for political theory is how to articulate the entire complex of unitary values with those of adversary democracy.

In this book, I have tried to move in this direction. I have looked only at the smallest units and have looked within these at the conflict between unitary and adversary values. Asking what is the nature of a good political life in this smallest unit, I have come to the practical conclusion that even in a unit of two people unitary and adversary systems are in tension. One cannot resolve their contradictions by adopting either a unitary or an adversary mode at all times and on all issues. Both couples and larger polities can and should shift from one system to the other, depending on the extent to which individual interests are actually in conflict.

This analysis directs attention to the question of objective interests rather than subjective preferences. It makes interests central to any normative discussion of democracy. Adversary theorists have been understandably reluctant to adopt this stance because objective interests are both definitionally elusive and usually impossible to measure. Yet only by asking to what extent objective interests are actually in conflict can one hope to answer such questions as when political equality is acceptable, when representatives should feel a duty to act for the common good and when they should represent the interests of their constituents, or when majoritarian systems and systems protecting individual rights should prevail over consensual systems that foster community.

As for the citizens themselves, they are most likely to come to understand their real interests in a small democracy, like a town or workplace, where members make a conscious effort to choose democratic procedures appropriate to the various issues that arise. Without an extensive program of decentralization and workplace democracy, few people are likely to have the political experiences necessary for understanding their interests.

Chapter 21

The Limits of Friendship

Lessons for the Small Collective

IN THE LATE 1960s and early 1970s, the thousands of small collectives that sprang up across the United States called themselves "participatory democracies."[1] They used the term not just as a slogan, but to define themselves as organizations that made decisions: (1) so that the members felt equal to one another; (2) by consensus rather than by majority rule; and (3) in face-to-face assembly, not through referenda or representation.

As Aristotle pointed out, these are the principles of friendship. Friendship is an equal relation: it does not grow or maintain itself well at a distance; and its expression is unanimity.[2] "Participatory democracy" tried to extend the ideals of friendship to larger, and in many cases less voluntary, associations.

But the small democracies that called themselves "participatory" faced a constant tension between the principles of friendship and their need for a universalistic and equitable decision rule that would apply when interests began to diverge. Their members espoused ideals—like that of equal power—that are the fruits of several centuries of adversary thought. Yet instead of learning to move back and forth between unitary and adversary forms of democracy, they tried to handle the tension by making the same political formulas—political equality, consensus, and face-to-face assembly—serve double duty. Each formula had both to create a community in which the individual was one with others and to protect the same individual against the others in that community.

When these small democracies grew from groups of close acquaintances to larger associations of strangers or when specific issues put the interests of the members in conflict, each distinctive feature of unitary democracy took on a new function. The ideal of equality, which a small group of friends experiences as mutual respect, became, as the group grew larger and more divergent in interests, an insistence on the equal protection of interests. The ideal of consensus, which among friends reflects similarity in goals, became an individual veto over the actions of the majority. The face-to-face contact that friends value for the pleasure of coming together became a guarantee that no decision could escape every individual's scrutiny. Although the procedures remained unitary in form, distrust replaced trust, and the natural equality, unanimity, and directness of friendship were transformed into rules whose major purpose was the protection of the individual.

This double function derived from the underlying attempt of these organizations to remain, in essence, friendships. While beginning to protect themselves against each other, their members continued to hope that some process, whether emotional or rational, would bring about solutions that were best for all. Yet the lesson of this volume for a small collective is that when a group grows larger and more diverse it must find a substitute for the discussion and genuine persuasion that friends use to discover their common interests. The two possible substitutes are intensified social pressure or the institution of adversary procedures. Many small democracies, still modeling themselves on friendships, end up using social pressure to bring minorities into line because invoking adversary procedures would require recognizing that the nature of their group had changed.

A sound instinct for self-preservation draws people to small, unitary associations where they can find refuge in mutual respect from a competitive and even hostile society. As their associations grow beyond the bounds of closely knit friendship, one can understand why they try to retain the equality of respect, the unanimity, and the face-to-face contact that marked the organization's earlier experience. Yet when such organizations expand and their members' interests diverge, they can better pursue both their old unitary and their new adversary goals by avoiding the double function of each of these formulas. Direct efforts to maintain equal status will usually be more effective than indirect efforts to do so by equalizing power; equal power works best to protect interests equally. The principles of consensus and face-to-face democracy, which can help maintain the unity of smaller unitary groups, can actually make it difficult in larger adversary groups for the shy and those without effective social contacts to protect their interests in the organization. After interests have begun to conflict in major ways, a combination of referenda, representation, and either majority rule or an emphasis on proportional outcomes will protect individual interests more equally than face-to-face assemblies and consensus.

Critics of modern democracy, like the participatory collectives themselves, must recognize both the philosophical tension between adversary and unitary democracy and the practical need to employ different procedures when interests conflict rather than converge. Hannah Arendt, for example, argues that only with a council system of small face-to-face assemblies can a democracy achieve the values that come with the "direct participation of every citizen in the public affairs of the country."[3] But Arendt's vision is limited by naiveté about how these small face-to-face assemblies would actually work. Her goal is "political freedom"—a citizen's ability to speak and act publicly, to be a "participator in government." She detests unanimity and the "role of a unanimously held 'public opinion,'" for she believes that "no formation of opinion is even possible where all opinions have become the same."[4] Arendt thus makes the small face-to-face assembly the ultimate defense against the tyranny of a unanimous public opinion. However, while decentralization to small councils might well produce the local differences and consequent national debate that she predicts, the face-to-face assemblies themselves would generate strong pressures toward unanimity, as did Selby, Helpline, and probably even the Greek polis to which she harks back.

Local assemblies will always tend to apply unitary procedures even when interests conflict. But if they could learn to guard against this tendency and to shift from unitary to adversary procedures and back again, depending on the goals they wish to pursue and the extent to which their members actually have interests in common, they would serve their members' interests better and might, in passing, help create a citizenry more able to judge the democratic performance of the nation-state. While no one will ever be able to determine common interests with perfect accuracy (since no one can ever know with certainty his or her own real interests, let alone the interests of others), asking the right question, and trying to determine those interests, makes one more likely to approximate that result. The members of small neighborhood and workplace democracies would be well placed to train themselves to recognize their self-regarding, public-regarding, and ideal-regarding interests, and they might learn how to pursue their interests against the interests of others without losing the capacity to shift back into the unitary mode whenever this again became possible.

Lessons for the Nation-State

I can summarize my argument regarding the nation-state in a syllogism. Its first premise, advanced in the last chapter, is that the larger the polity, the more likely it is that some individuals will have conflicting interests. Its second premise, advanced throughout the book, is that the more individual interests come in conflict, the more a democracy encompassing those interests must employ adversary procedures. These two premises demand the conclusion that democracies as large as the modern nation-state be primarily adversary democracies.

This is a bitter conclusion. It means rejecting the vision of national unitary democracy where interests coincide naturally, through unselfishness, or through the power of an idea. The unitary vision appeals to humanity's most exalted sentiments—the deep joy of spontaneous communion, unselfishness, and commitment to a larger good. When a powerful ideal or moment of transcendence unites millions of people, the result is even more inspiring than in a small community. Yet on this scale, the unitary goal is also more dangerous, because with increasing size the chances of real conflict increase, and so, consequently, do the chances that an appeal to unity will obscure conflict to the benefit of those who launch the appeal.

Appeals to unity on a national scale take many forms. One involves the institutionalization of communal charisma: each citizen inspires every other citizen, and all acquire, to a greater or lesser degree, that touch of the gods that makes human beings able to call forth in others the spirit of sacrifice and nobility. The goal is to weave into everyday life those "moments of madness"[5] in which each individual knows that he or she is a necessary part of the larger whole. The creation of such a national emotional communion is an integral part of most modern Marxian visions, partly because it helps to de-emphasize self-interested behavior when one does not want to rely fully on material incentives in production. Indeed, the communal energy kindled through mass mutual inspiration can, in the short run, produce extraordinary achievements. It can also ennoble each citizen's life. But as time goes on, the momentary exhilaration usually fades, to be replaced by social or institutional coercion on a national scale. The benefits diminish, while the costs become intolerable. Like war itself, efforts to create a unitary "moral equivalent of war"[6] lose their glamor after a year or two.

A second approach to national unitary democracy is purely definitional. The theory of democracy in Leninist nations depends on the idea that abolishing class-based society by definition abolishes all important conflicts of interest. With the abolition of classes, different groups will begin to work together in "deep harmony," and political decisions can be founded on the citizen's "undisputed and conscious, sincere preference for the public interests, the state's interests and the interests of the group, as opposed to private interests. . . ."[7] With only one class in the state, there will be no need for institutionalized conflict in the form of political parties and independent unions. So, for example, at the Tenth Party Congress of the Soviet Communist Party, Trotsky argued against the right of trade unions to strike on the grounds that, because the Soviet Union was a workers' state, the unions as workers' organizations had no reason to strike.[8]

A third, conservative, approach to a national unitary ideal holds that wise statesmen must identify the common good in the realm of right and wrong, not of individual preferences,[9] and either inspire the citizenry to follow that good or have the constitutional power to pursue it in spite of popular opposition. In this modified unitary democracy, the answer to "Who will guard the guardians?" comes from the constitutional process. The institutions that select an elite like the Justices of the U.S. Supreme Court and protect it from the short-run influence of the public are ulimately subject to the popular will. The constitutional aim is, in theory, only to delay popular retaliation long enough for citizens to consider their long-run as well as short-run interests. This approach usually assumes that citizens' interests are similar in the important issues that come before the polity. But when there are consistent conflicts of interest either among citizens or between the elite and the public, this procedure is difficult to reconcile with the principle of equal protection.

Still another approach to national unitary democracy is the Japanese. This approach recognizes conflicts of interest, but assumes that the conflicting groups all contribute to the common good in a relatively stable, recognizable way. In Japan, political elites allocate government benefits among interest groups by giving great weight to a group's traditional share, but expanding or contracting this share informally, depending on the group's political power and on a rough impression of its contribution to the general welfare. Politicians, businessmen, and citizens all avoid "zero-sum" conceptions of the polity in which whatever one group receives must be taken from another, emphasizing instead formulas in which all share in the good or bad fortunes of the whole.[10] Japan thus differs sharply from European consociational democracies, where zero-sum calculations predominate and allocations depend in theory on sheer numerical proportionality. Japan and countries like it are, in this sense, "pre-adversary."

A fifth approach to the unitary ideal, consistent with each of the above, assumes that the nation's major problems are susceptible of technically correct solutions, so that the polity can be concerned with the "administration of things, not the government of men."[11] While Mao, Marx, and Engels use the language of "correct solutions," progressives in American national politics and "good government" organizations on the state and local level make the same assumption, expecting elected officials to act only as facilitators, technocrats, and efficient managers of the business of government.

Each of these five approaches to unitary democracy at the national level has its separate appeal—creating a citizenry whose daily life brings out the noblest elements in their makeup, overthrowing the dehumanizing division between owner and worker, overcoming parochial divisions in the pursuit of what is right, orchestrating the several interests in a society in a way that emphasizes their connection to the common welfare, and eliminating the waste and misdirection endemic to political conflict. It would be absurd not to recognize the value of these goals. Yet the logic of this volume suggests that they are all dangerous. They all tend to obscure conflict in such a way that the initially disadvantaged become even more so. Although in this book I have subjected only the problem of political equality to close scrutiny, freedom is also in jeopardy. When the assumption of common interest makes conflict illegitimate, a polity may no longer tolerate dissent.

The depressing conclusion is that democratic institutions on a national scale can seldom be based on the assumption of a common good. To think otherwise is to stretch to untenability each method of achieving a common good. The method of overlapping private interests becomes the fantasy of "me-plus": you and you and all others add to my experience, take me out of and beyond myself, deepen my sensations and my thoughts, and take nothing away. Everyone adds; no one subtracts. The self expands, meeting no obstacles. So too with the method of making the good of others and the whole one's own. No individual can be completely and solely altruistic or wrapped up in the corporate good. A rhetoric, propaganda, or fantasy that praises altruism or reason of state while disparaging all self-regarding interests will make it much harder for those who believe in it to sort out their actual interests.

Because of the size and complexity of any modern nation-state, many citizens' interests will inevitably conflict. Yet a democracy based solely on the cold facts of national conflict will encourage selfishness based on perceiving others as opponents and discourage reasoned discussion among people of good will. The effect is particularly noticeable in the realm of ideals. Adversary democracy, which derives from a fundamental moral relativism, transforms the pursuit of ideals from a dialogue into a bargain. In an adversary system, one person's belief is no more right than any other's; ideals are no different from other interests; the way to deal with ideals is therefore to weight each person's ideal equally and sum them all up, letting the numerically preponderant ideals prevail. When a collectivity treats ideals as interests and decides to settle such issues with a vote, it has given up on the hope that discussion, good will, and intelligence can lead to agreement on the common good. Few politicians and even fewer ordinary citizens find these consequences acceptable. To avoid them, most people apply to the nation unitary assumptions and a unitary rhetoric that even they themselves do not quite believe. The resulting conceptual and moral confusions help undermine the legitimacy of what is, in fact, a primarily adversary polity.

There are alternatives to repeating myths one only half believes. To begin with, in the adversary realm, the members of a polity can realize that adversary democracy has its own ideals, which, although less emotionally inspiring than unitary ideals, will still appeal to the citizen's sense of equity. Nations organized primarily as adversary democracies have not generally faced up to the radical implications of the central adversary principle that each citizen's interests deserve equal protection. This is primarily because making genuine efforts to achieve the equal protection of interests would require major shifts in the balance of power in every modern national democracy. In no adversary democracy would it be in the interests of those who now have greater power to begin to protect all citizens' interests equally. But the position of the less powerful is further weakened by the way the underlying contradiction in democratic theory between unitary and adversary democracy obscures the importance of equal protection in moments of conflict. If any democratic nation were to try genuinely to protect individual interests equally, this in itself could become a source of pride to its citizens.

Taking adversary ideals seriously would go a long way toward relieving the simple self-interested focus of adversary politics. But a national polity can also try to make some forms of the unitary experience available to its citizens. The safest place to do this is on the most local level, either in the workplace or the neighborhood, where the greater information each citizen can have about any decision helps guard against false unity. With such decentralization, a nation operating primarily as an adversary democracy need not condemn its citizens to selfishness and amorality, any more than a state with no established church need condemn its citizens to atheism.

Moreover, even on the national level, some unitary, or almost unitary, moments can be preserved. First, even in a primary adversary democracy, citizens must agree to a significant extent on the ideals that sustain the adversary process itself and place them, by genuine consensus, somewhat beyond the adversary process.

Second, the pursuit of a higher goal—often responding to an external threat—can give citizens some common interests and convince them briefly that these are the only interests that count. These moments are precious, even though they must also be transitory. Just as couples can train themselves to acknowledge conflicts of interest, make explicit who wins and who loses, take turns in the winning, and yet return to a loving selflessness once a conflict is settled, so a nation can pull together in wartime or a natural emergency, then return to its normal bickering after the crisis. The transition is easier if a nation has made a deliberate effort to maintain its unitary institutions rather than letting them atrophy. And the national unitary moments are less dangerous the more a citizenry and its leadership has had the experience of consciously judging between unitary and adversary situations and choosing its democratic methods in accordance with this judgment.

Third, in the uninspiring arena of administration, a national bureaucracy can increase the frequency of a common good by handling technical decisions completely and by trying to resolve conflicts of interest on the basis of a rough principle of equal protection rather than denying the legitimacy of conflict.

Finally, and perhaps most importantly, an interdependent, less competitive economy can vastly increase the average worker's experience of common interest with others. The effect of economic structure on common interest has not been the focus of this book, partly because the theme has been treated extensively by others, and partly because I advance here a claim for the independent, although not necessarily large, effect of political institutions on the generation of common interest. Yet the effect of a more cooperative economy on citizens' moral experience is one of the strongest normative claims of socialism. A nation interested in expanding its citizens' unitary experience can always use its control over the economy to help achieve that end.

In short, by fostering decentralized and highly participative units, by maintaining a few crucial remnants of consensus, by instituting primarily cooperative economic relations, and by treating adversary methods not as an all-encompassing ideal but as an unavoidable and equitable re-course, a nation can maintain some of the conditions for community, comradeship, selflessness, and idealism without insisting that on most matters all its citizens have a common interest.

The national polity poses at its most difficult the problem that arises even in small groups when they try to move back and forth between unitary and adversary modes. We cajole and coerce ourselves into un-selfish behavior in ways that are often fragile and prone to slippage. We find it hard to dip in and out of the adversary mode without being tainted by it, hard to be selfish now and selfless ten minutes later. We can reach common interest with others in part by making their good our own, yet a too frequent recourse to adversary procedures undermines the habits of thought and feeling that induce such behavior.

The subversive effect of adversary procedure on unitary feeling makes it essential that the necessary dominance of adversary democracy in national politics not set the pattern of behavior for the nation as a whole. The effort to maintain unitary elements in the nation in turn depends on widespread rejection both of the cynical doctrine that interests always conflict and of the credulous assumption that they can always be harmonious.

Chapter 22

First Principles

WHENEVER a society becomes uncertain about the legitimacy of its institutions, its members inevitably discuss the possibility of reorganizing those institutions along lines consistent with a few of the society's most widely shared beliefs. In the United States, the steady expansion of both business and government has created precisely this kind of crisis, and the most commonly discussed remedy has been to make economic and political life more "democratic." Support for this notion was especially intense during the late 1960s and early 1970s. Since then, it has receded. But the crisis of legitimacy is still with us; indeed, some believe it has even grown more acute. Demands for democratization are therefore likely to recur. If these demands take account of the way "democracy" changes its meaning in different contexts, and if they can be reconciled with competing demands for freedom and efficiency, they may well end up transforming our political and economic institutions. Otherwise, the crisis of legitimacy is likely to make both big government and big business increasingly unworkable.

The student radicals of the 1960s were not much concerned with the contradictions inherent in our democratic ideals. The Port Huron Statement, which in 1962 set the goals for the emerging radical movement, urged that we make politics more "participatory" by subjecting both public and private bureaucracies to critical public scrutiny, by making representatives more accountable, and by giving people more voice in decisions that affected their lives. These measures, it predicted, would reduce apathy and improve not only the outcomes of decisions but the quality of citizens' lives. The Statement assumed at every point that politics would consist primarily of conflict. Thus, making democracy more participatory essentially meant making adversary institutions work better by giving citizens more equal power.

Yet in spite of its underlying assumption of conflict, the Port Huron Statement was at least as concerned with unitary as with adversary goals. Its authors wanted to create a society that would maintain deep human relationships, end loneliness, isolation, and estrangement, and develop individuals' capacity for love. An adversary system, unfortunately, cannot easily promote such goals. The Port Huron Statement's recommendations for more equal adversary participation might even have made a unitary society harder to reach. SDS implicitly recognized this in its own organization, for its local chapters came to operate on unitary principles that bore little relationship to anything in the Port Huron Statement. The experience of these small unitary chapters then offered no guidance to those concerned with maintaining cooperative relations among frequent adversaries or with democratizing the nation-state. The clash between unitary and adversary goals for the nation kept both SDS and other New Left groups from moving much beyond the vague agenda for transforming national institutions that the Port Huron Statement had sketched.

This book has argued that if we want to make our institutions conform more loosely to our democratic ideals, we must first sort out the contradictions in these ideals. Specifically, we must distinguish ideals appropriate to situations where we all have common interests from ideals appropriate to situations where we have conflicting interests. In the real world, we always have both. Thus, for a polity to embody our fundamental conceptions about democracy, it must deal with both common and conflicting interests in ways consistent with our ideals. As we have seen, a polity that purports to be either exclusively unitary or exclusively adversary cannot do this. To maintain its legitimacy, a democracy must have both a unitary and an adversary face. It must intertwine the unitary thesis and the adversary antithesis, embracing both unitary and adversary forms, becoming neither and absorbing neither, but holding them together so that when circumstances warrant, the constituent forms continue to appear.

On the national level, such a democracy must be primarily adversary. But it must be an adversary democracy that truly seeks to protect interests equally and consequently judges itself on its ability to produce proportional outcomes in moments of conflict. Very small democratic organizations must be primarily unitary. In small workplaces and neighborhood democracies, a citizen could learn the communal virtues, partake of a "community of values,"[1] become a genuine "participator in government,"[2] and at the same time, learn to adopt different democratic procedures for dealing with common and conflicting interests.

300

To state that people sometimes have common interests and sometimes have conflicting interests is to state the obvious. Yet most people's day-to-day thinking is dominated either by the assumption that interests always converge or by the assumption that they always conflict. The idealistic anarchist, the committed Marxist, the president of a corporation, the engineer, the city manager—none will let go of the notion that in the well-managed world (or organization) there will be no genuine conflicts of interest. They all assume that most, if not all, decisions can be genuinely in the best interests of all members of their polity.

The average political scientist is equally reluctant to give up his conviction that the combative forms of adversary democracy provide the only guarantees of freedom. In his eyes, unity is always a fraud. Proponents of the adversary model—in political science, in politics itself, and outside both these professional arenas—often love conflict. They enjoy making coalitions, calculating odds, forming strategies, and defeating their opponents. If they win, they try to extract as much as possible from their opponents. If they lose, they calculate ways of giving as little as possible. They reject consociational solutions that yield proportional outcomes or allow for taking turns, partly because such solutions drain the excitement from the battle. It was not just paranoia that made former President Nixon compile an "enemies list"; it was the spirit of adversary democracy.

As a people, we in America are starved for unitary democracy. Because our public life so often consists in the soulless aggregation of interests, we like our national leaders to raise our unitary goosebumps for a moment ("Ask not what your country can do for you, but what you can do for your country"). But our adversary training has also made us cynical about such appeals, so in the end we mostly ignore them. Unitary appeals fall into an institutional void. Most Americans experience democracy only in the voting booth. Citizens file into a curtained box, mark a preference, and file out. In special circumstances, if a big-city political machine is at work or if the community is small, they may see someone they know on the way in and out of the box, smile, and exchange a triviality. Most voters see no one they know. They sit in their homes; they consume information; they determine a preference; they go to the polling place; they register the preference; they return to their homes. Small wonder that the preferences so conceived and so expressed should tend toward the private and the selfish.

Yet in a polity with as few unitary institutions as ours, an effective national unitary appeal might well be dangerous. Our citizenry is not

educated to know its interests. Adversary issues that would raise consciousness often do not enter the realm of public decision. And even
when we have some idea of our self-regarding interests, we have not
usually tested this idea against either our ideals or our feeling for others
to determine what our "enlightened" choice would be. Because we have
had little experience in deciding when our interests converge and when
they conflict, we may hunger for a unitary appeal that we cannot wisely
evaluate.

A few philosophers have recently sounded the alarm against the increasingly self-interested focus of public life. They call for a return to
preadversary conceptions of the common good, to public discussion and
debate, and to relations of fellowship and community.[3] Some demand a
reform of the economy; others urge the return of politics to small face-to-
face forms of debate where citizens can be political actors rather than con-
sumers. To achieve these goals, such thinkers often advocate socialism,
decentralization of state functions, workplace democracy, or all three.
Yet their chorus has had virtually no impact on our actual political behavior. Government grows steadily more centralized, the economy not
greatly more cooperative, and workplaces remain as undemocratic as ever.

My purpose in this book has been to show that these recommendations
are not just reactions to specific abuses but to the entire conception of
adversary democracy. In many cases the recommendations implicitly call
for unitary democracy without recognizing the difficulties and limitations
of unitary institutions. My aim, on the contrary, has been to show that
preserving unitary virtues requires a mixed polity—part adversary, part
unitary—in which citizens understand their interests well enough to
participate effectively in both forms at once.

Appendixes
Notes
Bibliography
Index

Appendix A

Political Equality in Selby and Helpline: Tables

Key to Tables in Appendix A

Source: R = public records; I = interviews; Q = questionnaire; O = observations.

P = probability: The notation .05 or <.05 indicates that in a sample of this size there are fewer than 5 chances in 100 that the observed distribution could have arisen by chance in this sample if there had been no relation in the larger population. In the same way, .01 or <.01 indicates fewer than 1 chance in 100, and .001 or <.001 fewer than 1 chance in 1,000. The notation "—" indicates that the probability of the distribution reported here being random is greater than 5 in 100. (R) indicates a relation *reverse* to that expected.

Probability is based on the full rather than the dichotomous range of values, on the grounds that the simple dichotomy often distorts the true extent of the differences. All tests are one-tailed.

Selby is not typical of Vermont towns. I chose the town on the basis of a subjective impression that its meeting was the most democratic of any I had visited. Probability statistics reported for the town's population as a whole refer only to a hypothetical universe composed of other "similar" towns.

Helpline, too, is not representative of worker-controlled organizations. Again, I chose it on the basis of a subjective impression that it was more democratic than any of the other organizations I had encountered. The tests of statistical significance reported here, which are based on the entire Helpline staff, therefore have meaning insofar as the reader can imagine a universe composed of organizations similar to Helpline. They also indicate the likelihood that an observed association within Helpline is due to some systematic causal relation among the variables under study, and not to chance alone.

N = number of cases. N of cases in parentheses at top of table is the base N, divided into the two relevant categories. N's in parentheses under percentages are adjusted for nonresponse or nonapplicability. The percentage is calculated on the N in parentheses under the percentage.

Political Equality in Selby and Helpline: Tables

The number of cases on which each percentage is based differs from the total number in each of the two categories at the top of the table depending on the source and on the criteria for exclusion. "Don't know" responses have in all cases been excluded.

In Selby, tabulations derived from Selby voting records omit those residents who had lived in town less than one and one-half years, on the grounds that their failure to register represented only lack of time.

Tabulations derived from Selby's other public records include all cases.

Tabulations from Selby's interviews, which were generally free flowing and unstructured, do not encompass all the cases because in some interviews structured questions seemed inappropriate. For this reason, quantitative data derived from interviews should be relied on tentatively, in conjunction with other measures.

Tabulations from the Selby questionnaire encompass fifty-five cases or fewer after the "don't knows" have been eliminated. The group of people who answered the questionnaire seemed, however, to differ in no important respect from the group who did not.

At Helpline forty of the forty-one full-time staff had a full interview with me, and each filled out at least those parts of a structured questionnaire that I had indicated were crucial. Thirty-eight of the staff filled out the whole questionnaire or a large part of it.

$r = Pearson$ product-moment correlation coefficient. For example, if every man spoke once but no woman spoke, this perfect correlation would be represented by $+1.00$. If men and women were equally likely to speak, this absence of any correlation would be represented by .00. (The correlation between education and income in the United States is about .40.) Because many of these variables are noninterval and some may have nonlinear relationships, the correlations should be understood as approximations. They are presented only to facilitate comparisons of the strength of the relationships.

Indexes: For composition of indexes, see Appendix B.

Selby: Newcomers and Old-timers[a]

Source		Newcomers[b]	Old-timers[b]	P
	A. Political activity			
R	Attended more than a quarter of town meetings for which eligible in last ten years (calculated only on those in town long enough to vote)[c]	35%[d] (23)	57%[d] (35)	.01
R	Held town office at least once in last ten years	6%[d] (34)	31%[d] (35)	.01
I	Reports ever having contacted a town officer	57% (32)	79% (33)	.05
I	Reports having spoken "often" at town meeting (asked only of those who attended)	22% (9)	16% (25)	R (−)
	Index of local political activity $r = .48$ ($N = 69$)			.001
	B. Political efficacy			
Q	"In this town people like me don't have any say about what the town does."—Disagree	67% (30)	79% (24)	—
I	"Do you feel that the town here pays any attention to what people like you think?"— Often or always	42% (26)	56% (27)	—
	Index of local political efficacy $r = .17$ ($N = 68$)			—

C. Work and social ties

I	Works in town (calculated only on active work force)	32% (22)	59% (27)	.01
I	Spends free time outside the family	29% (31)	48% (29)	—
I	Could recognize at least a quarter of people in town	31% (32)	84% (31)	.001
	Index of social connection r = .29 (N = 67)			.05

D. Local information

Q	Knows names of two selectmen	47% (30)	84% (25)	.01
Q	Knows which day town meeting is held each year	43% (30)	64% (25)	—
I	"How about the local issues in this town? How well do you understand them?"—Fairly well or well	44% (27)	77% (26)	—
	Index of local information r = .25 (N = 63)			—

a For an explanation of symbols and discrepancies in the number of cases, see "Key to Tables," Appendix A. For composition of indexes and wording of questions, see Appendix B.

b "Newcomers" (N = 34) are those who have lived in town less than twelve years. "Old-timers" (N = 35) are those who have lived in town twelve years or longer. I chose this cut-off point so as to divide the sample in half.

c Tabulations derived from voting records omit those residents who had lived in town less than one and one-half years, on the ground that their failure to register represented only lack of time. This exclusion makes the differences in town meeting attendance less striking than they would be otherwise.

d As a partial check on these figures I examined public records on all adult residents of Selby (N = 379). Twenty-one percent (N = 79) were not registered, which is consistent with the interview sample. In the interview sample, only one of the sixteen nonregistrants had lived in town more than two years, and I assume that the same pattern held for the town as a whole. Of the 300 registered voters in the town, 147 had been registered more than ten years. Virtually all these individuals were presumably old-timers by my definition. However, the 153 individuals who had been registered for less than ten years also included a few old-timers who had lived in town twelve years or more but had reached voting age within the past ten years. Thus, splitting the electorate into those registered more than ten years and those registered for less than ten years confounds the effects of length of residence and age. Nonetheless, it is reassuring to find that those who had been registered ten years or more had attended 50 percent of the town meetings over the past ten years, while those who had been registered between one and one-half and ten years had attended only 33 percent of the meetings for which they were eligible—results quite compatible with those in the table. Likewise, 29 percent of those who had been registered ten years or more had held town office, compared with only 3 percent of those registered less than ten years.

TABLE A.2
Selby: Living in the Village[a]

Source		Nonvillagers	Villagers	
	A. Political activity			
R	Attended more than 25 percent of town meetings for which eligible in last ten years (calculated only on those in town long enough to vote)	39% (249)	55% (51)	—
R	Held town office at least once in last ten years	12% (326)	23% (53)	.05
I	Reports ever having contacted a town officer	64% (53)	83% (12)	—
I	Reports having spoken "often" at town meeting (asked only of those who attended)	15% (26)	25%[b] (8)	R (−)
	Index of local political activity $r = .20$ $(N = 69)$			—
	B. Political efficacy			
Q	"In this town people like me don't have any say about what the town does."—Disagree	67% (45)	100% (9)	—
I	"Do you feel that the town here pays any attention to what people like you think?"—Often or always	43% (42)	73% (11)	—
	Index of local political efficacy $r = .27$ $(N = 68)$			.05

C. Work and social ties

I	Works in town (calculated only on active work force)	45% (42)	57% (7)	—
I	Spends free time outside the family	30% (47)	69% (13)	.01
I	Could recognize at least one-quarter of people in town	53% (53)	80% (10)	—
	Index of social connection $r = .32$ ($N = 67$)			.01

D. Local information

Q	Knows names of two selectmen	61% (46)	78% (9)	—
Q	Knows which day town meeting is held each year	46% (46)	89% (9)	.05
I	"How about the local issues in this town? How well do you understand them?"—Fairly well or well	56% (43)	80% (10)	—
	Index of local information $r = .28$ ($N = 63$)			.05

[a] For an explanation of symbols and discrepancies in the number of cases, see "Key to Tables," Appendix A. For composition of indexes and wording of questions, see Appendix B.

The tabulation of town meeting attendance with living in the village is based on data covering all registered voters ($N = 300$). The tabulation of holding town office with living in the village is based on data covering all adult residents ($N = 379$). Among the residents, Nonvillager $N = 326$, Villager $N = 53$. In the interview sample, Nonvillager $N = 56$, Villager $N = 13$.

When data are available for both all adult residents and the interview sample, the sample follows much the same pattern as the population. In the interview sample, 46 percent of the eligible non-villagers ($N = 46$) had attended more than a quarter of the possible meetings in the last ten years, compared to 58 percent of the villagers ($N = 12$). Of the nonvillagers, 18 percent had held town office ($N = 56$), compared to 23 percent of the villagers ($N = 13$). In the interview sample, deter-mination of "village" status was made by measuring one mile from the town meeting hall to the actual residence. Such determination for the whole population was made by inspection of the mailing list, including in the village category only people who clearly lived in its center. Conse-quently, the proportion of "villagers" is somewhat smaller in the population than in the interview sample.

TABLE A.3
Selby: Youth and Age[a]

Source		Age 21-30	Age 31 and Above	P
	A. Political activity			
R	Attended more than 25% of town meetings for which eligible in last ten years (calculated only on those in town long enough to vote)	20% (15)	58% (43)	.01
R	Held town office at least once in last ten years	0% (19)	26% (50)	.001
I	Reports ever having contacted a town officer	47% (17)	75% (48)	.05
I	Reports having spoken "often" at town meeting (asked only of those who attended)	20% (5)	17% (24)	R (−)
	Index of local political activity $r = .41$ $(N = 69)$			.001
	B. Political efficacy			
Q	"In this town people like me don't have any say about what the town does."—Disagree	53% (15)	81% (39)	—
I	"Do you feel that the town here pays any attention to what people like you think?"—Often or always	41% (17)	53% (36)	—
	Index of local political efficacy $r = .14$ $(N = 68)$			—
	C. Work and social ties			
I	Works in town (calculated only on active work force)	36% (14)	51% (35)	.05
I	Spends free time outside the family	31% (16)	41% (44)	—
I	Could recognize at least one-quarter of people in town	50% (18)	60% (45)	—
	Index of social connection $r = .15$ $(N = 67)$			—
	D. Local information			
Q	Knows names of two selectmen	53% (15)	68% (40)	—
Q	Knows which day town meeting is held each year	13% (15)	68% (40)	.001
I	"How about the local issues in this town? How well do you understand them?"—Fairly well or well	44% (16)	68% (37)	.05
	Index of local information $r = .28$ $(N = 69)$			.05

[a] For an explanation of symbols and discrepancies in the number of cases, see "Key to Tables," Appendix A. For composition of indexes and wording of questions, see Appendix B. For ages 21-30, $N = 19$; for ages 31 and above, $N = 50$.

TABLE A.4
Selby: Gender[a]

Source		Females	Males	P
	A. Political activity			
R	Attended more than a quarter of town meetings for which eligible in last ten years (calculated only on those in town long enough to vote)	37% (143)	45% (157)	—
R	Held town office at least once in last ten years	12% (176)	14% (203)	—
I	Reports ever having contacted a town officer	66% (35)	70% (30)	—
I	Reports having spoken "often" at town meeting (asked only of those who attended)	22% (18)	13% (16)	—
	Index of local political activity $r = .03$ (N = 69)			—
	B. Political efficacy			
Q	"In this town people like me don't have any say about what the town does."—Disagree	15% (28)	29% (26)	—
I	"Do you feel that the town here pays any attention to what people like you think?"—Often or always	45% (31)	55% (22)	—
	Index of local political efficacy $r = .01$ (N = 68)			—
	C. Work and social ties			
I	Works in town (calculated only on active work force)	48% (23)	46% (26)	—
I	Spends free time outside the family	34% (32)	43% (28)	—
I	Could recognize at least a quarter of people in town	53% (32)	61% (31)	—
	Index of social connection $r = .20$ (N = 68)			—
	D. Local information			
Q	Knows names of two selectmen	59% (29)	69% (26)	—
Q	Knows which day town meeting is held each year	48% (29)	58% (26)	—
I	"How about the local issues in this town? How well do you understand them?"—Fairly well or well	50% (30)	74% (23)	—
	Index of local information $r = .07$ (N = 63)			—

[a] For an explanation of symbols and discrepancies in the number of cases, see "Key to Tables," Appendix A. For composition of indexes and wording of questions, see Appendix B.

The tabulation of town meeting attendance with gender is based on data covering all registered voters (N = 300). The tabulation of holding town office with gender is based on data covering all adult residents (N = 379). Among the residents, Female N = 176, Male N = 203. In the interview sample, Female N = 33, Male N = 31.

Again, the interview sample reflects fairly accurately trends in the town's population as a whole. In the interview sample 40 percent of the women had attended more than a quarter of the meetings for which they were eligible (N = 30), compared to 57 percent of the men (N = 28). Sixteen percent of the women had held town office (N = 38), compared to 23 percent of the men (N = 31).

TABLE A.5
Selby: Class[a]

Source		Low SES	High SES	P
	A. Political activity			
R	Attended more than a quarter of town meetings for which eligible in last ten years (calculated only on those in town long enough to vote)	38% (77)	51% (99)	.001
R	Held town office at least once in last ten years	14% (86)	20% (111)	—
I	Reports ever having contacted a town officer	63% (35)	73% (30)	—
I	Reports having spoken "often" at town meeting (asked only of those who attended)	12% (17)	24% (17)	—
	Index of local political activity $r = .20$ $(N = 69)$			.05
	B. Political efficacy			
Q	"In this town people like me don't have any say about what the town does."—Disagree	66% (29)	80% (25)	.01
I	"Do you feel that the town here pays any attention to what people like you think?"— Often or always	42% (33)	60% (20)	—
	Index of local political efficacy $r = .35$ $(N = 68)$			.01

C. Work and social ties

I	Works in town (calculated only on active work force)	31% (26)	66% (23)	.05
I	Spends free time outside the family	37% (35)	40% (25)	—
I	Could recognize at least a quarter of people in town	60% (37)	54% (26)	R (−)
	Index of social connection $r = .06$ $(N = 67)$			—

D. Local information

Q	Knows names of two selectmen	70% (30)	56% (25)	R (−)
Q	Knows which day town meeting is held each year	47% (30)	60% (25)	.05
I	"How about the local issues in this town? How well do you understand them?"—Fairly well or well	52% (29)	71% (29)	—
	Index of local information $r = .13$ $(N = 63)$			—

[a] For an explanation of symbols and discrepancies in the number of cases, see "Key to Tables," Appendix A. For composition of indexes, including the index of socioeconomic status, and wording of questions, see Appendix B.

The tabulation of town meeting attendance with socioeconomic status is based on registered voters who are also taxpayers ($N = 176$), dichotomized into those with residences valued below $8,000, and at $8,000 or more on the tax list. The tabulation of holding town office with socioeconomic status is based on all taxpayers ($N = 197$), dichotomized the same way. The other tabulations are based on the interview sample ($N = 69$), dichotomized into below average SES ($N = 39$) and above average SES ($N = 30$), with some variation for nonresponse.

The interview sample probably slightly underestimates the relationship between class and town meeting attendance in the town's population as a whole, although it reflects fairly accurately the relationship between class and holding town office. Among the town's taxpayers and registered voters (the only group for which measures of class and town meeting attendance are both available), the association in the town's population between appraised value of residence (a measure of class) and town meeting attendance is .25 ($N = 176$; p = $<$ .001); the same association in the interview sample is only .16 ($N = 33$; p = $<$ .05). Simply dichotomized, and compared to the below- and above-$8,000 residence categories in the population, the interview sample and the population look more alike. Of these below-average socioeconomic status in the interview sample, 42 percent had attended more than a quarter of the town meetings for which they were eligible ($N = 33$), compared to 56 percent of those above-average socioeconomic status ($N = 25$). Thirteen percent had held town office in the last ten years ($N = 39$), compared to 27 percent of those above-average socioeconomic status ($N = 30$).

Selby: Trust and Control[a]

	Low Trust	High Trust	P	Low Sense of Control	High Sense of Control	P
Political activity						
Attended more than a quarter of town meetings for which eligible in last ten years (calculated only on those in town long enough to vote)	41% (25)	55% (26)	—	35% (25)	59% (25)	—
Index of local political activity	r = .22 (N = 55)		—	r = .14 (N = 54)		—
"In this town people like me don't have any say about what the town does."—Disagree	59% (22)	81% (31)	—	67% (27)	78% (27)	—
Index of local political efficacy	r = .26 (N = 55)		.05	r = .27 (N = 54)		.05
Index of socioeconomic status	r = .30 (N = 55)		.05	r = .31 (N = 54)		.05

[a]Calculated only on those who answered one or more of the "trust" and "control" items on the questionnaire. For composition of indexes, including indexes of Trust and Control, and wording of questions, see Appendix B. Low Trust N = 27, High Trust N = 28; Low Control N = 27, High Control N = 27.

Helpline: Length of Time in Organization

Source		Less than 1½ years (N = 18)	1½ years or more (N = 23)[a]	P
	Speaking			
Q	Reports speaking an "average" amount or more at meetings	29% (17)	61% (23)	—
O	Among the five most frequent speakers at CPC[b]	0% (7)	33% (15)	—
O	Speaks more than average at Community Days	33% (18)	57% (23)	.05
	Index of speaking r = .26 (N = 41)			.05
	Attendance			
O	Attended at least one of the nineteen CPC meetings I observed	39% (18)	65% (23)	—
Q	Reports ever having been a representative to the CPC or the DPW	39% (18)	96% (23)	.001
O	Attended both of the two Community Days I observed	61% (18)	70% (23)	—
Q	Reports attending all or almost all possible Community Days since joined Helpline	72% (18)	61% (23)	R (−)
	Index of attendance r = .30 (N = 41)			.05
	Ascribed power			
I	Greater than median power score	22% (18)	65% (23)	.05
Q	Chosen by one or more people as having good judgment on Helpline issues	33% (18)	61% (23)	—
	Index of ascribed power r = .27 (N = 41)			.05
	Efficacy			
Q	Reports having greater than average say in service group	25% (16)	65% (23)	.05
Q	Reports having greater than average say at Helpline	6% (18)	44% (23)	.01
I	Gives self greater than median power score	36% (14)	53% (19)	—
	Index of efficacy r = .29 (N = 41)			.05
	Satisfaction			
Q	Reports being "never" or only "once in a while" dissatisfied with the outcomes of decisions at Helpline	25% (16)	17% (23)	R (−)
Q	Reports being "never" or only "once in a while" dissatisfied with the process of decision making at Helpline	31% (16)	22% (23)	R (−)
Q	Reports being "very" happy in general with Helpline	20% (15)	4% (23)	R (.05)
Q	More satisfied than average with outcomes and process of six specific decisions at Helpline	31% (13)	60% (20)	—
	Index of satisfaction r = .17 (N = 39)			R (−)

[a] For an explanation of symbols and discrepancies in the number of cases, see "Key to Tables," Appendix A. For composition of indexes, and wording of questions, see Appendix B.

[b] Calculated on CPC attenders only; percentage of times speaking per meeting attended.

TABLE A.8

Helpline: Physical Proximity to Social Center

Source		Shelter and Farm (distant)[a] (N = 14)	All other groups (close) (N = 27)[b]	P
	Speaking			
Q	Reports speaking an "average" amount or more at meetings	46% (13)	48% (27)	—
O	Among the five most frequent speakers at CPC[c]	50% (4)	17% (18)	R (−)
O	Speaks more than average at Community Days	36% (14)	52% (27)	—
	Index of speaking r = .25 (N = 41)			—
	Attendance			
O	Attended at least one of the nineteen CPC meetings I observed	29% (14)	66% (27)	—
Q	Reports ever having been a representative to the CPC or the DPW	64% (14)	74% (27)	—
O	Attended both of the two Community Days I observed	50% (14)	74% (27)	.05
Q	Reports attending all or almost all possible Community Days since joined Helpline	64% (14)	67% (27)	—
	Index of attendance r = .31 (N = 41)			.05
	Ascribed power			
I	Greater than median power score	29% (14)	56% (27)	.05
Q	Chosen by one or more people as having good judgment on Helpline issues	43% (14)	52% (27)	—
	Index of ascribed power r = .17 (N = 41)			—

Efficacy

Q	Reports having greater than average say at Helpline	29% (14)	26% (27)	R (−)
I	Gives self greater than median power score	25% (12)	57% (21)	.05
	Index of efficacy[d] $r = .38$ ($N = 41$)			.01

Satisfaction

Q	Reports being "never" or only "once in a while" dissatisfied with the outcomes of decisions at Helpline	14% (14)	24% (25)	.05
Q	Reports being "never" or only "once in a while" dissatisfied with the process of decision making at Helpline	21% (14)	28% (25)	−
Q	Reports being "very" happy in general with Helpline	7% (14)	13% (24)	−
Q	More satisfied than average with outcomes and process of six specific decisions at Helpline	33% (12)	57% (21)	−
	Index of satisfaction $r = .26$ ($N = 39$)			−

[a] The Farm is included here for completeness and comparability with the other tables. The two staff on the Farm worked at a much greater distance from most of the staff at Helpline than did those in the Shelter. Yet because of these two, one had to represent their group by attending the CPC, and giving the Farm's report on Community Days, etc., their combined participation score was somewhat higher than average. This explains the results in reverse of expectations in regard to speaking at the CPC. Eben and Pamela, as the representatives from the Farm and Shelter, spoke frequently at CPC meetings. Few others from their groups attended CPC meetings at all, and were therefore excluded from the CPC calculations. Thus Eben's and Pamela's high scores had a major effect on the average speaking score for their groups. The same phenomenon explains why the Farm has a high percentage reporting greater than average say at Helpline, although I have no explanations for the relatively large percentage of the Shelter (25 percent) reporting a greater than average say. Eliminating the Farm from these calculations does not greatly affect the correlation between proximity and power (the coefficients .25, .31, .34, .38, and .26 reported in Table 5 in the text become .30, .34, .29, .42, and .22).

[b] For an explanation of symbols and discrepancies in the number of cases, see "Key to Tables," Appendix A. For composition of indexes, and wording of questions, see Appendix B.

[c] Calculated on CPC attenders only; percentage of times speaking per meeting attended.

[d] This efficacy index omits "Reports having greater say than average in own service group."

TABLE A.9
Helpline: Age

Source		Ages 19-24 (N = 15)	Ages 25-38 (N = 23)[a]	P
	Speaking			
Q	Reports speaking an "average" amount or more at meetings	13% (15)	59% (22)	.05
O	Among the five most frequent speakers at CPC[b]	20% (5)	13% (15)	R (−)
O	Speaks more than average at Community Days	27% (15)	57% (23)	—
	Index of speaking *r* = .20 (N = 38)			—
	Attendance			
O	Attended at least one of the nineteen CPC meetings I observed	33% (15)	65% (23)	—
Q	Reports ever having been a representative to the CPC or the DPW	40% (15)	57% (23)	.01
O	Attended both of the two Community Days I observed	60% (15)	65% (23)	—
Q	Reports attending all or almost all possible Community Days since joined Helpline	73% (15)	65% (23)	R (−)
	Index of attendance *r* = .30 (N = 38)			.05
	Ascribed power			
I	Greater than median power score	20% (15)	61% (22)	—
Q	Chosen by one or more people as having good judgment on Helpline issues	27% (15)	57% (23)	—
	Index of ascribed power *r* = .20 (N = 38)			—
	Efficacy			
Q	Reports having greater than average say in service group	39% (13)	57% (23)	.05
Q	Reports having greater than average say at Helpline	13% (15)	30% (23)	—
I	Gives self greater than median power score	33% (12)	56% (18)	—
	Index of efficacy *r* = .25 (N = 38)			—
	Satisfaction			
Q	Reports being "never" or only "once in a while" dissatisfied with the outcomes of decisions at Helpline	15% (13)	22% (23)	—
Q	Reports being "never" or only "once in a while" dissatisfied with the process of decision making at Helpline	23% (13)	26% (23)	—
Q	Reports being "very" happy in general with Helpline	23% (13)	0% (22)	R (−)
Q	More satisfied than average with outcomes and process of six specific decisions at Helpline	27% (11)	58% (19)	.05
	Index of satisfaction *r* = .17 (N = 36)			—

[a] Only thirty-eight of the forty-one staff answered this question on the questionnaire.
    For an explanation of symbols and discrepancies in the number of cases, see "Key to Tables," Appendix A. For composition of indexes, and wording of questions, see Appendix B.
[b] Calculated on CPC attenders only; percentage of times speaking per meeting attended.

TABLE A.10
Helpline: Gender

Source		Female (N = 17)	Male (N = 24)[a]	P
	Speaking			
Q	Reports speaking an "average" amount or more at meetings	41% (17)	52% (23)	—
O	Among the five most frequent speakers at CPC[b]	14% (7)	27% (15)	—[c]
O	Speaks more than average at Community Days	29% (17)	58% (24)	—
	Index of speaking $r = .11$ (N = 41)			—
	Attendance			
O	Attended at least one of the nineteen CPC meetings I observed	41% (17)	63% (24)	—
Q	Reports ever having been a representative to the CPC or the DPW	71% (17)	71% (24)	—
O	Attended both of the two Community Days I observed	71% (17)	63% (24)	—[c]
Q	Reports attending all or almost all possible Community Days since joined Helpline	53% (19)	75% (24)	.05
	Index of attendance $r = .17$ (N = 41)			—
	Ascribed power			
I	Greater than median power score	41% (17)	50% (24)	—
Q	Chosen by one or more people as having good judgment on Helpline issues	53% (17)	46% (24)	—[c]
	Index of ascribed power $r = .04$ (N = 41)			—
	Efficacy			
Q	Reports having greater than average say in service group	44% (16)	52% (23)	—
Q	Reports having greater than average say at Helpline	18% (17)	33% (24)	—
I	Gives self greater than median power score	40% (15)	50% (18)	—
	Index of efficacy $r = .21$ (N = 41)			—
	Satisfaction			
Q	Reports being "never" or only "once in a while" dissatisfied with the outcomes of decisions at Helpline	19% (16)	22% (23)	—
Q	Reports being "never" or only "once in a while" dissatisfied with the process of decision making at Helpline	19% (16)	30% (23)	—
Q	Reports being "very" happy in general with Helpline	7% (15)	13% (23)	—
Q	More satisfied than average with outcomes and process of six specific decisions at Helpline	33% (12)	57% (21)	.05
	Index of satisfaction $r = .25$ (N = 39)			—

[a] For an explanation of symbols and discrepancies in the number of cases, see "Key to Tables," Appendix A. For composition of indexes, see Appendix B.

[b] Calculated on CPC attenders only; percentage of times speaking per meeting attended.

[c] Because these relationships are so close to zero, in these cases the dichotomized variable does not reflect the direction of the relationship as expressed in the Pearson correlation coefficient.

Helpline: Race

Source		Black (N = 3)	White (N = 38)[a]	P
	Speaking			
Q	Reports speaking an "average" amount or more at meetings	67% (3)	46% (37)	R (−)
O	Among the five most frequent speakers at CPC[b]	0%[c] (1)	24% (21)	—
O	Speaks more than average at Community Days	33% (3)	47% (38)	—
	Index of speaking r = .01 (N = 41)			—
	Attendance			
O	Attended at least one of the nineteen CPC meetings I observed	33% (3)	55% (38)	
Q	Reports ever having been a representative to the CPC or the DPW	67% (3)	71% (38)	—
O	Attended both of the two Community Days I observed	67% (3)	66% (38)	R (−)
Q	Reports attending all or almost all possible Community Days since joined Helpline	33% (3)	68% (38)	—
	Index of attendance r = .09 (N = 41)			—
	Ascribed power			
I	Greater than median power score	0%[c] (3)	50% (38)	—
Q	Chosen by one or more people as having good judgment on Helpline issues	67% (3)	47% (38)	R (−)
	Index of ascribed power r = .04 (N = 41)			—
	Efficacy			
Q	Reports having greater than average say in service group	33% (3)	50% (36)	—
Q	Reports having greater than average say at Helpline	0%[c] (3)	29% (38)	—
I	Gives self greater than median power score	33% (3)	47% (30)	—
	Index of efficacy r = .11 (N = 41)			—
	Satisfaction			
Q	Reports being "never" or only "once in a while" dissatisfied with the outcomes of decisions at Helpline	0%[c] (3)	22% (36)	—
Q	Reports being "never" or only "once in a while" dissatisfied with the process of decision making at Helpline	0%[c] (3)	28% (36)	—
Q	Reports being "very" happy in general with Helpline	0%[c] (3)	11% (35)	—
Q	More satisfied than average with outcomes and process of six specific decisions at Helpline	0%[c] (3)	53% (30)	—
	Index of satisfaction r = .07 (N = 39)			—

[a] For an explanation of symbols and discrepancies in the number of cases, see "Key to Tables," Appendix A. For composition of indexes, and wording of questions, see Appendix B.

[b] Calculated on CPC attenders only; percentage of times speaking per meeting attended.

[c] With only three individuals in this category, the dichotomous division of each variable into, for example, "greater than average" and "average or less" creates a misleading impression. In these cases, the black members clustered just under the cutoff point, while the white members distributed themselves around it. By reflecting the entire distribution of values in the variable, the indexes give a better picture of the actual association.

Helpline: Parents' Class

Source		Working Class	Lower Middle to Upper Class	P
		(N = 3)	(N = 36)[a]	
	Speaking			
Q	Reports speaking an "average" amount or more at meetings	0% (3)	54% (35)	.01
O	Among the five most frequent speakers at the CPC	[0]%[b]	24% (21)	b
O	Speaks more than average at Community Days	0% (3)	53% (36)	—
	Index of speaking r = .37 (N = 39)			.01
	Attendance			
O	Attended at least one of the nineteen CPC meetings I observed	0% (3)	58% (36)	—
Q	Reports ever having been a representative to the CPC or the DPW	33% (3)	72% (36)	—
O	Attended both of the two Community Days I observed	0% (3)	75% (36)	.001
Q	Reports attending all or almost all possible Community Days since joined Helpline	0% (3)	72% (36)	.01
	Index of attendance r = .47 (N = 39)			.01
	Ascribed power			
I	Greater than median power score	0% (3)	53% (36)	—
Q	Chosen by one or more people as having good judgment on Helpline issues	33% (3)	53% (36)	—
	Index of ascribed power r = .21 (N = 39)			—
	Efficacy			
Q	Reports having greater than average say in service group	0% (3)	53% (34)	—
Q	Reports having greater than average say at Helpline	0% (3)	31% (36)	.05
I	Gives self greater than median power score	0% (3)	52% (29)	.05
	Index of efficacy r = .36 (N = 39)			.05
	Satisfaction			
Q	Reports being "never" or only "once in a while" dissatisfied with the outcomes of decisions at Helpline	0% (3)	21% (34)	.05
Q	Reports being "never" or only "once in a while" dissatisfied with the process of decision making at Helpline	0% (3)	27% (34)	—
Q	Reports being "very" happy in general with Helpline	0% (3)	12% (33)	—
Q	More satisfied than average with outcomes and process of six specific decisions at Helpline	0% (3)	55% (29)	.01
	Index of satisfaction r = .31 (N = 37)			.05

[a] Only thirty-nine of the forty-one staff members answered this question. I am fairly certain, however, that the other two members' parents were middle class. For an explanation of symbols and discrepancies in the number of cases in the table, see "Key to Tables," Appendix A. For composition of indexes, and wording of questions, see Appendix B.

[b] Calculated on CPC attenders only. No working-class members attended the nineteen CPC meetings I observed.

Appendix B

Variables and Indexes

Composition of Indexes

In every case, either a typical component or all the components of the index appear in tables in Appendix A. The indexes are designed only to provide, with an easily readable summary statistic, an approximate overview of the association between a cluster of variables and another single variable or similar cluster. All indexes are composed of standardized variables (mean = 0; s.d. = 1), equally weighted, coded in one direction for purposes of the index. (Source: R = public records; Q = questionnaire; I = interview; O = observations.)

SELBY: INDEXES

Index of Local Political Activity

(1) Percentage town meeting attendance in last ten years.   (R)[a]

0–100%:   continuous variable

0	1–10	11–20	21–30	31–40	41–50	51–60	61–70	71–80	81–90	100
(18)	(2)	(6)	(4)	(6)	(6)	(2)	(4)	(3)	(4)	(3)

[a] Calculated only on the fifty-eight people in town more than one and a half years (long enough to register and vote). Due to an error, those not registered were coded as −1, not 0 (reported here with 0). Since this could not substantively affect the results, the analysis was not rerun.

(2) "Have you ever gone to see, or phoned an official of the town?"   (I)

    1: no   (21)
    2: yes   (44)

(3) "Have you ever spoken at a town meeting—asked a question or said something?"   (I)

    1: never spoke, but been   (6)
    2: rarely   (13)
    3: sometimes   (6)
    4: often   (9)

(4) "Have you ever done anything to try to influence a local decision?"   (I)

    1: no   (31)
    2: yes   (17)

(5) Ties to town in last ten years   (R and I)[b]

1: no ties	(41)
2: unofficial participant (e.g., Fire Department)	(6)
3: spouse small officer	(5)
4: spouse selectman or school director	(4)
5: self small officer	(9)
6: self selectman or school director	(4)

[b] As a check on the validity of including spouses and unofficial participants in this index in the position shown, I also created dichotomous and trichotomous variables distinguishing town officers from others, and selectmen-school directors from lesser town officers and from others. These latter variables had lower correlations with other measures of participation and efficacy and with the independent variables.

INTERCORRELATION: LOCAL POLITICAL ACTIVITY

	1	*2*	*3*	*4*	*5*
1	—				
2	.36	—			
3	.30	.15	—		
4	.46	.36	.43	—	
5	.60	.28	.33	.61	—

Index of Local Political Efficacy

(1) "In this town people like me don't have any say about what the town does." (Q)

1: strongly agree	(3)
2: agree	(9)
3: not sure; neutral	(3)
4: disagree	(32)
5: strongly disagree	(7)

(2) "I don't think the selectmen care much what people like me think."   (Q)

1: strongly agree	(2)
2: agree	(8)
3: not sure; neutral	(13)
4: disagree	(28)
5: strongly disagree	(8)

(3) "Often the same people are elected year after year to the same jobs. Why do you think this is?" (I)

1: they are all related; high up guys, etc. (negative toward those elected)	(4)
2: everybody wants to be nice to one another, etc. (neutral)	(5)
3: the people who have the jobs are qualified, etc. (positive toward those elected)	(47)

(4) "How about this town? Do you feel that the town here pays any attention to what people like you think?"   (I)

1: never	(3)
2: rarely	(9)
3: sometimes	(15)
4: often	(21)
5: always	(5)

(5) "These are some of the reasons people give for not going to town meeting. Do you agree with any of them?"   (I)

(1) "The decisions are really made by a few important people anyway."
(2) "No one cares what I think."

(3) "They would make the same decisions whether I went or not."
—3: chose all three reasons (2)
—2: chose two reasons (9)
—1: chose one reason (15)
0: chose no reasons (33)
+1: volunteered that never felt this way about one reason (3)
+2: volunteered that never felt this way about two reasons (3)
+3: volunteered that never felt this way about three reasons (1)

(6) Spontaneously said something about feeling powerless in the town. (I)

0: no mention (35)
1: mention (33)

(7) "Suppose a regulation were being considered by the town that you thought very unjust or harmful (this could be a zoning regulation or an unfair tax, for example). What do you think you could do?" (I)

1: nothing (8)
2: talk to people about it (14)
3: speak at town meeting, vote, go to town official (28)
4: petition, form a committee, call a town meeting (16)

INTERCORRELATION: LOCAL POLITICAL EFFICACY

	1	2	3	4	5	6	7
1	—						
2	.79	—					
3	.35	.44	—				
4	.49	.47	.36	—			
5	.38	.49	.18	.29	—		
6	.42	.53	.31	.48	.32	—	
7	.29	.15	—.01	.23	.18	.33	—

Index of Social Connection

(1) "About how many people who live in Selby would you recognize by sight if you saw them in a crowd?" (I)

1: 5 to 10 (5)
2: 10 to 25 (13)
3: 25 to 50 (9)
4: quarter to half (16)
5: three quarters (10)
6: all except newcomers (9)
7: everyone (1)

(2) "Aside from your work and family, do you have any activities that interest you, that you like to spend your free time on?" (I)

1: mentions individual and family activities only (37)
2: mentions social activities with individuals outside family (23)

(3) Working in town—active labor force only (I)

1: works in town (23)
2: works out of town (26)

INTERCORRELATION: SOCIAL CONNECTION

	1	2	3
1	—		
2	.36	—	
3	.29	.07	—

Variables and Indexes

Index of Local Information

(1) "Can you give the names of any two of the Selby selectmen?" (Q)
    1: none correct or no answer to this question (12)
    2: one correct (8)
    3: two correct (35)

(2) "On what day does the Selby town meeting meet each year?" (Q)
    1: incorrect or no answer to this question (19)
    2: half correct (7)
    3: correct (29)

(3) "How about the local issues in this town? How well do you understand them?" (I)
    1: not at all (0)
    2: not well (13)
    3: moderately well (8)
    4: very well (32)

INTERCORRELATION: LOCAL INFORMATION

	1	2	3
1	—		
2	.53	—	
3	.45	.37	-—

Index of Socioeconomic Status

(1) Residence value, at half-value assessment. (R)
    1: under $2,499 (8)
    2: $2,500–$3,999 (13)
    3: $4,000–$5,999 (12)
    4: $6,000+ (11)

(2) "Would you place your family income in one of the following income groups?" (Q)
    1: under $1,000 (1)
    2: $1,000–$1,999 (0)
    3: $2,000–$2,999 (2)
    4: $3,000–$4,999 (4)
    5: $5,000–$7,499 (10)
    6: $7,500–$9,999 (17)
    7: $10,000–$14,999 (5)
    8: $15,000+ (5)

(3) "What is the last grade or year in school that you completed?" (Q)
    1: elementary, but not complete (3)
    2: complete elementary (6)
    3: some high school (11)
    4: complete high school (24)
    5: some college (7)
    6: complete college (4)
    7: higher than college (3)

(4) Categorization of job (I)
    1: welfare (2)
    2: odd jobs, retired on scant Social Security (3)
    3: laborer, operative, service, poor farmer (12)
    4: transport equip. operator, craftsman, clerical (25)

5: lower management/professional, prosperous farmer   (10)
6: higher management/professional   (17)

INTERCORRELATION: SOCIOECONOMIC STATUS

	1	2	3	4
1	—			
2	.08	—		
3	·34	·39	—	
4	·41	·54	·52	—

Index of Trust

(1) "Generally speaking, would you say that most people can be trusted or that you can't be too careful in dealing with people?"   (Q)
     1: can't be too careful   (20)
     2: it depends   (5)
     3: most people can be trusted   (30)

(2) "Do you think most people would try to take advantage of you if they had a chance, or would they try to be fair?"   (Q)
     1: would take advantage   (15)
     2: it depends   (8)
     3: would try to be fair   (29)

(3) "Would you say that most of the time people try to be helpful or that they are just looking out for themselves?"   (Q)
     1: just look out for themselves   (14)
     2: it depends   (9)
     3: try to be helpful   (30)

INTERCORRELATION: TRUST

	1	2	3
1	—		
2	.71	—	
3	·57	.62	—

Index of Control

(1) "Have you usually felt pretty sure your life would work out the way you wanted it to, or have there been times when you haven't been very sure about it?"   (Q)
     1: sometimes not very sure   (15)
     2: it depends   (7)
     3: pretty sure   (26)

(2) "When you make plans ahead, do you usually get to carry things out the way you expected, or do things usually come up to make you change your plans?" (Q)
     1: have to change plans   (25)
     2: it depends   (11)
     3: things work out as expected   (15)

(3) "Do you feel that you are the kind of person who gets his share of bad luck, or do you feel that you have mostly good luck?"   (Q)
     1: bad luck   (3)
     2: it depends   (5)
     3: mostly good luck   (26)

Variables and Indexes

INTERCORRELATION: CONTROL

	1	2	3
1	—		
2	.29	—	
3	.28	.23	—

Index of Being "Talkative"

(1) "I am a better talker than listener."   (Q)

1: never true	(9)
2: seldom true	(23)
3: sometimes true	(15)
4: often true	(5)
5: almost always true	(0)

(2) "Here are some of the reasons people give for not going to town meeting. Do you agree with any of them?"   (I)

A: "I don't like to speak in public."

—1: chose this reason	(11)
0: no mention	(48)
1: volunteered that never felt this way	(7)

(3) Length of interview

1: curtailed	(2)
2: short	(33)
3: medium	(30)
4: long	(4)

INTERCORRELATION: BEING "TALKATIVE"

	1	2	3
1	—		
2	.27	—	
3	.15	−.04	—

SELBY: INTERCORRELATIONS OF MAJOR INDEPENDENT VARIABLES

	Time in town	Village	Age	Gender	Socio-economic Status
Length of time in town	—				
Living in village	.08	—			
Age	.13	.39	—		
Gender (f., m.)	−.13	.06	−.02	—	
Socioeconomic status	−.10	.03	.11	.11	—

HELPLINE: INDEXES

Index of Speaking

(1) "Do you usually speak at meetings?"   (Q)

1: no	(1)
2: hardly at all	(6)
3: less than average	(14)
4: average	(7)
5: more than average	(9)
6: a lot	(3)

(2) Average number of times speaking at the CPC (O). Total times recorded as having spoken divided by number of meetings attended. Those never attending the CPC not present in calculations.

0–28 continuous variable:

0	1	4	5	7	9	10	12	13	14	15	17	18	19	28
(1)	(1)	(2)	(2)	(1)	(2)	(2)	(1)	(1)	(2)	(2)	(2)	(1)	(1)	(1)

(3) Average number of times speaking at large meetings on two Community Days (O). Total times recorded as having spoken divided by number of meetings attended. Those not attending either Community Day excluded from calculations.

0–10 continuous variable:

0	.1–1	1.1–2	2.1–3	3.1–4	4.1–5	5.1–6	6.1–7	7.1–8	8.1–9	9.1–10
(4)	(7)	(4)	(5)	(5)	(4)	(5)	(1)	(0)	(2)	(2)

INTERCORRELATION: SPEAKING

	1	2	3
1	—		
2	.79	—	
3	.62	.75	—

Index of Attendance

(1) Attended two Community Days (O)

    0: none   (2)
    1: one   (12)
    2: two   (27)

(2) "Have you usually gone to the full Community meetings?" (Q)

    1: skipped a lot   (4)
    2: skipped some   (10)
    3: skipped one or two   (18)
    4: attended all   (9)

(3) Attended nineteen CPC meetings (O)

0–9 continuous variable:

0	1	2	3	6	8	10	11	12	15	16	17	19
(19)	(2)	(3)	(3)	(1)	(2)	(1)	(1)	(1)	(3)	(3)	(1)	(1)

(4) CPC representative (O; Q)

    0: no   (22)
    1: yes   (9)

(5) DPW representative (O; Q)

    0: no   (22)
    1: yes   (19)

(6) "Have you ever been to a CPC meeting?" (Q) Asked only of non-CPC representatives

    1: never   (6)
    2: sat in 1–2 times   (6)
    3: sat in 3–4 times   (3)
    4: sat in 5–10 times   (4)
    5: sat in 10+ times   (3)

(7) "Have you ever been to a DPW meeting?" (Q) Asked only of non-DPW representatives

    1: never   (7)
    2: sat in 1–2 times   (5)

```
3: sat in 3–4 times      (5)
4: sat in 5–10 times     (1)
5: sat in 10+ times      (1)
```

INTERCORRELATION: ATTENDANCE

	1	2	3	4	5	6	7
1	—						
2	.59	—					
3	.30	.23	—				
4	−.11	.03	.66	—			
5	−.22	−.48	−.10	−.06	—		
6	.59	.01	.68	—	.39	—	
7	.18	.20	.56	.52	—	.16	—

Index of Ascribed Power

(1) Average of the power rankings given each respondent by the other staff.
0–15 continuous variable:

4	5	6	7	8	9	10	11	12	13	14
(2)	(7)	(4)	(9)	(5)	(4)	(2)	(4)	(1)	(1)	(2)

(2) Chosen by other staff in response to the question, "If you wanted to discuss Helpline issues with someone, who are two people whose judgment you would most respect?" (Q)
0–9 continuous variable:

0	1	2	3	4	7	8	9
(21)	(7)	(6)	(3)	(1)	(1)	(1)	(1)

INTERCORRELATION: ASCRIBED POWER

	1
2	.77

Index of Efficacy ("Reports self high in 'say' and 'power' ")

(1) "How much say do you have on decisions in your service group?" (Q)
```
1: less than average     (1)
2: average               (19)
3: more than average     (19)
```

(2) "How much say do you have on decisions in Helpline as a whole?" (Q)
```
1: less than average     (15)
2: average               (15)
3: more than average     (11)
```

(3) Power ranking the respondent gives self in power-ranking exercise.
0–15 continuous variable:

0	1	3	4	5	6	7	8	9	10	11	12	13	14	15
(1)	(1)	(2)	(2)	(1)	(1)	(3)	(2)	(5)	(4)	(3)	(2)	(2)	(1)	(3)

INTERCORRELATION: EFFICACY

	1	2	3
1	—		
2	.45	—	
3	.40	.58	—

Index of Satisfaction

(1) "How often are you dissatisfied with the *outcome* of decisions made in Helpline as a whole?" (Q)

1: very often   (1)
2: often   (7)
3: sometimes   (20)
4: once in a while   (9)
5: never   (2)

(2) "How often are you dissatisfied with *the way* decisions are made in Helpline as a whole?" (Q)

1: very often   (1)
2: often   (9)
3: sometimes   (13)
4: once in a while   (12)
5: never   (4)

(3) "How happy are you with the overall functioning of Helpline?" (Q)

1: not at all   (3)
2: a little   (11)
3: reasonably   (20)
4: very   (4)

(4) "How satisfied were you with the outcome and the process of the following decisions?" (Q) (1: serious reservations; 2: minor reservations; 3: pretty satisfied; 4: very much satisfied) Lists: a. [Grant] proposal with [professor's] salary. b. Dispersing office manager's job. c. Dropping . . . Air Force hotline. d. Overall Helpline budget cutting. e. Choosing new coordinator. f. Renting Farm to present renters. (Average scores for each decision, both on "outcome" and on "process.")

12–48 continuous variable:

13	17	18	22	23	24	25	26	28	29	31	32	33	34	35	39
(1)	(1)	(2)	(2)	(3)	(3)	(2)	(3)	(1)	(3)	(1)	(1)	(3)	(4)	(2)	(1)

INTERCORRELATION: SATISFACTION

	1	2	3	4
1	—			
2	.77	—		
3	.43	.44	—	
4	.45	.39	.30	—

Index of Power and Responsibility

(1) "I enjoy power." (Q)

1: always true   (6)
2: often true   (9)
3: sometimes true   (11)
4: seldom true   (2)
5: never true   (1)

(2) "I hate to tell others what to do." (Q)

1: always true   (2)
2: often true   (8)
3: sometimes true   (15)
4: seldom true   (7)
5: never true   (0)

(3) "I enjoy planning things and taking charge." (Q)

1: always true   (0)
2: often true   (4)
3: sometimes true   (9)

4: seldom true   (7)
5: never true   (0)

(4) "I like competition."   (Q)
     1: always true   (4)
     2: often true   (4)
     3: sometimes true   (12)
     4: seldom true   (8)
     5: never true   (3)

(5) "I like taking responsibility."   (Q)
     1: always true   (0)
     2: often true   (0)
     3: sometimes true   (8)
     4: seldom true   (17)
     5: never true   (6)

(6) "I don't like to 'operate.' "   (Q)
     1: always true   (1)
     2: often true   (5)
     3: sometimes true   (5)
     4: seldom true   (6)
     5: never true   (2)

(7) "If you had your choice, would you rather have a job where you gave the orders or a job where somebody else told you what to do?"   (Q)
     1: rather be told what to do   (10)
     2: depends   (1)
     3: rather give orders   (17)

INTERCORRELATION: POWER AND RESPONSIBILITY

	1	2	3	4	5	6	7
1	—						
2	.33	—					
3	.73	.45	—				
4	.38	.53	.49	—			
5	.31	.44	.32	.35	—		
6	.36	.42	.44	.36	.66	—	
7	.60	.40	.53	.30	.52	.46	—

Index of Verbalism

(1) "Articulate people intimidate me."   (Q)
     1: always true   (8)
     2: often true   (15)
     3: sometimes true   (4)
     4: seldom true   (3)
     5: never true   (2)

(2) "I express myself well in words."   (Q)
     1: always true   (0)
     2: often true   (3)
     3: sometimes true   (11)
     4: seldom true   (12)
     5: never true   (5)

INTERCORRELATION: VERBALISM

	1
2	.64

HELPLINE: INTERCORRELATIONS OF MAJOR INDEPENDENT VARIABLES

	Time	Proximity	Age	Race	Gender	Parents' Class
Length of time in organization	—					
Physical proximity to social center	.00	—				
Age	.16	.17	—			
Race	.23	−.07	.18	—		
Gender (f., m.)	.09	.06	.08	.05	—	
Parents' class (working class, other)	−.22	.21	.31	.28	.05	—

Notes

Preface

1. For example, the Bread and Roses Collective (1971), p. 184. From about 1968 to 1974, the American radical women's movement was preoccupied with questions of internal equality of power—a concern that continued, somewhat abated, thereafter. See, for example, "The Women's Liberation Movement in England" (1972), p. 7; and "Power Relationships" (1972), p. 13. Mehrhof (1970, p. 12) exemplifies the concerns of the time:

> Who are these women who have risen to the top of the women's movement and how are they able to maintain a leadership position? In general, they come from either the middle or the upper classes . . . they are often equipped with many of the same advantages and attitudes as males—educational privileges, self-confidence (if not toward men, at least toward other women), feelings of superiority toward the masses, etc. . . . [Like males,] they often accuse the grumblers at the bottom of suffering from personality or psychological disorders. . . .

2. The 1970s had a benign effect on this situation. Using aggregate data, Bryan is preparing a major comparative study of the correlates of town meeting participation in Vermont (for one portion of this study, see Bryan, 1975). Hixon (1971), comparing citizens of one Vermont town under a modified town meeting government to citizens of a matched Michigan town under city council government, found, among other things, that the citizens in the Vermont town had more information on their town's political life. Kotler (1972, 1974) suggested that participation in town meeting has become over time less "community-oriented" and more "consumer-oriented." None of these studies, however, includes data appropriate to a detailed analysis of the political dynamics of the meeting itself or many of the variables affecting attendance.

3. For example, a radical women's organization to which I belonged seemed to be dominated by former SDS members. In a left wing research organization, the two organizers and fund raisers had a dominant influence.

4. The young people in this workplace, most of whom were unencumbered by the financial responsibilities of a family, generally expected to stay in the job only a few years. This would not be so true of an older workforce. Indeed, older employees are almost as captive as residents. In the most comparable data available, 17 percent of the people in the United States moved to a different address between 1975 and 1976, while only 14 percent of the work force changed employers between 1972 and 1973. U.S. Department of Commerce (1977), p. 1; U.S. Department of Labor (1976), p. 57.

5. This can be conceived both as "triangulation" (fixing the point one aims at by charting its position from more than one angle) or as a form of controlling for other variables that might influence the outcome. Within each study, I also tried to triangulate by finding measures from different sources for each important variable. Thus, whenever possible, I use public records; quantitative measures of public behavior; my own impressions of that behavior; the conclusions and estimates of members of the group about others' behavior; in-depth interviews with the participants; and closed-ended, replicable, and quantifiable questions in an interview or questionnaire format. I also pretested a thematic apperception test (TAT) projective measure of "need for power" (see Winter, 1973) for use with the radical workplace but rejected it on grounds of the time it took, the irritations and suspicions it raised, and my doubts about the standard coding, which lumped together expressions of desire to help with more obvious references to power.

Pursuing my goal of combining differing approaches and differing cases, I also carried out a third study, a women's center organized on anarcho-feminist lines. In contrast to my combination of survey research, interviews, and short duration observations in the town meeting and my participant observation in the workplace, I was an active participant in the women's center. I decided not to use the data from this study because both the case and the approach had major limitations. First, because the women's center was a voluntary association with an extremely fluid membership, it was next to impossible to determine who was affected by decisions. Thus, the meaning of nonparticipation was unclear. Second, my own involvement kept me from keeping the accurate records of public behavior on which I relied heavily in the other studies. The quantitative questionnaire data from the women's center study, however, reflect all but one of the patterns of inequality in other studies. Here, measures of socioeconomic background and a subjective estimate of parents' class showed a significant *inverse* relation with ranked power and participation. By the time I did the questionnaire part of the study, all but two working-class women had left the center, and a group of women from lower-middle-class backgrounds had begun to set the dominant tone. Women from upper-middle-class backgrounds tended to feel left out of the friendship network and were thus less likely to participate actively.

6. Face-to-face meetings and consensus can be justified on the egalitarian grounds that representatives inevitably acquire more power than those they represent and that consensus gives each member an irreducibly equal veto. These same procedures can also be justified on the libertarian grounds that no group can legitimately require an individual to abide by any decision he or she has not agreed to in person.

Chapter 1: Introduction

1. Lively begins his *Democracy* (1977) by discussing the traditional "identification of democracy with political equality," which he defines as an equal distribution of power (p. 8). His later discussion consistently equates democracy with political equality, always defined as "actual equality in the ability to determine decisions" (p. 16). See also pp. 10, 13, 17, 21, 24, 26–28, 35, 50, 109. Berg (1965, p. 157) describes ideal democracy as "governance by all the citizens equally"; Nagel (1975, p. 5) says that "Democracy ideally prescribes that everyone have equal power"; Sartori (1965, p. 91) sums up his comparison of norms and practice with the conclusion: "prescriptively—and therefore potentially—democracy is 'equal power for everybody.'"

Even earlier writers sometimes made the same equation. Carritt (1940, p. 61) uses phrases like "democracy, that is political equality," "democracy or political equality," and even (interpreting another's remarks) "democracy means political equality." Russell (1962, p. 108) took it for granted that in "a completely democratic government," "every man has an equal voice in joint decisions, and if there are (say) a million members, every man has a millionth part of the power over the whole million. . . ."

Ranney and Kendall (1951, p. 439) conclude that among all the contradictions about what "democracy" means, there are only three areas of "minimum common ground," and the first of these is "political equality," meaning that "in a democracy political power must be equally shared by all its citizens, no man having a larger share than any other."

Chapter 2: Unitary versus Adversary Democracy

1. Although Aristotle (*Ethics*, 1155a22–23) distinguishes between justice and friendship (e.g., 1155a23), he does not seem to allocate the first to the political and the second to the purely personal realm. Kinds of friendship correspond to kinds of community, not only below the level of political community (1160a28) but also, it seems, at that level. Quantitative equality, for instance, characterizes the friendship (as well as the justice) appropriate to a democracy, while proportional equality characterizes the friendship (as well as the justice) appropriate to a monarchy and aristocracy (*Ethics* 1161a10ff., and *Politics* 1317b10ff.).

2. Aristotle, *Ethics*, 1156b9. See Adkins (1963, p. 37ff.) on this passage.

3. Service (1975), pp. 47–70.

4. Sahlins (1972), pp. 9–13. Although domesticating the horse made possible economic inequality, some nomadic Indian tribes nevertheless retained relatively egalitarian economic, social, and political norms after this innovation.

5. Service (1975), p. 52.

6. Father Le Jeune, 1634, describing the Montagnais-Naskapi of Labrador (cited in Service, 1975, p. 5). The anthropologist Sharp wrote of the Yir Yoront of Australia that they "cannot even tolerate mild chiefs or headmen, while a leader with absolute authority over the whole group would be unthinkable" (cited in Service, 1975, p. 52). For similar quotations from seventeenth-century traders, explorers, and military officers in the western Great Lakes region of North America, see Miller (1963), pp. 94–95.

7. Miller (1963), p. 108.

8. Zurcher (1970), p. 273. For a full discussion of this incident, see pp. 268–331. The Indians' sentiment had deep roots in their childhood training. One participant reported his father's telling him that "if . . . you wanted to be a Number One man, then you'd give other people a feeling that you thought you were better than they were, and that would be the worst kind of bad manners there is." Another recalled his grandfather's "good advice" about sports: "Don't make anybody else look bad! I suppose there's nothing wrong with winning, but don't forget that it might be one of your brothers who's going to lose" (p. 288).

9. Marshall (1961), p. 231.

10. They even expected that citizens would often have inimical interests. Plato has Meno describe a man's excellence (*arete*) as consisting in "managing the city's affairs capably, and so that he will help his friends and injure his foes while taking care to come to no harm himself" (Plato, *Meno*, 71e; see also *The Republic*, 331e, both in *Collected Dialogues*, 1961). This was a common formulation. See examples in Dover (1974), p. 180, and Pearson (1962), pp. 87–88. In many ways, the Athenians revealed their enmity openly (Dover, 1974, pp. 180–183). For an extended commentary on helping one's friends and injuring one's foes, see Connor (1971), pp. 42ff. and passim.

11. Aristotle, *Politics*, 1261b18–19, referring to Plato's *Republic*, 462c and 463e. In the *Politics*, Book II, Chapters 1–3, Aristotle argues that the polis differs from a tribe precisely in being composed of "different kinds of men," of "elements which differ in kind" (*Politics*, 1261a22–30). Therefore, Plato's principle in *The Republic*, that "the greatest possible unity of the whole polis is the supreme good," must be mistaken (*Politics*, 1261a16ff.). In Aristotle's view, the goal of the polis ought to be "harmony" [*symphonia*] rather than mere "unison" [*homophonia*] (*Politics*, 1263b34–35).

12. Aristotle, *Politics*, 1294a11ff. Larsen (1948) indicates that the Greeks of the seventh century B.C. may well have invented the formal vote with majority rule. Glotz (1930), p. 56, suggests that the Greeks introduced majority rule as "a prophylactic against civil war." See also his p. 168, n. 2.

13. Breed and Seaman (1971) cite Aristophanes and Thucydides to support their conflictual interpretation of Athenian democracy. They also point out that in Broneer's (1938) excavation report one find of 191 potsherds of the sort used as ballots in

votes of ostracism, all bearing the name of "Themistocles," was analyzed as the work of only fourteen different hands, a circumstance that indicates the functioning of some form of political machine. Finally, they quote Calhoun (1913, p. 642) as concluding that the Athenian political clubs organized and held preassembly meetings to test and select the best speakers and review speeches. Calhoun claims the clubs also tried to influence voters before the assembly meeting by persuasion, bribes, and threats and that they sometimes packed the assembly, initiated applause and appropriate interruptions, and filibustered to postpone a vote. Connor (1971, pp. 25–29) reviews and supports this interpretation.

14. Popular morality as well as political philosophy in ancient Greece maintained that the good citizen was bound to put public above private interest (Dover, 1974, p. 301). This is in spite of the fact that on the individual level, "no Greek doubted . . . that an individual is very apt to give precedence to his own interest over the interests of others; or that . . . individuals . . . have a natural inclination to aggrandisement when an opportunity presents itself" (pp. 81–82).

15. Thucydides assures us that "leaders of parties in cities had programs which appeared admirable . . . but in professing to serve the public interest they were seeking to win prizes for themselves" (1966, III, 5, p. 201). This recognition did not shake his faith in the importance of the public good.

16. It is unclear how often the Athenian assembly actually made decisions by consensus rather than by majority rule. It seems most likely that a formal majority rule was joined to a strong informal preference for unanimity.

On the one hand, majority rule was firmly established as the formal decision rule in all Greek constitutions and did not have to contend against the claims of the rule of consensus. Aristotle states as a matter of undisputed fact that "the principle of the rule of majority-decision is present in all constitutions. Alike in oligarchies, in aristocracies, and in democracies, the decision of the majority of those who share in constitutional rights is final and sovereign" (*Politics*, 1294a11ff.). He makes the "conception of the sovereignty of the majority" one of "two conceptions that are generally held to be characteristic of a democracy" (*Politics*, 1310a28–29, also 1317b9–10; see also 1318a19).

On the other hand, some fragmentary evidence suggests that the assembly had an informal preference for consensus. First, in the only two descriptions of the mechanics of voting in the assembly that I have discovered, the vote was unanimous. Aeschylus' *Suppliants*, probably dated about 490 B.C., describes two such votes in a Greek assembly, both unanimous: "The air was moved by the whole people proclaiming their decision with favorable hands," and the people "cast their vote with their hands without a herald that it be so" (607, 621, both cited in Ehrenberg, 1950, p. 521. Ehrenberg explains that the "herald" was probably a voteteller, whose services would not be necessary when a vote was unanimous).

Second, Demosthenes characterized the "good citizen" as "making the same choice as the majority" and "grieving when the majority grieve and rejoicing when they rejoice" (xviii 280, 292, cited in Dover, 1974, p. 300). He even suggested that disagreement with the majority was unpatriotic and that a good citizen ought not to consider possible arguments against Athenian policy (xv 25, 33, cited in Dover, 1974, p. 291). This would explain why potential dissenters had to stress the importance of free expression and exhort one another not to be intimidated (Thucydides vi 24.4, iii 42.5, cited in Dover, 1974, p. 291). The oath that Athenian citizens had to take to pursue likemindedness (*homonoia*) may also have affected the tendency to consensus. Xenophon's Socrates says, "I don't believe the purpose of this oath is merely to ensure that the people vote for the same dramatic companies . . . it is to ensure that they obey the law" (Xenophon, Mem. IV 4, 16, cited in Ferguson, 1958, p. 119). Others may have thought the oath was meant to encourage consensus.

Third, although votes of ostracism and trials produced split votes, only one record of an actual numerical division in the assembly seems to have survived. See Zimmern (1952), p. 164.

Fourth, the early Greek assemblies voted by vocal acclamation and the later assemblies by a visible show of hands (Larsen, 1948, pp. 164–181), both techniques that could lead to intimidation.

Fifth, popular democratic opinion may have believed that a majority should not simply outvote a minority. Xenophon reports a probably imaginary conversation between Pericles and Alcibiades in which Pericles defines violence and lawlessness as "when the stronger does not persuade the weaker but compels him by force to do what he wants." Xenophon, however, then has Pericles avoid Alcibiades' crucial question as to whether a majority enacting a measure without persuading a minority would be violence rather than law (Mem. I.ii.40–46, cited in Jones, 1966, p. 51). Jones also cites Demosthenes as asserting that the assembly's laws are "enacted by persuasion" (XXIV.76, cited idem.). On the basis of these two rather weak examples, Jones concludes: "Some democrats then conceived of the law as the *considered* will of the majority, adding the rider that the majority should persuade the minority and consider the interests of all" (pp. 51–52).

17. Aristotle, *Ethics*, 1155a24ff. The equation of unanimity and friendship must have been a common maxim, or at least a commonly accepted concept, for Aristotle also writes: "Unanimity [*homonoia*] seems, then, to be political friendship [*philia*], as indeed it is *commonly held to be*" (*Ethics* 1167b2ff.; my emphasis).

Havelock contends that the central ideal of the Greek "liberals" was "natural amity . . . the basic identity of interest among human beings" (1957, p. 222; see also passim and pp. 222–247, 310–313, 379, 393, 402). This is in spite of the fact that some of these "liberals" (e.g., Callicles in Plato's *Gorgias* and Thrasymachus in *The Republic*) were more than familiar with the language of "interest" and "advantage."

18. Aristotle, *Ethics*, 1167a26–28. As examples of instances in which citizens could and should achieve unanimity (*homonoia*), Aristotle gives: (1) that the offices in a city be elective (procedure); (2) that a city should form an alliance with another (foreign affairs); and (3) that all classes wish the best men to rule (the criterion of competence). Aristotle concludes that unanimity is found among good men, who are of one mind. Bad men, on the contrary, "aim at getting *more than their share* of advantages . . . each man wishing for advantage to himself." The pursuit of private advantage destroys the commonwealth through faction because each wants to use the state to compel others, but none is willing to take responsibility for the whole and "do what is just" (*Ethics*, 1167b4ff.; my emphasis).

At the time Aristotle wrote, both democratic and aristocratic theorists seem to have perceived *homonoia* as central to a good polity. The word, meaning literally "of one mind," is usually opposed to *stasis*, or faction, and seems to signify primarily "unanimity among interest groups, often simply the well-to-do and the poor" (West, 1977, p. 307).

One reason for the centrality of *homonoia* must have been purely practical: division at home frequently meant weakness abroad. As the democrat Democritus wrote:

> Faction [*stasis*] within the clan is a bad thing for both sides. Those who win and those who lose share impartially in common disaster.
>
> It is consensus [*homonoia*] that makes possible for cities the [execution of] mighty works enabling them to execute and carry through wars.
>
> [B229, B250, cited in Havelock, 1957, pp. 134–142.]

This practical reason alone may have accounted for the common requirement in Athens and the other Greek cities that citizens take an oath swearing to uphold *homonoia* (Xenophon, *Mem.* 4.4.16; Thucydides, *Hist.* 8.75.2; Lysias 25.27; Andocides, *Myst.* 76—all cited in West, 1977, pp. 309–310).

Yet evidence suggests that "being of one mind" had a value that exceeded expediency. Both Aristotle and Democritus, for example, link their arguments about equality to *homonoia*. As we have seen, Aristotle argues that *homonoia* is achieved through inequality: "when both the common people and those of the better class wish the best men to rule" and when they do not "try to get" more than their deservedly unequal share of advantages (*Ethics*, 1167a32ff.; see also Plato, *The Republic*, IV, 432A, 433C). Democritus, on the other hand, argues that *homonoia* is achieved when the rich give to the poor, thus creating greater equality:

> At that time when the powerful [classes] confronting the have-nots take it on themselves to pay toll to them and to do things for them and to please them: This is the [situation] in which you get [the phenomenon of] compassion and

337

the end of the isolation and the creation of comradeship and mutual defense and then civic consensus [*homonoia*]. . . . [FVS B255, cited in Havelock, 1957, p. 142.] Another probable democrat repeats the argument that *homonoia* is achieved when rich give to poor and adds that each therefore receives, not the Aristotelian unequal "share of advantages," but rather an "egalitarian equivalence."

19. Aristotle, *Ethics*, 1168b8. See also 1157b3a and 1159b2–3. Plato approved the maxim, "equality gives birth to friendship" only after he had modified "equality" to mean not only quantitative equality but also proportionate rewards to unequals (Plato, *Laws*, VI, 757e (ed. 1961). Like Plato, Aristotle argued that a "kind" or type of friendship can exist between unequals, for example, between father and son, elder and younger, husband and wife, ruler and subject, in which cases love must be proportional to merit, this proportion being, "in a sense," equality (*Ethics*, 1158b20–28). Aristotle's confidence in the force of these examples seems weak. Not only does he guard himself with phrases like "in a sense," but he concludes, first, that under conditions of great inequality "the possibility of friendship ceases" (1159a5) and, second, that "in friendship quantitative equality is primary and proportion to merit secondary (1158b31–34).

The apothegm "Friendship is equality" is originally attributed to Pythagoras. The Pythagorian disciples shared all their possessions in common, although some evidence suggests that an original arithmetical equality of sharing gave way later in the history of the school to a geometrical equality of proportion, justifying distinctions within the community (Ferguson, 1958, p. 55). This evolution may have influenced Plato's and Aristotle's distinction between arithmetical and proportional equality, as may the earlier formulation of *isê dias*, or "fair portion" (Motto and Clark, 1969, 118ff.).

On what he calls Aristotle's "semantic contortions" while trying to reinterpret the essentially democratic maxim, "Friendship is equality," see Havelock (1957), pp. 297–326.

20. Euripides' *Phoenician Maidens*, quoted in Sabine (1950), p. 26. The nature of Greek friendship, and presumably of the equality in friendship, may have changed between the time of Homer and that of Aristotle. *Philotes* in Homer denotes a relationship of formal or informal mutual expectation, and things or persons that are *philos* are things one can depend on for reliable positive actions. "The relationship has objective character; it does not depend on emotional inclination" (Adkins, 1972, pp. 16–18; see also 1963, pp. 30–36). Even by the time of Aristotle, people still speak of a friend as the mightiest of all possessions, but by then, the elements of delight in companionship, mutual affection, and love are more predominant (Plato, *Lysis*, 221B. See also Xenophon, *Hieron*, c.V, cited in Ferguson, 1958, pp. 61–62). Aristotle begins to introduce the note of pure altruism, saying that friendship consists in giving rather than receiving affection and in benefiting a friend for his own sake (Aristotle, *Ethics*, 1155b3; Ferguson, 1958, p. 64), but even here he has to "create a civic morality out of the primitive and intractable materials which lay to hand" (Adkins, 1963, p. 45).

21. We cannot know whether Greek democratic theorists used the equality of friendship as an argument for democracy. The conclusions—"Equality holds cities together," and "Equality is good for the city"—could be derived, roughly, from the two premises: "Friendship holds cities together" (probable maxim, cited in Aristotle, *Ethics*, 1155a22), and "Friendship is equality" (maxim, cited in ibid., 1168b8); and from the three premises: "*Homonoia* (unanimity) is good for the city" (or even "the greatest good," as in "You would agree that *homonoia* is the greatest good," sons of Eucrates, 18.17–18, cited in West, 1977, p. 311), "*Homonoia* is political friendship" (maxim, cited in Aristotle, *Ethics*, 1167b2–3), and "Friendship is equality" (see above). Without making the line of argument as explicit as I have done here, Havelock (1957, p. 380), postulating a strong connection in Greek democratic theory between friendship and the polity, sees this as one reason why Plato and Aristotle had to address themselves seriously to the maxim, "Friendship is equality."

If the Greek democrats ever in fact made such an argument, the kind of equality that is good for the city would be the same kind of equality that is central to friendship—equality of respect or status.

22. Plato, *Menexenus*, 238e. This speech, in the mouth of Socrates, is probably a

parody of orations in praise of Athens. It should therefore not be taken as the opinion of either Socrates or Plato, but rather as typical of Greek democratic thought in the fifth and fourth centuries B.C. (see note by Hamilton in Plato, *Collected Dialogues*, 1961, p. 186).

That democratic theory emphasized an underlying equality of status does not mean that the ordinary citizen of Athens ignored social distinctions. On the contrary, all the evidence suggests that many citizens of every class in Athens believed that, by and large, those born to higher social ranks could give the best advice to the city. See in particular the comic plays of Aristophanes and the orations of Demosthenes as analyzed in Ehrenberg (1943), pp. 73–85, and Dover (1974), pp. 30–45. The equality of status stressed in Greek democracy would not therefore have been as far-reaching as that in hunter-gatherer tribes.

23. It is perilous to generalize about Greek democratic theory because so much has been lost. By all evidence, Democritus was a strong democrat, however, and he seems not only to have assumed that the citizens had a common good but also to have been concerned almost totally with good administration:

> If inferior [citizens] proceed to the prerogatives of office
> the more unfit they are when they proceed
> the more negligible they become
> and are filled with witlessness and overconfidence.
>
> . . .
>
> The exercise of authority is by nature proper
> to the superior.
>
> . . .
>
> A man in authority is expected to perform well
> and not badly.
> This is the formal assumption on which he was elected.
> [FVS B254, B267, and B265c, cited in Havelock, 1957, pp. 147–148.]

On the basis of this and other scattered evidence, Havelock (1957, p. 171) concludes that the Greek democratic writers did not defend democracy as an egalitarian society but "as a participating society, in which the opinion forming capacities of all men are involved."

This supports my contention that the crucial form of equality for the democrats was probably not equality of power, but equality of status. Socrates comments in the *Menexenus* (just before stating that the basis of the government was equality of birth) that the Athenian government was really a kind of "aristocracy, or government of the best with the approval of the many" and Pericles' statement that in Athens merit brings advancement in public life lend support to this interpretation (Plato, *Menexenus*, 238d. and Thucydides, 2.37). However, see Larsen's (1948, pp. 13–14) interpretation of this passage from Pericles.

Although Aristotle implies in the *Politics* (1317b14ff.) that Greek democrats were more concerned with equality of power than the quotations from Democritus, Socrates, and Pericles suggest, he may draw his conclusions less from the democratic theory of the time than from his own analysis of the implications of democratic practice.

24. See Neale (1949), pp. 384, 398; and Kishlansky (1977), passim, on the English Parliament.

25. This quotation and the preceding summary derive from Walzer (1965), pp. 199–207.

26. Kishlansky (1977) makes a persuasive case for the pre-1640 English Parliament as, in my terms, a "unitary" institution. He argues that "the primacy of reasoned debate and unanimous decision-making and the rhetoric that eschewed faction and interest suggests not an adversary system of politics, but a consensual one" (p. 618). "Debate was considered to be persuasive discussion: reasoned argument among men uncommitted to predetermined positions. It was designed to convince, not to conquer. And during debate the members of the socially stratified House of Commons acted as equals" (p. 620). The House would defer issues in the hope of reaching unanimity, or reconsider a question even after a vote was taken, if its members thought the dissenter might have good reason. If they had to take a vote and divide an issue,

which was rare, both sides would nevertheless present the bill together to the Speaker "as the sense of the unified membership" (p. 623).

This ideal of unanimity was little different from that of seventeenth-century town meetings in the United States (Zuckerman, 1970). In Dedham and Watertown, Massachusetts and probably in other large towns as well, the "communal spirit" with its "marked stress on consensus" had begun to "slacken perceptibly" by the 1670s, and by the 1690s may "be said to have disappeared" (Lockridge and Krieder, 1966, p. 567). These towns thus experienced the adversary revolution one or two generations after the English Parliament.

27. Colonel Rainborough, the Putney Debates, 29 October 1647, in Woodhouse (1957), pp. 59, 67.

28. Kishlansky (1977), p. 626.

29. In regard to majority rule, Locke also argues that the majority has a "right" to conclude the rest because every individual implicitly agreed that the community should act as one body (II.8.96).

Kendall (1965) advances several other arguments by which Locke supports the doctrine of majority rule, including the idea that because individual consents were the "only rightful title to the exercise of power, the right of the majority flows as a matter of course from the fact that it can point to more consents than the minority" (p. 117). Kendall also concludes that Locke would never have promoted majority rule had he not believed that a "'safe' majority of men (thus the 'average' man) are rational and just" (p. 134). This interpretation allows Locke to reconcile the adversary procedure of majority rule with the unitary goal of the public good.

Although Locke's *Second Treatise* is punctuated with central elements of self-interest, the public good plays a vital role in it. The public good, for example, becomes a major criterion by which a citizen may judge whether or not a government has kept its trust and may legitimately be rebelled against (see II.11.135; II.d 11.142; II.d 15.171; II.d 19.216; II.d 19.240). However, even here Locke breaks with tradition to define the public good as an aggregate of individual interests: "the good of every particular member of that society, as far as by common rules it can be provided for" (I. 9.92).

30. Madison, "Ten Federalist" (1961), p. 79.

31. For example, Bentley (1949), p. 222: "We shall never find a group interest of the society as a whole"; Truman (1959), p. 51: "We do not have to account for a totally inclusive interest, because one does not exist"; MacIver (1947), p. 416: "We should never imply that the people are a unity on any matter of policy. The people are always divided"; or Sorauf (1957), p. 625: "It seems clear that no interest motivates all citizens."

32. For an early formulation of this model, see Schumpeter (1962), chapters 21–23. No political scientist, to my knowledge, has adopted this model in its entirety. Contact with political reality makes it clear that self-interest provides too weak a support for the kinds of negotiations and development of skills that a functioning democracy requires. Schumpeter himself realized this (e.g., pp. 287–288, 294–295).

Indeed, just as capitalism cannot work without a substantial leaven of non-self-interested economic behavior among the entrepreneurs and the citizenry (see Hirsch, 1976, pp. 11–12 and passim), so adversary democracy cannot work without a substantial leaven of the morality and concern for others developed under unitary conditions. Successful legislators usually need to grease the wheels of self-interest with the loyalty and camaraderie of friendship. Nor could adversary democracy, with its reliance on majority rule and formal elections of representatives, maintain itself among a citizenry devoid of political trust. Ironically, the system depends for its continuance on the very impulses its own assumptions and procedures tend to erode.

33. Rousseau (1950), pp. 94, 96. Rousseau was referring to "sovereignty," the framing of general laws, not day-to-day "government." See Shklar (1969), pp. 19–20.

34. Rousseau (1950), p. 23.

35. Ibid., pp. 102, 103.

36. Ibid., p. 50.

37. Ibid., p. 68.

38. Marx and Engels (1954), p. 18.

39. Toennies (1957), pp. 33–78.

40. Mao (1960), pp. 31–33 and Alexandrov (1948), criticized adversary democracy from the perspectives of, respectively, mixed-size and large-scale unitary democracy; Louis Veuillot and Joseph de Maistre from the perspective of monarchy (see Soltau, 1959, pp. 17 and 179).

41. See Proudhon, excerpted in Shatz (1972), p. 103 and pp. 88–89 on "the identity of interests"; and against "the intermediary of representatives." See also Kropotkin, excerpted in Shatz (1972), p. 205, on "the inherent vices of the representative principle."

Bookchin's 1968 essay, "The Forms of Freedom," is the most extended anarchist statement on governmental forms. Attacking indirect structures like the Paris Commune of 1871 and the Russian soviets of 1905 and 1917, Bookchin praises the face-to-face assemblies of Athens in the fifth century B.C. and Paris in 1792. He concludes: "The factory committees, which will almost certainly be the forms that will take over industry, must be managed directly by workers' assemblies in the factories. By the same token, neighborhood committees, councils and boards must be rooted completely in the neighborhood assembly. . . . The specific gravity of society, in short, must be shifted to its base—the armed people in permanent assembly" (1971, pp. 168–169).

42. Dolgoff, personal communication to the author. However, Martha A. Ackelsberg (Department of Government, Smith College) concludes on the basis of her 1979 interviews with former members of Spanish rural anarchist collectives from the period 1936–1939 that, at least in the eight or ten collectives for which she has information, consensus was more frequently the goal than the formal decision rule.

43. Mills (1959), p. 5.

44. At this point, it stabilized. The proportions were 40 percent in 1974, and 41 percent in 1976 (American National Election Studies, Center for Policy Studies, University of Michigan).

45. Richard M. Nixon, State of the Union Address, 1971, cited in Cook and Morgan 1971, p. ix. It may be a triumph for the New Left that this phrasing has become a political commonplace. The queen of England, in her November 1978 speech on the opening of Parliament, also declared, "My Government are resolved to strengthen our democracy by providing new opportunities for citizens to take part in the decisions that affect their lives" (*The Times*, November 2, 1978, p. 10).

46. Zablocki (1971), p. 315. For the experiments of SDS with direct democracy, see Sale (1973), pp. 75, 92, 106–107, 206–207, 217, 225, 235, 241, 247, 249, 257, 258, 273, 280ff., 291, 355–357, 365, 393, 464, 594–595, 621. While the national organization made some decisions in a face-to-face general assembly (Sale, 1973, p. 207), it often submitted the most controversial decisions to a membership referendum (Sale, 1973, pp. 208, 241, 254, 273).

47. The Port Huron Statement diagnosed the problem as both a subjective sense of powerlessness and the "actual structural separation of people from power":

The apathy here is first, subjective—the felt powerlessness of ordinary people, the resignation before the enormity of events. But subjective apathy is encouraged by the objective American situation—the actual structural separation of people from power, from relevant knowledge, from pinnacles of decision-making. . . .

With the great mass of people structurally remote and psychologically hesitant with respect to democratic institutions, those institutions themselves attenuate and become, in the fashion of the vicious circle, progressively less accessible to those few who aspire to serious participation in social affairs.

It proposed to remedy the situation through "the establishment of a democracy of individual participation":

"In a participatory democracy political life would be based on several root principles, [one of which would be that] decision making of basic social consequence be carried on by public groupings." However, the Statement never made clear how "public groupings" would be organized ("The Port Huron Statement," in Jacobs and Landau, 1966, pp. 159, 160).

48. The only exception I am aware of comes from Dee Jacobsen, "We've Got to Reach Our Own People" (1967), quoted in Lynd (1971), p. 22. In one paragraph of the article, Jacobsen urges groups in the Resistance to make their decisions by consensus (see below, chapter 18, p. 253).

Chapter 3: The Inner Logic of Unitary Democracy

1. For example, Wall (1975) or Marxists who believe that interests can be determined solely through the analysis of an individual's historical and economic position.

2. Theorists in the liberal tradition have been chary of any definition of interests that discounts an individual's current, subjective preferences. These thinkers argue that, because there is no way of knowing with accuracy an individual's true interests, one must accept subjective preferences at a given moment as the best available guide to individual interests. Barry (1965, p. 175, n. 1), for instance, cites C. B. Hagen as making "*x* is in *A*'s interests" equivalent to "*A* wants *x*." Held (1970, pp. 23–26) adds Roscoe Pound and David Truman to the list and interprets John Plamenatz as holding a modified form of this position. Nelson Polsby seems to take this position since he denies that one can lack awareness of and identification with one's "objective interests," but in correspondence with Connolly, he has also denied that he defines interest as preference (Connolly, 1972, p. 461).

In real political life, one might want to balance the mandate to aggregate enlightened preferences against the practical problems of ascertaining enlightened preferences correctly and the dangers of tyranny and paternalism involved in anyone's deciding for others that their enlightened preferences would not be the same as their current preferences. But balancing one good against another in this matter is different from deciding that in every case one will define interests as current subjective preferences.

3. My working definition of interest therefore follows Connolly:

Policy *x* is more in *A*'s interest than policy *y* if *A*, were he to experience the *results* of both *x* and *y*, would *choose x* as the result he would rather have for himself [1972, p. 472].

My definition adds, however, that this criterion is part of a criterion of perfect knowledge. This addition has the advantage of admitting other criteria for knowledge than that of experience-choice but the disadvantage of making the definition of interest vague and in some sense circular (e.g., perfect knowledge would include knowledge of interests).

4. This is not solely an operational difficulty. Logically, the question remains open in this exercise as to how different choices can ever be intersubjectively comparable without specifying a fixed point that allows one to say what values one brings to the process of choosing between different trajectories.

The exercise could be saved from this difficulty if one assumed, as Socrates is often said to assume, that in the most important areas of human choice every person able to experience the full consequences of an array of choices would inevitably, by virtue of his or her nature as a human being, make the same choice. If this interpretation is correct, the Socratic theory eliminates the possibility of free will (since knowing the good entails willing the good) and bases choice on hedonism, for it assumes that, with perfect knowledge, what one wants (desires for one's own happiness) will correspond with what one ought to do. It therefore differs fundamentally both from the Christian tradition, which postulates not only the possibility but the likelihood of a corrupt will, and from Kantian analysis, which opposes desires to duties.

My analysis of interests does not assume that only one choice is possible under conditions of perfect knowledge. Without this assumption, however, the definition of interest advanced here is open to Wall's criticism of Connolly. Wall (1975, pp. 487–510) argues that the criterion of having experienced the results of each choice still "makes each individual the final arbiter of what is in his interest" and thus "signals a collapse back into subjectivism" (p. 499). The definition of interests I have adopted might thus best be considered "quasi-objective," for its assumes that even people's enlightened preferences will sometimes differ.

My definition of interests has no relation to the idea that interests involve justifiable claims (as argued by Benn, 1960, pp. 123–140; Fried, 1963, pp. 755–778; and Held, 1970, p. 31).

5. Including matters of taste makes it clear that this concept of interest is not fully "objective."

6. This example involves a policy choice. Interest, as the word is used here, has to do with "an interest in something being *done,* or enacted, or brought about, or maintained. It is an interest in action of some kind . . ." (Held, 1970, p. 19). It is also an interest in lack of action, in nondecision, when a policy of nondecision benefits or harms the individual whose interest is in question. Interests are therefore a subset of enlightened preferences that have to do with the choice between two or more policies or actions (cf. Barry, 1965, pp. 179–180, 192, and Connolly, 1972, p. 472; see *per contra*, Wall, 1975, p. 498, n. 20).

7. See, on this point, Barry (1965, pp. 176–178, 181, 182, and note E, pp. 297–298). Barry indeed suggests going further, to exclude publicly oriented wants from the adversary process itself (pp. 63–65).

8. Held (1970, pp. 22–23) and Flathman (1966, pp. 26–27) also take this position. Connolly (1972, pp. 466–468) takes a position halfway between mine (with Held and Flathman) and Barry's. Connolly includes in interests "the interests a person has as a social being" (e.g., "the interests of maintaining a relationship of trust with another"), but excludes "act[s] of altruism" (p. 467).

9. Unfortunately for analytical clarity, in almost every conceivable situation, alternatives could in theory be structured so that the individuals making the decision would not have the same enlightened preferences. For example, in the first case study in this book, I contend that the townspeople of Selby had a "common interest" in building a town garage as cheaply and efficiently as possible and that they correctly approached the decision on how to build it as if there were one solution (a technical solution in this case) that would be best for all (see pp. 77–78, 88). In the second case study, I contend that the staff members of Helpline arguably had a "common interest" in refusing to accept a training contract from a local Air Force base and that they were not mistaken in approaching this problem as if there were one solution (based on their shared ideals) that would be best for all (see pp. 178–81 and 238–39). However, in each of these cases, one can conceive of a policy alternative being suggested that would have prevented the coincidence of enlightened preferences. In the case of the town garage, introducing the alternative that the town spend $1 million on the garage and give the building contract entirely to Joe Smith would probably have swung Mr. Smith's enlightened preference away from the most cost-efficient alternative. The townspeople would then no longer have had a "common interest," as I define it, in the cost-efficient solution. Some similar alternative would no doubt have sufficed to detach the interests of one of the Helpline staff members from those of the rest of the group in the Air Force contract decision.

Some limitation of the available choices is therefore necessary if the concept of "common interest" is to make sense. Yet I do not want to restrict the meaning of "common interest" to situations in which the participants would make the same enlightened policy choice only as between the alternatives with which chance and perhaps manipulation presented them. This would force me to say that A and B have common interests in a situation where B has arranged the alternatives so that it is in A's interest, given those alternatives, to make the choice most acceptable to B. I see no satisfactory solution to this problem. One must therefore concede that the "common interest" must always be understood in relation to a specific and limited list of alternatives. These alternatives will always reflect the norms of the community in which they arise, but one must nonetheless constantly ask whether the alternatives under consideration exhaust the list of "plausible" possibilities. What constitutes a "plausible possibility" will, of course, be a matter for controversy.

10. Common interests do not always arise from similar circumstances. Two people could both have an interest in obtaining food, but if food were scarce, those interests, identical in content, would conflict.

11. When we praise people, as Rousseau does, for putting the collective good above their particular interests, we are generally referring to this process. In my terminology, we praise them for making a change in their intrapsychic costs and benefits so that the good of the collectivity weighs more than their own private good.

This usage runs the risk that readers will confuse the "collective good" with "common interests," as defined earlier. Two or more people have "common interests" when their net interests, including private interests, lead them all to choose one policy rather than another from a given array of alternatives. When one makes the "collective good" one's own, this need not encompass the good of *all* individuals in the collectivity. It is a loose term for contrasting the interests of most others to one's self-regarding interest.

12. Johnson (1789), p. 564.

13. The importance of this finding grew on Homans in the ten years between *The Human Group* (1950), where it is one point among many (cf. pp. 116–117, 243, 246), and *Social Behavior: Its Elementary Forms* (1961), where it forms the leitmotif of the entire work. A central chapter, "Equality," in *Social Behavior* concludes on the basis of social-psychological evidence that friendship requires "similarity of esteem" (p. 316) because of the greater social and emotional costs of associating with inferiors or superiors.

14. Homans chose as the epigraph to *Social Behavior* the following selection from Chaucer's fourteenth-century *The Franklin's Tale*:

> For o thyng, sires, saufly dar I seye,
> That freends everych oother moot obeye,
> If they wol longe holden compaignye.
> Love wol nat been constreyned by maistrye.
> Whan maistrie comth, the God of Love anon
> Beteth his wynges, and farewel, he is gon!

15. Brain (1976), p. 20. Some cultures institute formal "friendships" between un-equals in the patron-client relation. By tying an economic and political relationship to friendship, these arrangements import some symbols of equality and affection into an otherwise unequal and self-interested relation.

16. For a discussion of James C. Davies, John Rawls, Robert Lane, J. R. Lucas, Bernard Williams, and W. G. Runciman on the ideal of "equal respect," see Mansbridge (1976b), p. 267, n. 7.

17. See Williams (1962), pp. 117–118. For more on the relationship of equal respect to identification, see Mansbridge (1976b), p. 268, n. 9.

18. Lucas argues that fraternity is opposed to equality because fraternity demands that we treat each person "as a person for him- or herself and not simply as the bearer of certain characteristics" (Lucas, 1965, pp. 306–307). However, the process of being recognized for oneself must begin with others' empathy, their having had to some extent the same experiences themselves.

19. Schelling (1960), p. 67. The three most obvious solutions to the problem of distribution are: (1) the maintenance of the status quo or the customary standard; (2) proportionality, and (3) equality. For a fuller discussion of this issue, see Barry (1965), pp. 319–322.

20. Berlin (1969), p. 17. See also Kelsen (1955), p. 38 on the derivation of the norm of political equality from philosophical relativism.

21. For purposes of this analysis, I will follow Nagel in defining "power," actual or potential, as requiring "an actual or potential causal relation between the preferences of an actor regarding an outcome and the outcome itself" (Nagel, 1975, p. 29). I will restrict the analysis to power actually or potentially causally related to the outcomes of issues that in a given polity do or could plausibly (nonfancifully) come up for communal decision, affecting some or all members of that polity.

23. It is worth repeating that this volume addresses itself only to democracy and democratic theory, although other types of polity also run the spectrum from

common to conflicting interests. A two-by-two table indicates the most obvious alternatives:

	Democracy	Hierarchy
Common Interests	Unitary democracy	Benevolent dictatorship or oligarchy
Conflicting Interests	Adversary democracy	Tyranny, slavery

24. See below, chapters 14 and 18.
25. Steiner and Dorff (1980) call this a "decision by interpretation."
26. Rousseau (1950), p. 102.

Chapter 4: Life in Small-town Selby

1. de Tocqueville (1954), vol. 1, p. 63.
2. Bryce (1894), vol. 2, p. 284. He introduces certain caveats elsewhere, however, when he writes that "no better school of politics can be imagined" than the town meeting as long as the citizenry is of native American stock, farmers rather than factory operatives, and the meeting itself is composed of fewer than 800 persons (vol. 1, p. 595).
3. Jefferson, "Letter to Samuel Kercheval" (1905), vol. 12, p. 9. Jefferson also defined a "republic" as having a town-meeting form, and claimed that "every other government is more or less republican as it has in its composition more or less of this ingredient of the direct action of the citizens." "Such a government is evidently restrained to very narrow limits of space and population. I doubt if it would be practicable beyond the extent of a New England township" (Jefferson, "Letter to John Taylor" (1905), vol. 11, p. 529). For a fuller discussion, see Baker (1977), pp. 5–18.
4. The interview sample was chosen by a random numbers table from a list generated by combining the list of registered voters, the postmaster's list of residents, and the town clerk's list of residents subject to the poll tax. Of the seventy-seven people originally chosen, six had moved from town and one was hospitalized. Of the remaining seventy, only one totally refused an interview. He was an older man, born in town, a large landowner, a frequent voter, and a small officeholder. I used public record data on property ownership and value, registering to vote, having been registered ten years ago, actual voting and town meeting attendance, holding town office, sex, and place of residence to compare my sample to the full population. My sample slightly overrepresents property owners, voters, and officeholders. The addition of the one refusal would have accentuated this overrepresentation.

The sample indicates that because the public records were not completely up to date, two or three dozen individuals covered by these records (and thus included in the N of 379 used as a base in line 2 of Table 2 and section A.2 of Tables A.2 and A.4 in Appendix A) had probably moved from town by the time I did my interviews.
5. Of the total interview sample of sixty-nine, fifty-five filled out a written questionnaire. Nine asked not to fill out the questionnaire, and one was too old to concentrate fully on the structured questions. Four others, whom I interviewed on the last day and left a mail-back questionnaire rather than picking it up in person the following day, failed to mail it back. Those who answered the questionnaire, however, seemed not to differ in any important respect from those who did not.
6. I hope, indeed, that their goodwill has not been betrayed in this book. I have

taken some care to disguise and alter details about the town and the individuals described here, and I urge the reader to collaborate with me in this endeavor. It would not be useful to anyone, and could cause pain for some, to invest energy in penetrating these disguises.

7. Barber (1974), p. 263.

8. See below, chapter 11.

9. Stephens (1974) shows that by 1969 local governments in Vermont had fewer powers than local governments in most other states. But local governments in Vermont are also far smaller on the average than those in other states. Indeed, Vermont towns are smaller than most of the urban neighborhoods to which radicals (e.g., Kramer, 1972) wished to decentralize powers of the type Vermont towns exercise. Bedford-Stuyvesant in New York City, for example, has a larger population than the entire state of Vermont. Thus, to assert, as Stephens does, that New York state is more decentralized than Vermont because local governments have more powers in New York state than in Vermont, is quite misleading. If one were to measure the size of the units exercising any given power, the averages would be far smaller in Vermont than in New York or almost any other state.

Chapter 5: The Town Meeting

1. In 1970, Bryan found an average of 25 percent attendance in 82 Vermont towns ranging in size from 196 to 3,187, with a high of 42 percent attendance in one town of 751 people and a low of 8 percent in a town of 1,061 (Bryan, 1975, pp. 26–27).

2. The towns of Broome and Conesville, New York, comparable to Selby in physical size, population, percentage of land in average size of farm, and average value of land per acre, had in 1969 a turnout for town elections of, respectively, 83 percent and 93 percent of the eligible voters. Other small towns, not so exactly comparable in physical characteristics, had almost as high turnouts. In New York State, town elections are not only partisan but also are combined with the election of county officers (sheriff, county clerk, county treasurer, and county coroner), and occasionally of an associate judge of the State Court of Appeals.

3. By Vermont law, employers must give their employees town meeting day off without pay if the employee so requests. Large towns, which have mandated their selectmen or finance committees to do most of the legislation of the town, often have their meetings at night. In a small town like Selby, however, many of the issues are discussed and much of the legislation for the next year hammered out at the meeting itself. The amount of business always fills one whole day and sometimes even requires a second town meeting.

4. I attended three town meetings in Selby. Some people picked the same seat or vicinity in which to sit each time.

Chapter 6: Unitary Forces in a Face-to-Face Assembly

1. Hicks (1947), p. 140.

2. Rosenberg (1954–55), p. 349.

3. Nathan Leites has pointed out to me, however, that these jokes themselves mask reminders of potential hostility: "I'll get him later"; "[They'll] be out in the cold!"

4. Zuckerman (1970), p. 136.

5. See p. 95.

Chapter 8: Conflicting Interests

1. Among the taxpayers, the correlation between length of residence in Selby and amount of town property tax is .22. The correlation between length of residence in Selby and farming is .45. In assessing correlations reported in the Notes, readers may want some indication of the likelihood that the observed value could arise entirely by chance. In the full Selby sample of 69, one correlation in twenty will exceed .24 by chance, one in a hundred will exceed .32, and one in a thousand will exceed .42. In the full Helpline sample of 41, the analogous values are .32, .42, and .54. Because of missing data on specific items, some of the Selby correlations are calculated on samples closer to 41 than to 69. Because there is less missing data in Helpline, almost all the Helpline correlations are calculated on samples close to .41. All correlations are Pearson product-moment.

2. The correlation between length of residence in Selby and self-employment is .21.

3. In the year 1971, only three (8 percent) of the thirty-seven people forty-four years old and under in my sample paid a town tax of more than $840. This group had a total of fifty-one children in the town school. In the same year, almost half (47 percent) of the thirty-two people over forty-four in my sample paid a town property tax of more than $840, but this group had only fifteen children in the town's schools. The correlation between age and having children in school is −.27; the correlation between age and amount of town property tax is .40.

4. He also tells me that he does not "want to complain" about any of the decisions that are made because if he were to take the selectman's job, "I'd probably ruin the town."

Chapter 9: Political Inequality: Selby

1. Locke (1965), p. 346 (II, 158). See also pp. 419–420.

2. The U.S. Supreme Court, *Wesberry v. Sanders* 276 U.S. 1 (1964) at 7. The Court based its conclusion on no more than the assertion in Article I, Section 2 of the U.S. Constitution that members of the U.S. House of Representatives should be chosen "by the People of the several States."

3. These are two of the more traditional measures of community power. See Hunter (1953), Dahl (1961), and Polsby (1963) for examples of the reputational and decisional methods and for a brief analysis of the controversy surrounding these methods. For other methods of measuring power, see Shapley and Shubik (1954), and March (1955). For a critique of the Shapley-Shubik and other methods, see Riker (1964). In Helpline, the second case study, I was able to pursue both decisional and reputational approaches. The results were consistent with objective measures of participation, self-assessments of participation, and, in most cases, respondents' subjective assessments of their power—the types of measures I have in Selby.

4. See, for example, Kasarda and Janowitz (1974).

5. Among the newcomers, being "talkative" and town meeting attendance (times attended as a percentage of times registered) are positively correlated, .44. This correlation may not adequately capture the true relationship, however, since the index of talkativeness may not be reliable. This index is based on the length of time people spoke in their interview with me, whether they cited not liking to speak in public as a reason for not attending town meeting, and whether they described themselves as better talkers than listeners. These three measures are not highly correlated with one another, the values ranging from −.04 to .27. Unfortunately, I did not develop more satisfactory measures of talkativeness until I studied Helpline.

6. Among the old-timers being "talkative" and town meeting attendance are nega-

tively correlated, −.19. This is in itself a nonsignificant deviation from zero. It differs significantly, however, from the newcomers. Newcomers in the meetings I attended were also more likely than the old-timers to make striking nonverbal impressions on the meeting. Mr. Gretsch's dramatic striding to the front of the room to make his case, followed by his towering over Clayton Bedell to threaten him with a lawsuit, contrasts visibly with the avoidance of confrontation, the soft voices, and the embarrassed mumbles of some of the older residents. An older resident confirmed my impression by telling me, "The people 'in the know' don't ever get to their feet [to speak]!"

7. In the town's full population, there is only a −.02 correlation between being in town more than ten years and class as measured by the appraised value of one's residence. (The correlation between length of residence and socioeconomic status in the sample is −.10.) Among those who attend the meeting, the twenty oldest residents in my sample show only the slightest correlation between class and reporting frequent speaking at town meeting (.09). Among the twenty most recent residents who attend, however, the relationship between class and reported speaking is quite strong (.41).

8. The standardized coefficient of length of residence when predicting local political activity (.37) is reduced to .30 by controlling for social connection (as measured by my three-variable index). It is reduced to .26 by controlling for local political information (as measured by my three-variable index). It is reduced to .20 by controlling for both social connection and information together.

Length of residence did not predict localism as opposed to cosmopolitanism as much as I had expected. I found a slight association between length of residence and disagreeing with a questionnaire statement that local elections were not important (.14), and some association between length of residence and two statements of local loyalty ("Newcomers may be all right, but if I were picking someone for a position of responsibility in Selby, I'd pick an old-timer," .21; "The local community is the backbone of America," .26). However, I found no association between length of residence and responses to questions on the effect of local government on one's life, the comparative interest of local as against national news, and the likelihood of town meeting deciding anything anyway.

9. Dependence on informal rates of communication would help explain the "friends and neighbors" effect in a one-party state like Alabama. See Key (1949), pp. 37–52. See also Greenstone (1965), p. 350; and Peterson (1970), p. 502.

10. It is an indication of the processes of change in Selby that some of the residents have begun to hire others to take their garbage to the dump for them.

11. However, as with length of residence, there seems to be no correlation between living in the village and my measures of local interest. There is also no correlation between living in the village and my two measures of local loyalty.

12. Festinger, Schachter, and Bach (1950), p. 112.

13. All eight villagers who answered the questionnaire item: "Do you think of yourself as outgoing, or do you keep pretty much to yourself?" answered "outgoing" or "depends," compared to 41 percent of the forty-four nonvillagers who answered. Due to nonresponse, the numbers are small. However, in the unlikely event that all the village nonresponders "kept to themselves" and all the non-village responders were "outgoing," the villagers in this sample would still consider themselves marginally more outgoing than the nonvillagers (61.5 percent to 53.6 percent). All of the twelve villagers who had been in town long enough to vote had voted in more than a quarter of the state and national elections in the past ten years, compared to 56 percent of the forty-six nonvillagers.

14. The standardized coefficient of living in the village when predicting political activity (.21) is reduced to .05 by controlling for age. It is reduced to .09 by controlling for social connection, and also to .09 by controlling for information. Controlling all three variables makes the coefficient of living in the village negative, although insignificantly so.

15. The coefficient of age when predicting political activity (.43) is only slightly reduced (to .38) by controlling for social connection. It is reduced to .32 by controlling for information. It is reduced to .31 by controlling for both social connections and information together.

16. March (1953–54), p. 461. The women in my sample are marginally more likely than the men to be interested more in local than in national affairs (.11) and more likely to say that the local government has a great effect on their lives (.32).

As for the schools, even before American women won the vote in 1920, several of the states had allowed women to vote in school elections alone.

17. Frank M. Bryan has provided me with the following data for purposes of comparison. The gender-related division of political labor is even more striking in Selby than in the rest of Vermont.

TABLE A
Officeholding by Gender in Vermont and Selby, 1962-72

| Office[a] | 1969-72, 99 Vermont towns, pop. 3,000 | | 1962-71 Selby, pop. c. 500 | |
	Office-Years Possible[b]	Percent Held by Women	Office-Years Possible	Percent Held by Women
Selectman (3)	1,188	0.9	30	0
Moderator (1)	396	0.8	10	0
Lister (3)	1,188	4	30	0
Auditor (3)	1,188	50	30	90
Treasurer (1)	396	64	10	100
Clerk (1)	396	69	10	100

[a]Numbers in parentheses indicate number of incumbents at any one time.

[b]Office years = number of terms × number of years measured × number of incumbents at any one time.

18. Women are actually more likely to hold elective office in Selby than in most Vermont towns. From 1969 to 1972, for example, only 24 percent of all town office-holders and in 1974, 41 percent of all Vermont school directors in towns this size were women, compared to 40 percent and 50 percent in Selby between 1962 and 1971. For several years before reapportionment Selby had a female representative in the state legislature, whereas in the same era (1961–65) 78 percent of other Vermont towns of similar size had male representatives. (Vermont town office statistics from Bryan, 1975, p. 24, measuring a sample of towns with populations from 196 to 3,187 in the years 1969 to 1972. The Vermont school director statistic is an average from the Vermont Town Reports of all Vermont towns of 500–599 population in 1974. State legislature statistics from Bryan, 1974, pp. 52–53.)

19. Again, women participate more in Selby than in Vermont as a whole. Bryan (1975, p. 27) reports that women constituted 44 percent of those attending town meetings in Vermont from 1970 to 1972, and 20 percent of those speaking, compared to 49 percent and 29 percent in Selby from 1970 through 1972.

20. Indirect techniques can sometimes be important. At a crucial point in Selby's zoning debate, for example, one woman asked quietly, "If we do like the state says now and join, can we get out?" When the lawyer for the Planning Commission had to answer in the negative, this changed the direction of the debate, for it helped put the commission on the defensive.

21. The men and women in the interview sample did not, however, differ appreciably from those in the town's population as a whole on other measures that I had for both groups. In both the interview sample and the town as a whole, men were no more likely than women to attend town meetings (.02 correlation between gender [f = o, m = l] and town meeting attendance in both the town as a whole and the interview sample.) Nor were men, in either the interview sample or the town as a whole, much more likely than women to hold town office (.04 correlation between gender and office holding in town as a whole, .09 in interview sample.) There was a greater discrepancy between the sample and the town population for voting in national elections. Women voted more than men in both the town as a whole and the interview sample, but the imbalance was greater in the sample (−.07 correlation between gender and national voting in the town as a whole, −.22 in the interview sample.) The small differences between the sample and the whole popula-

tion do not seem adequate to explain the serious discrepancy between my observations, in which I have some faith, and the reports of the men and women in my interview sample of how often they spoke in town meeting. Because I asked people for their subjective assessments of how often they spoke, not for an objective count, there may have been gender differences in the way my respondents defined terms like "often."

22. The women in my sample were no more likely than the men, however, to be among the sixteen people who singled out as a reason for not attending town meeting: "I don't like to speak in public" or to be among the ten who singled this reason out for disagreement ($-.01$).

23. One woman, who had strong opinions on basic education, said she would never express them in town meeting: "No, my husband does the talking." And another woman agreed: "I don't like to be in the limelight. I'd rather be behind, pushing."

Such attitudes derive from a traditional culture in which the men are expected to make the important decisions. One more-than-competent farmer's wife, for instance, explained to me that "in a family the one that is most capable should make most of the decisions and be head of the family, so I leave that up to him." Another woman, who cleans in a hospital morgue and whose husband constantly interrupted our interview with comments of his own, mentioned toward the end of our interview that "I'll be joining the Elks Club because my husband's let me become a member."

24. Men and women who hold blue-collar manual jobs comprise 43.5 percent of my sample. Poor farmers comprise 7.2 percent. Women working in clerical jobs make up another 10.1 percent. See Chapter 4, pp. 42–43.

25. Within the group of both taxpayers and registered voters, the correlation between percentage town meeting attendance and a four category variable measuring appraised value of residence was .16 for the thirty-three individuals in my sample, and .25 for the 179 individuals in the entire town. This difference is easily explicable in terms of sampling error, but it suggests that class differences in my sample are likely to be slightly smaller than in the population.

26. Forty-four percent of the fifty-two people who could think of a reason volunteered this one. The second most popular reason (28 percent) was some variant of "Things would go the way they want anyway."

27. The correlation between class and talking for a long time in the interview is .06, and between class and reporting oneself as "a better talker than listener," .09.

28. Indeed, controlling for trust reduces the standardized coefficient of socioeconomic status when predicting political activity from .20 to .13. Controlling for sense of control also reduces the coefficient to .13. Controlling for both trust and sense of control reduces the coefficient to .10.

Chapter 10: Free Choice in Selby

1. That this is literally an article of faith among the Selby townspeople can be seen from the frequency and the identical wording with which it appears in interview after interview: "You can get up and say what you think"; "You can get up and voice your opinion, you know, really, and you can stand up and the people can talk back and forth"; "It gives all a chance to really have their say"; "People can voice their opinions"; "The individual can voice his opinion"; "At least you have a voice"; "At least you can ask questions"; "You [can] express your views on things. . . . You have a right to express your opinion"; "It gives an individual a chance to air their feelings"; "It gives people a chance to get some of their ideas and feelings out of their system"; "For many people, it is the one day that they will say their piece, whether it's good or bad. This is their one chance; they save up for it all year long . . . they can air their feelings"; "A lot of things get aired that wouldn't if dependent only on a motion that got voted on. The less literate people that wouldn't write an article do get on

their feet and speak. . . . That's one thing about these slow meetings—you have plenty of time to get up and voice your opinion."

2. Again, the formula of "sit back and complain" has widespread currency: "People bitch all year long, but refuse to *do* anything about it"; "Some of the people who find most fault have never been to town meeting since I've been in town"; "These other people sit back and complain, but yet they didn't do anything about it"; "They'd rather sit back and criticize than get up and do something constructive about it"; "There are so many people in town who have so much to say about it at the coffee counter or somewhere, but they are the ones who don't come out to the town meeting. When the town report comes out, that's when they start . . . making all their complaints, but they don't do anything about it"; "Too many people will sit back and bitch, and not speak much at all. They wouldn't get off their cans and do something about it. They'd sit back and they won't go the day of town meeting"; "A lot of people don't take advantage of town meetings, and sit home and squawk about what goes on; where if they would go and take a part in it, it would change a lot of things they don't like."

3. See, for example, Barnlund (1959), Maier (1953, 1972), Hall (1971), and Collaros and Anderson (1969).

4. The conclusions of Morris-Jones (1954) and Berelson et al. (1954) also have this implication.

Chapter 11: Was There a Golden Era?

1. Emerson (1833), pp. 50–52.
2. d'Agostino (1948), pp. 14–18.
3. "Each inhabited town in this state may, forever and hereafter, hold elections therein and choose each one Representative to represent them in the House of Representatives." The Vermont Constitution of 1777, cited in Nuquist and Nuquist (1966), p. 32.
4. Bogart (1959), p. 21. Bogart also estimates that only "in a few [states] does the influence of local government begin to approach that which prevails in Vermont" (p. 19).
5. For a discussion of the effect of reapportionment on the Vermont legislature, see Bryan (1974).
6. This pattern is typical when towns of different sizes are consolidated into one representative district. Bryan (1974), pp. 133–134.
7. Nuquist and Nuquist (1966), p. 263.
8. Ibid., p. 275. The authors also point out that in 1966 the Vermont state government bore only 20 percent of the cost of public education, compared to a national average of 50 percent.
9. Title 16, *Vermont Statutes Annotated* (hereafter referred to as VSA), Sec. 165 (1969).
10. d'Agostino (1948), pp. 40ff. See also Title 33, VSA, pp. 701ff., passim, prior to 1967.
11. Green (1941, p. 39) argues that the transfer of responsibility for others to a bureaucracy constitutes an irretrievable moral loss. For a more recent, less philosophical statement of this position, see Suttles and Street (1969), reprinted in Laumann, Siegel, and Hodge (1970), pp. 744–755.
12. Title 10, VSA, Sec. 1259, History, 1943.
13. The ban was actually promulgated by a state-created agency: Agency of Environmental Conservation, *Environmental Protection Regulations*, Ch. 5–2011.
14. Title 24, VSA, Sect. 2201 (1967).
15. Title 24, VSA, Sect. 4301ff. (The Vermont Planning and Development Act, 1967). As of 1974, one-third of the towns in the state had acted with Selby in refusing

to join or fund the state-sponsored regional planning commissions. (Personal communication to the author from Schuyler Jackson, chairman, Agency of Environmental Conservation, Montpelier, Vermont, November 18, 1974.)

16. Title 10, *VSA*, Sect. 6001ff. (Vermont's Act 250—Land Use and Development, 1970). See also Myers (1974). As a gesture to Vermont antipathy toward state control, Act 250 established "local" panels to judge initial requests for the permits it required. However, as the governor appointed each panel's three commissioners and as their jurisdiction encompassed an average of twenty-eight towns, the system had little in common with traditional town control.

17. *The Early Records of the Town of Dedham* (hereafter cited as *Dedham Town Records*), III, p. 4. The fine established was one shilling for more than a half hour lateness, two shillings sixpence for absence. A year later (1637), the fines were raised:

> Wheras meetings haue ben agreed vpon & tymes apoynted accordingly, it hath often happened y^t by ye slacknes of many their comeing, others haue by long attendance waested much tyme to their greate damage. It is nowe for p^{r}vention therof agreed & ordered that whosoever shall haue Received notice of such a meeteing & shall absent himselfe one halfe houer after ye beateing of the drume shall forfet twelve pence. And yf any shall wholly absent himselfe shall forfet the sum of Three shillings & Fower pence. except ther be some greate occasions to the contrary. . . [III, p. 30].

The first extant dated record of any town meeting in the United States (Cambridge, Massachusetts, 1632) institutes a fine for nonattendance at town meeting (Sly, 1930, p. 30). According to Sly (p. 43) attendance at town meeting was compulsory in most early Massachusetts towns.

18. My calculations, using the first ten years in *Dedham Town Records*, III, pp. 20–113. In all but five of the fifteen town meetings from 18 August 1636 (old style) through 1 January 1646 (old style), Dedham's early minutes record the names of the men who attended the meeting. I counted a man as absent only when his name appeared on the list of attenders both at some point before and at some point after his nonattendance. This measure probably underestimates the degree of absenteeism. For further discussion of these records, see Brown (1967).

19. My calculations, using data from Powell (1963, pp. 120–125). Brown (1967, p. 385, and 1954, p. 877) indicates that after 1647 the adult male population is the correct base on which to calculate town meeting attendance.

20. My calculations. The Dorchester voting records come from Blake (1846, vol. 2). Robert A. Gross (Department of History, Amherst College) supplied the Concord voting records. Edward M. Cook (Department of History, University of Chicago) supplied the voting records from Andover (*Town Meeting Records*, 12 October 1708), Barnstable (*Records* N.E.H.G.S. copy, p. 15), and Dedham (*Town Records*, III, p. 146; III, p. 246; IV, p. 249).

The calculations in the text assume that 90 percent of the estimated male population over twenty-one was eligible to vote (see Lockridge and Kreider, 1966). Robert Gross, however, suggests that only 70 to 80 percent of the male population over twenty-one was eligible to vote in eighteenth-century Concord. If Gross's estimates were to apply to towns other than Concord, the figures in the text would be higher by about 10 to 15 percent.

21. My calculations, using data supplied by Robert Gross, and adopting as a base the number of adult male taxpayers on the Concord assessment lists in the relevant years.

22. My calculations, using data from contested elections in the town meeting minutes of Bedford, 1833–46; Lincoln, 1821–29; Acton, 1821–39; Carlyle, 1835–40; and Lexington, 1822–37. These microfilmed town records, in *Early Massachusetts Records* (1154 Boylston Street, Boston, Massachusetts 02215), are available at the Charles Warren Center for the Study of American History, Harvard University. Unfortunately, the number of male taxpayers in these towns was not readily available. I have consequently calculated these percentages on a base of "adult males" extrapolated from the 1830 and 1840 census statistics. When the census lists the number of males over twenty-one in a town, I have extrapolated for intercensal years. When

the census gives only the number of total inhabitants in the town and the number of males over twenty-one in the county, I have extrapolated for intercensal years assuming a parallel with the countywide age structure. This procedure introduces a considerable margin of error. If I had used this technique instead of the assessment lists in Concord, I would have produced percentages between 1 percent and 8 percent lower than those reported here. It may be, therefore, that these percentages are also between 1 percent and 8 percent too low.

23. My calculations, using *The Old Records of the Town of Fitchburgh* (1902), vol. 6, p. 21, March 7, 1831.

24. My calculations, using Selby town meeting minutes.

25. See Brown (1954, pp. 868–882) for seventeenth-century meetings, and Brown (1955, pp. 78–79, especially pp. 90, 93) for eighteenth-century meetings.

26. My calculations, using the first ten years in *Dedham Town Records*, III, pp. 20–113 both for a record of town meeting attendance and, through the tax rolls, to indicate relative wealth.

27. Powell (1963), p. 125.

28. Data supplied by Robert Gross.

29. Lockridge and Kreider (1966), p. 566. Brown (1967, p. 395) argues to the contrary that there does not "appear to be any important correlation between being consistently elected selectman and being wealthy" in Dedham between 1636 and 1659. Yet her own table demonstrates that while the estate valuation of all Dedham townsmen averaged £108, that of selectmen elected to fewer than eight terms averaged £123, and that of selectmen elected to eight or more terms averaged £202.

30. Lockridge and Kreider (1966), p. 566. However, Brown (1955, p. 98) points out that in Northampton in 1765 "the bottom 57 percent of the population had 65 percent of all the town officials, and three of the five selectmen."

31. Data supplied by Robert Gross.

32. Grant (1961), p. 113.

33. Data supplied by Robert Gross.

34. "The Peticion" of the town of Dedham, 1636, to the Massachusetts General Court, requested that the town be named "Contentment" (*Dedham Town Records*, III, p. 1). In this respect, the petition was denied, and the town was named Dedham.

35. In the full passage from which these excerpts are taken, the adult male householders of Dedham promised "amongst ourselves and each to other to pffesse and practice one trueth according to that most pfect rule. the foundacion where of is Euerlasing Loue: (2) That we shall by all meanes Laboure to keepe of from vs all such. as ar contrarye minded. And receau onlely such vnto vs as be such as may be pbably of one harte, with vs as that we either knowe or may well and truely be informed to walke in a peaceable conuersation with all meekenes of spirit for the edification of each other in the knowledg and faith of the Lord Jesus: And the mutuall encouragmt vnto all Temporall comforts in all things: seekeing the good of each other out of all which may be deriued true Peace" (original punctuation and spelling preserved; *Dedham Town Records*, III, p. 3).

36. Ibid., III, p. 3.

37. Ibid., III, p. 10.

38. Hosmer (1885), p. 423.

Chapter 12: Helpline: A Crisis Center

1. This does not mean that the members of Helpline were more radical, egalitarian, or committed than the members of other collectives. They were less militantly radical than some collectives I knew well. Yet the kind of work they did, which diffused expertise, and their history of having overthrown their founder and original fund raisers made Helpline more able to practice equality. In contrast, radical schools

and universities are inherently divided into the trained and the trainees, and need formal credentials for accreditation; voluntary associations have major differences in potential time commitment among the members; and in new collectives of all sorts the founders or original fund raisers have greater power.

My own political activity, along with the extensive pretests I did in a number of organizations before settling on Helpline, gave me a vivid picture of the obstacles to equality in most participatory democracies. This understanding in turn made it possible for me to talk with the members of Helpline frankly and on the basis of common experience.

From the beginning, the members of Helpline welcomed me. A friend in the city had introduced me to a former fund raiser at Helpline, who, on learning of my plan to study the problems of participatory democracy, told me to phone Kaye, Helpline's "vice-coordinator." She suggested that I visit a meeting of the CPC, Helpline's central policy committee. At that meeting, I explained my goal of coming to understand better the problems of egalitarian decision making, and got permission to sit in on the weekly meetings of the CPC. As one of a group of twelve to twenty or so people, I not only took notes, but occasionally added a piece of information to the meeting. Once I took and typed the minutes.

Helpline, as a social work agency (although one with radical aspirations), was used to studying and being studied. My steady attendance convinced people fairly quickly that I was serious; and by the time I had been there four months, no one, I think, even considered not giving me an interview.

At Helpline I attended five straight months of CPC meetings (as well as an extra set of meetings later on), two Community Days, and various meetings of the service groups. In each of these meetings I took notes on the extent as well as the content of each member's participation. For the Community Day in which I measured participation in the small groups as well as in the large, I asked one person whom I knew well in each small group other than the one I joined, to record the participation of the members of that group. My method of recording participation was simply to place an *X* or a question mark next to a persons name whenever that person spoke or asked a question.

After I had been at Helpline four months, I interviewed forty of the forty-one members (one was on vacation) in a generally unstructured format for an hour or more, ending with the exercise described on page 183 of the text. Every member also filled out a structured written questionnaire. On the questionnaire I requested that those who did not have time to complete the whole form at least answer the few questions I had starred (these covered my major independent and dependent variables); six people took this option.

2. For example, volunteers typically give widely varying amounts of time to an organization and are affected by that organization in varying degrees. The boundaries to membership in most voluntary associations are extremely permeable and the membership is transitory.

3. The worker-controlled enterprise of classic theory makes a physical product—shoes, cans, tea, tiles. Yet a greater and growing percentage of the work force in all industrial countries is now employed in fields other than manufacturing, mining, farming, or the transportation of these products. For example, 61 percent of the 1975 U.S. work force was employed in fields other than direct production or transportation (U.S. Bureau of the Census, 1977, Table 56, p. 246).

Chapter 13: Fears of Conflict in a Face-to-Face Democracy

1. Bruce, the treasurer, made much the same point:

We've done well when we've broken down into these small working groups. And then we come back into a big group, and when you've got sixty people in a room all of whom are invested in the issue, all of whom want to be heard, all of whom are somewhat "on stage"—when you are talking to that many people, it's just very hard to focus, very hard to work out disagreements; it's very hard to have a dialogue; it's very hard to get compromises.

2. The staff repeatedly worried about how the meetings got "into heavy personal issues," "personality things, conflicts—they really shouldn't be brought up at the meetings," "I really get upset, like in an obvious personality clash," and "everything is brought down here to a kind of personal level."

People are so frightened of such conflict that they exaggerate its impact. In one meeting, what I would call a minor skirmish between two participants ended in an amicable exchange of apologies and a move to other business. But one new staff member remembered that:

> Someone started something with somebody else and then they said, "OK, Lets' quit," and that was the only thing to do. . . . So the meeting was over. When things like that happen, that's the way they have to end.

So too in Selby, one nonparticipant summed up the meeting in which Clayton Bedell had tangled with Robert Gretsch by saying, "This year, they had a big fight, and they all went home."

3. Of the sixty-six friends named in response to the question, "Who are your two closest friends at Helpline?" forty-three (65 percent) were in the respondent's service group. But other ties cut across the service groups. Half the people at Helpline lived with others in the organization, and the people they lived with were often not in their service group. Members also worked, dated, and shared training sessions across groups. As a consequence, as many as 57 percent said that they felt close to more than three people outside their service groups.

Even the staff at the Shelter had cross-cutting friendships with CCC. As one Shelter member put it, after the budget-cutting Community Day:

> I didn't feel good about CCC being so picked on. I wasn't laying the blame on anyone; I think they set it up for themselves as much as we set them up, but it was just a nasty dynamic that I didn't like. . . . I know Greg and I know Ellen [both from CCC], and it was really hard to come down on CCC. They believe in CCC just as much as we believe in the Shelter. And maybe they don't believe in the Shelter as much as I don't believe in CCC. It was really hard to see their group put on the defensive. I went out to Yellow Springs to do some recruiting with Evie and Penny [both from the CCC], so it was sort of a marathon encounter group, going back and forth with them. (laugh) . . . Evie and Penny I know pretty well.

Lipset (1963, p. 211ff.) concludes that as individuals experience pressures from opposing directions they become more likely to withdraw by losing interest and deciding not to vote. For the same reasons, cross-cutting friendships at Helpline probably drove the staff to avoid conflict. But those cross-cutting friendships did not reduce participation. Rather, one's number of friends outside the service group was highly correlated with participation in communitywide decisions (see below, Chapter 15, note 71).

Chapter 14: Consensus and the Common Interest

1. Although I had attended the relevant CPC meetings, I too had been misled by the consensus on "information sharing" into not knowing which decision had been made. Only my notes from the two meetings revealed how the process of searching for agreement had led to confusion. In the first CPC meeting, Nate, who favored self-determination for the service groups and opposed open criticism at the Community Day, stated, "I have trust in the service groups—that they'll be able to make the kind of decisions that have to be made." But he added, perhaps prompted by the desire to achieve consensus, "It hasn't always happened in the past, and if it doesn't, then *the other groups must say so*" (my emphasis). Kaye, who supported the right of the assembly to use criticism to pressure the service groups, seconded this double message: "We've got to try to start with the service groups. And *also give*

the groups feedback about whether we think they're doing their jobs" (my emphasis). Pamela, a proponent of assembly criticism, at first suggested baldly that on a Community Day the whole body had the power to "decide the big issues," but when asked what she meant, she fell back to the words "information sharing."

The second CPC meeting, after the agenda committee meeting, began with Eben's report that the agenda committee had decided the Community Day would *not* be a "'prove it to me' session." Kaye agreed with the general sentiment but added that somewhere in the Community Day she felt "a need for an explicit statement that people are 'comfortable' or 'not comfortable' with [what] the service groups [had decided]" and that this should take the form of a "community statement" and not happen only in the discussion groups into which a major part of the Community Day would be broken. The agenda committee agreed to "tack it on," but no one noticed that "tacking on" a community response to the service groups' determinations explicitly added a dimension of evaluation, with its potential for criticism and pressure.

A little later in the same meeting, a proponent of critical evaluation remarked offhandedly that the Community Day would be "evaluating, in a short period of time, the service groups." Eben, from the agenda committee, broke in immediately: "But we're *not* evaluating service groups!" The first speaker, tired and impatient, countered: "That's just semantics," to which Eben reiterated: "*No,* it's real!" But the meeting immediately moved on to the new issue at hand. It never resolved how the agenda committee's determination not to have a "prove it to me" session could be reconciled with Kaye's request for a community statement of how "comfortable" people felt with the service groups' reports. As the first speaker put it later:

> One of the major questions around the whole meeting was whether it was just going to be an information-sharing meeting or whether there were going to be evaluations. I was certainly among those who were pushing for license to evaluate. I think that actually was never decided. . . .

2. Center for New Schools (1972), p. 322. See also Freeman (1972–73), p. 161.

3. The minority of nine had as high a percentage of speakers (78 percent) as the majority of sixteen (72 percent). But the seven speakers in the minority each spoke on the average 3.3 times in the two hours it took to make the decision; the twelve speakers in the majority each spoke on the average 4.4 times.

4. In this, in his comments on work, and in several other points, Eddie's analysis was much like that of Marcuse (see Wolff, Moore, and Marcuse, 1965). Although four years later, Eddie told me that he had in fact read a good deal of Marcuse, at the time of the interview, I did not realize the closeness of the fit and therefore did not ask about it. Of all the staff at Helpline, Ken and Eddie presented the most Marxist analysis.

5. Leon thought "people listened with great sensitivity. . . . My opinion changed." Deborah, the office manager, called it "the most exciting thing that has happened to me yet":

> At the first meeting, I was just looking at it on a very superficial plane. During the next meeting, when everyone presented their cases so articulately, I really started to think about it. I found myself thinking "Yes, we should do it" for about the first half hour, and then I was totally against it. (laugh) It was really a hard decision to make. And you could tell a lot of people weren't sure for a long time. But we kept talking about it until everyone was sure. I thought that was really good.

Chapter 15: Political Inequality: Helpline

1. A network analysis of choices of friends, persons "whose judgment you would most respect" on a Helpline issue, and persons not known by the respondent yields no distinct pattern of deference or hierarchy, no interlocked "ruling group." Moreover, although certain individuals within each friendship group had characteristics

associated with greater participation, no one friendship group (as defined by block model analysis of friendship choices) was composed primarily of individuals whose participation rates were greater than average. Certainly no one friendship group collected together the high participants in an interlocking clique.

Helpline's history suggests that this may have been deliberate. The acts of deposing the founder and his circle, who had specialized in administration, and dispersing fund raising among the service groups weakened the administrative group, Administrative Backup, to the point where it became noticeably the least cohesive group at Helpline.

I am indebted for the block model analysis of this data to Roberto M. Fernandèz, Chris Winship, and Ronald Breiger.

2. This question was designed by Barber (1966), p. 172.

3. Others confirmed my observations. For four of the six decisions, I asked the staff which people they thought had most influence. Six people were generally held to have influenced one or another decision. But none of the six, including the coordinator, was generally held to have had influence on more than one decision.

4. Comparisons of participation in Selby and Helpline are problematic because the meaning of a political act in the two contexts is not strictly comparable. However, there is some basis for comparison. At Helpline, only two people did not attend either full assembly while I was there. These two had both attended many assemblies in the past. They had attended many meetings of their own small groups and had taken some form of responsibility for the whole. The participation of the least active members of Helpline seems therefore comparable to the participation of someone in the most active tenth of the Selby population. One might diagram the comparison as follows:

Helpline: 0 ∟⎯⎯⎯⎯⎯⎯⎯⎯⎯⏌ 100

Selby: 0 ∟⎯⎯⎯⎯⎯⎯⎯⎯⎯⎯⎯⎯⎯⎯⎯⎯⎯⎯⎯⎯⎯⎯⎯⎯⎯⏌ 100

5. The correlation between a person's length of time in the organization and the percentage of the forty-one staff members that person knows is .43. The correlation between a person's length of time in the organization and the percentage of the forty-one staff members who know that person is .52.

6. The correlation between length of time in the organization and feeling sure about where to place others on the "power circle" is .60; the correlation between length of time and being chosen as someone whose judgment on a Helpline issue another would respect is .23.

7. Responses to the question, "How many people in Helpline outside your service group do you feel personally close to?" correlated .56 with attendance at organization-wide meetings, .45 with speaking at such meetings, .50 with other members' estimate of one's power, and .52 with self-estimate of power.

8. Using a standardized measure of feeling close to people in Helpline outside one's service group (mean = 0; S.D. = 1), the mean scores were .55 for the Switchboard, .29 for both Administrative Backup and the Van, .14 for the CCC, and −.61 for the Shelter.

9. Controlling for friendships outside one's service group reduces the standardized coefficient of centrality when predicting attendance at meetings from .35 to .15 and when predicting ranked power from .37 to .19. The direction of the causal connection between friendship patterns and participation is obviously ambiguous. There is, however, no evidence of self-selection bias since, unlike Selby's villagers, Switchboard members were *less* likely than others to describe themselves as outgoing. Compare also Festinger, Schachter, and Bach (1950).

10. Controlling for education reduces the standardized coefficient of age when predicting attendance at meetings from .30 to .09. Controlling for how long a staff member had been in the organization reduces the coefficient to .20. Controlling for both education and length of time in the organization reduces the coefficient of age when predicting attendance at meetings to .02. As for ranked power, controlling for education reduces the coefficient of age when predicting ranked power from .22 to −.05. Controlling for both education and length of time in the organization makes the coefficient even more strongly negative. The same pattern holds with the other partici-pation, efficacy, and satisfaction measures.

11. Table B reports the means of men and women at Helpline to questions in which the possible responses ranged from "Never true" (1) to "Almost always true" (5).

TABLE B
Reported Personality Attributes by Gender

Correlation with ranked "power"[a]		Women (N = 12)	Men (N = 20)[b]	Difference[c]	Probability
−.35	Articulate people intimidate me	2.0	.8	1.2	< .01
.40*	I express myself well in words	2.2	2.9	.7	< .05
.35*	People seem to respect my opinion about things	2.7	3.2	.5	—
−.43	I don't like to "operate"	2.2	1.7	.5	—
.25	I have strong political opinions	2.3	2.7	.4	—
.48*	I like competition	1.9	2.2	.3	—
.29	I'm good at making decisions quickly	2.4	2.7	.3	—
.41*	I enjoy planning things and taking charge	2.6	2.8	.2	—
−.57***	I hate to tell others what to do	2.3	2.1	.2	—
−.24	I am easily downed in an argument	1.5	1.3	.2	—
.22	I can usually find a way of giving criticism without upsetting a person	2.5	2.6	.1	—
−.28	Meetings bore me	2.3	2.2	.1	—
.38*	I enjoy power	2.6	2.6	0	—
.60***	I like taking responsibility	3.0	2.9	−.1	—

[a] Pearson product-moment correlation of reported personality attribute with average "power" rank at Helpline. In this, as in subsequent tables in the notes, probability will be reported either directly, with the notations < .05 etc., or with asterisks: * = p < .05; ** = p < .01; *** = p < .001. Correlations below .2 not reported here.

[b] Only thirty-two of the forty-one staff members answered this optional portion of the questionnaire.

[c] Difference between male and female scores is reported positively both when males score higher and trait is positively correlated with power, and when males score lower and trait is negatively correlated with power.

12. Suter and Miller (1973), passim.

13. On the generation of trust by accumulating personal information, see Suttles (1968), p. 194.

14. Because the two people who described their parents as "lower middle class" were very powerful at Helpline, correlations using the full range of values (working class, lower middle class, middle middle class, upper middle class, upper class) do not express the predicament of the staff with working-class parents at Helpline. To provide a comparison with Table 5, in text, Table C reports the correlation of major dependent variables with the full range of values in reported parents' class and with an index of parents' socioeconomic status (SES) composed of reported parents' income, reported parents' occupation, and reported parents' class.

TABLE C
Participation, Ranked Power, Sense of Efficacy and Satisfaction by Parents' Class and Socioeconomic Status

	Parents' Class	Parents' SES
Speaking at meeting	.21	.19
Attending meetings	.26	.22
Ranked high in "power" by other staff	.09	.11
Reports self as high in "say" and "power"	.26	.22
Reports satisfaction with decisions	.01	−.05

15. Among the thirty-one cases with responses to the verbal items on the questionnaire, controlling for verbal self-confidence reduces the coefficient of parents' class (dichotomized: working class vs. others) when predicting attendance from .51 to .31, and when predicting power ranking from .28 to .09.

16. Moreover, at one point Clarence argued:

> Maybe if you're a white middle-class kid, this is your trip. You're taught to be able to abstract . . . and that is a legacy of the middle class—how to abstract from certain situations. [But] I know this is not my trip.

17. See Rothschild-Whitt (1979), pp. 219–221.

18. The left-wing Institute for Policy Studies in Washington, D.C., initiated an age-graded salary structure. In other collectives, I was told of marked differences in interest between older and younger members: "The older people who come here have a greater commitment. Their career and emotional flexibility isn't as great, while younger people see it as an adventure, learning things to go on somewhere else."

19. The correlation between age and valuing equal salaries was .22. If this correlation had been stronger, one might argue that cognitive dissonance was at work and that the longer one stayed at Helpline, accepting a low, equal salary, the more important the ideology of equal salaries would become. As it stands, however, the correlation seems more than adequately explained by self-selection.

20. The correlation between length of time at Helpline and subscribing to countercultural values like "making decisions by consensus, not majority vote" and "belonging to a unified sharing community" was .23 and .29, respectively. This does not mean that the old-timers were more middle class than the newcomers. Rather, the reverse was true. The association between length of time at Helpline and reported parents' class was −.26, with parents' income −.37, and with one's own education, controlled for age, −24.

One policy effect of the old-timers' longer tenure and stronger commitment to communitarian values was that they were more likely than the newcomers to have visited the Farm for pleasure and were therefore less willing to rent it. The correlation between length of time at Helpline and having visited the Farm for pleasure was .50; and with dissatisfaction on the policy of renting the Farm, .44.

But despite the old-timers' generally greater power, the advocates of countercultural values were collectively not a great deal more powerful than anyone else. The old-timers' greater power must have been balanced by the lower power of others who subscribed to countercultural values. All told, for example, the correlation of ranked power with valuing community was −.08. The supporters of decisions by consensus had somewhat greater ranked power ($r = .22$).

21. All three members with working-class parents indicated that they considered "efficiency of decision making" and "accountability—ensuring that people do their work" "very crucial" to making Helpline what they wanted it to be. These 100 percent endorsements compare to 29 percent and 48 percent, respectively, among the rest of the staff.

22. All three members with working-class parents indicated that they considered "equality of political power in internal decisions" and "equal influence in all internal decisions" "very crucial" to making Helpline what they wanted it to be. These 100 percent endorsements compare to 59 percent and 29 percent, respectively, among the rest of the staff. (Along with efficiency and accountability, these were the only values endorsed as "very crucial" by all three members with working-class parents.

23. The correlation between education and considering crucial "equal salaries (with more for dependents), not salaries based on the outside market" was .46. Thirty-three percent of those with some college, 73 percent of those with complete college, and 93 percent of those with graduate education considered equal salaries "very crucial" to making Helpline what they wanted it to be. It stands to reason that those who stayed at Helpline making $5,000 a year when they could have been making $15,000 would be more committed than others to the principle of equal salaries. The more educated were not more idealistic than the others across the board. The correlations between education and considering other ideals crucial were in two cases negative and in no cases reached significance.

Chapter 16: The Lust for Power

1. I will define "administration" at Helpline as including the CPC representatives (but not the representatives to the DPW), all the members of Administrative Backup (except the office manager and carpenter-janitor), the fund raisers, the coordinator, the vice-coordinator, and the treasurer. Table D (I) indicates that the fourteen incumbents of Helpline's administrative positions were more likely to be active in every kind of meeting at Helpline than were the other staff. They were also very high in attendance, ranked power, and efficiency, although not in satisfaction.

Table D (II) lets us compare the CPC and DPW representatives. The staff who came to represent their service groups at CPC spoke more than their colleagues in all varieties of meetings, were ranked as higher in power, and ranked themselves higher in power compared to their colleagues. This was not true of those who came to represent their service groups at DPW. Another contrast is that while the past and present CPC representatives attended Community Days no more or less than the rest of the staff, the past and present representatives of the DPW were distinctly less likely to attend (although the reasons for the DPW representatives' aversion to Community Days are not clear). The representative position on the DPW seems to have allowed people who were not likely to be active in more public ways to take a responsible job that benefited the community as a whole. In this way, the DPW position functioned very like the small town offices in Selby.

TABLE D

Participation, Ranked Power, Sense of Efficacy and Satisfaction by Administrative Position
("Administration," "CPC representative ever," and "DPW representative ever"
are dichotomized dummy variables; for example, "nonadministration vs. administration")

	I	II	
Power and Participation	Administration	CPC representative ever	DPW representative ever
Self reported speaking at meetings	.58**	.69***	.03
Average number of times speaking at Community Days	.60***	.55***	−.04
Average number of times speaking at CPC (per time attended)	.60**	.63***	.01
Speaking at meetings (index)	.66***	.67***	.10
Attending two Community Days	.40**	−.11	−.22
Self reported attendance at Community Days	.29*	.03	−.48***
Attending meetings (index) (includes CPC meetings)	.70***	.52***	.09
Ranked high in "power" by other staff	.55***	.47***	.15
Efficacy and Satisfaction			
Reports self high in "say" and "power"	.42**	.45**	.11
Reports satisfaction with decisions	.06	−.02	−.15

2. For a journalist's description of this satisfaction, see Wolfe (1969), pp. 238–244.

3. The correlation between the index of liking power and responsibility and holding an administrative position (as defined in note 1) is .33.

The seven items of which the index of liking power and responsibility is composed were the seven that loaded most heavily on the first factor in a factor analysis of all twenty-nine "personality trait" items on the questionnaire. The intercorrelations are reported in Appendix B. Within the index of liking power and responsibility, there seems to be no internal ordering that distinguishes between impersonal and personal power, between liking to get things done and liking to tell others what to do.

4. For example, six of the staff never heard about the professor's salary decision (presumably because the speed with which the decision was made meant that missing one business meeting meant missing the entire issue), and two did not hear about the Air Force contract decision. In the first meeting on the Air Force contract, Pamela from the Shelter, Ken from the CCC, and Alex from the Van failed to understand and report the mix of opinions within their service groups.

5. Four told me they liked power; three appeared indifferent to power; one did not say outright that he liked power, although others in the organization suspected him of liking power. This person mentioned his parents in the interview.

6. Frank spoke quite a lot about leadership in our interview:

I've done a tremendous amount of studying leadership roles. I've been reading a lot on it for the last six or seven months. I've been reading a tremendous amount of French history. There's a lot of analogies about what goes on here because the French have always been split between anarchy and centralized leadership. . . . I'm really dedicated to that, to providing the process of centralization.

. . . some person will eventually come out in a leadership position.

7. In a discussion of leadership, for example, when I asked Nate how he felt about a director's getting other people to do his typing, he equivocated: "Not *here*—it's against the organization's ideas":

JM: But it wouldn't disturb you in another organization?

NATE: Are you asking me if I'm opposed to secretaries?

JM: Yes.

NATE: I don't know. (blandly) I don't really ever think about it very much. [Our discussion came after the decision to eliminate the job of office manager, or secretary, a decision I had heard him discuss in a meeting.]

JM: Well, here we are.

NATE: Am I opposed to secretaries? (pause) Yeah, I guess. If *pushed*. (pause) Because I guess I believe that it's a total shitwork job.

8. The average number of times talking per CPC meeting was for men 11.1, for women 8.5, and for Kaye 28.0. The average number of times talking per Community Day was for men 3.6, for women 2.6, and for Kay 10.0. In response to the question, "Do you usually speak at meetings," which was coded from "No" (1) to "A lot" (6), the average man scored 3.8; the average woman, 3.3, and Kaye, 6. The average man attended CPC 5.8 times; the average woman 2.9 times; and Kaye, 17 times. Men and women averaged the same attendance (1.8) for the two Community Days I observed; Kaye attended both Days.

9. Kaye used the phrase "making a lot of noise" six times throughout the interview. Five of these described the exercise of power by women. The sixth described a man she did not trust, whom she felt "has no scruples." When I asked who had been influential in particular decisions, Kaye mentioned only four people by name, two of them women, two men. The interchange went like this:

JM: [Who do you think was most influential] in the office manager decisions?

KAYE: Deborah and Paula made a lot of noise. That's why it happened.

JM: In the Air Force decision?

KAYE: Ken and Tom had the greatest influence, I think.

10. The association between ranked power and positive responses to the question, "On the average, would you say that you worked harder or less hard than most of the paid staff at Helpline?" was .47. I cannot vouch for the accuracy of the self-rating on hard work. In one case, I know it to be incorrect. However, I observed that, among the most powerful eight staff members, six did work very hard.

11. Many people at Helpline dreamed about the work or the decisions, and Tom put his fantasy of equality into a dream:

I had a dream when I had only been with Helpline, Inc., for a while, and it was in this room. And there was only room for, like, twenty people, and there were thirty people in the room. And ten people had to leave. And it was the ten people who worked the hardest! (laugh) So they decided it was time to split. [And you were among them?] I always am! (laugh) [How did you feel?] Really good, really good. . . . I felt good that I was leaving and giving other people a chance to do something 'cause they said they were going to. It's a kind of agreement we made. Like there's ten people leaving: you stay here and take care of everything.

12. The other three facilitators made similar comments. Amy remembered one decision: "That felt good, to be able to synthesize some of the differences and come up with things that would compromise positions so that everyone could accept them. . . . I see the Switchboard [her group] as the group that mediates more disputes than any other group in the community." Pamela told me: "I don't thrive on conflict, personally; in fact, I don't think I particularly like it. On a spectrum, like at the Shelter, *I* usually say, "Now I think it's time we sat down and talked about it." Bruce, the treasurer, belived that his biggest task was to "put together the financial side of our operations well enough [to provide] the kind of clear information that is needed for decisions."

13. The three "power hungry" spoke with so much force that the transcriber thought it required an exclamation point an average of .63 times a page (.85 with Kaye included), compared to an average of .13 among the four facilitators. The three "power hungry" used the words "I" or "me" an average of twenty-three times a page (twenty-four with Kaye included), compared to an average of sixteen among the facilitators.

14. Amy, another facilitator, explained participation at a Community Day in the same way: "The people who had made the decision to get involved organizationally were the ones who participated the most."

15. The treasurer, another facilitator, had a similar ambition. Because the previous treasurer had alone understood Helpline's tangled finances, he had been able to pressure the Shelter into making decisions they might not otherwise have made. Bruce was determined to make the accounts clear enough so that this would not happen again.

16. Pamela also spoke of being "intimidated" at meetings and of being very "upset with myself for not saying anything," in a way that suggested a nonpowerful self-concept. Yet neither of these women gave herself a power score lower than the high average score that the rest of the group gave her.

17. For example, Vidich and Bensman (1968, p. 119) report that in Springdale it is "difficult to find a qualified person willing to stand for election not because such persons are not flattered by being considered but rather because they do not want to appear to be eager 'to seek public office.' "

18. Zurcher (1970), p. 289, emphasis in original.

19. Plato, *The Republic* 520d; see also 347 a–d. For a modern instance, see Center for New Schools (1972), p. 320.

20. Michels (1962), p. 71.

21. The correlation between reporting that one enjoys power and considering equal power critical to making the organization what one would like it to be is —.31.

Chapter 17: Equality

1. The word "trust" appeared over and over in these responses: "There was trust; I respected [her]"; "There's a high level of trust of people in the middle [of the power circle]"; "It seems perfectly natural to me, as long as I trust [them]"; "Those people don't misuse their power . . . we trust [them]"; "People feel they can trust [him] and [him]"; "I trust [him] because of his ideals"; "I trust [him]."

2. Colonel Rainborough in the Putney Debates, 29 October 1647, in Woodhouse (1957), p. 59.

3. Locke (1965), p. 419.

4. See, for example, Held (1970), pp. 99–161. My reading of Marx, however,

differs from hers. She understands Marx as concluding that "the proletariat will eventually succeed in achieving a society in which interests no longer conflict" (p. 148). It seems clear to me that Marx was interested in eliminating only differences between classes. While other conflicts of interest would remain in the eventual socialist society, these would not deeply affect the fundamental relationship between human beings. The Strausian reading of *The Republic* would exempt Plato from this list (see Bloom, 1968, 1977).

5. See chapter 2, note 31.

6. Leys (1978, p. 169), for example, defines politics as "that which pertains to divisions, disagreements and conflicts." He concludes on the basis of this definition that Plato was "non-political."

7. Because the influential staff members in this decision employed rational persuasion rather than the threat of sanction and because, according to our assumption, their interests were very similar to those of the others, some political theorists would say that they exercised unequal "authority" rather than unequal "power." Bachrach and Baratz (1963, pp. 638–639) and Lukes (1974, p. 32), for example, suggest that whatever was exercised in this situation should be termed a form of "authority" rather than of "power." Under the Bachrach–Baratz definition of "power," no power was exercised in this decision because no one got anyone else to do anything by threat of sanction, even the smallest sanction like threatening to be angry. Threats were made in the course of a heated two weeks: one man implied that he would be personally very hurt if the decision went one way rather than the other; another implied that he might leave the organization. But as far as I was able to judge by observing the decision and by talking with people afterward, everyone at Helpline made up his or her mind on the basis of the issues.

If the members had common interests in this decision, no power was exercised under the Lukes definition of power as well, because no one got anyone else to do anything against his or her own interests. Terminology like this, which adopts a term implying greater legitimacy for A's relationship to B when interests converge, strongly underscores the normative point made here. In regard to the protection of interests, an egalitarian would find unequal "authority" acceptable.

The argument for political inequality when interests are similar does not contradict the assertion that widespread participation often helps produce the right decision. Even when there is a correct answer to a problem, the decision is often best made not by a single talented individual but by a group with different points of view. (See Barnlund, 1959; Barry, 1965, p. 292–293; Aristotle, *Politics*, 1281b.) Moreover, rough equality in a communications network will sometimes produce faster correct answers (see Leavitt, 1964, pp. 231–234). Yet as far as I know, no one has produced evidence that correct answers are more likely to emerge from decision-making procedures designed so that the capacity of each individual to influence outcomes is exactly equal.

8. Compare Michels (1962), pp. 338, 358.

9. Keniston (1968), p. 166.

10. Because all societies have norms—rules regarding what is and is not valued—some inequalities of status always remain (Dahrendorf, 1962). The important questions are what consequences inequalities in status have and whether the norms that produce them are just, both in the eyes of the losers and in the eyes of outside observers. Attempting to eliminate these inequalities entirely or to ignore what Walzer, in an Aristotelian vein, calls the "distributive reasons that are somehow right, that are naturally part of our ideas about the things themselves" (Walzer, 1973, p. 403), can only make questions of status more rather than less salient.

11. Indeed, in most societies, from the kibbutzim to Indian caste societies, increases in material inequalities seem to be accompanied by increases in status inequalities and vice versa.

12. Kaufman (1960), p. 277 and passim.

13. The Port Huron Statement (1966), p. 156 and passim.

14. Pateman (1970), pp. 45–66.

15. Bachrach (1967), passim.

16. Pateman (1970), pp. 22–25, 35–40.

17. Mill (1958), p. 214.

18. Only Pateman (1970, pp. 43, 67–71) argues that "equal" power is a necessary means to this end.

19. See, for example, Bennis and Slater (1969). For a discussion of the "participation hypothesis" that people will accept change more easily if they participate in the decision to make the change, see Verba (1961), pp. 206–243. For the "contingency theory" argument that democratic participation in decisions raises production only on some tasks and among some individuals, see Lawrence and Lorsch (1967).

20. A competent organizer in the women's movement, 1972, quoted in Mansbridge (1976b), p. 255.

21. For a fuller analysis of these costs, see Mansbridge (1973) passim, and Mansbridge (1976b), pp. 253–256.

I have not explored in these pages anything like the full range of trade-offs between equality of power and other values. Equal power can have ideal-regarding costs as well as benefits. For example, if one defines liberty or justice as getting whatever reward in money, prestige, or power that the marketplace of supply and demand would offer in the absence of any social or political mandate to the contrary, then the pursuit of equal power must be traded off against the demands of liberty and justice so defined.

22. Robert Dahl once defined political equality as "the indefinitely enduring opportunity to exercise as much power as any other citizen," cited in Bachrach (1967), pp. 83–92. Rawls (1971, pp. 15, 74) calls for "fair access to participation."

23. See Verba, Nie, and Kim (1978), pp. 168–171, 307.

24. In ancient Athens, the state paid citizens to attend the assembly, as well as to take jury duty (see Jones, 1966, p. 5, for a discussion of the value of the payment). Indeed, Aristotle (*Politics* 1317b–1318a) considered payment for attending assemblies to be one of the "attributes common to democracies generally." Seventeenth-century town meetings fined their members for failure to attend (see chapter 11, note 17). The Netherlands and Australia today levy small fines for failure to vote in national elections. (For an analysis of the effects of these fines on class differences in electoral participation in the Netherlands and Australia, see Verba, Nie, and Kim, [1978], p. 8; and Douglas [1973], pp. 56–58, respectively).

Chapter 18: Consensus

1. Whyte (1943), p. 96.

2. Quoted in Lynd (1971), p. 22.

3. Mansbridge, food co-op interview, 1972.

4. Mansbridge, women's liberation interview, 1972.

5. See the analysis of consensus in draft resistance groups in Ferber and Lynd (1971), p. 158.

6. Simmel argues that "In such (jury) cases, the requirement of unanimity (found, for instance, in England and America) is based on the more or less unconscious assumption that the objective truth must always also be subjectively convincing, and that, inversely, the identity of subjective convictions is the criterion of objective truth" (1950, p. 241; parentheses in original). Today, the jury is beginning to be seen as a mini-legislature deciding questions of conflicting interest rather than discovering the truth, and as this evolution progresses, equal representation and majority rule will also seem more appropriate to the task.

7. The declining number of unanimous decisions in the Supreme Court since the 1930s is thus a mark of the growing tendency of the Justices to think of their role in adversary terms.

8. Working committees thus very frequently come out with unanimous recommendations. In Barber's (1966) study of twelve Connecticut town boards of finance, eleven of the twelve reached unanimous decisions on every issue, including the "hot" issue

the investigator had assigned. Barber concludes: "The analyst attempting to explore intragroup alliances and conflicts through voting records would have no material to work with. In the course of discussion there is often considerable controversy. But by the time the group gets down to making a final decision, the conclusion is almost always in this form:

CHAIRMAN: 'All right, all in favor of the proposal?'
ALL: 'Aye.'
CHAIRMAN: 'Opposed? (Silence) Carried.' [Barber, 1966, p. 110]

Barber attributes the unanimity on the boards of finance neither to spontaneous adherence to a single opinion, nor to coercive pressures toward conformity, but rather to the committees' efforts: (1) to forego political partisanship; (2) to control personal animosity; and (3) to encourage active integration of views, not passivity (pp. 110–114). However, his account of these committees reveals that by and large his committee members believed they all had a common interest—in not hurting the taxpayer, in reaching a "reasonable solution," and in getting the job done (pp. 113–114).

Because they assume common interest, many experts in business management and organization recommend consensual decision making. Maier, in his early and influential *Principles of Human Relations* (1952, p. 22), advises that "the objective of decisions under democratic leadership is to obtain *unanimous* agreement, and the skilled leader can obtain this degree of agreement in a high percentage of instances." Maier's three reasons for preferring unanimity to majority rule (fewer divided loyalties, less exclusion of potential minorities, and less "trickery" beforehand) have to do primarily with the quality of the relations among members of the group. They differ little from the reasons members of Helpline gave for preferring consensus to majority rule, and they assume throughout that the members of the group have a common interest in the decision.

William C. Schutz (excerpted in Bennis, Benne, and Chin, 1961, p. 294) also supports consensus, assuming a common interest through identification with the good of the group as a whole. He argues that decisions by majority rule are often quicker, but the group "pays" in later delays and subtle resistance. By "consensus," Schutz means that "everyone in the group is agreed that a certain course of action is best for the group, regardless of whether or not he individually agrees with it."

Zaleznik and Moment also assert that "consensus is necessary for obtaining effective results *after* the decision has been reached" (1964, p. 142; their emphasis). They accordingly define consensus in terms of commitment to the result:

Consensus as we define it is quite different . . . from the idea that 100 percent agreement has to be reached. Our meaning of consensus lies in the degree of personal commitment the members feel toward the group decision after it is reached. This means, for example, that even though some members might disagree with the decision on principle, they will accept it and personally carry out their part.

Logically, their definition would hold no matter how much the interests of the members came in conflict and no matter what forms of manipulation the group applied to make its members accept the final decision and carry out their part in the implementation. But in fact, like other writers in this field, they too seem to assume a high degree of common interest. See also Follett (1949), pp. 65–66, and (1940), p. 32.

None of these writers seems to advocate consensus for Buchanan and Tullock's (1971) reason, that with side payments it produces the most equitable solution. They all seem to assume that in some respects the members of the group will have no conflicts of interest. For critiques of the managerial approach to consensus, see Verba (1961), pp. 222–224, on the "no-conflict assumption," and Coser (1956), p. 24, on the Mayo school.

9. The Quaker *Book of Discipline* reads: "We deprecate division in our Meetings and desire unanimity. It is in the unity of common fellowship, we believe, that we shall most surely learn the will of God" (Pollard, Pollard, and Polland, 1950, p. 44). In the Bruderhof, the unanimity rule is "based on the assumption that the right decision exists. The task of the Bruderhof is to find it." One former Bruderhof member described the process as follows: "In line with the theory of the preexistent decision, defined as God's will, one had to *listen* and *look* to find the decision. But to do this

properly, one had to be empty of self . . . transparent . . . so that the spirit of God could flow through you . . ." (Zablocki, 1971, p. 155).

10. The Bruderhof believe that they cannot pray collectively without *gemeinde*—that is, a congregation free from disunity and filled with the Holy Spirit (Zablocki, 1971, pp. 152–155).

11. See Mansbridge (1976b), pp. 257–258.

12. Pollard, Pollard, and Pollard (1950), p. 45.

This care for the feelings of others in the group was a marked feature of the participatory democracies of the 1960s and early 1970s. Jacobs and Landau (1966, p. 30) write of the 1965 Cleveland SDS: "they exhibit great tolerance, and no speaker is silenced, no matter how irrelevant or repetitious." Keniston (1968, p. 167) reports on the 1967 Vietnam Summer radicals that "everyone is to be completely honest, open, and direct with everyone else, and . . . all are to have a full say regardless of experience and competence." A radical women's newspaper exhorted its readers to "commit ourselves to respecting each other (really listening to a problem stated and hearing the person struggle with that problem)" (Hammond, 1970, p. 9). Zablocki (1971, p. 316) also reports of the consensual process in the communes he visited from 1965 to 1970: "These discussions were remarkable for the ability of the participants really to listen to one another. At Hobbit Hole the tone was combative; at Geodesic Village, urbane and witty; and at Mandala, psychoanalytic and spiritual. But in all of them the process was essentially the same: deeper and deeper probing into meanings and motivations until a common ground was found."

13. Zablocki (1971), p. 185.

14. Ibid., p. 316.

15. Bailey (1965), p. 20 n. 1, citing Robert A. Scalapino and Junnosuke Masumi, *Parties and Politics in Contemporary Japan* (Berkeley: University of California Press, 1962), p. 145.

16. Ibid., p. 3, citing Jayaprakash Narayan, *A Plea for Reconstruction of Indian Polity*, c. 1960, pp. 47–48, 51.

17. Ibid., p. 1.

18. Westerners often explain consensus in other countries by, for example, stressing Japanese concepts of propriety that "place a heavy premium on the appearance of unanimous conformity" and attach "extraordinary importance to the outward preservation of a common, harmonious, and undifferentiated front" (Beardsley, Hall, and Ward, 1959, pp. 354–355).

19. Zuckerman (1970), p. 133.

20. Ibid., p. 132.

21. Pollard, Pollard, and Pollard (1950), p. 33.

22. Ibid., p. 59.

23. Vidich and Bensman (1968), p. 110.

24. Ibid., pp. 127–128.

25. Ibid., p. 115. In their analysis this factor also helps explain why the village board made as few decisions as possible and tended to surrender its jurisdictional prerogatives.

26. Ibid., p. 116.

27. Ibid., p. 127.

28. Ibid., pp. 127–133. Vidich and Bensman also argue that a latent function of such unanimity is to "kill public interest" in town politics, thus allowing relatively few citizens to vote and control elections (p. 213).

29. Ibid., p. 45. See also p. 303.

30. Ibid., pp. 182–183.

31. Ibid., p. 127.

32. Ibid., p. 152. This was a prosperous farmer, one of those whom Vidich and Bensman believe "make sure their roads get preferential treatment" (p. 153).

33. The phrase is taken from Zuckerman's 1970 title.

34. Simmel (1950), p. 240.

35. Ibid.

36. Ibid., p. 245.

37. Buchanan and Tullock (1971), p. 74.

38. Ibid., p. 17.

39. Ibid., p. 4: "Indeed, when individual interests are assumed to be identical, the main body of economic theory vanishes." Buchanan and Tullock thus seem to assume that economic activity equals "trade" and consequently exclude from their calculus the possibility of two or more individuals with common interests cooperating in productive economic activity (e.g., by putting two shoulders to the wheel to push a truck out of a ditch).

40. Ibid., p. 18: "The theory of markets postulates only that the relationship be *economic*, that the interest of his opposite number in the exchange be excluded from consideration" (their emphasis).

41. Wolff (1970), pp. 17, 23.

42. Buchanan and Tullock (1971), p. 69. See also pp. 106, 110, 115.

43. Bailey (1965), pp. 8–9.

44. Kuper (1970), pp. 119–123.

45. See ibid., p. 121.

46. Other tasks require unanimity because the group faces an outside adversary. Helpline's Shelter needed to have a consistent policy toward the young people living there because otherwise the runaways would have played one counselor off against another. The staff needed genuine unanimity, in other words, because it could not enforce the spirit as well as the letter of a nonunanimous policy.

47. Calhoun (1953), for example, combines both self-protective and unitary arguments. He argues for giving major interest groups the veto on the basis of "the great law of self-preservation (p. 5, also p. 9) and makes the veto the central protection that any interest group can have against being "depressed to abject poverty and dependence" by the majority. Yet the result, in his view, is to "unite the community" and to promote "kind feelings . . . harmony, and a [concern for] the common good of the whole" (pp. 37–38).

48. Barber (1965), p. 124.

49. See Berg (1965), pp. 138–139.

50. Locke (1965), VIII: 96, p. 375.

51. See above, chapter 17, n. 7, for arguments that the opinions of the majority will tend to reflect the common good.

52. Bentham (1843), p. 19.

53. Barry (1979, pp. 161–163) suggests that five men in a railway car, some smokers and some not, could resolve their opposing interests only by majority vote. Yet the men could in principle have divided the time into five equal segments allotted to smokers and nonsmokers on a proportional basis, instead of giving the entire time to one faction after a majority vote.

54. Walzer, for example, argues that, by participating in the process of majority decision making, minorities agree to the legitimacy of the final decision, "hoping that one day they will not lose out and will be deferred to in turn" (1970, p. 47).

55. Kruijt (1959), reprinted in McRae (1974), p. 134.

56. Lijphart (1968), reprinted in McRae (1974), p. 141.

57. Ibid., p. 139.

58. In Switzerland, all four major parties are represented on the multimember executive; the same was tried for the two major parties in the now defunct Uruguay government. When the executive consists of one person, as in Colombia, the position is alternated for four-year terms between the two parties. In Lebanon, the president of the republic comes from one of the two contending religious groups, the president of the council from the other. Lijphart (1969), reprinted in McRae (1974), pp. 76–77.

59. Steiner (1970), reprinted in McRae (1974), p. 98. In practice the division of benefits is also influenced by historic political deals and compromises. To the degree that these compromises produce results that differ from pure numerical proportionality, they do not protect interests equally and thus do not fulfill their adversary function.

60. Although when resources are at stake proportionality implies that they should be divided among groups according to their numbers, many decisions do not involve resources or other divisible goods. Other decisions involve matters of right and wrong that people are not willing to settle by an adversary process. In still others, divisible

and indivisible goods, and adversary and non-adversary matters are mixed inextricably. Finally, trying to weight decisions by their importance to all parties often produces insuperable practical difficulties. Proportionality thus often is a better normative standard than a political tool.

61. First, every decision-rule requires, in a sense, some form of unanimity. Even majority rule requires some prior unanimity in the form of agreement to use the procedure (see Friedrich, 1969, p. 238 and Partridge, 1971, pp. 79–138 on agreement on fundamentals). Consociationalism and bargaining require increasing degrees of unanimity on specific packages of issues, and the more unanimity is required, the more a system favors the status quo, and hence benefits those groups, usually the more powerful, who can afford to pay the costs of waiting—costs such as time itself, legal counsel, or tying up financial or emotional capital.

Second, consociationalism usually ensures equal representation of a very limited variety of interests. None of the four European consociational systems tries to guarantee proportional outcomes to more than five groups.

Third, ensuring that each group gets its proportional share does not ensure that each member of each group will get the same. Indeed, since consociationalism requires that each group's elite meet regularly on a face-to-face basis with the elites of other groups, it encourages elites to develop interests and understandings that differ from those of rank and file members of their group and to accept solutions that may not serve the rank and file as well as they serve the elite.

Beyond these drawbacks in not producing fully proportional outcomes, consociational democracies are also inefficient. They are cumbersome and require a great deal of negotiation. They are susceptible to deadlock and consequent immobility. They duplicate effort. Because they demand that a large number of citizens staff the various bureaucracies and representative bodies in each sector, the quality of personnel is not always high.

Finally, consociational democracies have a further disadvantage in the realm of democratic ideals, because the process of proportional allocation requires close, trusting, and relatively secret negotiations among elites, and this process in turn tends to produce passivity among the rank and file (although the duplication of positions creates more responsible activity for the relatively active citizens).

62. The proportionality rule does not guarantee that a government will act justly, because justice invariably implies more than minimal egalitarian equity. Nor does the proportionality rule imply that each individual has a claim to equal satisfaction. On the contrary, the proportionality rule ensures greater satisfaction to those individuals fortunate enough to have the same interests as most of their fellow citizens, and less satisfaction to those individuals so unfortunate as to have different interests.

Chapter 19: Face-to-Face Assembly

1. Laslett (1956), p. 157.
2. Ibid., p. 158.
3. Ibid.
4. Ibid., p. 167.
5. Ibid., p. 166.
6. Ibid., p. 170.
7. Ibid., p. 171.
8. Latané and Darley (1970), p. 117. An alternate explanation they suggest for this finding is that the face-to-face meeting gave those who had had the experience a sense of specific responsibility since they were the only ones who had met the "victim."
9. Milgram (1974), Chapter 4: "Closeness of the Victim," especially Experiment 3, p. 34. See also Tilker (1970); and for the most recent summary of the literature, Savitsky and Eby (1979).

10. Leavitt (1964), pp. 141–150. In these experiments, two-way face-to-face communication produced more accurate judgments, both about the external stimulus and about the subjects' own accuracy, than did one-way communication with facial expressions hidden. Leavitt did not, however, measure the effects of the two variables separately.

11. Kotler (1974), p. 9.

12. This presumes that hostility is under control. When a high level of hostility would make either party feel uncomfortable in the negotiation, face-to-face meetings of proxies are usually substituted for face-to-face meetings of the principles.

13. Verba (1961), pp. 22–29; Lewin (1947) in Newcomb and Hartley (1947); and Bennett (1955), pp. 251–273.

14. See Deutsch and Gerard (1955).

15. Rosenberg (1954–55), pp. 349–351, based on interviews from Ithaca, New York, in 1954. One of Rosenberg's respondents steers away from politics because "I don't like to get into arguments." Another does the same because "there is no harm in avoiding unnecessary conflicts." At Helpline also, a newcomer equates meetings with "politics" and conflict:

> I don't put much merit on meetings . . . as soon as you start having a meeting, you start running into people with different opinions. . . . As soon as you get into meetings, you get into a lot of politics. . . . I'm really not into politics. That's why I don't like meetings.

16. Hixon (1971), p. 85.

17. Center for New Schools (1972), p. 319.

18. Rousseau (1950), p. 95. Rousseau pictured the people of ancient Rome being in assembly "several times" every few weeks (p. 89) and those of ancient Greece "constantly assembled in the public square" (p. 95).

19. See above, chapter 2, n. 33.

Chapter 20: Size and the Two Forms of Democracy

1. Lincoln (1976), pp. 7–8. In some cases, of course, small governments perform the same functions as large ones. A snowplow operation has the same effect on a given voter's life whether it plows the roads of 500 or of 500,000 others. Yet the larger operation affects more people, and its activities may get more attention from the media. This may produce the illusion that large local governments have more effect than small ones even when both render identical services.

2. Survey results are consistent with this proposition. In national surveys, people tend to say they understand local issues better than national ones. They also tend to say they have more control over local than over national government. However, they are *less* likely to say about local than about national government that it has a great effect on their lives (see Table E, Column I). Selby's citizens respond in the same way (see Table E, Column II).

The same pattern recurs when we compare small local governments to large ones. Most Americans live in towns and cities much larger than Selby. Most Americans also reported less local understanding, less local efficacy, and less local political activity in 1961 than my Selby sample reported in 1971 (compare "Local" figures in Table E). Large local governments tend to have more power (i.e., they make more collective choices) than smaller units. And most Americans felt in 1961 that their local governments had a greater effect on their lives than the citizens of Selby felt it did in 1971 (compare "Local" figures for "Effect" in Table E). None of the differences between Selby and larger localities is statistically significant, and some may be explained either by trends between 1961 and 1971 or by peculiarities of Selby rather than by size per se. Nonetheless, the basic paradox is clear even within the large national sample. Although the ordinary citizen feels more fully informed, feels more efficacious, and is more likely to try to influence the government in a smaller

TABLE E

The Paradox of Decentralization

		I	II
		U.S. 1961[a]	Selby 1971
Understanding:			
Percentage responding that they understood issues moderately or very well[b]	National	46% (959)	49% (59)
	Local	65% (957)	75% (54)
Control (feelings of efficacy):			
Percentage responding that they could do something to prevent an unjust or harmful government action[c]	National	78% (924)	67% (66)
	Local	82% (904)	88% (66)
Control (activity):			
Percentage reporting an actual attempt to influence the government	National	16% (964)	23% (61)
	Local	28% (966)	35% (48)[d]
Effect:			
Percentage reporting that governmental decisions have a great effect on their lives	National	43% (932)	49% (51)
	Local	36% (950)	27% (51)

[a] Gabriel Almond and Sidney Verba, *Civic Culture* survey, unpublished data. The data differ slightly from those in Dahl and Tufte (1973), pp. 54, 56, 59, as they were recalculated without the "don't know" responses.

[b] The Almond and Verba questions were Q15: "Thinking of the important national and international issues facing the country, how well do you think you can understand these issues?" and Q16: "How about the local issues in this town or part of the country? How well do you understand them?" The Selby questions were: "Nowadays many people think the issues facing the country are very complex. How well do you think you understand the big international and national issues facing the country?" and "How about the local issues in this town? How well do you understand them?" The wording of the other Selby questions was the same as in the Almond-Verba survey.

[c] The question was, "Suppose a regulation were being considered by ["the town of Selby" or the U.S. Congress"] that you considered very unjust or harmful . . . , what could you do?" Any positive response was coded as being able to do "something." I did not ask Almond and Verba's next question. "If you made an effort to change this regulation, how likely is it that you succeed?" because in the pretest it so often aroused the scornful response, "It would depend on how many others agreed with me!" I tried to avoid questions like this that seemed to the respondent stupid and irritating. The distribution of responses, however, is much the same as that put forward by Dahl and Tufte (1973), p. 58, who used the second of Almond and Verba's questions.

[d] I did not ask this question when respondents seemed to be tiring of the structured format, so the results may not be representative. (The small numbers in the questions on understanding and effect, however, come from the questionnaire sample, which is fairly representative of the Selby population.)

governmental unit, the citizen's vote affects fewer other individuals outside that unit, and citizens typically believe the smaller unit has less effect on their lives.

The relation between size and information holds up in Germany, Sweden, and other countries (Dahl and Tufte, 1973, pp. 54, 55, 64). In Selby, the reason is clear, for there many decisions still involve people the townfolk have grown up with and see every week; buildings like the schoolhouse, with whose furniture, paint, and even textbooks many citizens have spent a good number of years; or land the men have hunted and know well enough to identify casually in town meeting as "that patch of brush on the hill past Northrup's Pond." Many of Selby's residents have an immediate grip on the transactions that make up their political lives; almost half say they understood local issues *very* well, compared to only 19 percent who can say the same about national issues.

The relation between size and overall participation does not hold up with Verba and Nie's 1967 data (Verba and Nie, 1972, pp. 232–242), but even in their data, citizens in *isolated* villages and rural areas are more likely to engage in *nonconflictual*, *communal* political activity than those in larger towns and cities. This is especially true when participation rates are corrected for socioeconomic status (p. 239). Verba and Nie have potentially better data than any previous American survey for testing the effects of size at the lower end of the scale because they oversampled from communities of 50,000 or under (pp. 347–348). However, because they do not have reliable measures of the degree of local community control, the meaning of their data on small political units is problematic.

Dahl and Tufte (1973) provide evidence from countries other than the United States for a generally positive relationship between size and both efficacy and attempts to influence government and a negative relationship between size and sense of a government's effect on one's life.

For more on what I have termed "the paradox of decentralization," see Dahl (1970), pp. 100–101, and Dahl and Tufte (1973), pp. 13, 23, 43, 65 (points 4 and 5), 129, and passim. Indeed, the paradox becomes an integrating theme in the later work, with "citizen effectiveness" (possibly greater in a small setting) being set, to some degree, against "system capacity" (greater in a large setting).

3. Rochen and Deutsch (1969). Dahl and Tufte (1973) provide the best summary to date on the pros and cons of governmental units of different sizes for citizen effectiveness and system capacity.

4. McConnell (1966), pp. 6, 107.

5. Thompson (1970), pp. 175–176. In the deleted part of this sentence, Thompson deliberately restricted his prediction to nonvoting activities, where presumably he thought the effect of class would be strongest.

6. If other conditions are equal, the smaller the unit, the closer to equal in power its members will be. This equation is best illustrated by comparing different sized groups on the distribution of one power resource, speaking. Consecutive debate requires that each speaker have time to develop an argument and reply to objections. As a group grows larger, it usually preserves consecutive debate, which gives fewer people time to speak. Each added member widens the gulf between the small elite of speakers and the large mass of silent. For other statements of this effect, see Hare (1976, pp. 219–221), who cites a series of studies from 1934 to 1971; Thomas and Fink (1963, pp. 373–374), who note one exception to the rule (in N. E. Miller, Jr., "The Effect of Group Size on Decision-making Discussions," unpublished doctoral dissertation, University of Michigan, 1951); de Jouvenal (1961); and Dahl and Tufte (1973, pp. 66–75).

On the same theme, Dahl and Tufte (1973) note that increasing size increases the asymmetry between the communications of leaders and followers. As a group grows larger, it becomes harder for a leader to hear and absorb all the communications from ordinary citizens, while citizens can still as easily hear and absorb communications from the leader. The problem is compounded by the more active members tending to have different preferences (and presumably different interests) from those of the less active: "To the extent that formal or informal representative institutions do not develop, then the larger the political system, the less representative of the views of citizens the leaders are likely to be" (p. 72).

Finally, small group research indicates that the smaller the group, the more equal the distribution of leadership activity. The smaller the group, the more likely the marginal participants are to speak effectively, seem interested, know about the topic, show initiative, define problems, motivate others, lead discussion, offer good solutions, and try to influence others. See Bass and Norton (1951), pp. 397–398 (measuring groups of two, four, five, eight, and twelve members only), and studies cited in Hare (1976), pp. 218–219.

At least in the already egalitarian context of Helpline, however, smaller units did not reduce inequality between advantaged and disadvantaged groups. Partly in order to encourage more equal participation, Helpline devoted part of each Community Day to small group discussions. Both logic and small group research suggest that this strategy should reduce disparities between the advantaged and the disadvantaged. Yet the one time that I measured speaking both in the large assembly and in the small groups into which the assembly broke down, the association of speaking with seniority in the organization, proximity to the social center, age, gender, race, and class in the small groups was about the same as in the large assembly.

7. Small settings are "understaffed." Just as three bridge players look hungrily around for a fourth, or a few children playing baseball accept almost anyone as outfielder, so a small town will press a high proportion of its citizens into public service. In Selby, for instance, the proliferation of minor offices (fence viewer, trustee of public funds, surveyor of wood and lumber) combined with the tiny population to ensure that more than half the families that had lived in town over ten years had had at least one member pressed into service as a town officer. This process allowed an unusually varied collection of people to hold office. While those people who described themselves as "outgoing" were more likely to attend Selby's town meeting, talk at the meeting, and go to see a town officer, none of the nine members of my sample who held small town offices described him or herself this way. Being a fence viewer, a surveyor of wood and lumber, a lister, a trustee of public funds, or a trustee of the library provided the less outgoing citizens with an opportunity to exert influence in an informal way suited to their personalities.

Students in small high schools are also more likely than those in large schools to participate actively in a variety of student activities (Larson, 1949; Barker and Hall, 1964; Wicker, 1968; Baird, 1969). Members of a small church are more apt to participate in church activities, hold leadership positions, contribute money, and support activities more warmly than are members of a larger church (Wicker, 1969). Marginal contributors, such as children, the elderly, and those of lower social standing, are particularly likely to participate in a wider range of activities, fill more essential positions, become more intensely involved, and participate for longer periods of time in small settings (Willems, 1967).

These arguments suggest that social class should have less impact on political participation in very small polities than in larger ones, but direct evidence for this hypothesis is hard to find. Most studies of the relationship between size and participation compare polities that are all too large for the influences I have just described to be important. When I compared polities with fewer than 5,000 residents from Verba and Nie's (1972) national survey of political participation in 1967, I found that town size had no impact on the participation gap between the economically advantaged and the economically disadvantaged. This finding is not conclusive, however, because town size is a poor proxy for the size of the various local governmental jurisdictions in which a town's residents participate. Local school boards and many other governmental units often cover an area larger than a single small town. I tried to resolve this problem by corresponding with the jurisdictions in question, but I was not able to obtain satisfactory information.

8. Dahl and Tufte (1973), pp. 84–86. The effect is similar in small union shops (see Lipset, Trow, and Coleman, 1962, p. 214). Selby's experience too supports Dahl and Tufte's data. The plumber, laborer, and housewife who served as Selby's school directors, and the carpenter, repairman, and store owner who served as Selby's selectmen, resembled the average citizen of Selby more closely than the professional people who usually hold these positions in larger towns resemble the average citizen of such towns. Personal contact in a small town like Selby also allows subtle opportunities for political control—both of the townspeople by their officers and vice versa. Selby's officials, like most politicians, want to be liked. Unlike most politicians, they find themselves in daily, neighborly contact with their constituents. While in 1967 only 20 percent of all Americans had contacted a local official (Verba and

Nie, 1972, p. 31), 68 percent had done so in Selby. The Selby resident who wants to criticize a selectman can usually find him and tell him off to his face. Even a more cautious type, who only voices a gripe at the lunch counter, can be fairly sure this complaint will eventually find its way back to its intended target. This kind of control can further the equal protection of interests.

9. Among those who both owned property and registered to vote in Selby ($N =$ 176), the correlation between socioeconomic status and town meeting attendance was only .25, while the correlation between socioeconomic status and voting in national elections was .43. The same pattern recurred in my sample. These data on participation support Thompson. However, in the same sample the correlation between socio-economic status and feeling that people like oneself had a "say" in government fell from .26, when the question dealt with the town government, to .08 when it dealt with the national government. These data on subjective power support McConnell.

Such results illustrate the argument in the text that size can affect the class gap in different ways depending on which outcome one emphasizes. The specific correlations should not, however, be treated as having general significance. The correlations that involve having a say in local or national government have sampling errors of ±.13 and the difference between the national and local values is not statistically significant. The correlations involving actual participation do differ significantly, but Selby may nonetheless be atypical. Selby lost its home-grown elite with the death of "Uncle" Horace Fletcher, owner of the sawmill, and the influx of newly arrived professionals is not yet large enough to have created a new elite. This provides Selby's working-class residents with unusual opportunities for participation. When a foreman like Mr. Waite sees that a laborer, a housewife, and a plumber "run the biggest budget in town" while a repairman and a carpenter become selectmen, he can begin to nurse ambitions of being a selectman himself in a way that he would not elsewhere. He pores over the town report when it arrives and goes to the town meeting believing that his presence contributes something. At the town meeting itself, Mr. Gretsch is one of the few participants who makes Mr. Waite feel outclassed. The other voices he hears are like his own. In short, it may not be Selby's size but its relatively high percentage of working-class residents, creating a feeling of homogeneous working-class dominance, that encourages working-class citizens to participate (Tingsten, 1937, pp. 126–127; Lane, 1959, pp. 262–263).

Homogeneous working-class neighborhoods are also related to working-class political participation in Finland, Sweden, Norway, and Canada (Lipset, 1960; Pesonen, 1960; Rokkan and Campbell, 1960; Rokkan, 1962; Milbrath, 1965).

10. Peterson (1979, pp. 295–296, and passim). Peterson argues that only the more inclusive levels of government reap benefits as well as incurring costs from redistributive policies.

11. Coleman (1966, p. 616), analyzing situations in which each actor strives only to maximize his own utility, points out that with two actors there are four possibilities: "Neither A nor B finds the action beneficial; A finds it beneficial, but B does not; B finds it beneficial, but A does not; or both A and B find it beneficial." If action occurs only when the last of these conditions holds, "almost any action on the part of a large collectivity would be impossible, because as the actors increase to A, B, C, then A, B, C, D—A, B, C, D, E, and so on, the number of no-action conditions increases to 7, 15, 31, and so on, in powers of 2, while there remains only one condition for action."

12. Dahl and Tufte (1973, pp. 32–35) provide evidence that within countries large communities have greater linguistic, religious, cultural, and economic diversity than small communities. That is not true among countries, probably because, they speculate, at the national level historical and other factors override the effect of size.

13. Newcomb (1961), p. 12 and passim.

14. Dahl and Tufte (1973), pp. 36–39.

15. Ibid., pp. 98–109.

16. Lipset, Trow, and Coleman [1962], p. 189.

17. Hare (1952), p. 264.

18. Asch (1951), p. 185. See also Dahl and Tufte (1973), pp. 90–91.

19. This generalization is based on extensive qualitative evidence. I also tried to

gather quantitative evidence on the propensity of citizens in small communities to avoid conflict, but the results are ambiguous. Verba and Nie (1972) for example, asked: "In many communities there are groups that are opposed to each other. Thinking still about this community (previously named local government unit), what are the major groups that oppose each other here?" (Probe, if needed: "I mean, the groups that have differences of interest, or who have controversies?") When I reanalyzed their 1967 data I found a correlation of .33 between the log of community size and whether a respondent reported conflict in the community (see also Verba and Nie, 1972, p. 99). Unfortunately, when I wrote to the towns in Verba and Nie's sample, asking how much local autonomy they had, I learned that many of the smallest units had very little local control. And when I looked at the 163 towns that I determined had significant local control, I found no correlation between community size and the probability of a respondent's reporting no conflict in the community. The fact that residents of smaller communities report fewer political conflicts may therefore derive simply from the fact that smaller political units make fewer political decisions.

20. Walsh (1973), pp. 25, 28, 31.

21. Ibid., p. 22. Other studies indicate that participants in small groups have a greater sense of group unity and of belonging to the group, and are rated by outside observers as more responsible toward the other members than participants in large groups (Walsh 1973, pp. 28–30).

22. Interviews with recently elected rural representatives to the Connecticut state lower house, 1959 (Barber, 1965, pp. 148, 124). Barber cites instance after instance of these small town legislators using the word "politics" derogatorily to mean "conflict" (pp. 145–149). As one of these legislators put it, "You know, there are people who are trained politicians, and I'm afraid I'm at their mercy, because I don't know anything about campaigning, I don't know anything about how to *create discontent* and what have you" (p. 145; emphasis mine).

Another of these legislators considered a situation undesirable when "if we're talking on opposite points, we'll soon have an argument perhaps on our hands" (p. 143). A third summed it up by saying, "I don't want any enemies at all" (p. 143).

23. Ibid., p. 148.

24. In explaining the association between small size and lack of conflict, British and American social scientists almost always cite the greater and more certain punishment others can deliver in the smaller context. For example, Barber (1965, p. 123) attributes the lack of conflict to the sanctions afforded one's neighbors by the narrowness of social contacts in a small town, by the continuity of interpersonal ties over the years, and by overlapping social roles ("unless one prefers solitude, he cannot afford to alienate those he meets again and again, at church, in the store, in social gatherings"). Bailey (1965, p. 5) summarzies this analysis as follows:

> Where relationships tend to be multiplex . . . disagreements cannot easily be isolated with one realm of social action. . . . You can quarrel bitterly with your neighbor if you live in certain areas of London, Manchester, or Leeds and still get on with the business of making a living, taking part in politics, worshipping your God, and maintaining amicable relationships with your kinsmen, because all these activities have nothing to do with your neighbor; but you cannot do this in Bisipara, Tikopia, or even Pentrediwaith, because some or even all of these activities are likely to involve you with the same set of people.

Sherwood Anderson also has one of his small town characters explain:

> You have to go on living with people, day after day, week after week. You can't just ignore your brother-in-law, forget him as you might in a city. Tomorrow you will meet him in the street. You will be meeting him in the stores and in the postoffice. Better make it up, start over again. [Wood, 1958, p. 273]

See also Frankenberg (1957), p. 18:

> [I]n village conditions open and continuous breach is not possible. If it did occur it would place in conflict not only friends but different members of the same family. Thus . . . committees of the village, like the village itself, must maintain an appearance of impersonal, unanimous, even leaderless unity.

Dahl and Tufte (1973) summarize this approach in their schema on p. 92.

Simmel (1955, pp. 43–44) explains the greater avoidance of conflict in small towns and small groups by postulating that conflict becomes more threatening the more facets of one's personality one opens to or shares with one's antagonists. In Simmel's view, the more like someone else one feels, the more intense conflict with that person becomes. Fear of such a personally destructive conflict then may lead one to suppress hostile feelings, only to have the feelings break out even more destructively later on. According to this hypothesis, both the intimacy and the homogeneity of a small community would make conflict relatively threatening and therefore likely to be suppressed. See also Coser (1956), p. 75ff., and Dahl and Tufte (1973), p. 94.

25. Kephart (1950), p. 548.

26. This was Matthew Arnold's argument against J. S. Mill's contention in *On Liberty* that the battlefield of ideas was the best guarantor of truth. See Himmelfarb (1974), p. 293.

27. In the epileptic experiment described earlier, all the subjects who believed they were alone with an epileptic responded to his cries for help, while only 85 percent responded if they believed a second person was present (Latané and Darley 1970, p. 97).

Other simulated emergencies and thefts produce the same result: responsibility for others weakens as the number who share that responsibility grows. Indeed the sum total of responsibility for others may actually shrink as the number who might feel responsible grows: a woman purportedly falling from a chair and breaking her ankle is actually more likely to get help if only one person hears her (help arrives 70 percent of the time) than if two people together hear her (help arrives 40 percent of the time) (Latané and Darley 1970, p. 61).

28. While students in small schools are generally more likely than students in large schools to report a sense of obligation to support group activities, the difference arises mainly among students with IQs below 99, two or more grades of D, and low socio-economic status. In small schools, these marginal students report as great a sense of responsibility toward school activities as the regular students. In large schools, however, they report hardly any sense of obligation or responsibility at all (Willems 1967, p. 1254).

29. Latané and Darley (1970), p. 117.

30. Percentage attendance from Breed and Seamon (1971), p. 634; governmental responsibilities from Sabine (1950), pp. 13–14. Sabine's estimates are drawn from Aristotle's *Constitution of Athens.*

31. I am indebted for this experiment to my research assistant, Pamela Kraus of the University of California at Santa Barbara. According to her calculations, a person with 20-20 vision can no longer perceive closed eyes at 115 feet or a stuck-out tongue at 155 feet. A person with normal hearing can no longer make out the words of someone speaking fairly loudly at 285 feet, without the aid of an acoustically constructed auditorium. See also Davis (1969) on the role of eye contact in communication.

32. The Strahor Stadium in Prague, built in 1934, can accommodate 240,000 spectators (McWhirter and McWhirter (1976), p. 256).

33. If the population of the Swiss canton of Appenzell Exterieur were 57,000 in 1904 (see Bridel, 1952, n. 1, p. 49), if about one-third of these were registered voters and if 63 percent to 79 percent of the registered voters attended the Landesgemeinde in that year (Brooks, 1930, p. 123), then from 12,000 to 15,000 citizens must have attended the Landesgemeinde that year. If all these figures are correct, this event may have been the largest face-to-face democracy in recorded history.

34. Late in the sixth century B.C., the Pnyx, where the Athenian assembly usually met, could accommodate about 5,000 citizens (votes of ostracism, however, took place in the *perischoinisma,* "a roped-off place" in the agora). Its renovation in the fifth century, when Aristotle wrote, does not seem to have much expanded its capacity. Later, in the fourth century B.C., it may have been enlarged enough to hold 10,000 (Wycherley 1976, pp. 120–122).

35. Brooks (1930), pp. 120, 124.

36. Dahl and Tufte (1973), p. 5.

37. Ibid., p. 6, referring especially to Rousseau's *Social Contract.*

38. Ibid., p. 7.

39. Ibid., p. 14.

40. Even the evidence Dahl and Tufte marshal regarding the greater homogeneity of smaller units and their lesser tendency to develop organized factions with their own interests and goals (pp. 30–40, esp. p. 39, and, pp. 91–109, esp. p. 93) deals only with the advantages and disadvantages of smallness for the articulation of individual interests within the political system. They mention once that in a small system "overall solidarity is greater" (p. 93), but this consideration appears in a discussion of the problems of dissent in a homogeneous community and does not figure in their discussion of the advantages of such a community.

Chapter 21: The Limits of Friendship

1. The term was apparently coined by Kaufman (1960). It came into widespread use after 1962, when SDS gave it a central place in its founding Port Huron Statement (1962). What the term meant then was unclear, and it became less clear afterward, as it was applied to virtually every form of organization that brought more people into the decision-making process. In the actual organizations of the New Left, however, the term came to be associated quite quickly with the combination of equality, consensus, and face-to-face assembly.

2. See Aristotle, *Ethics*, on equality, 1157b, 1159b, 1168b; on direct association, 1157b, 1171b–1172a; on unanimity, 155a, 1167a–1167b.

3. Arendt (1965), p. 243.

4. Ibid., p. 267. Arendt, of course, concerns herself less with the average citizen than with "the best" who select themselves into active attendance, who "care," who take the initiative, who "have a taste for public freedom and cannot be 'happy' without it" (pp. 282–283). This strong and self-directed elite might be impervious to the usual forces at work in a face-to-face assembly.

On the other hand, Arendt indicates that the small assemblies she proposes should never switch into the adversary mode (p. 230). In her mind, the republic has become corrupt and perverse when "private interests invade the public domain" (p. 255) and voters:

> force their representatives to execute their wishes at the expense of the wishes and interests of other groups of voters. In all these instances the voter acts out of concern with his private life and well-being, and the residue of power he still holds in his hands resembles rather the reckless coercion with which a black-mailer forces his victim into obedience than the power that arises out of joint action and joint deliberation. [p. 273]

I argue, to the contrary, that if local assemblies are to be lawmaking bodies as well as debating societies they must be able to handle equitably conflicting interests, including private interests. The fully unitary approach that Arendt proposes would accentuate the tendency in small assemblies toward a false consensus that benefits the more powerful.

5. Zolberg (1972), pp. 183–207.

6. James (1967). James stressed primarily "hardihood" but included in the "martial virtues" the "surrender of private interest" (p. 668).

7. Alexandrov (1948), pp. 11, 12. See also Andrei Y. Vyshinsky, ed., *The Law of the Soviet State*, as cited in Berg (1965), pp. 5–10.

8. Deutscher (1950), p. 56.

9. See Pitkin (1972), pp. 168–184, on Edmund Burke.

10. Vogel (1979), Chapter 5: "Politics: Higher Interests and Fair Shares."

11. In *Socialism: Utopian and Scientific* (1975, p. 38), Engels states that the Marxist theory of the "abolition of the state" was derived directly from St. Simon's idea of "the future conversion of political role over men into an administration of

things and a direction of processes of production." St. Simon, in turn, almost certainly derived his doctrine from Francis Bacon's dictum, in *Novum Organum,* that the progress of the arts and sciences would result in the replacement of dominion over man by "the empire of man over things." See Taylor (1975), pp. 36–38, 53.

Chapter 22: First Principles

1. Unger (1975), p. 20 and passim, esp. pp. 262–263. For Unger's differences from my conception, see, among others, pp. 247–248, 260, 266.

2. Arendt (1965), p. 221.

3. See, among others, Arendt (1965), Macpherson (1977), Barber (1977), and, most recently, Shumer (1979).

Bibliography

Adkins, A. W. H. 1963. " 'Friendship' and 'Self-Sufficiency' in Homer and Aristotle." *Classical Quarterly* 13:30–45.

———. 1972. *Moral Values and Political Behavior in Ancient Greece.* New York: W. W. Norton.

Agency of Environmental Conservation. 1970. *Environmental Protection Regulations*: Ch 5–201, Washington, D.C.: United States Government Printing Office.

Alexandrov, George F. 1948. *The Pattern of Soviet Democracy.* [1946] Trans. Leo Grulsow. Washington, D.C.: Public Affairs Press.

Arendt, Hannah. 1965. *On Revolution.* New York: Viking.

Aristotle. 1946. *Politics.* Trans. Ernest Barker. London: Oxford University Press.

———. 1954. *Ethics.* Trans. Sir David Ross. London: Oxford University Press.

Asch, Solomon E. 1951. "Effects of Group Pressure upon the Modification and Distortion of Judgements," in H. Guetzkow, ed., *Groups, Leadership and Men.* Pittsburgh: Carnegie Press.

Bachrach, Peter. 1967. *The Theory of Democratic Elitism: A Critique.* Boston: Little, Brown.

———. 1974. "Interest, Participation and Democratic Theory," in J. Roland Pennock and John W. Chapman, eds. *Participation in Politics: NOMOS XVI.* New York: Lieber-Atherton.

———, and Baratz, Morton. 1963. "Decisions and Non-Decisions: An Analytic Framework." *American Political Science Review* 57:632–644.

Bailey, F. G. 1965. "Decisions by Consensus in Councils and Committees," in Michael Banton, ed., *Political Systems and the Distribution of Power.* London: Tavistock.

Baird, L. L. 1969. "Big School, Small School: A Critical Examination of the Hypothesis." *Journal of Educational Psychology* 60:253–260.

Baker, Gordon. 1977. "American Conceptions of Direct vis-a-vis Representative Governance." *Claremont Journal of Public Affairs* 4:5–18.

Barber, Benjamin R. 1974. *The Death of Communal Liberty.* Princeton, N.J.: Princeton University Press.

———. 1977. *Political Participation and the Creation of Res Publica.* Bloomington, Ind.: The Poynter Center.

Barber, James David. 1965. *The Lawmakers.* New Haven: Yale University Press.

———. 1966. *Power in Committees.* Chicago: Rand-McNally.

Barker, R. G., and Hall, E. R. 1964. "Participation in Interschool Events and Extracurricular Activities," in R. G. Barker and P. V. Gump, eds., *Big School, Small School.* Stanford, Calif.: Stanford University Press.

Barnlund, D. C. 1959. "A Comparative Study of Individual, Majority and Group Judgment." *Journal of Abnormal Psychology* 58:55–60.

Barry, Brian. 1965. *Political Argument.* London: Routledge and Kegan Paul.

———. 1979. "Is Democracy Special?" in Peter Laslett and James Fishkin, eds. *Philosophy, Politics and Society. Fifth series.* Oxford: Blackwell.

Bass, Bernard M., and Norton, Fay-Tyler M. 1951. "Group Size and Leaderless Discussions." *Journal of Applied Psychology* 35:397–400.

Beardsley, Richard K., Hall, John W., and Ward, Robert E. 1959. *Village Japan.* Chicago: Chicago University Press.

Benn, Stanley I. 1960. " 'Interests' in Politics." *Proceedings of the Aristotelian Society* 60:123–140.

———. 1967. "Egalitarianism and the Equal Consideration of Interests," in J. Roland Pennock and John W. Chapman, eds. *Equality: NOMOS IX.* New York: Atherton Press.

Bibliography

Bennett, Edith. 1955. "Discussion, Decision, Commitment and Consensus in 'Group Decision.'" *Human Relations* 8:251–273.

Bennis, Warren G., Benne, Kenneth D., and Chin, Robert, eds. 1961. *The Planning of Change*. New York: Holt, Rinehart and Winston.

———, and Slater, Philip E. 1969. *The Temporary Society*. New York: Harper and Row.

Bentham, Jeremy. 1843. "Constitutional Code," [1827] in John Bowring, ed., *Works*, vol. 9. Edinburgh: W. Tait.

Bentley, Arthur. 1949. *The Process of Government* [1908]. Evanston, Ill.: Principia Press.

Berelson, Bernard R., Lazarfeld, Paul F., and McPhee, William N. 1954. *Voting*. Chicago: University of Chicago Press.

Berg, Elias. 1965. *Democracy and the Majority Principle*. Stockholm: Ivar Hæggstroms Tryckeri AB.

Berlin, Isaiah. 1969. "Equality." *Proceedings of the Aristotelian Society* 56 (1955–56), reprinted in W. T. Blackstone, ed. *The Concept of Equality*. Minneapolis, Minn.: Burgess.

Blake, James. 1846. "Annals of the Town of Dorchester." *Collections of the Dorchester Antiquarian and Historical Society*. Boston: David Clapp, vol. 2.

Bloom, Alan. 1968. *The Republic of Plato*. New York: Basic Books.

———. 1977. "Response to Hall." *Political Theory* 5:315–330.

Bogart, Walter T. 1959. "State-Local Relations in Vermont," in Rolf N. B. Haugen and E. William Steele, eds., *Vermont—the 14th Original State*. Burlington, Vt.: Government Clearing House.

Bookchin, Murray. 1971. *Post-Scarcity Anarchism*. Berkeley, Calif.: Ramparts Press.

Brain, Robert. 1976. *Friends and Lovers*. New York: Basic Books.

Bread and Roses Collective. 1972. "Getting Together," *The Old Mole*, 1971, reprinted in Richard Fairfield, ed., *Utopia, U.S.A.* San Francisco: Alternative Foundation.

Breed, Warren, and Seaman, Sally M. 1971. "Indirect Democracy and Social Process in Periclean Athens." *Social Science Quarterly* 52:631–645.

Bridel, Marcel, ed. 1952. *La Democratie Directe dans les Communes Suisses*. Zurich: Editions Polygraphiques SA.

Brinton, Howard. 1952. *Friends for 300 Years*. New York: Harper.

Broneer, Oscar. 1938. "Excavations on the North Slope of the Acropolis, 1937." *Hesperia* 7:228–243.

Brooks, Robert Clarkson. 1930. *Civic Training in Switzerland*. Chicago: University of Chicago Press.

Brown, Katharine B. 1954. "Freemanship in Puritan Massachusetts." *American Historical Review* 59:865–883.

———. 1967. "Puritan Democracy in Dedham, Massachusetts: Another Case Study," *William and Mary Quarterly* 24:378–393.

Brown, Robert E. 1955. *Middle-Class Democracy and the Revolution in Massachusetts, 1691–1780*. Ithaca, N.Y.: Cornell University Press.

Bryan, Frank M. 1974. *Yankee Politics in Rural Vermont*. Hanover, N.H.: University Press of New England.

———. 1975. "Comparative Town Meetings: A Search for Causative Models of Feminine Involvement in Politics." Paper delivered at the annual meeting of the Rural Sociological Society.

———. 1976. "Open Democracy: Correlations of Participation in the New England Town Meeting. Unpublished manuscript, p. 46.

Bryce, Lord. 1894. *The American Commonwealth*. New York: Macmillan.

Buchanan, James M., and Tullock, Gordon. 1971. *Calculus of Consent*. Ann Arbor, Mich.: University of Michigan Press.

Calhoun, John C. 1953. A Disquisition on Government. [1853] New York: Bobbs-Merrill.

Calhoun, George M. 1913. "Athenian Clubs in Politics and Litigation." *Bulletin of the University of Texas*. No. 262, Humanistic Series No. 14.

Carritt, E. F. 1964. "Liberty and Equality." *Law Quarterly Review* 56 (1940): 61–74. Reprinted in Anthony Quinton, ed., *Political Philosophy*. Oxford: Oxford University Press.

Center for New Schools. 1972. "Strengthening Alternative High Schools." *Harvard Educational Review* 42:313–350.

Coleman, James S. 1966. "Foundations for a Theory of Collective Decisions." *American Journal of Sociology* 71:615–627.

Collaros, Panajiota A. and Anderson, Lynn R. 1969. "Effects of Perceived Expertness upon Creativity of Members of Brainstorming Groups." *Journal of Applied Psychology* 53:159–163.

Connolly, William A. 1972. "On 'Interests' in Politics." *Politics and Society* 2:459–477.

Connor, W. Robert. 1971. *The New Politicians of Fifth Century Athens*. Princeton, N.J.: Princeton University Press.

Cook, Terrence E., and Morgan, Patrick M., eds. *Participatory Democracy*. San Francisco: Canfield Press.

Cooley, Charles. 1929. *Social Organization*. New York: Charles Scribner Sons.

Coser, Lewis A. 1956. *The Functions of Social Conflict*. New York: Free Press.

d'Agostino, Lorenzo. 1948. *The History of Public Welfare in Vermont*. Winooski Park, Vt.: St. Michael's College Press.

Dahl, Robert A. 1957. "The Concept of Power." *Behavioral Science* 2:201–215.

———. 1961. *Who Governs*. New Haven: Yale University Press.

———. 1967. *Pluralist Democracy in the United States: Conflict and Consent*. Chicago: Rand McNally.

———. 1970. *After the Revolution*. New Haven: Yale University Press.

———, and Tufte, Edward R. 1973. *Size and Democracy*. Stanford, Calif.: Stanford University Press.

Dahrendorf, Ralf. 1962. "On the Origin of Social Inequality," in Peter Laslett and W. G. Runciman, eds., *Philosophy, Politics, and Society*. Oxford: Blackwell.

Douglas, Roger. 1973. "Some Effects of Compulsory Voting." *Melbourne Journal of Politics*, 6:53–62.

Davies, James C. 1963. *Human Nature in Politics*. New York: Wiley.

Davis, James H. 1969. *Group Performance*. Reading, Mass.: Addison-Wesley.

de Jouvenel, Bertrand. 1961. "The Chairman's Problem." *American Political Science Review* 55:382–392.

Deutsch, Morton, and Gerard, Harold B. 1955. "A Study of Normative and Informal Social Influences upon Individual Judgment." *Journal of Abnormal and Social Psychology* 51:629–636.

Deutscher, Isaac. 1950. *Soviet Trade Unions*. London: Oxford University Press.

Dolgoff, Sam. 1974. *The Anarchist Collectives: Workers' Self-Management in the Spanish Revolution 1936–39*. Montreal: Black Rose.

Dover, Kenneth. 1974. *Greek Popular Morality in the Time of Plato and Aristotle*. Berkeley: University of California Press.

The Early Records of the Town of Dedham, Massachusetts, 1636–1659. 1892. Don Gleason Hill, ed. Dedham, Mass.: vol. III.

Ehrenberg, Victor. 1943. *The People of Aristophanes*. Oxford: Blackwell.

———. 1950. "Origins of Democracy." *Historia* 1:515–548.

Emerson, Ralph Waldo. 1883. "Historical Discourse at Concord (1835)." *Miscellaneous Collected Works*. Boston: Houghton Mifflin, vol. 11.

Engels, Frederick. 1975. *Socialism: Utopian and Scientific*. [1880] New York: International Publishers.

Ferber, Michael, and Lynd, Staughton. 1971. *The Resistance*. Boston: Beacon Press.

Ferguson, John. 1958. *Moral Values in the Ancient World*. London: Methuen.

Festinger, Leon, Schachter, Stanley, and Bach, Kurt. 1950. *Social Pressures in Informal Groups*. Stanford, Calif.: Stanford University Press.

Finifter, Ada W. 1970. "Dimensions of Political Alienation." *American Political Science Review* 4:389–410.

Flathman, Richard E. 1966. *The Public Interest*. New York: Wiley.

Follet, Mary Parker. 1940. *Dynamic Administration*. New York: Harper.

———. 1949. *Freedom and Coordination*. London: Management Publications Trust.

Bibliography

Freeman, Jo. 1972–73. "The Tyranny of Structurelessness." *Berkeley Journal of Sociology* 17:151–164.

Frankenberg, Ronald. 1957. *Village on the Border.* London: Cohen and West.

Fried, Charles. 1963. "Two Concepts of Interest." *Harvard Law Review* 76:755–778.

Friedrich, Carl J. 1959. "The Concept of Community in the History of Political and Legal Philosophy," in Carl J. Friedrich, ed., *Community: NOMOS II.* New York: Liberal Arts Press.

————. 1963. *Man and His Government.* New York: McGraw Hill.

Glotz, Gustav. 1930. *The Greek City and Its Institutions.* N. Mallison, trans. New York: Knopf.

Grant, Charles S. 1961. *Democracy in the Connecticut Frontier Town of Kent.* New York: Columbia University Press.

Green, T. H. 1941. *Political Obligation.* London: Longmans, Green.

Greenstone, J. David. 1965. "Political Norms and Group Process in Private Government: The Case of a Local Union." *Midwest Journal of Political Science* 9:339–360.

Hall, Jay. 1971. "Decisions." *Psychology Today* 5:51–88.

Hammond, Lore. 1970. "On Community." *It Ain't Me, Babe* 1 (4–7 September):9.

Hare, A. Paul. 1952. "A Study of Interaction and Consensus in Different Sized Groups." *American Sociological Review* 17:261–267.

————. 1973. "Group Decision by Consensus: Reaching Unity in the Society of Friends." *Sociological Inquiry* 43:75–84.

————. 1976. *Handbook of Small Group Research.* New York: Free Press.

Havelock, Eric A. 1957. *The Liberal Temper in Greek Politics.* New Haven: Yale University Press.

Held, Virginia. 1970. *The Public Interest and Individual Interests.* New York: Basic Books.

Hicks, Granville. 1947. *Small Town.* New York: Macmillan.

Himmelfarb, Gertrude. 1974. *On Liberty and Liberalism: The Case of John Stuart Mill.* New York: Knopf.

Hirsch, Fred. 1976. *The Social Limits of Growth.* Cambridge, Mass.: Harvard University Press.

Hixon, Vivian Scott. 1971. "The New Town Meeting Democracy: A Study of Matched Towns." Ph.D. thesis, Department of Philosophy, Michigan State University.

Homans, George. 1950. *The Human Group.* New York: Harcourt, Brace and World.

————. 1961. *Social Behavior: Its Elementary Forms.* New York: Harcourt, Brace and World.

Hosmer, James K. 1885. *Samuel Adams.* Boston: Houghton Mifflin.

Hunter, Floyd. 1953. *Community Power Structure.* New York: Doubleday-Anchor.

Jacobs, Paul, and Landau, Saul. 1966. "The Port Huron Statement," in *The New Radicals.* New York: Random House.

James, William. 1967. "The Moral Equivalent of War." [1910] in John J. McDermott, ed., *Writings.* New York: Random House.

Jefferson, Thomas. 1905. "Letter to John Taylor" [1816], in Paul L. Ford, ed., *The Works of Thomas Jefferson.* New York: Putnam, vol. 11.

Johnson, Samuel. 1789. *The Rambler.* London: Rivington, vol. 2.

Jones, A. H. M. 1966. *Athenian Democracy.* Oxford: Blackwell.

Kasarda, John D., and Janowitz, Morris. 1974. "Community Attachment in Mass Society." *American Sociological Review* 39:328–339.

Kaufman, Arnold. 1960. "Human Nature and Participatory Democracy," in Carl J. Friedrich, ed. *Responsibility: NOMOS III.* New York: Liberal Arts Press.

————. 1971. "Participatory Democracy: Ten Years Later." *La Table Ronde,* No. 251–252 (1968):216–228, reprinted in William E. Connolly, ed., *The Bias of Pluralism.* New York: Atherton Press.

Kelsen, Hans. 1955. "Foundations of Democracy." *Ethics* 66:1–101.

Kendall, Wilmoore. 1965. *John Locke and the Doctrine of Majority Rule.* Urbana, Ill.: University of Illinois Press.

Keniston, Kenneth. 1968. *The Young Radicals.* New York: Harcourt Brace Jovanovich.

Kephart, William M. 1950. "A Quantitative Analysis of Intragroup Relationships." *American Journal of Sociology* 55:548–549.

Key, V. O. 1949. *Southern Politics.* New York: Random House.

Kishlansky, Mark. 1977. "The Emergence of Adversary Politics in the Long Parliament." *Journal of Modern History* 49:617–640.

Kotler, Neil G. 1972. "Politics and Citizenship in the New England Town: A Study of Values of Participatory Democracy." Ph.D. Dissertation, Department of Political Science, University of Chicago.

———. 1974. "The Decline of Political Community in New England Towns: The Impact on Citizen Participation and Education." Paper delivered at the 1974 Annual Meeting of the American Political Science Association, Chicago, Ill.

Kramer, Daniel C. 1972. *Participatory Democracy: Developing Ideals of the Political Left.* Cambridge, Mass.: Schenkman Publishing Company.

Kropotkin, Peter. 1972. *The Conquest of Bread.* [1892] London: Chapman and Hall, 1906, excerpted in Marshall F. Shatz, ed., *The Essential Works of Anarchism.* New York: Quadrangle.

Kruijt, J. P. 1959. "The Netherlands: The Influence of Denominationalism on Social Life and Organizational Patterns." *Archives de Sociologie des Religions* 4:105–111.

Kuper, Adam. 1970. *Kalahari Village Politics.* Cambridge: Cambridge University Press.

Lane, Robert E. 1959. *Political Life.* New York: Free Press.

———. 1962. *Political Ideology.* New York: Free Press.

Larsen, J. A. O. 1948. "Cliesthenes and the Development of the Theory of Democracy at Athens," in *Essays in Political Theory Presented to George Sabine.*

———. 1949. "The Origin and Significance of the Counting of Votes." *Classical Philology* 44:164–181.

Larson, C. M. 1949. *School Size as a Factor in the Adjustment of High School Seniors.* Bulletin No. 511, Youth Series No. 6, State College of Washington.

Laslett, Peter. 1956. "The Face to Face Society," in Peter Laslett, ed. *Philosophy, Politics and Society.* Oxford: Blackwell.

Latané, Bibb, and Darley, John M. 1970. *The Unresponsive Bystander: Why Doesn't He Help?* Englewood Cliffs, N.J.: Prentice-Hall, Inc.

Laumann, Edward O., Siegel, Paul M., and Hodge, Robert N. 1970. *The Logic of Social Hierarchies.* Chicago: Markham.

Lawrence, Paul R., and Lorsch, Jay W. 1967. *Organization and Environment.* Boston: Division of Research, Harvard University Graduate School of Business Administration.

Leavitt, Harold J. 1964. *Managerial Psychology.* Chicago: University of Chicago Press.

Lewin, Kurt. 1947. "Group Decision and Social Change" in Theodore M. Newcomb and Eugene L. Hartley, eds. *Readings in Social Psychology.* New York: Henry Holt.

Leys, Wayne A. R. 1978. "Was Plato Non-Political?" [1964] in Gregory Vlastos, ed. *Plato: A Collection of Critical Essays.* Notre Dame, Indiana: University of Notre Dame, vol. 2.

Lijphart, Arend. 1968. "The Netherlands: The Rules of the Game," in *The Politics of Accommodation.* Berkeley: University of California Press, reprinted in *Consociational Democracy.* Kenneth McRae, ed. Ottawa: McClelland and Stewart, 1974.

———. 1969. "Consociational Democracy." *World Politics* 21:207–225, reprinted in *Consociational Democracy.* Kenneth McRae, ed. Ottawa: McClelland and Stewart, 1974.

Lincoln, James R. 1976. "Power and Mobilization in the Urban Community: Reconsidering the Ecological Approach." *American Sociological Review* 41:1–15.

Lipset, Seymour Martin. 1950. *Agrarian Socialism.* Berkeley: University of California Press.

———. 1963. *Political Man.* [1960] Garden City, N.Y.: Andover Books, Doubleday.

———, Trow, Martin, and Coleman, James. 1962. *Union Democracy.* [1956] Garden City, N.Y.: Anchor Books, Doubleday.

Lively, Jack. 1977. *Democracy* [1975]. New York: Putnam.

Locke, John. 1965. *Two Treatises of Government* [1689]. Peter Laslett, ed. New York: New American Library.

Lockridge, Kenneth A., and Kreider, Alan. 1966. "The Evolution of Massachusetts Town Government, 1640–1740." *William and Mary Quarterly* 23:548–574.

Lucas, J. R. 1965. "Against Equality." *Philosophy* 40:296–307.

Bibliography

Lukes, Steven. 1974. *Power: A Radical View.* London: Macmillan.
Lynd, Staughton. 1971. "Prospects for the New Left." *Liberation* 13:20–28.
McConnell, Grant. 1966. *Private Power in American Democracy.* New York: Knopf.
MacIver, Robert. 1947. *The Web of Government.* New York: Macmillan.
McKeon, Richard, ed. 1951. *Democracy in a World of Tension.* Chicago: University of Chicago Press.
Macpherson, C. B. 1977. *The Life and Times of Liberal Democracy.* Oxford: Oxford University Press.
McRae, Kenneth, ed. 1974. *Consociational Democracy: Political Accommodation in Segmented Societies.* Toronto: McClelland and Stewart/Macmillan.
McWhirter, Norris, and McWhirter, Ross, eds. 1976. *Guiness Book of World Records.* New York: Sterling.
Madison, James. 1961. "Ten Federalist" [1787], *The Federalist Papers.* New York: New American Library.
Maier, Norman R. F. 1952. *Principles of Human Relations.* New York: Wiley.
———. 1953. "An Experimental Test of the Effects of Training on Discussion Leadership." *Human Relations* 6:161–173.
———. 1972. "Effects of Training on Decision-making." *Psychological Report* 30: 159–164.
Mansbridge, Jane J. 1973. "Time, Emotion, and Inequality: Three Problems of Participatory Groups." *Journal of Applied Behavioral Science* 9:351–368.
———. 1976a. "Conflict in a New England Town Meeting." *Massachusetts Review* 17:631–633.
———. 1976b. "The Limits of Friendship," in J. Roland Pennock and John W. Chapman, eds. *Participation in Politics: NOMOS XVI.* New York: Lieber-Atherton.
———. 1977. "Acceptable Inequalities." *British Journal of Political Science* 7:321–336.
Mao Tse-Tung. 1960. "Combat Liberalism." *Selected Works of Mao Tse-Tung.* Peking: Foreign Language Press.
March, James G. 1953–54. "Husband-Wife Interaction Over Political Issues." *Public Opinion Quarterly* 17:461–470.
———. 1955. "An Introduction to the Theory and Measurement of Influence." *American Political Science Review* 49:431–449.
Marshall, Lorna. 1961. "Sharing, Talking and Giving: Relief of Social Tensions among !Kung Bushmen." *Africa* 31:231–249.
Marx, Karl, and Engels, Frederich. 1954. *The Communist Manifesto* [1848]. Chicago: Henry Regenery.
Mehrhof, Barbara. 1970. "Notes from the Second Year" reprinted in *Off Our Backs* 1 (July 10):12
Michels, Robert. 1962. *Political Parties* [1915]. New York: Collier.
Milbrath, Lester W. 1965. *Political Participation.* Chicago: Rand McNally.
Milgram, Stanley. 1974. *Obedience to Authority: An Experimental View.* New York: Harper Colophon Books.
Mill, John Stuart. 1958. *On Representative Government* [1861]. Indianapolis, Ind.: Bobbs-Merrill.
Miller, Walter B. 1963. "Two Concepts of Authority." *The American Anthropologist,* 1955, reprinted in James D. Thompson, Peter Hammond, Robert W. Hawkes, Buford H. Junker, and Arthur Tuden, eds., *Comparative Studies in Administration.* Pittsburgh, Pa.: University of Pittsburgh Press.
Mills, C. Wright. 1959. *The Power Elite.* [1956] New York: Oxford University Press.
Morris-Jones, W. H. 1954. "In Defense of Political Apathy." *Political Studies,* pp. 25–37.
Motto, Anna Lydia, and Clark, John R. 1969. "Isè Dias: The Honor of Achilles." *Arethusa* 2:109–125.
Myers, Phyllis. 1974. *So Goes Vermont.* Washington, D.C.: The Conservative Foundation.
Nagel, Jack H. 1975. *The Descriptive Analysis of Power.* New Haven: Yale University Press.
Neale, J. E. 1949. *The Elizabethan House of Commons.* Harmondsworth, Eng.: Penguin.

Newcomb, Theodore M. 1961. *The Acquaintance Process.* New York: Holt, Rinehart & Winston.

Nuquist, Andrew E., and Nuquist, Edith W. 1966. *Vermont State Government and Administration.* Burlington, Vt.: Government Research Center.

Partridge, P. H. 1971. *Consent and Consensus.* London: Macmillan.

Pateman, Carole. 1970. *Participation and Democratic Theory.* Cambridge: Cambridge University Press.

Pearson, Lionel. 1962. *Popular Ethics in Ancient Greece.* Stanford, Calif.: Stanford University Press.

Pesonen, Perti. 1960. "The Voting Behavior of Finnish Students." *Democracy in Finland.* Helsinki: Finnish Political Science Association.

Peterson, Paul E. 1970. "Forms of Representation: Participation of the Poor in the Community Action Programs." *American Political Science Review* 64:491–507.

————. 1979. "A Unitary Model of Local Taxation and Expenditure Policies in the United States," *British Journal of Political Science* 9:281–314.

Pitkin, Hanna Fenichel. 1972. *The Concept of Representation.* Berkeley: University of California Press.

Plamenatz, John P. 1957. "Equality of Opportunity," in Lyman Bryson, Clarence H. Frank, Louis Finkelstein, and R. M. MacIver, eds., *Aspects of Human Equality.* New York: Harper & Row.

Plato. 1961. *Collected Dialogues.* Edith Hamilton and Huntington Cairns, eds. Princeton, N.J.: Princeton University Press.

Pollard, Francis E., Pollard, Beatrice E., and Pollard, Robert S. W. 1950. *Democracy and the Quaker Method.* New York: Philosophical Library.

Polsby, Nelson W. 1963. *Community Power and Political Theory.* New Haven: Yale University Press.

"The Port Huron Statement." 1966. In Paul Jacobs and Saul Landau. *The New Radicals.* New York: Random House.

Powell, Sumner Chilton. 1963. *Puritan Village.* Middletown, Conn.: Wesleyan University Press.

"Power Relationships." 1972. *Pedestal* 4:13.

Proudhon, Pierre-Joseph. 1972. *General Idea of the Revolution in the Nineteenth Century* [1851]. John B. Robinson, trans. London: Freedom Press, 1923, excerpted in Martin F. Shatz, ed., *The Essential Works of Anarchism.* New York: Quadrangle.

Ranney, Austin, and Kendall, Wilmoore. 1951. "Democracy: Confusion and Agreement." *Western Political Quarterly* 4:430–439.

Rawls, John. 1971. *A Theory of Justice.* Cambridge: Harvard University Press.

Redfield, Robert. 1947. "The Folk Society." *The American Journal of Sociology* 52:293–308.

Riker, William. 1964. "Some Ambiguities in the Notion of Power." *American Political Science Review* 58:341–349.

Rochen, M., and Deutsch, Karl W. 1969. "Toward a Rational Theory of Decentralization." *American Political Science Review* 63:734–749.

Rokkan, Stein. 1962. "The Comparative Study of Political Participation: Notes Toward a Perspective on Current Research," in Austin Ranney, ed. *Essays on the Behavioral Study of Politics.* Urbana, Ill.: Uuniversity of Illinois Press.

————, and Campbell, Angus. 1960. "Norway and the United States of America." *Citizen Participation in Political Life, International Social Science Journal* 12:69–99.

Rosenberg, Morris. 1954–55. "Some Determinants of Political Apathy." *Public Opinion Quarterly* 18:349–366.

Rothschild-Whitt, Joyce. 1979. "Conditions for Democracy: Making Participatory Organizations Work" in John Case and Rosemary Taylor, eds., *Co-ops, Communes, and Collectives.* New York: Pantheon.

Rousseau, Jean Jačques. 1950. *The Social Contract* [1762]. G. D. H. Cole, trans. New York: Dutton.

Runciman, W. G. 1966. *Relative Deprivation and Social Justice.* London: Routledge and Kegan Paul.

Russell, Bertrand. 1962. *Power.* [1938] New York: Barnes and Noble.

Sabine, George H. 1950. *A History of Political Theory.* New York: Henry Holt.

Sahlins, Marshall. 1972. *Stone Age Economics.* Chicago: Aldine.

Bibliography

Sale, Kirkpatrick. 1973. *SDS*. New York: Random House.
Sartori, Giovanni. 1965. *Democratic Theory*. [1958] New York: Praeger.
Savitsky, Jeffrey C., and Eby, Thomas. 1979. "Emotion Awareness and Antisocial Behavior" in Carroll E. Izard, ed., *Emotions in Personality and Psychopathology*. New York: Plenum Press.
Schelling, Thomas C. 1960. *The Strategy of Conflict*. Cambridge: Harvard University Press.
Schumpeter, Joseph A. 1962. *Capitalism, Socialism and Democracy* [1942, 1947]. New York: Harper and Row.
Schutz, William C. 1958. "Interpersonal Underworld." *Harvard Business Review* 36:123–135.
Service, Elman R. 1975. *Origins of the State and Civilization*. New York: W. W. Norton.
Shapley, L. S., and Shubik, Martin. 1954. "A Method for Evaluating the Distribution of Power in a Committee System." *American Political Science Review* 48:787–792.
Shklar, Judith N. 1969. *Men and Citizens*. Cambridge: Cambridge University Press.
Shumer, S. M. 1979. "Machiavelli: Republican Politics and Its Corruption." *Political Theory* 7:5–34.
Simmel, Georg. 1950. "The Phenomenon of Outvoting" [1908], in Kurt H. Wolff, ed. and trans. *The Sociology of George Simmel*. New York: Free Press.
———. 1955. *Conflict and the Web of Group Affiliations* [1908; 1923], Kurt H. Wolff, trans. New York: Free Press.
Sly, John F. 1930. *Town Government in Massachusetts* [1620–1930]. Cambridge: Harvard University Press.
Soltau, Roger Henry. 1959. *French Political Thought in the Nineteenth Century*. New York: Russell and Russell.
Sorauf, Frank H. 1957. "The Public Interest Reconsidered." *Journal of Politics* 29: 616–639.
Steiner, Jurg. 1974. "The Principles of Majority and Proportionality." *British Journal of Political Science* 1 (1970):63–70, reprinted in Kenneth McRae, ed. *Consociational Democracy*. Toronto: McClelland and Stewart.
———, and Dorff, Robert H. 1980. *A Theory of Political Decision Modes*. Chapel Hill: University of North Carolina Press.
Suter, L. E., and Miller, H. P. 1973. "Income Differences Between Men and Career Women." *American Journal of Sociology* 78:962–974.
Suttles, Gerald D. 1968. *The Social Order of the Slum*. Chicago: University of Chicago Press.
———, and Street, David. 1969. "Aid to the Poor and Social Exchange." Working Paper No. 110, Center for Organization Studies, University of Chicago.
Taylor, Keith, ed. and trans. 1975. *Henri Saint-Simon: Selected Writings*. New York: Holms and Meier.
Thomas, Edwin J., and Fink, Clinton F. 1963. "Effects of Group Size." *Psychological Bulletin* 60:371–384.
Thompson, Dennis F. 1970. *The Democratic Citizen*. Cambridge: Cambridge University Press.
Thucydides. 1966. *The Peloponnesian War*. Rex Warner, trans. Baltimore, Md.: Penguin.
Tilker, Harvey. 1970. "Socially Responsible Behavior as a Function of Observer Responsibility and Victim Feedback." *Journal of Personality and Social Psychology* 14 (2):95–100.
Tingsten, Herbert. 1937. *Political Behavior, Studies in Election Statistics*. London: P. S. King.
Tocqueville, Alexis de. 1954. *Democracy in America* [1835–40]. Henry Reeve and Phillips Bradley, trans., ed. New York: Vintage, 2 vol.
Toennies, Ferdinand. 1961. *Community and Society* [1887]. Charles P. Loomis, trans. East Lansing: Michigan State University Press, 1957. Reprinted in *Theories of Society*. New York: Free Press.
Toffler, Alvin. 1970. *Future Shock*. New York: Bantam Books.
Truman, David. 1959. *The Governmental Process*. New York: Knopf.
Unger, Roberto Mangabeira. 1975. *Knowledge and Politics*. New York: The Free Press.

U.S. Department of Commerce, Bureau of the Census. 1977a. "Geographical Mobility: March 1975 to March 1976." *Current Population Reports Series P-60, No. 305.* Washington, D.C.: U.S. Government Printing Office.

U.S. Department of Commerce, Bureau of the Census. 1977b. "Money Income in 1975 of Families and Persons in the United States," *Current Population Reports Series P-60,* No. 105. Washington, D.C.: U.S. Government Printing Office.

U.S. Department of Labor, Bureau of Labor Statistics. 1975. "Occupational Mobility of Workers." *Special Labor Force Report 176.* Washington, D.C.: U.S. Government Printing Office.

Verba, Sidney. 1961. *Small Groups and Political Behavior.* Princeton, N.J.: Princeton University Press.

Verba, Sidney, and Nie, Norman H. 1972. *Political Participation in America: Political Democracy and Social Equality.* New York: Harper and Row.

Verba, Sidney, Nie, Norman H., and Kim, Jae-on. 1978. *Participation and Political Equality.* Cambridge: Cambridge University Press.

Vermont State Highway Board. 1970a. *The Highway Fund in Perspective.* Montpelier, Vt.: Vermont State Highway Board, 1970.

————. 1970b. *A Report on Vermont Highways: Twenty-fifth Biennial Report.* Montpelier, Vt.: Vermont State Highway Board.

Vidich, Arthur J., and Bensman, Joseph. 1968. *Small Town in Mass Society: Class, Power and Religion in a Rural Community.* Princeton, N.J.: Princeton University Press.

Vogel, Ezra F. 1979. *Japan as Number One.* Cambridge, Mass.: Harvard University Press.

Vonnegut, Kurt, Jr. 1972. "Fiftieth Annual Address." *Proceedings,* Second Series no. 22, The American Academy of Arts and Letters and the National Institute of Arts and Letters.

Wall, Grenville. 1975. "The Concept of Interest in Politics." *Politics and Society* 5:487–510.

Walsh, Bruce. 1973. *Theories of Person-Environment Interaction: Implications for the College Student.* Iowa City: The American College Testing Program.

Walzer, Michael. 1965. *Revolution of the Saints.* Cambridge: Harvard University Press.

————. 1970. "The Obligations of Oppressed Minorities." *Obligations.* Cambridge: Harvard University Press.

————. 1973. "In Defense of Equality." *Dissent* 20:399–408.

Wesberry v. Sanders. 1963. 376 U.S. 1 at 7.

West, William C. 1977. "Hellenic Homonoia." *Greek, Roman and Byzantine Studies* 16:307–319.

Whyte, William F. 1943. *Street Corner Society.* Chicago: University of Chicago Press.

Wicker, A. W. 1968. "Undermanning, Performances, and Students' Subjective Experiences in Behavior Settings of Large and Small High Schools." *Journal of Personality and Social Psychology* 10:255–261.

————. 1969. "Size of Church Membership and Members' Support of Church Behavior Settings." *Journal of Personality and Social Psychology* 13:278–288.

Williams, Bernard. 1962. "The Idea of Equality," in Peter Laslett and W. G. Runciman, eds., *Philosophy, Politics and Society.* Oxford: Blackwell.

Willems, E. P. 1967. "Sense of Obligation to High School Activities as Related to School Size and Marginality of Student." *Child Development* 38:1247–1260.

Winter, David. 1973. *The Power Motive.* New York: Free Press.

Wolfe, Tom. 1969. "The Ultimate Power: Seeing 'Em Jump," in Clay Felker, ed., *The Power Game.* New York: Simon & Schuster.

Wolff, Robert Paul. 1970. *In Defense of Anarchism.* New York: Harper & Row.

————, Moore, Barrington, Jr., and Marcuse, Herbert. 1965. *A Critique of Pure Tolerance.* Boston: Beacon Press.

"The Women's Liberation Movement in England." 1972. *Me Jane* 1:7.

Wood, Robert C., 1958. *Suburbia.* Boston: Houghton-Mifflin.

Woodhouse, A. S. 1957. *Puritanism and Liberty.* Chicago: University of Chicago Press.

Wycherley, R. E. 1976. *How the Greeks Built Cities*. New York: W. W. Norton.
Zablocki, Benjamin D. 1971. *The Joyful Community*. Baltimore: Penguin.
Zaleznik, Abraham, and Moment, David. 1964. *Dynamics of Interpersonal Behavior*. New York: Wiley.
Zimmern, Alfred. 1952. *The Greek Commonwealth*. Oxford: Oxford University Press.
Zolberg, Aristide R. 1972. "Moments of Madness." *Politics and Society* 1:183–207.
Zuckerman, Michael. 1970. *Peaceable Kingdoms*. New York: Knopf.
Zurcher, Louis A. 1970. *Poverty Warriors*. Austin: University of Texas Press.

INDEX

References that begin with A and are followed by a period and a numeral (for example, A.2, A.3) refer to tables in Appendix A, which begins on page 304.

Index

Index

Hixon, Vivian Scott, 333n
Hobbes, Thomas, 15–16
Homans, George, 29, 344n
"Home Dem" Club of Selby, 44, 101
Homer, 338n
Homestead Act, 44
Homonoia, 14, 336n–338n; *see also* Consensus
Hunter, Floyd, 347n
Hunter-gatherer bands, 10–12, 28, 228

Ideals: adversary treatment of, 296; included in interests, 26; of national unitary and adversary democracy, 293–97
Identical interests, definition of, 26–27
India, village communities of, 256–57, 262, 263
Indians, American, unitary democracy among, 11, 12, 228, 335n
Individual development, *see* Education, political
Inequality, political: causes of, *see* Age, Class, Gender, Geographical centrality, Length of residence in Selby, Length of time in organization at Helpline, Power (enjoyment of), Race; in early town meetings, 132–33; in Helpline, 183–209; Helpline staff's explanations for, 234–35; other participatory collectives' explanations for, vii; in Selby, 97–114; unitary rationale for, 30–31
Informality: at Helpline, 160–61; in Selby, 66–70
Institute for Policy Studies, 359n
Interests, 24–26; centrality of, xi, 5–6, 289; definition of, 25–26, 342n–43n; equal protection of, x, xii, 5, 17, 30–31, 114, 235, 237–40, 265–68, 282, 291, 296, 300; gaining understanding of, 292, 296, 302; psychological, 91, 93–94, 95, 123; *see also* Common interests; Conflicting interests
Israeli kibbutzim, 243

Jackson, Schuyler, 352n
Jacobs, Paul, 366n
Jacobsen, Dee, 342n
James, William, 376n

Japan: consensus beliefs in, 256, 366n; unitary approach in, 294–95
Jefferson, Thomas, 41, 261, 345n
Johnson, Samuel, 28
Joking: at Helpline, 160–61; in Selby, 66, 68, 70
Jones, A. H., 337n, 364n

Kassarda, John D., 347n
Kaufman, Arnold, 244, 376n
Kelsen, Hans, 344n
Kendall, Wilmoore, 334n, 340n
Keniston, Kenneth, 363n, 366n
Kennedy, John F., 119
Kent, Conn., political inequality in, 133
Kentucky Resolution (1798), 261
Kephart, William M., 375n
Key, V. O., 348n
Kibbutzim, 243
Kishlansky, Mark, 339n, 340n
Kotler, Neil G., 333n, 369n
Kramer, Daniel C., 346n
Kraus, Pamela, 375n
Kropotkin, Peter, 341n
Kruijt, J. P., 367n
Kruper, Adam, 367n

Laissez-faire economics, 17
Land-use laws, Vermont, 129
Landau, Saul, 366n
Landesgemeinde, 286, 375n
Lane, Robert E., 344n, 373n
Larsen, J. A. O., 335n
Larson, C. M., 372n
Laslett, Peter, 270–71, 288
Latané, Bibb, 272, 368n, 375n
Laumann, Edward O., 351n
Lawrence, Paul R., 364n
Le Jeune, Father, 335n
Leavitt, Harold J., 363n, 369n
Lebanon, political parties in, 367n
Legitimacy, crises of, 3, 299
Leninist nations, 293
Length of residence in Selby, 81–93, 98–102, 111–12
Length of time in organization at Helpline, 184, 186–89, 206–7
Levellers, 16, 237
Lewin, Kurt, 369n

Index